Study Guide

West Federal Taxation
Corporations, Partnerships, Estates & Trusts
2003 Edition

William H. Hoffman, Jr.
University of Houston

William A. Raabe
Capital University

James E. Smith
College of William and Mary

David M. Maloney
University of Virginia

Prepared by

James C. Young, Ph.D., CPA
Northern Illinois University

Australia · Canada · Mexico · Singapore · Spain · United Kingdom · United States

Corporations, Partnerships, Estates & Trusts Study Guide 2003 Edition
William H. Hoffman, Jr., William A. Raabe, James E. Smith, David M. Maloney,
prepared by Jim Young

Editor-in-Chief:
Jack W. Calhoun

Publisher:
Melissa S. Acuña

Acquisitions Editor:
Jennifer L. Codner

Developmental Editor:
Craig Avery

Marketing Manager:
Mark Linton

Senior Production Editor:
Marci Combs

Manufacturing Coordinator:
Doug Wilke

Printer:
Globus
Minster, Ohio

Design Project Manager:
Michelle Kunkler

Cover Designer:
Paul Neff Design, Cincinnati

COPYRIGHT © 2003
by South-Western, a division of
Thomson Learning. Thomson
Learning™ is a trademark used herein
under license.

ISBN: 0-324-15568-9

Printed in the United States of America
1 2 3 4 5 05 04 03 02

For more information
contact South-Western,
5191 Natorp Boulevard,
Mason, Ohio 45040.
Or you can visit our Internet site at:
http://www.swcollege.com

ALL RIGHTS RESERVED
No part of this work covered by the
copyright hereon may be reproduced or
used in any form or by any means—
graphic, electronic, or mechanical,
including photocopying, recording,
taping, Web distribution or information
storage and retrieval systems—without
the written permission of the publisher.

For permission to use material from this
text or product, contact us by
Tel (800) 730-2214
Fax (800) 730-2215
http://www.thomsonrights.com

CONTENTS

Chapter 1	UNDERSTANDING AND WORKING WITH THE FEDERAL TAX LAW	1-1
Chapter 2	CORPORATIONS: INTRODUCTION, OPERATING RULES, AND RELATED CORPORATIONS	2-1
Chapter 3	CORPORATIONS: ORGANIZATION AND CAPITAL STRUCTURE	3-1
Chapter 4	CORPORATIONS: EARNINGS & PROFITS AND DIVIDEND DISTRIBUTIONS	4-1
Chapter 5	CORPORATIONS: REDEMPTIONS AND LIQUIDATIONS	5-1
Chapter 6	ALTERNATIVE MINIMUM TAX AND CERTAIN PENALTY TAXES IMPOSED ON CORPORATIONS	6-1
Chapter 7	CORPORATIONS: REORGANIZATIONS	7-1
Chapter 8	CONSOLIDATED TAX RETURNS	8-1
Chapter 9	TAXATION OF INTERNATIONAL TRANSACTIONS	9-1
Chapter 10	PARTNERSHIPS: FORMATION, OPERATIONS, AND BASIS	10-1
Chapter 11	PARTNERSHIPS: DISTRIBUTIONS, TRANSFER OF INTERESTS, AND TERMINATIONS	11-1
Chapter 12	S CORPORATIONS	12-1
Chapter 13	COMPARATIVE FORMS OF DOING BUSINESS	13-1
Chapter 14	EXEMPT ENTITIES	14-1
Chapter 15	MULTISTATE CORPORATE TAXATION	15-1
Chapter 16	TAX ADMINISTRATION AND PRACTICE	16-1
Chapter 17	THE FEDERAL GIFT AND ESTATE TAXES	17-1
Chapter 18	FAMILY TAX PLANNING	18-1
Chapter 19	INCOME TAXATION OF TRUSTS AND ESTATES	19-1

CHAPTER 1

Understanding and Working with the Federal Tax Law

LEARNING OBJECTIVES

After completing Chapter 1, you should be able to:

1. Realize the importance of revenue needs as an objective of Federal tax law.
2. Appreciate the influence of economic, social, equity, and political considerations on the development of the tax law.
3. Understand how the IRS, as the protector of the revenue, has affected tax law.
4. Recognize the role of the courts in interpreting and shaping tax law.
5. Identify tax law sources—statutory, administrative, and judicial.
6. Locate tax law sources.
7. Assess the validity and weight of tax law sources.
8. Make use of various tax planning procedures.
9. Have an awareness of computer-assisted tax research.

KEY TERMS

Acquiescence
Arm's length concept
Business purpose concept
Certiorari
Continuity of interest concept
Determination letters
Indexation
Letter rulings
Nonacquiescence
Proposed Regulations
Revenue neutral
Revenue Procedures
Revenue Rulings
Tax benefit rule
Temporary Regulations
Wherewithal to pay

OUTLINE

I. **THE WHYS OF THE TAX LAW**
   A. Revenue Needs
      1. The major objective of the Federal tax law is raising revenue to absorb the cost of government operations.
      2. Over the years, budget deficit considerations have emphasized the concept of revenue neutrality.
      3. Revenue neutral changes in the tax law neither reduce nor increase the deficit—the net revenue raised remains the same.
   B. Economic Considerations
      1. Control of the economy
         a. Capital outlays for business property are:
            1. encouraged through shorter asset lives and accelerated methods of depreciation.
            2. discouraged through longer asset lives and slower methods of depreciation.
         b. Tax rate changes often have a more immediate impact on the economy.
      2. Encouragement of certain activities
         a. Technological progress is encouraged by favorable tax provisions concerning the treatment of:
            1. research and development expenditures.
            2. inventors and patents.
         b. A healthy environment is encouraged through amortization of pollution control facilities.
         c. Low income rental housing is encouraged through tax credits.
         d. Savings is encouraged by making contributions to private retirement accounts deductible and allowing earnings to accumulate tax-free.
      3. Encouragement of certain industries
         a. Farmers are allowed to expense certain soil and water conservation expenditures and defer gain recognition on crop insurance proceeds.
         b. Extractors of gas, oil and some minerals are allowed to use percentage depletion and may expense rather than capitalize some exploration costs.
      4. Encouragement of small business
         a. Ordinary loss treatment allowed on sales of certain small business corporation's stock encourages investments.
         b. The S corporation election allows the corporation to pass through profits and losses to shareholders without a corporate level income tax.
         c. Provisions for corporate reorganization allow corporations to combine without adverse tax consequences.
   C. Social Considerations
      1. Congress uses the Tax Code to address social concerns. Examples include:
         a. The refundable earned income credit reduces the number of people on welfare.
         b. Employer paid insurance coverage for employees (a tax-free fringe benefit that encourages private sector financial support for employees and their families in the event of an employee's illness, injury, or death).
         c. Deferred taxability of private retirement plans encourages saving to supplement social security benefits in post-employment years.
         d. The charitable contribution deduction encourages private sector support for socially desirable programs.
         e. The child and dependent care tax credit encourages taxpayers to work.
         f. Educational credits and the student loan interest deduction encourage higher educational achievement.
   D. Equity Considerations
      1. The equity concept (a Congressional measure of tax system "fairness") appears in various Tax Code provisions.

2. To alleviate the effect of multiple taxation:
   a. deductions are allowed for state and local income taxes.
   b. credits or deductions are allowed for foreign income taxes paid.
   c. corporations are allowed a deduction for certain dividends received.
3. The wherewithal to pay concept allows deferral of gain recognition in specific situations where a taxpayer's economic position has not significantly changed.
4. The annual accounting period concept is modified in certain instances to simplify the computation of taxable income.

E. Political Considerations
1. Special interest legislation is an inevitable product of our political system; certain groups influence Congress to promote the enactment of laws providing special tax treatment for their particular business or interest.
2. Political expediency refers to tax provisions developed in response to popular opinion at the time of enactment.
3. State and local law also influences the Federal tax law. The Federal tax benefit that resulted from taxpayers living in community property states (v. common law states) forced the Congress to change the tax law.

F. Influence of the Internal Revenue Service
1. The IRS as protector of the revenue has been instrumental in securing passage of legislation designed to close tax loopholes.
2. Administrative feasibility of the tax laws is aided by provisions which place taxpayers on a pay-as-you-go basis and impose interest and penalties on taxpayers for noncompliance.

G. Influence of the Courts
1. Judicial concepts relating to tax law serve as guides in applying various tax provisions. Examples include the substance over form, continuity of interest, and business purpose doctrines.
2. Congress may incorporate key court decisions into Federal tax law.

II. **WORKING WITH THE TAX LAW—TAX SOURCES**
A. Statutory Sources of the Tax Law
1. Origin of the Internal Revenue Code
   a. The Internal Revenue Code of 1939 arranged all Federal tax provisions enacted by Congress prior to that time in a separate part of the Federal statutes.
   b. The Internal Revenue Code of 1954 was a revision of the 1939 Code.
   c. The Internal Revenue Code of 1986 added to, deleted, and amended various provisions of the 1954 Code.
   d. Statutory amendments to the tax law, such as the Tax Relief Reconciliation Act of 2001, are integrated into the existing Code.
2. The Legislative Process
   a. Tax legislation generally originates in the House of Representatives, where the enactment process is accomplished in a step-by-step manner, normally starting in the House of Representatives, proceeding to the Senate, and then to the President for signature (see pages 1–18 and 1–19 of your text for a visual representation of this process).
   b. Tax bills may originate in the Senate as riders to other legislation.
   c. When the House and Senate versions of a bill differ, the Joint Conference Committee attempts to resolve the differences.

B. Administrative Sources of the Tax Law
1. Treasury Department Regulations
   a. Regulations provide taxpayers with guidance on the meaning and application of the Code.
   b. Regulations are usually first issued in proposed form before finalization to permit comment from taxpayers.
   c. Temporary Regulations are issued when immediate guidance is critical.

d. Temporary Regulations are simultaneously issued as Proposed Regulations and automatically expire within three years.
e. Final Regulations are issued as Treasury Decisions.
2. Revenue Rulings and Revenue Procedures
   a. A Revenue Ruling provides interpretation of the tax law as it applies to a particular set of circumstances.
   b. Revenue Procedures deal with the internal management practices and procedures of the IRS.
3. Other Administrative Pronouncements
   a. Treasury Decisions are issued to make known Final Regulations, to change existing Regulations, and to announce the Government's position on selected court decisions.
   b. Technical Information Releases are issued to announce the publication of various IRS pronouncements.
   c. A letter ruling is issued, upon a taxpayer's request, to describe how a proposed transaction will be treated for tax purposes.
      1. A letter ruling generally applies only to the requesting taxpayer.
      2. The issuance of letter rulings is limited to restricted, preannounced areas.
   d. A technical advice memorandum is issued in response to a request of IRS personnel during an audit and gives the IRS's position on a specific issue.
   e. A determination letter is issued at the request of a taxpayer to provide guidance concerning the tax laws that are applicable to a *completed* transaction.

C. Judicial Sources of the Tax Law
1. The Judicial Process
   a. If no satisfactory settlement has been reached with the IRS, the dispute can be taken to Federal court (see Figure 1–1).
   b. The case is first considered by a court of original jurisdiction, including:
      1. Federal District Court.
      2. U.S. Court of Federal Claims.
      3. Tax Court (including its Small Cases Division).
   c. Any appeal is taken to the appropriate appellate court, including:
      1. Court of Appeals of appropriate jurisdiction.
      2. Court of Appeals for the Federal Circuit.
      3. Supreme Court.
2. Judicial Decisions
   a. American law is frequently *made* by judicial decisions. Under the doctrine of *stare decisis*, each case has precedential value for future cases having the same controlling set of facts.
   b. The Tax Court hears only tax cases and issues two types of decisions.
      1. Regular decisions involve issues not previously resolved by the Court.
      2. Memorandum decisions involve application of already established principles of law.
   c. If the IRS loses in a decision, it usually indicates agreement (acquiescence) or disagreement (nonacquiescence).

III. **WORKING WITH THE TAX LAW – TAX RESEARCH**
A. Identify the Problem
   1. Gather all of the facts that might have a bearing on the problem.
   2. Refine the problem and determine the tax consequences of each possibility.
B. Locate the Appropriate Tax Law Sources
   1. Various tax services provide access to tax law and provide commentary.
   2. Key words derived from the facts are used to explore tax services.
   3. Make sure your information is up to date.
C. Assess the Validity of Tax Law Sources
   1. Assess the relevance of the tax law source in light of the facts and circumstances of the problem at hand.

2. Assess the weight of the tax law source in light of the facts and circumstances of the problem at hand.
3. Different sources have varying degrees of authority.
D. Arrive at the Solution or at Alternative Solutions
E. Communicate Tax Research
1. Present a clear statement of the issue.
2. Provide a short review of the factual pattern that raised the issue.
3. Provide a review of the pertinent tax law sources.
4. Describe any assumptions made in arriving at the solution.
5. State the recommended solution and the reasoning to support it.
6. List the references consulted.

IV. **WORKING WITH THE TAX LAW—TAX PLANNING**
A. The primary purpose of effective tax planning is to reduce the taxpayer's total tax bill.
B. A secondary objective is to reduce, defer, or eliminate the tax.
C. These objectives must be consistent with the taxpayer's legitimate business goals and consider the impact of a particular action over time (not just the current year).
D. Tax avoidance minimizes tax liabilities through legal means; tax evasion implies the use of subterfuge and fraud to minimize taxes.

TEST FOR SELF-EVALUATION—CHAPTER 1

True or False

Indicate which of the following statements is true or false by circling the correct answer.

T F 1. Revenue Procedures are official IRS statements of internal management practices and procedures that either affect the rights or duties of taxpayers or other members of the public, or concern matters of public knowledge. (IRS 97 4A-7)

T F 2. Nonacquiescence by the Commissioner of Internal Revenue to an adverse decision in a regular Tax Court case means the Internal Revenue Service will NOT accept the decision and will NOT follow it in cases involving similar facts. (IRS 96 4A-27)

T F 3. A Memorandum Decision is a report of a Tax Court decision thought to be of lesser value as a precedent because the issue has been decided many times. (IRS 96 4A-28)

T F 4. An income tax case NOT resolved at an appeals conference can proceed to the United States Tax Court WITHOUT the taxpayer paying the disputed tax, but generally, the United States District Court and United States Court of Federal Claims hear tax cases ONLY after the tax is paid and a claim for credit or refund is filed by the taxpayer and is rejected by the IRS or the IRS has not acted on the taxpayer's claim within six months from the date of filing the claim for refund. (IRS 95 4A-11)

T F 5. All courts except the Tax Court are bound by legislative regulations. (IRS 95 4A-24)

T F 6. Proposed regulations automatically replace the temporary regulations. (IRS 95 4A-25)

T F 7. Revenue rulings are the published interpretations of the IRS concerning the application of tax law to a specific set of facts. (IRS 95 4A-26)

T F 8. The courts are NOT bound by interpretive Treasury Regulations. (IRS 94 4A-27)

T F 9. Decisions of the courts other than the Supreme Court are binding on the Commissioner of Internal Revenue ONLY for the particular taxpayer and for the years litigated. (IRS 94 4A-28)

T F 10. If the Supreme Court determines that various lower courts are deciding a tax issue in an inconsistent manner, it may review a decision and resolve the contradiction. (IRS 94 4A-29)

Fill in the Blanks

Complete the following statements with the appropriate word(s) or amount(s).

1. _____, _____, _____, and _____ play a significant role in the development of Federal tax law.

2. _____, _____, and _____ are examples of political considerations.

3. The courts have influenced and formulated tax law through the two techniques of _____ and _____.

4. If the IRS loses in a Regular decision of the Tax Court, it will indicate _____ or _____ with the result reached by the Court.

5. Appeal to the U.S. Supreme Court is by _____.

6. _____ are issued at the request of taxpayers and provide guidance concerning the application of tax law to completed transactions.

7. Tax reform legislation which does not change net revenues raised is _____.

8. The _____ concept applies to situations in which a taxpayer's economic position has not significantly changed; gain recognition is postponed.

9. _____ is the method whereby one determines the best solution or series of solutions to a particular problem with tax ramifications.

10. _____ is the minimization of tax payments through legal means.

Multiple Choice

Choose the best answer for each of the following questions.

_____ 1. Which of the following statements is correct with respect to procedures of the Small Cases Division of the United States Tax Court? (IRS 97 4B-67)

   a. The amount in the case must be $5,000 or less for any one tax year or period.
   b. The taxpayer can request small case procedures without any approval from the Tax Court.
   c. Small case procedures require the taxpayer and the IRS to submit briefs presenting their positions on the issues.
   d. The Tax Court decision is final and you CANNOT appeal.

_____ 2. With respect to procedures of the Small Cases Division of the United States Tax Court, all of the following statements are correct except: (IRS 95 4B-70)

   a. Within 90 days of receiving a statutory notice of deficiency, the taxpayer must pay a filing fee and file a petition with the Tax Court in Washington, D.C.
   b. The total disputed deficiency (tax and penalties) for ALL tax years at issue must be $10,000 or less.
   c. The decision of the Tax Court CANNOT be appealed to another court and CANNOT be used as a precedent for any other case.
   d. The proceedings are conducted in accordance with such rules of evidence and procedures as the Tax Court may prescribe.

_____ 3. With regard to Revenue Rulings and Revenue Procedures, all of the following statements are correct except: (IRS 96 4B-69)

   a. A Revenue Ruling is a published official interpretation of tax law by the IRS that sets forth the holding of the IRS as to how the tax law applies to a particular set of facts.
   b. Revenue Rulings have the force and effect of Treasury Regulations.
   c. A Revenue Procedure is a published official statement of practice or procedure that either affects the rights or duties of taxpayers or other members of the public under the Internal Revenue Code and related statutes and regulations or, if not necessarily affecting the rights and duties of the public, should be a matter of public knowledge.
   d. Revenue Procedures are directive and NOT mandatory so that a taxpayer has no vested right to the benefit of the procedures when the IRS deviates from its internal rules.

_____ 4. Which of the following statements BEST describes the applicability of a constitutionally valid Internal Revenue Code section on the various courts? (IRS 95 4B-70)

    a. Only the Supreme Court is NOT bound to follow the Code section. All other courts are bound to the Code section.
    b. Only the Tax Court is bound to the Code section, all other courts may waiver from the Code section.
    c. Only District, Claims, and Appellate Courts are bound by the Code section, the Supreme and Tax Courts may waiver from it.
    d. All courts are bound by the Code section.

_____ 5. All of the following statements with respect to classes of regulations are CORRECT except: (IRS 95 4B-71)

    a. All regulations are written by the Office of the Chief Counsel, IRS, and approved by the Secretary of the Treasury.
    b. Public hearings are NOT held on temporary regulations.
    c. Although IRS employees are bound by the regulations, the courts are NOT.
    d. Public hearings are NOT held on proposed regulations.

_____ 6. Which of the following is NOT one of the three classes of Treasury Regulations? (IRS 95 4B-72)

    a. Temporary
    b. Judicial
    c. Final
    d. Proposed

_____ 7. Which of the following statements is FALSE? (IRS 95 4B-73)

    a. The Tax Court will issue either a regular report or a memorandum decision depending upon the issues involved and the relative value of the decision being made.
    b. The Commissioner of Internal Revenue may issue a public acquiescence or nonacquiescence on District or Court of Federal Claims court cases.
    c. Interpretative regulations are issued under the general authority of Internal Revenue Code Section 7805(a) and legislative regulations are issued under the authority of the specific Internal Revenue Code section to which they relate.
    d. The government prints the regular and memorandum Tax Court decisions in bound volumes.

_____ 8. With regard to procedures of the Small Cases Division of the United States Tax Court, all of the following statements are correct except: (IRS 94 4B-41)

    a. The amount of tax involved in the case must be $50,000 or less for any one tax year or period.
    b. The taxpayer must request small case procedures and the Tax Court must approve the request.
    c. The taxpayer must pay the tax and file a claim for credit or refund that the IRS rejects.
    d. The Tax Court decision is final and you CANNOT appeal.

_____ 9. With regard to Treasury Regulations, all of the following statements are correct except: (IRS 94 4B-69)

    a. Notices of proposed rulemaking are REQUIRED for proposed regulations and are published in the Federal Register so that interested parties have an opportunity to participate in the rulemaking process.
    b. Until final regulations are issued, unexpired temporary regulations have the same force and effect of law as final regulations.

c. Legislative regulations are those for which the IRS is specifically authorized by the Code to provide the details of the meaning and rules for particular Code sections.

d. Interpretative regulations, which explain the IRS's position on the various sections of the Code, are NOT accorded great weight by the courts.

_____ 10. The concept of equity appears to explain all of the following provisions of the tax law, except:

a. Anita has had three surgeries this year and is allowed a deduction for her paid extraordinary, unreimbursed, medical expenses.

b. This year, Kerrie's house was destroyed by fire, thereby allowing Kerrie a deduction for her extraordinary casualty loss.

c. Keith has taxable income that is exactly 3 times more than Edward's taxable income. Even though Keith and Edward are both single, Keith pays a tax that is more than 3 times the amount of tax that Edward pays.

d. This year, John realized a gain on the sale of his house. In exchange for his house, John accepted a promissory note (secured by his house) for the entire purchase price. John will begin receiving principal and interest payments next year. John may defer any gain realized on the sale of his house until John begins receiving principal payments (next year).

e. This year, Laura is allowed to deduct the interest paid to a financial institution on $300,000 of indebtedness (secured by her principal residence), the proceeds of which were used to acquire her principal residence.

_____ 11. If a taxpayer with a statutory notice of deficiency wishes his/her case heard by a court before paying the tax, which court would the taxpayer petition? (IRS 94 4B-71)

a. United States Tax Court
b. United States Court of Federal Claims
c. United States District Court
d. United States Court of Appeals

_____ 12. With regard to terminology relating to court decisions, all of the following statements are correct except: (IRS 94 4B-72)

a. DECISION, the court's formal answer to the principal issue in litigation, has legal sanction and is enforceable by the authority of the court.

b. DICTUM, a court's statement of opinion on a legal point NOT raised by the facts of the case, is NOT controlling, but may be persuasive to another court deciding the issue dealt with by the dictum.

c. Acquiescence by the Commissioner of Internal Revenue Service on adverse regular Tax Court decisions, generally means the IRS will follow the Court's decision in cases involving similar facts.

d. *Writ of Certiorari* is a petition issued by the lower appellate court to the Supreme Court to hear a case that is NOT subject to obligatory review by the Supreme Court.

SOLUTIONS TO CHAPTER 1 QUESTIONS

True or False

1. T (p. 1–22)

    - Revenue Procedures are issued by the National Office of the IRS and relate to internal management practices and procedures. The IRS issues these statements to publicly address the specific manner in which it carries out certain aspects of its administrative function that may affect the rights and duties of taxpayers.

2. T (p. 1–32)

    - IF the IRS loses a tax case in Tax Court, it issues an acquiescence or non-acquiescence position for the purpose of guiding the taxpayer. However, IF the IRS loses a case in either the District Court or the Court of Federal Claims, it may choose to issue an acquiescence or non-acquiescence position in the form of an information release. An acquiescence (non-acquiescence) position indicates that the IRS will follow (not follow) the adverse decision of the court in a subsequent case with substantially the same facts. The determination of such position depends upon the IRS's perception of revenue implications, policy implications, and litigation costs.

3. T (p. 1–30)

    - The U.S. Tax Court. The U.S. Tax Court issues the following two types of decisions.
        - Regular decisions. A regular decision generally deals with a case where some issue relating to the application of tax law to a particular set of facts has not been previously adjudged.
        - Memorandum decisions. A memorandum decision is a case where the issues surrounding the case have all been previously adjudged. Although the taxpayer should be aware of both types of decisions, memorandum decisions have less weight in terms of authority.

4. T (p. 1–26)

    Throughout this entire process (audit, assessment, and collection of a tax), the taxpayer may:

    - First, pay the alleged deficiency, deficiency, or assessed deficiency, either:
        - during the audit process (before or after the issuance of the 30-day letter) or
        - after the issuance of the 90-day letter (before or after the 90 day period has expired).
    - Second, file a claim for refund.

    Under Section 7422, no suit for the recovery of any tax shall be maintained unless a formal claim for refund has been filed with the IRS Further, to file a claim alleging an overpayment of tax in either the U.S. Court of Federal Claims or the U.S. District Court, the claim for refund filed with the [IRS] must have been either:

    - disallowed by the IRS in a statutory notice of claim disallowance or
    - filed at least 6 months before without any IRS action being taken.

    However, to enable the taxpayer to more quickly file a claim alleging an overpayment of tax in either the U.S. Court of Federal Claims or the U.S. District Court, the taxpayer may request in writing that the IRS immediately issue a statutory notice of claim disallowance. Otherwise, the taxpayer may be waiting 6 months after the claim for refund is filed with the IRS.

5. F (p. 1–37; no exceptions, truly possess the force and effect of law)

    Primary sources of the tax law include:

    - Statutory sources, which include:
        - The U.S. Constitution.
        - The Internal Revenue Code.

STUDY GUIDE | CHAPTER 1 | 1–11
Understanding and Working with the Federal Tax Law

- Judicial sources, which include trial court and appellate court cases.
- Administrative sources, which include statements of:
  - The Internal Revenue Service (revenue rulings and procedures and statements of acquiescence or nonacquiescence).
  - Treasury Department regulations.

6. F   (p. 1–22; temporary regulations are simultaneously issued as proposed regulations)

- Proposed regulations. Under the APA, Treasury Regulations are first published in the Federal Register as proposed regulations to satisfy the APA's requirements of notice and to give an opportunity for public comment. Proposed regulations are issued at least 30 days before final regulations are issued. These regulations do not have the force and effect of law and they expire after 3 years.
- Final regulations. Final regulations are issued to replace proposed regulations, but only after the 30-day notice and public comment period has expired.
- Temporary regulations. Some regulations may not be first issued as proposed regulations, thereby avoiding the APA's notice and public hearing requirements. For example, temporary regulations may be issued pursuant to a change in the tax law to assist taxpayers and practitioners in interpreting the new law. This type of interpretive regulation (similar to a final interpretive regulation) has the force and effect of law, unless it is found to be inconsistent with the statute for which it was written. Further, there is no public comment opportunity. Temporary regulations are not replaced by proposed regulations. Instead, such regulations are contemporaneously published as proposed regulations, so that under Section 7805(f) they expire after 3 years, for temporary regulations issued after September 10, 1988.

7. F   (p. 1–22; interpretive holdings)

- The Internal Revenue Service (IRS), includes statements on:
  - Revenue Rulings. Revenue Rulings are issued by the National Office of the IRS published in the *Internal Revenue Bulletin* and discuss the tax consequences of a prospective transaction within a particular framework. Such framework incorporates:
    - A description of a particular set of facts and circumstances that relate to a person or a set of persons.
    - An issue that is relevant to a person or a set of persons.
    - Identification of the appropriate tax law and its authoritative weight.
    - Application of the law to the set of facts.

8. T   (p. 1–38)

- Interpretive regulations. Under Section 7805(a), interpretive regulations are issued under the Treasury's general authority to interpret the laws of the Internal Revenue Code. Generally, an interpretive regulation has the force and effect of law, unless it is found to be inconsistent with the statute for which it was written. Thus, an interpretive regulation is not necessarily controlling, thereby precluding judicial deference. The weight a court gives to an interpretive regulation depends upon all facts and circumstances. However, interpretive regulations are not given as much weight as legislative regulations.

9. T   (p. 1–30)

   The U.S. Tax Court issues the following two types of decisions.

- Regular decisions. A regular decision generally deals with a case where some issue relating to the application of tax law to a particular set of facts has not been previously adjudged.
- Memorandum decisions. A memorandum decision is a case where the issues surrounding the case have all been previously adjudged. Although the taxpayer should be aware of both types of decisions, memorandum decisions have less weight in terms of authority.

   Appellate court cases include cases of:

- The U.S. Court of Appeals.
- The U.S. Court of Appeals for the Court of Federal Claims.

- The U.S. Supreme Court. A taxpayer does not have an automatic right to have the Supreme Court hear his/her case. Instead, the taxpayer must request that the Supreme Court issue a *Writ of Certiorari*. The writ is a demand by the Supreme Court to a lower court for the lower court to send the case up to the Supreme Court. Generally, the Supreme Court hears tax cases only if:
  - An issue of national import arises.
  - There is a conflict among the lower appellate courts.

  Because the Supreme Court is the ultimate arbiter (i.e., the sovereign legal authority) concerning the interpretation of Federal law under the U.S. Constitution, the IRS is bound by its decisions. However, such status has not been conferred on lower appellate (or trial) courts. Thus, the IRS is technically bound by a court's decision (other than a decision of the Supreme Court) with respect to only the particular litigant and to only the years litigated.

10. T (p. 1–29)

- U.S. Supreme Court. A taxpayer does not have an automatic right to have the Supreme Court hear his/her case. Instead, the taxpayer must request that the Supreme Court issue a *Writ of Certiorari*. The writ is a demand by the Supreme Court to a lower court for the lower court to send the case up to the Supreme Court. Generally, the Supreme Court hears tax cases only if:
  - An issue of national import arises.
  - There is a conflict among the lower appellate courts.

Fill in the Blanks

1. Economic, social, equity, political factors (p. 1–2)

   The Federal tax law is amazingly intimidating in its complexity. The major objective of the Federal tax system is revenue collection. However, other underlying considerations of specific provisions may include:

   - Economic factors. For example, economic considerations underlie provisions designed to influence certain aspects of the economy.
   - Social factors. For example, societal considerations underlie provisions designed to achieve public policy goals without the need for direct government intervention.
   - Equity factors. For example, equity considerations underlie provisions designed to provide for fairness across all taxpayers.
   - Political factors. Political factors that affect the enactment of specific revenue provisions include the influence of special interest groups, the role of political expediency, and state and local influences.

2. Special interest legislation, political expediency, and state and local influences (p. 1–10)

   - Political factors. Political factors that affect the enactment of specific revenue provisions include:
     - The influence of special interest groups. For example, special interest groups lobby for special interest legislation.
     - The role of political expediency. For example, that which is determined to be suitable to obtain a specific objective may give rise to political compromise resulting in legislation to obtain such objective.
     - State and local influences. For example, the Federal tax law generally follows state property law in determining the rights and obligations of persons who own interests in property.

3. Formulating judicial concepts, making key decisions (p. 1–13)

   Trial court cases include cases of:

   - The U.S. District Court.
   - The U.S. Court of Federal Claims.
   - The U.S. Tax Court.

The U.S. Tax Court issues the following two types of decisions.
- Regular decisions. A regular decision generally deals with a case where some issue relating to the application of tax law to a particular set of facts has not been previously adjudged.
- Memorandum decisions. A memorandum decision is a case where the issues surrounding the case have all been previously adjudged. Although the taxpayer should be aware of both types of decisions, memorandum decisions have less weight in terms of authority.

Appellate court cases include cases of:

- The U.S. Court of Appeals.
- The U.S. Court of Appeals for the Court of Federal Claims.
- The U.S. Supreme Court.

The judiciary provides a source for tax law through:

- The formation of common law (judicial) concepts that are employed in applying Federal tax law.
- The holding of a case that interprets the Federal tax law.

4. Acquiescence, nonacquiescence (p. 1–32)

- Statements of acquiescence or non-acquiescence. The IRS has an acquiescence/non-acquiescence program whereby IF the IRS loses a tax case in Tax Court, it issues an acquiescence or non-acquiescence position published in the *Internal Revenue Bulletin* for the purpose of guiding the taxpayer. However, IF the IRS loses a case in either the District Court or the Court of Federal Claims, it may choose to issue an acquiescence or non-acquiescence position in a form of an information release. An acquiescence (non-acquiescence) position indicates that the IRS will follow (not follow) the adverse decision of the court in a subsequent case with substantially the same facts. The determination of such position depends upon the IRS's perception of:
  - Revenue implications.
  - Policy implications.
  - Litigation costs.

5. *Writ of centiorari* (p. 1–29)

- U.S. Supreme Court. A taxpayer does not have an automatic right to have the Supreme Court hear his/her case. Instead, the taxpayer must request that the Supreme Court issue a *Writ of Certiorari*. The writ is a demand by the Supreme Court to a lower court for the lower court to send the case up to the Supreme Court. Generally, the Supreme Court hears tax cases only if:
  - An issue of national import arises.
  - There is a conflict among the lower appellate courts.

6. Determination Letters (p. 1–24)

During an examination audit, the taxpayer can seek official advice from the IRS concerning a disputed tax issue:

- In the form of a Determination Letter. A Determination Letter is issued by the District Director's Office that has jurisdiction over the taxpayer's audit. Such letter is written only if the response to the issue presented is within the specific scope of statutory, administrative or judicial tax law.
- In the form of a Technical Advice Memorandum. A Technical Advice Memorandum is issued by the National Office of the IRS to a District Office in connection with a disputed tax issue with a view toward maintaining consistent positions within the examination function across District Offices. It applies statutory, administrative or judicial tax law to the facts at issue.

7. Revenue neutral (p. 1–3)

The Federal tax law is amazingly intimidating in its complexity. The major objective of the Federal tax system is revenue collection. In fact, the revenue implications of any change in the tax law must be determined prior to consideration for enactment. In evaluating the merits of a revenue bill, Congress may mandate that such bill be revenue neutral, where the aggregate of all changes produces no change in total revenue.

8. Wherewithal to pay (p. 1–7)

The Federal tax law is amazingly intimidating in its complexity. The major objective of the Federal tax system is revenue collection. However, other underlying considerations of specific provisions may include:

- Economic factors. For example, economic considerations underlie provisions designed to influence certain aspects of the economy.
- Social factors. For example, societal considerations underlie provisions designed to achieve public policy goals without the need for direct government intervention.
- Equity factors. For example, equity considerations underlie provisions designed to provide for fairness across all taxpayers (e.g., the wherewithal to pay doctrine is applied to defer the gain (or loss) in certain exchanges where the essential economic position of the taxpayer has not changed).
- Political factors. Political factors that affect the enactment of specific revenue provisions include the influence of special interest groups, the role of political expediency, and state and local influences.

9. Tax research (p. 1–33)

Tax research is defined as a process incorporating the following steps:

- A finding of a particular set of facts and circumstances that relate to a person or a set of persons.
- An issue that is relevant to a person or a set of persons.
- Identification of the appropriate tax law and its authoritative weight.
- Application of the law to the set of facts.
- A conclusion pertaining to the issue based upon professional judgment arising from application of the law to the set of facts.
- Communication of the conclusion to the relevant parties.

10. Tax avoidance (p. 1–43)

Tax avoidance is defined as the systematic structuring of a person's transactions to minimize his/her/its tax burden. Tax avoidance (evasion) necessarily involves tax planning through legal (illegal) means. Judge Learned Hand commented:

> Over and over again courts have said that there is nothing sinister in so arranging one's affairs as to keep taxes as low as possible. Everybody does so, rich or poor; and all do right, for nobody owes any public duty to pay more than the law demands: taxes are enforced exactions, not voluntary contributions. To demand more in the name of morals is mere cant. *Commissioner v. Newman*, 159 F2d 848 (CA–2, 1947).

Multiple Choice

1. d (p. 1–25)

The U.S. Tax Court also has the Small Cases Division. Under Section 7463(a), the subject matter jurisdiction of the Small Claims Division covers deficiencies (including penalties) and overpayments of not more than $50,000. A taxpayer must have approval from the Tax Court to be heard by the Small Cases Division. A hearing (case) within the Small Cases Division is:

- Informal, where the taxpayer may represent himself or herself in a Small Cases Division proceeding conducted in accordance with Tax Court rules.
- Does not require extensive briefs or formal presentment but requires the filing of a petition under Tax Court Rule 34(b) that must be approved by the Tax Court.
- Not published and, accordingly, does not have precedential value.

Since cases in the Small Cases Division are heard informally according to the special rules of evidence and procedure promulgated by the U.S. Tax Court, the taxpayer's appeal is precluded.

Thus, in the instant case, item d is correct. Further, the following choice items are incorrect.

- Item a is incorrect because the subject matter jurisdiction of the Small Claims Division covers deficiencies (including penalties) and overpayments of not more than $50,000.
- Item b is incorrect because the taxpayer needs approval from the Tax Court.
- Item c is incorrect because a case within the Small Cases Division is informal, where the taxpayer may represent himself or herself and where extensive briefs or formal presentment is not required.

2. b (p. 1–25; $50,000)

The U.S. Tax Court also has the Small Cases Division. Under Section 7463(a), the subject matter jurisdiction of the Small Claims Division covers deficiencies (including penalties) and overpayments of not more than $50,000. A taxpayer must have approval from the Tax Court to be heard by the Small Cases Division.

Thus, in the instant case, item b is the right answer because it is not true that the subject matter jurisdiction of the Small Claims Division covers deficiencies (including penalties) and overpayments of not more than $10,000. Rather, such amount is $50,000. Further, each of the choice items a, c, and d is not the right answer because each is correct.

3. b (p. 1–22; do not have the same force and effect, deal with more restrictive problems)

- Revenue Rulings. Revenue Rulings are issued by the National Office of the IRS published in the *Internal Revenue Bulletin* and discuss the tax consequences of a prospective transaction within a particular framework.

  Revenue Rulings have less precedential weight than Treasury Regulations.

  Thus, item b is the right answer because it is not true that Revenue Rulings have the force and effect of Treasury Regulations. Further, each of the choice items a, c, and d is not the right answer because each is correct.

4. d (p. 1–13; subject to interpretation)

- The Internal Revenue Code. The Internal Revenue Code (Title 26 of the United States Code) embodies statutory Federal tax law in its entirety. All Federal administrative agencies and the Federal judiciary are bound to statutory Federal tax law, unless such law is found unconstitutional. Administrative agencies are charged with administering statutory law. The judiciary is charged with interpreting and applying statutory law.

  Thus, item d is correct. Further, choice items a, b, and c are incorrect because they each are inconsistent with item d.

5. d (p. 1–22; public comment period, not hearings)

- The manner in which regulations are promulgated. Treasury Regulations are promulgated under the formal rule-making procedures of the Administrative Procedure Act (APA).
  - Proposed regulations. Under the APA, Treasury Regulations are first published in the Federal Register as proposed regulations to satisfy the APA's requirements of notice and opportunity for public comment. Proposed regulations are issued at least 30 days before final regulations are issued. These regulations do not have the force and effect of law and they expire after 3 years.
  - Final regulations. Final regulations are issued to replace proposed regulations, but only after the 30-day notice and public comment period has expired.
  - Temporary regulations. Some regulations may not be first issued as proposed regulations, thereby avoiding the APA's notice and public hearing requirements. For example, temporary regulations may be issued pursuant to a change in the tax law to assist taxpayers and practitioners in interpreting the new law. This type of interpretive regulation (similar to a final interpretive regulation) has the force and effect of law, unless it is found to be inconsistent with the statute for which it was written. Further, there is no public comment opportunity. Temporary regulations are not replaced by proposed

regulations. Instead, such regulations are contemporaneously published as proposed regulations, so that under Section 7805(f) they expire after 3 years, for temporary regulations issued after September 10, 1988.

Thus, item d is the right answer because it is not true that public hearings are not held upon issuance of proposed regulations. In fact, they are held. Further, each of the choice items a, b, and c is not the right answer because each is correct.

6. b (p. 1–22)

- The 3 classes of Treasury Regulations are:
  - Proposed regulations. Proposed regulations are issued at least 30 days before final regulations are issued. These regulations do not have the force and effect of law and they expire after 3 years.
  - Final regulations. Final regulations are issued to replace proposed regulations, but only after the 30-day notice and public comment period has expired.
  - Temporary regulations. Some regulations may not be first issued as proposed regulations, thereby avoiding the APA's notice and public hearing requirements. Temporary regulations are not replaced by proposed regulations. Instead, such regulations are contemporaneously published as proposed regulations, so that under Section 7805(f) they expire after 3 years, for temporary regulations issued after September 10, 1988.

Thus, item b is the right answer because it is not true that a Judicial Regulation is a class of Treasury Regulation. Further, the each of choice items a, c, and d is not the right answer because each represents a class of Treasury Regulation.

7. d (p. 1–30; Memorandum decisions printed in mimeograph form only)

- The U.S. Tax Court. The U.S. Tax Court issues the following two types of decisions.
  - Regular reports. A regular report generally deals with a case where some issue relating to the application of tax law to a particular set of facts has not been previously adjudged.
  - Memorandum decisions. A memorandum decision is a case where the issues surrounding the case have all been previously adjudged. Although the taxpayer should be aware of both types of decisions, memorandum decisions have less weight in terms of authority.

Item d is the right answer because it is not true that the government prints regular and memorandum Tax Court decisions. Rather, only regular Tax Court decisions are published. Further, each of the choice items a, b, and c is not the right answer because each is correct.

8. c (p. 1–26; taxpayer is not required to pay tax)

The U.S. Tax Court has the Small Cases Division. Under Section 7463(a), the subject matter jurisdiction of the Small Cases Division covers deficiencies (including penalties) and overpayments of not more than $50,000. A taxpayer must have approval from the Tax Court to be heard by the Small Cases Division. A hearing (case) within the Small Cases Division is:

- Informal, where the taxpayer may represent himself or herself in a Small Cases Division proceeding conducted in accordance with Tax Court rules.
- Does not require extensive briefs or formal presentment but requires the filing of a petition under Tax Court Rule 34(b) that must be approved by the Tax Court.
- Not published and, accordingly, does not have precedential value.

Since cases in the Small Cases Division are heard informally according to the special rules of evidence and procedure promulgated by the U.S. Tax Court, the taxpayer's right of appeal is precluded.

Item c is the right answer because it is not true that a prerequisite to filing a petition in Tax Court is to first pay the tax. Further, each of the choice items a, b, and d is not the right answer because each is correct.

STUDY GUIDE **CHAPTER 1** 1–17
Understanding and Working with the Federal Tax Law

9. d (p. 1–21, 38; generally have the force and effect of law)

   - Interpretive regulations. Under Section 7805(a), interpretive regulations are issued under the Treasury's general authority to interpret the laws of the Internal Revenue Code. Generally, an interpretive regulation has the force and effect of law, unless it is found to be inconsistent with the statute for which it was written. Thus, an interpretive regulation is not necessarily controlling, thereby precluding judicial deference. The weight a court gives to an interpretive regulation depends upon all facts and circumstances. However, interpretive regulations are not given as much weight as legislative regulations.
   - Legislative regulations. Legislative regulations arise from Congress' specific delegation of authority to write regulations associated with a particular statute. As such, these regulations effectively have the authoritative weight of statutory law. Thus, legislative regulations are generally binding on all courts as statutory law, as long as such regulations are:
     Issued within the power of the agency.
     Issued consistent with proper procedure.
     Reasonable.

   Thus, in the instant case, item d is the right answer because it is not true that courts do NOT accord great weight to interpretive regulations. Generally, an interpretive regulation is upheld unless unreasonable and plainly inconsistent with the statute. Further, each of the choice items a, b, and c is not the right answer because each is correct.

10. e (p. 1–5)

   In the instant case, item e is the right answer because it it not true that enactment of the qualified residence interest deduction was motivated by a Congressional equity concern. Rather, such enactment was motivated by a societal concern. Because Congress believes that home ownership is a positive societal virtual, subsidizing home ownership is a public policy goal. Further, each of the choice items a, b, c, and d is not the right answer because each represents a provision whose enactment arose out of an equity concern of either (1) a taxpayer's ability to pay or (2) a taxpayer's wherewithal to pay.

   - In item a and b, Anita (Kerrie) has a lesser ability to pay as a result of her extraordinary medical expenses (casualty loss).
   - In item c, vertical equity suggests that Keith should pay more tax than Edward pays because Keith has a greater ability to pay. In the enactment of the progressive income tax structure, Congress has translated vertical equity into Keith paying a tax that is more than 3 times the tax that Edward pays.
   - In item d, John does not have the wherewithal to pay the tax on the gain from the sale of his house, since John sold his house on an installment basis.

11. a (p. 1–30)

   - The U.S. Tax Court.
     The U.S. Tax Court issues the following two types of decisions.
     - Regular decisions. A regular decision generally deals with a case where some issue relating to the application of tax law to a particular set of facts has not been previously adjudged.
     - Memorandum decisions. A memorandum decision is a case where the issues surrounding the case have all been previously adjudged. Although the taxpayer should be aware of both types of decisions, memorandum decisions have less weight in terms of authority.

   Thus, in the instant case, item a is correct. Further, the choice items b, c, and d are incorrect because each is inconsistent with item a.

12. d (p. 1–29; order issued by the Supreme Court)

   - U.S. Supreme Court. A taxpayer does not have an automatic right to have the Supreme Court hear his/her case. Instead, the taxpayer must request that the Supreme Court issue a *Writ of Certiorari*. The writ is a demand by the Supreme Court to a lower court for the lower court to send the case up to the Supreme Court. Generally, the Supreme Court hears tax cases only if:

- An issue of national import arises.
- There is a conflict among the lower appellate courts.

Because the Supreme Court is the ultimate arbiter (i.e., the sovereign legal authority) concerning the interpretation of Federal law under the U.S. Constitution, the IRS is bound by its decisions. However, such status has not been conferred on lower appellate (or trial) courts. Thus, the IRS is technically bound by a court's decision (other than a decision of the Supreme Court) with respect to only the particular litigant and to only the years litigated.

Thus, in the instant case, item d is the right answer because it is not true that the *Writ of Certiorari* is a petition by the lower court to the Supreme Court. Rather, it is a demand by the Supreme Court to the lower court for the lower court to send the case up. Further, each of the choice items a, b, and c is not the right answer because each is correct.

CHAPTER 2

Corporations: Introduction, Operating Rules, and Related Corporations

LEARNING OBJECTIVES

After completing Chapter 2, you should be able to:

1. Summarize the various forms of conducting a business.
2. Compare the taxation of individuals and corporations.
3. Discuss the tax rules unique to corporations.
4. Compute the corporate income tax.
5. Explain the tax rules unique to multiple corporations.
6. Describe the reporting process for corporations.
7. Evaluate the corporation as a form of business organization.

KEY TERMS

Affiliated group
Brother-sister controlled group
Check-the-box Regulations
Controlled group
Dividends received deduction
Limited liability company (LLC)

Limited partnership
Organizational expenditures
Parent-subsidiary controlled group
Passive loss

Personal service corporation (PSC)
Regular C corporation
Related corporations
S corporation
Schedule M–1

OUTLINE

I. **TAX TREATMENT OF VARIOUS BUSINESS FORMS**
   A. A Sole Proprietorship reports all business activity on the individual owner's Schedule C, Form 1040.
   B. A Partnership reports all of the partnership's business activity on Form 1065 and each partner's distributive share on Schedule K–1; this information is then transferred to and included in each partner's Form 1040.
   C. S corporations are similar to partnerships; each S corporation reports its activities on Form 1120S and K–1's are issued to each shareholder; and each individual shareholder incorporates the K–1 information on his/her Form 1040.
   D. Regular C corporations report all business activity on Form 1120. These corporations are taxable entities separate and distinct from their owners (shareholders).
   E. Limited liability companies (LLCs) may be taxed as partnerships, regular corporations, or sole proprietorships.
   F. Check-the-box entity regulations permit a business entity to choose its tax status regardless of its corporate or noncorporate characteristics.

II. **INCOME TAXATION OF CORPORATIONS**
   A. Overview
      1. The gross income of a corporation, including gains and losses from property transactions, is determined in much the same manner as it is for individuals.
      2. Business deductions of corporations parallel those of individuals—deductions are allowed for all ordinary and necessary expenses paid or incurred in carrying on a trade or business.
      3. Corporations are subject to a different tax rate structure than individuals.
   B. Specific Provisions
      1. Accounting periods and methods
         a. Regular C corporations may choose a calendar or fiscal tax year.
         b. A personal service corporation (PSC) must generally use a calendar year. A corporation is a PSC if owner-employees substantially perform services in the fields of health, law, engineering, architecture, accounting, actuarial science, performing arts, or consulting. PSCs are allowed to elect a fiscal year if certain requirements are met.
         c. Generally, a regular corporation must use the accrual method of accounting.
         d. The cash method may be used by:
            1. corporations engaged in the trade or business of farming and timber.
            2. corporations having average annual gross receipts of $5 million or less.
            3. qualified PSCs.
            4. S corporations.
            5. qualified service providers with average annual gross receipts of $10 million or less.
      2. Capital gains and losses
         a. Net capital gain is fully included in a corporation's taxable income.
         b. Capital losses can offset only capital gains.
         c. Net capital losses may be carried back 3 years and forward 5 years.
         d. When carried back or forward, all capital losses are treated as short-term.
      3. Passive losses
         a. Closely held C corporations may offset passive losses against active income, but not against portfolio income.
         b. A corporation is closely held if more than 50% of the value of the corporation's outstanding stock is held by 5 or fewer individuals at any time during the tax year.
         c. PSCs cannot offset passive losses against either active income or portfolio income.

4. Charitable contributions
   a. A contribution deduction is allowed if the recipient is a qualified charitable organization. Special rules apply to accrual basis corporations and property contributions.
   b. An accrual basis corporation may claim the deduction in the year preceding payment if:
      1. the contribution has been authorized by the end of that year and
      2. the payment is made on or before the 15th day of the 3rd month of the next year.
   c. Property contributions
      1. The deduction for long-term capital gain property donated is, generally, fair market value.
      2. The deduction for ordinary income property donated is, generally, limited to its basis (FMV-ordinary income potential).
      3. The flowchart following this chapter outline reviews exceptions for property contributions.
   d. A corporate taxpayer's charitable contribution deduction for any one year is limited to 10% of modified taxable income. Modified taxable income is taxable income computed without regard to the charitable contribution deduction, any net operating loss carryback, any net capital loss carryback, and the dividends received deduction.
5. Net operating losses may be carried back 2 years and forward 20 years to offset taxable income.
6. Deductions available only to corporations
   a. The dividends received deduction mitigates triple taxation.
      1. A corporation may deduct 70, 80, or 100% of the amount of dividends received from domestic corporations.
      2. The percentage of ownership in the payor corporation determines the deductible percentage.
      3. This deduction may be limited by the corporation's adjusted taxable income.
   b. Organizational expenditures
      1. A corporation may elect to amortize organizational expenditures over a period of 60 months or more.
      2. Amortizable expenses include:
         a. legal services incident to organization.
         b. necessary accounting services.
         c. expenses of temporary directors.
         d. expenses of organizational meetings of directors or shareholders.
         e. fees paid to the state of incorporation.
      3. The expenditures must be incurred before the end of the taxable year in which the corporation begins business.

III. DETERMINING THE CORPORATION INCOME TAX LIABILITY
   A. Corporate Income Tax Rates:

Taxable Income Over—	But Not Over—	Tax Is:	Of the Amount Over—
$ 0	$ 50,000	15%	$ 0
50,000	75,000	$ 7,500 + 25%	50,000
75,000	100,000	13,750 + 34%	75,000
100,000	335,000	22,250 + 39%	100,000
335,000	10,000,000	113,900 + 34%	335,000
10,000,000	15,000,000	3,400,000 + 35%	10,000,000
15,000,000	18,333,333	5,150,000 + 38%	15,000,000
18,333,333	—	5,150,000 + 35%	0

B. PSCs are taxed at a flat 35% rate on all taxable income.
C. Corporations are subject to the Alternative Minimum Tax.
D. Certain related corporations (controlled groups of corporations) are subject to special rules for computing the income tax, the alternative minimum tax, and certain other provisions.
 1. Controlled corporate groups include:
    a. Parent-subsidiary groups (one or more chains of corporations connected through stock ownership with a common parent corporation).
    b. Brother-sister groups (multiple corporations owned by five or fewer persons).
    c. Combined groups (a combination of parent-subsidiary corporations and brother-sister corporations).
 2. Various 80 percent and 50 percent tests are applied to see if a controlled group exists.
 3. If a controlled group of corporations exists, taxable income is limited in the tax brackets below 35% to the amount the corporations in the group would have if they were one corporation.

IV. **PROCEDURAL MATTERS**
A. A corporation, whether or not it has taxable income, must file its return by the 15th day of the 3rd month after the close of its tax year.
B. An automatic extension of six months for filing the corporate return may be requested on Form 7004.
C. Estimated tax payments are required of corporations expecting a tax liability of $500 or more.
D. Schedule M–1 on page 4 of Form 1120 is used to reconcile financial accounting net income to taxable income.

V. **TAX PLANNING CONSIDERATIONS**
A. Tax planning to reduce corporate income taxes should occur before year end.
B. Particular attention should be focused on:
 1. charitable contributions.
 2. timing capital gains and losses.
 3. net operating losses.
 4. dividends received deductions.
 5. organizational expenditures.
 6. shareholder-employee payment of corporate expense.

Section 234–Dividends Received Deductions

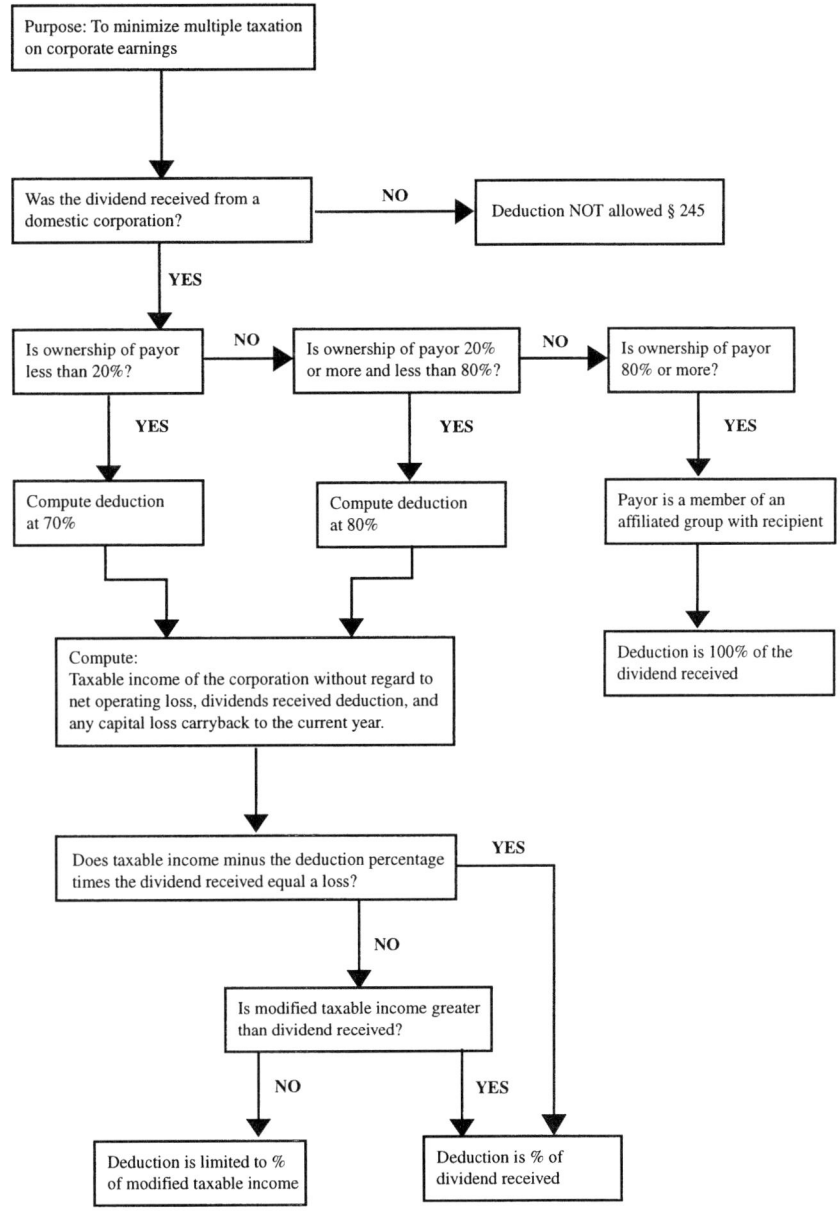

Section 170–Charitable Contributions

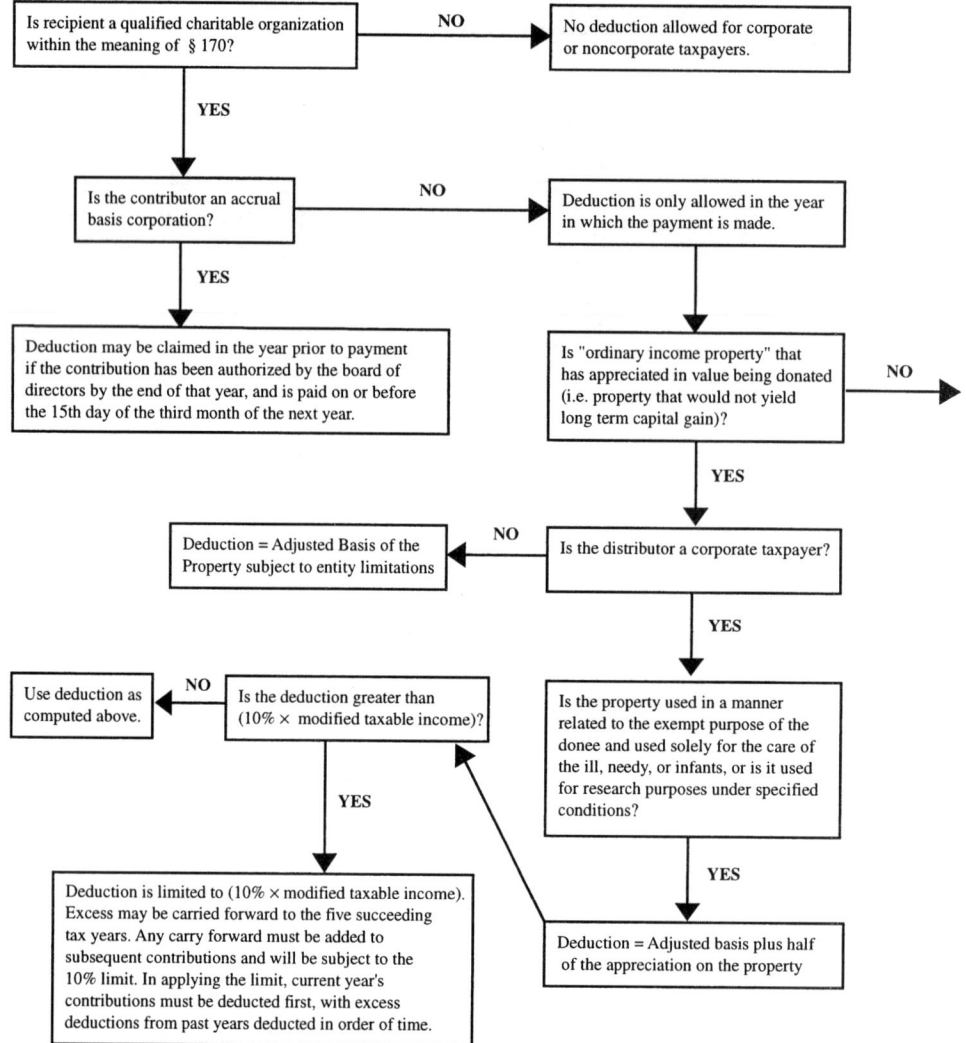

STUDY GUIDE
CHAPTER 2
Corporations: Introduction, Operating Rules, and Related Corporations

2-7

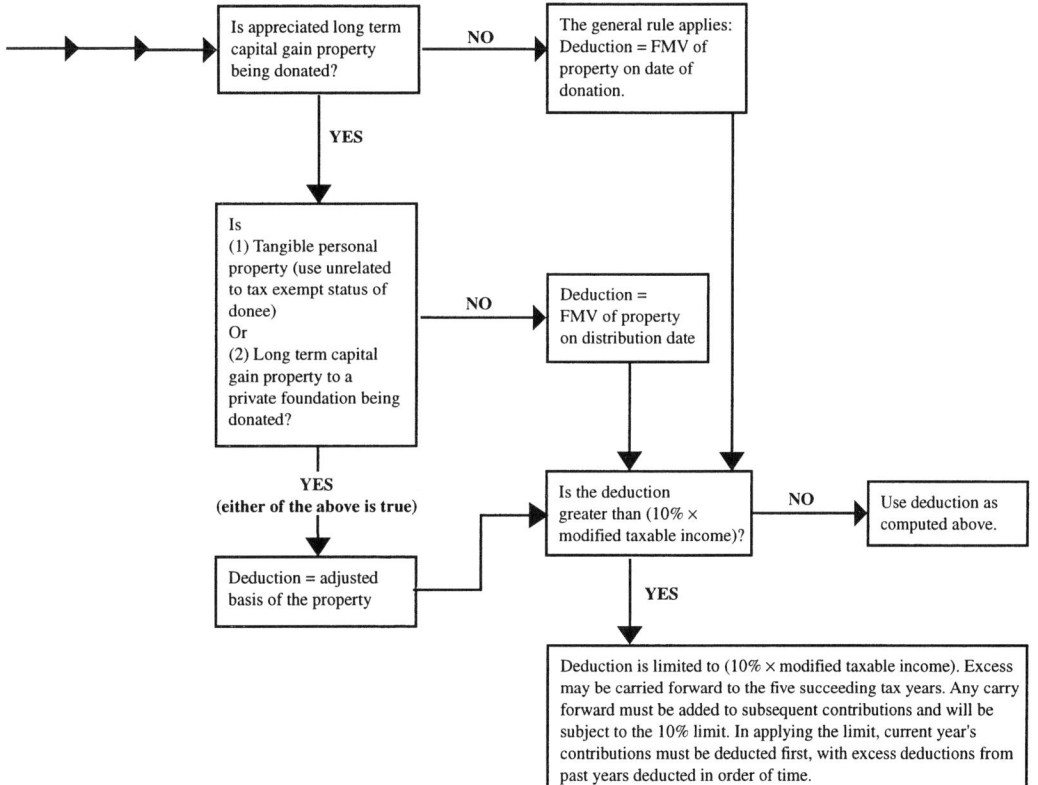

TEST FOR SELF-EVALUATION—CHAPTER 2

True or False

Indicate which of the following statements is true or false by circling the correct answer.

T F 1. A professional service organization must be BOTH organized and operated as a corporation to be necessarily classified as a corporation under the check-the-box entity regulations. (IRS 97 3A-1)

T F 2. In 2002, CDS, a C corporation, has a net short-term capital gain of $3,000 and a net long-term capital loss of $9,000. The short-term gain offsets some of the long-term loss, leaving a net capital loss of $6,000. CDS treats this $6,000 as a short-term loss when carried back or forward. (IRS 97 3A-15)

T F 3. A corporation will receive an automatic 6-month extension of time for filing its return by submitting an application for extension on Form 7004. The IRS can terminate this extension at any time by mailing a notice of termination to the corporation. (IRS 96 3A-1)

T F 4. Corporation Y, a calendar year corporation, incurred qualifying organizational expenses of $7,000, and started business on January 1, 2002. Corporation Y may elect to deduct the organizational expenses in full in 2002 or treat them as deferred expenses and amortize them over a period of no less than 60 months. (IRS 96 3A-4)

T F 5. Advertising expenses for the opening of a business of a corporation that has not yet begun its business operations MUST be considered a start-up expense. (IRS 95 3A-3)

T F 6. In 2002, Rock Corporation incurred a net operating loss and elected to forgo the carryback period. Rock incurred another net operating loss in 2003. Since Rock elected to forgo the carryback period for 2002, it CANNOT carry the 2003 net operating loss back to 2001. (IRS 95 3A-7)

T F 7. Corporation W, a calendar year corporation, incurred organizational expenses of $1,000 and started business on January 1, 2002. It filed its return on March 20, 2003, without an extension. Corporation W can automatically amortize some of its organizational expenses in 2002. (IRS 91 3A-4)

T F 8. Generally, the total deduction for dividends received is limited to 70% (or 80%) of the modified taxable income of a corporation. In figuring this limitation, modified taxable income is determined without regard to any capital loss carryback to the tax year. (IRS 90 3A-6)

T F 9. During 2002, a corporation set up a contingent liability on its books to take into account a customer's claim. The claim was NOT settled in 2002. The contingent liability is NOT deductible in determining the corporation's 2002 taxable income but it does REDUCE unappropriated retained earnings and is shown as an adjustment on Schedule M–2 of Form 1120. (IRS 93 3A-7)

T F 10. The component members of a controlled group of corporations are generally limited to one apportionable $50,000 amount and one $25,000 amount (in that order) in each taxable income bracket below 34%. Unless the component members of the controlled group agree to a different allocation, the $50,000 and $25,000 (in that order) amount is to be divided equally among all members. (IRS 91 3A-11)

T F 11. If a corporation's capital losses from two or more years are carried to the same year, the loss from the earliest year is deducted first. When that loss is completely used up, the loss from the next earliest year is deducted, and so on. (IRS 91 3A-9)

Fill in the Blanks

Complete the following statements with the appropriate word(s) or amount(s).

1. Corporations are to include the amount of net long-term capital gain in _____.

2. Corporations may carryback capital losses to the _____ preceding years.

3. Generally charitable contributions of long-term capital gain property are measured at their _____ on the date of their donation.

4. The charitable deduction for "ordinary income property" that has appreciated in value is generally limited to the _____ of the property.

5. For net operating losses of a corporation, the carryback period is _____ years and forward _____ years.

6. A corporation is required to file its tax return on or before the 15th day of the _____ month following the close of its fiscal year.

7. A group of corporations form a _____ if each corporation is a member of either a parent-subsidiary controlled group or a brother-sister controlled group, at least one of the corporations is a _____ of a parent-subsidiary controlled group and the parent corporation is also a member of a _____.

Multiple Choice

Choose the best answer for each of the following questions.

_____ 1. All of the following are considered characteristics of a C corporation except: (IRS 97 3B-21)

   a. Continuity of life.
   b. Free transferability of corporate ownership interests.
   c. Limited liability of shareholders for corporate debts.
   d. A limited number of shareholders.

_____ 2. Rabid Corporation uses a fiscal year ending November 30 and receives an automatic extension of time for filing its tax return for the fiscal year ending November 30, 2002. Including the extension, what is the due date for filing Rabid's tax return (not considering weekends and holidays)? (IRS 97 3B-34)

   a. February 15, 2003
   b. June 30, 2003
   c. July 15, 2003
   d. August 15, 2003

_____ 3. The dividends received deduction (IRS 97 3B-38)

   a. May be claimed by S corporations.
   b. Must exceed the applicable percentage of the recipient shareholder's taxable income.

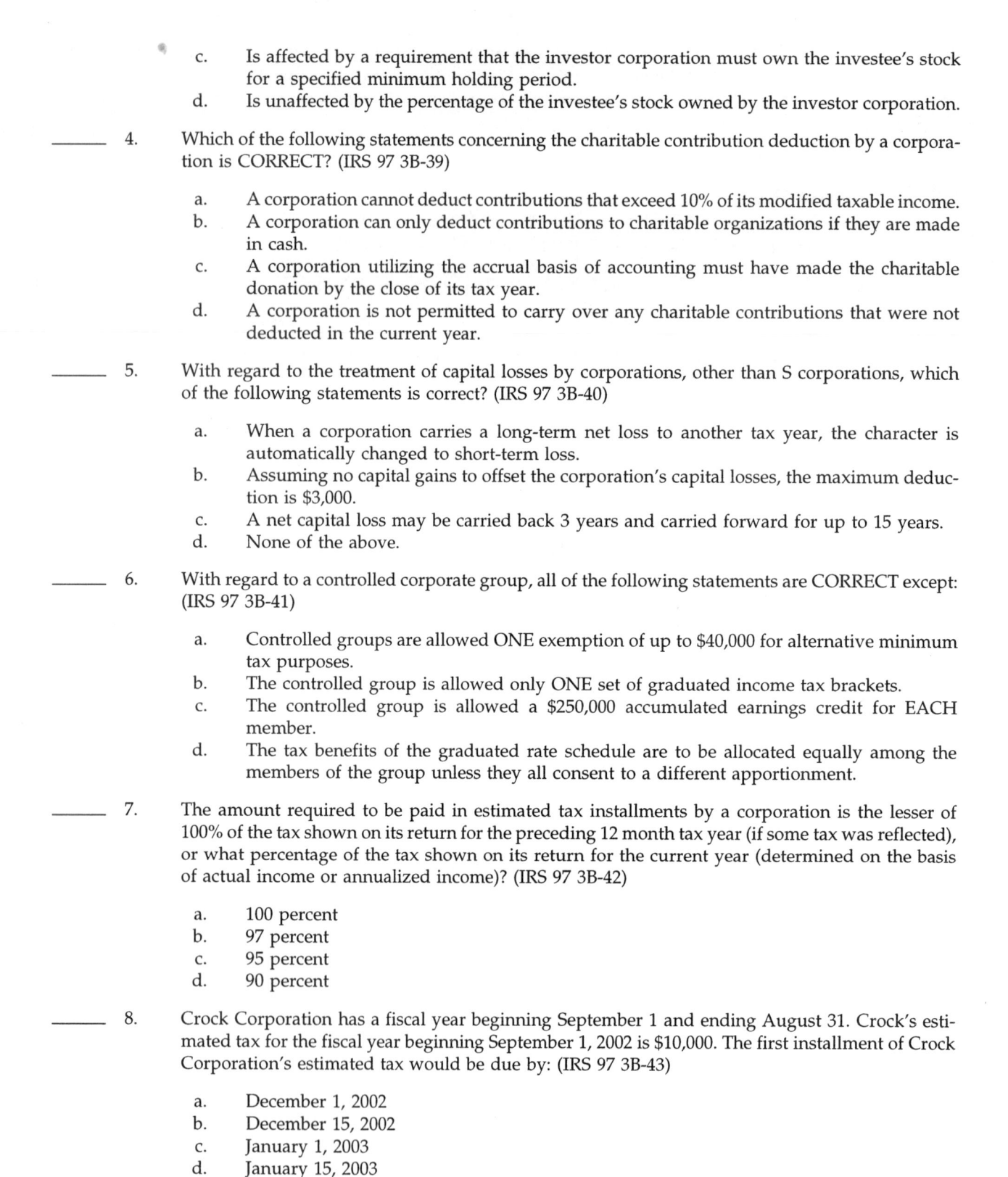

c. Is affected by a requirement that the investor corporation must own the investee's stock for a specified minimum holding period.
d. Is unaffected by the percentage of the investee's stock owned by the investor corporation.

_____ 4. Which of the following statements concerning the charitable contribution deduction by a corporation is CORRECT? (IRS 97 3B-39)

a. A corporation cannot deduct contributions that exceed 10% of its modified taxable income.
b. A corporation can only deduct contributions to charitable organizations if they are made in cash.
c. A corporation utilizing the accrual basis of accounting must have made the charitable donation by the close of its tax year.
d. A corporation is not permitted to carry over any charitable contributions that were not deducted in the current year.

_____ 5. With regard to the treatment of capital losses by corporations, other than S corporations, which of the following statements is correct? (IRS 97 3B-40)

a. When a corporation carries a long-term net loss to another tax year, the character is automatically changed to short-term loss.
b. Assuming no capital gains to offset the corporation's capital losses, the maximum deduction is $3,000.
c. A net capital loss may be carried back 3 years and carried forward for up to 15 years.
d. None of the above.

_____ 6. With regard to a controlled corporate group, all of the following statements are CORRECT except: (IRS 97 3B-41)

a. Controlled groups are allowed ONE exemption of up to $40,000 for alternative minimum tax purposes.
b. The controlled group is allowed only ONE set of graduated income tax brackets.
c. The controlled group is allowed a $250,000 accumulated earnings credit for EACH member.
d. The tax benefits of the graduated rate schedule are to be allocated equally among the members of the group unless they all consent to a different apportionment.

_____ 7. The amount required to be paid in estimated tax installments by a corporation is the lesser of 100% of the tax shown on its return for the preceding 12 month tax year (if some tax was reflected), or what percentage of the tax shown on its return for the current year (determined on the basis of actual income or annualized income)? (IRS 97 3B-42)

a. 100 percent
b. 97 percent
c. 95 percent
d. 90 percent

_____ 8. Crock Corporation has a fiscal year beginning September 1 and ending August 31. Crock's estimated tax for the fiscal year beginning September 1, 2002 is $10,000. The first installment of Crock Corporation's estimated tax would be due by: (IRS 97 3B-43)

a. December 1, 2002
b. December 15, 2002
c. January 1, 2003
d. January 15, 2003

STUDY GUIDE **CHAPTER 2** 2–11
Corporations: Introduction, Operating Rules, and Related Corporations

_____ 9. Vagabond Corporation was organized and began active business on January 2, 2002. Vagabond incurred the following expenses in connection with creating the business.

State incorporation fee	2,000
Legal fees for drafting the charter	6,000
Printing costs for stock certificates	1,500
Professional fees for issuance of stock	4,000
Broker's commission on sale of stock	7,000
Expense for temporary directors	5,000
Total	25,000

What is the maximum amount of organizational expense that Vagabond Corporation may deduct on its 2002 income tax return? (IRS 97 3C-58)

a. $2,600
b. $5,100
c. $17,000
d. $25,000

_____ 10. Kappa Corporation owns 20% interest in Sigma Corporation, a domestic corporation. For 2002, Kappa had gross receipts of $390,000, operating expenses of $400,000, and dividend income of $120,000 from Sigma Corporation. The dividends were NOT from debt-financed portfolio stock. What is the amount of Kappa Corporation's dividends received deduction for 2002? (IRS 97 3C-61)

a. $96,000
b. $88,000
c. $84,000
d. $24,000

_____ 11. During 2002, HOOS Corporation had the following income and expenses:

Gross receipts	$700,000
Salaries	300,000
Contributions to qualified charitable organizations	60,000
Capital gains	7,000
Depreciation expense	28,000
Dividend income	60,000
Dividends received deduction	42,000

What is the amount of HOOS Corporation's charitable contribution deduction for 2002? (IRS 97 3C-62)

a. $33,400
b. $43,900
c. $46,900
d. $60,000

_____ 12. During 2002, Glitz, a C corporation, realized a long-term capital gain of $5,000 from the sale of a tract of land, a long-term capital gain of $10,000 from the sale of stock of Meg Corporation, and a long-term capital loss of $23,000 from the sale of U. S. Government securities. What amount of the long-term capital loss may Glitz deduct on its 2002 income tax return? (IRS 97 3C-63)

    a. $8,000
    b. $15,000
    c. $18,000
    d. $23,000

_____ 13. For the tax year ended December 31, 2002, Muncie Corporation had gross income of $300,000 and operating expenses of $450,000. Contributions of $2,500 were included in the expenses, Muncie had a net operating loss carryover of $8,000. What is the amount of Muncie Corporation's net operating loss for 2002? (IRS 97 3C-64)

    a. $156,500
    b. $152,500
    c. $150,000
    d. $147,500

_____ 14. For the calendar year 2002, Cincy Cooperation had operating income of $80,000, exclusive of the following capital gains and losses:

Long-term capital gain	$14,000
Short-term capital gain	6,000
Long-term capital loss	(2,000)
Short-term capital loss	(8,000)

What is Cincy's income tax liability for 2002? (IRS 97 3C-66)

    a. $22,250
    b. $18,850
    c. $18,250
    d. $15,450

_____ 15. For tax year 2002, Bosse Corporation's books and records reflect the following:

Net income per books	$76,000
Tax-exempt interest	4,000
Excess contributions	2,000
Meal in excess of 50% limitation	8,000
Accrued federal income taxes	18,000

What is the amount of Bosse's taxable income as it would be shown on Schedule M–1 of its corporate income tax return? (IRS 97 3C-68)

    a. $92,000
    b. $100,000
    c. $104,000
    d. $108,000

SOLUTIONS TO CHAPTER 2 QUESTIONS

True or False

1. T (p. 2–7)

    Under the check-the-box regulations, to be necessarily classified as a corporation for tax purposes, a professional service organization must be incorporated under state law (organized as a corporation). In addition, such organization must be operated in a manner that does not lack substance (e.g., the owners recognize the organization as a separate entity and not merely for tax avoidance purposes).

2. T (p. 2–12)

    In the instant case, under the capital gain and loss netting process of CDS Corporation, the 2002 net long term capital loss of $9,000 is netted against the net short term capital gain of $3,000 to yield a $6,000 net capital loss. This capital loss is not deductible in the current year, but (as a short term capital loss) may be carried back 3 years and forward 5 years to offset any capital gains in those years.

3. T (p. 2–25)

    By filing Form 7004 on or before the due date of the federal income tax return, a corporation automatically receives a six-month extension for filing such return (but not for paying the associated tax liability). However, by mailing a 10-day notice to the corporation, the IRS may terminate this automatic six-month extension

4. F (p. 2–18; amortize or capitalize, not deductible)

    In the instant case, Corporation Y's $7,000 of qualifying organizational expenses are NOT deductible. Instead, they are generally chargeable to a capital account, since such expenses lack a determinable and limited estimated useful life. However, under I.R.C. Sec. 248, Corporation Y may elect (on its first income tax return) to (a) capitalize these expenses and (b) amortize such capitalized amount over a period of 60 months (or more) beginning with the month business begins (January, 2002).

5. T (p. 2–19)

    Start-up expenses include operating-type expenses that are incurred before business begins. Hence, they are not deductible as ordinary and necessary business expenses. However, under I.R.C. Sec. 195, a corporation may elect (on its first income tax return) to (a) capitalize these expenses and (b) amortize such capitalized amount over a period of 60 months (or more) beginning with the month business begins.

6. F (p. 2–16; the election is made on a year by year basis)

    In the instant case, Rock Corporation incurs a NOL in 2003. Rock Corporation can carry such NOL back to 2001 for the purpose of offsetting 2001 income. The fact that Rock Corporation elected to forgo carrying back its 2002 NOL to 2000 is NOT relevant. Such election is made on a year-by-year basis and does not impact the treatment of future NOLs.

7. F (p. 2–18; the election must be timely made)

    Corporation W's $1,000 of organizational expenses are not deductible. Instead, they are generally chargeable to a capital account, since such expenses lack a determinable and limited estimated useful life. However, under I.R.C. Sec. 248, Corporation W may elect (on its first income tax return) to (a) capitalize these expenses and (b) amortize such capitalized amount ($1,000) over a period of 60 months (or more) beginning with the month business begins. To effectively elect under I.R.C. Sec. 248, in the instant case, Corporation W must (a) attach a statement of election to its first return and (b) file its first return no later than the due date (including extensions). Here, the election was made March 20, 2003 (without a timely filed extension), 5 days after the due date of the return. Thus, the election was NOT effective, since the first return of Corporation W was NOT filed no later than the due date.

8. T (p. 2–16)

In certain situations, a taxable income ceiling limitation applies to the dividends received deduction of a corporation. The taxable income ceiling limitation is computed by multiplying modified taxable income by the applicable percentage (70% or 80%). For this purpose, modified taxable income is computed without regard to a NOL deduction, the dividends received deduction, and a capital loss carry back.

9. T (p. 2–26)

Under GAAP, a contingent liability from a estimated loss due to a lawsuit (e.g., a customer's claim), which is not either probable or reasonably estimable, does not generate an expense, but can prudently result in an amount of retained earning being transferred from unappropriated to appropriated. In contrast, under the tax law, a contingent liability results in a deduction only when paid. In the instant case, since neither an expense nor a deduction has been recognized by the corporation, the contingent liability does not constitute an Schedule M-1 adjustment. However, as an adjustment to the beginning balance of unappropriated retained earnings, it may result in a Schedule M-2 adjustment.

10. T (p. 2–21)

A controlled group of corporations is subject to special rules in the computation of each member's federal income tax liability. To preclude each member of the controlled group from receiving the benefits of the progressive nature of the corporate tax rate structure (i.e., taxable income being taxed at 15% or 25%, rather than 34%), the tax law limits the aggregate amount of each member's taxable income to $50,000 ($25,000) for the 15% (25%) bracket. The $50,000 (or $25,000) aggregate amount is allocated equally across all members of the controlled group, unless otherwise agreed.

11. T (p. 2–12)

Under the capital gain and loss netting process of a corporation, if a net capital loss results, the capital loss is not deductible in the current year. Instead (as a short term capital loss), it may be carried back 3 years and forward 5 years to offset any net capital gain in those carry back (forward) years. If multiple net capital losses are either carried back (or forward), net capital losses of earlier years are first used to offset a net capital gain of a carry back (forward) year.

Fill in the Blanks

1. ordinary income (p. 2–11)

Under the capital gain and loss netting process of a corporation, a net capital gain is treated as ordinary income and is not preferentially treated. In contrast, a net capital gain of an individual is preferentially treated and is generally taxed at a maximum tax rate of 20%.

2. three (p. 2–12)

Under the capital gain and loss netting process of a corporation, if a net capital loss results, such capital loss is not deductible in the current year. Instead (as a net short term capital loss), it may be carried back 3 years and forward 5 years to offset any net capital gain in those carry back (forward) years.

3. fair market value (p. 2–13)

Capital gain property is property that, if sold, would result in the recognition of long term capital gain. A deduction for a charitable contribution of capital gain property is measured by such property's fair market value, as long as such property is not tangible personal property that is not expected to be used by the charitable organization within the scope of its charitable purpose.

4. adjusted basis (p. 2–13)

Appreciated ordinary income property is property that, if sold, would result in the recognition of ordinary income. A deduction for a charitable contribution of ordinary income property is measured by an amount equal to such property's fair market value less such property's ordinary income potential, which is essentially equal to such property's tax adjusted basis.

5. two; twenty (p. 2–16)

   A NOL of a corporation in the current year may be carried back 2 years and forward 20 years to offset taxable income in such carry back (forward) years.

6. third (p. 2–25)

   A corporation must file a federal income tax return (Form 1120, 1120A or 1120S), whether or not it has taxable income. The due date for the filing of such return is the fifteenth day of the third month after the close of its taxable year (fiscal or calendar).

7. combined group; parent; brother-sister controlled group (p. 2–24)

   Each member of a controlled group of corporations is subject to special rules in the computation of such member's federal income tax liability. A controlled group of corporations includes a parent-subsidiary controlled group, a brother-sister controlled group, or a combined group. A combined group includes a group of corporations where (a) each member of the group is a member of either a parent-subsidiary controlled group or a brother-sister controlled group, (b) at least one member of the combined group is a parent of a parent-subsidiary controlled group and (c) such parent corporation is also a member of a brother-sister controlled group.

Multiple Choice

1. d (p. 2–7; no limit on number of shareholders)

   Item d is correct, because a limited number of shareholders is a requirement of an S corporation, but NOT of a C corporation. Further, items a, b, and c are incorrect because:

   - Item a: continuity of life (generally, events that occur at the shareholder level have no impact on a corporation's existence),
   - Item b: free transferability of ownership interests, and
   - Item c: limited liability of shareholders

   are C corporation characteristics.

2. d (p. 2–25; fifteenth day of the third month plus 6 months)

   A corporation must file a federal income tax return (Form 1120, 1120A or 1120S), whether or not it has taxable income. The due date for the filing of such return is the fifteenth day of the third month after the close of the corporation's tax year (fiscal or calendar). However, by filing Form 7004 on or before the due date of the return, the corporation can receive an automatic 6-month extension. In the instant case, Rabid Corporation's fiscal year-end for the current year is November 30, 2002. Thus, the due date for the filing of Rabid's federal income tax return for the current year is February 15, 2003. With a timely made extension, the extended due date for such filing is August 15, 2003. Thus, item d is correct. Further, choice items a, b, and c are incorrect because they are each inconsistent with item d.

3. c (p. 2–16; investor corporation must hold stock for a minimum period before or after ex-dividend date)

   To qualify for the dividends received deduction, the investor must own the stock (on which the dividend is paid) on the record date and must hold such stock for a period of at least 46 days either before or after the ex-dividend date. Thus, item c is correct. Further, the following items are incorrect:

   - Item a is incorrect because the dividends received deduction is NOT deductible by an S corporation. With certain qualifications, the taxable income of an S corporation is computed in the same manner as in the case of an individual, the rules of which do not allow for a dividends received deduction.

- Item b is incorrect because if the taxable income ceiling limitation applies to the dividends received deduction, the dividends received deduction is less than (or equal to) BUT NOT MORE THAN an amount equal to the applicable percentage multiplied by the shareholder's modified taxable income.
- Item d is incorrect because in the calculation of the dividends received deduction, the applicable percentage (70% or 80%) depends on (RATHER THAN BEING UNAFFECTED BY) the percentage of the investee's stock owned by the investor corporation.

4. a (p. 2–13)

The charitable contribution deduction allowable to a corporation is subject to a taxable income ceiling limitation. Such deduction is limited to 10% of modified taxable income. Thus, item a is correct. Further, the following items are incorrect:

- Item b is incorrect because charitable contribution deductions ARE allowed for contributions of noncash property.
- Item c is incorrect because an exception to the general rule (i.e., charitable contribution deductions are only allowed when paid) IS made for accrual basis corporations. Under this exception, such corporation may claim a charitable contribution deduction in the year preceding payment if (a) the contribution is authorized by the board of directors before the end of the preceding year and (b) such contribution is paid on or before the fifteenth day of the third month of the payment year.
- Item d is incorrect because any amount of charitable contribution not allowed as a corporate deduction (because of the taxable income ceiling limitation) MAY be carried over to the five succeeding tax years.

5. a (p. 2–12)

Under the capital gain and loss netting process of a corporation, if a net long term capital loss is netted against a net short term capital gain to yield a net capital loss, this capital loss is not deductible in the current year. Rather, such loss (as a short term capital loss) is carried back 3 years and forward 5 years to offset any capital gains in those years. Thus, in the instant case, item a is correct. Further, the following items are incorrect:

- Item b is incorrect because a net capital loss is NOT deductible by a corporation.
- Item c is incorrect because a net capital loss IS carried back 3 years and forward 5 years (NOT forward 15 years).
- Item d is incorrect because it is inconsistent with item a.

6. c (p. 2–21; accumulated earnings credit allocated across all members)

Each member of a controlled group of corporations is subject to special rules in the computation of such member's federal income tax liability. It is incorrect to say that each member of the controlled group is allowed ONE $250,000 accumulated earnings credit. Instead, such credit must be allocated across all members of the controlled group. Thus, item c is the right answer. Further, each of the following items is not the right answer:

- Item a is not the right answer because the controlled group IS allowed ONE $40,000 exemption for AMT purposes, which is allocated across all members of the controlled group.
- Item b is not the right answer because the aggregate amount of taxable income associated with each tax bracket (for the controlled group as a whole) IS limited to an amount equal to the taxable income associated each tax bracket as if the controlled group was ONE corporation.
- Item d is not the right answer because equal allocation of the benefits of the progressive income tax structure IS required unless all members of the controlled group consent to an apportionment plan providing for an unequal allocation.

7. a (p. 2–26)

The required annual payment of estimated tax is the lesser of (a) 100% of the tax for the preceding year or (2) 100% of the tax shown on the return for the current year. Thus, in the instant case, item a is correct. Further, choice items b, c, and d are incorrect because they are each inconsistent with item a.

STUDY GUIDE **CHAPTER 2** 2–17
Corporations: Introduction, Operating Rules, and Related Corporations

8. b (p. 2–26; fifteenth day of fourth month after year end)

The first installment of estimated tax is due on or before the fifteenth day of the fourth month of its fiscal year. Thus, in the instant case, because Crock's current fiscal year begins September 1, 2002 Crock's first installment of estimated tax is due on or before the fifteenth day of December 2002. It follows that item b is correct. Further, choice items a, c, and d are incorrect because they are each inconsistent with item b.

9. a (p. 2–18; ($2,000 + $6,000 + $5,000)/60 × 12)

Qualifying organizational expenses do NOT include expenses of stock issuance, including:

- Printing costs for stock certificates.
- Professional fees for issuance of stock.
- Broker's commission on sale of stock.

The maximum amount of a corporation's amortization deduction for organization expenses is calculated by (a) capitalizing such corporation's qualifying organizational expenses and (b) amortizing such capitalized amount over 60 months beginning with the month business begins. Thus, in the instant case, Vagabond's 2001 deduction for amortization is calculated as follows:

$$12 \text{ months} \times \frac{\text{Qualifying Organizational Expenses of } \$13,000 \ (\$2,000 + \$6,000 + \$5,000)}{60 \text{ months}} = \$2,600$$

It follows that item a is correct. Further, choice items b, c, and d are incorrect because they are each inconsistent with item a.

10. b (p. 2–16; 80% of taxable income, without dividend received deduction)

Kappa's dividends received deduction is equal to the applicable percentage as applied against the dividends received, but is limited to an amount equal to the applicable percentage as applied against the Kappa's modified taxable income (taxable income, without the dividends received deduction). Kappa's dividends received deduction is calculated as follows: Kappa's applicable percentage (80%) as applied against the dividends received ($120,000) Equals $96,000. However, such amount is limited to $88,000 [Kappa's applicable percentage (80%) as applied against Kappa's modified taxable income ($110,000 = $390,000 + $120,000 − $400,000)].

11. b (p. 2–15; ($700,000 + $7,000 + $60,000 − $300,000 − $28,000) × 10%)

The charitable contribution deduction of a corporation is subject to a taxable income ceiling limitation. Such deduction is limited to 10% of modified taxable income. Modified taxable income is taxable income, without consideration for the charitable contribution deduction and the dividends received deduction. Thus, in the instant case, HOOS' charitable contribution deduction of $60,000 is limited to its taxable income ceiling limitation of $43,900 ($439,000 × 10%), where HOOS' modified taxable income equals $439,000 ($700,000 + $7,000 + $60,000 − $300,000 − $28,000). It follows that item b is correct. Further, choices a, c, and d are incorrect because they are each inconsistent with item b.

12. b (p. 2–12; limited to capital gain)

Under the capital gain and loss netting process of a corporation, a long-term capital loss may only offset capital gains (first long-term capital gains and then any net short-term capital gain). A long-term capital loss may not be used to offset other income. Thus, in the instant case, Glitz's long-term capital loss of $23,000 may only offset capital gains of $15,000 ($10,000 + $5,000). It follows that item b is correct. Further, items a, c, and d are incorrect because they are each inconsistent with item b.

13. d (p. 2–16; (−$150,000 + $2,500))

A NOL of a corporation may be carried back 2 years and forward 20 years to offset taxable income in such carry back (forward) years. Thus, in the instant case, Muncie's 2002 NOL is calculated by adjusting Muncie's taxable loss of $155,500 ($300,000 − $450,000 + $2,500 − $8,000) by the amount of Muncie's 2002

NOL deduction of $8,000. Thus, Muncie's 2002 NOL is $147,500 ($155,500 + $8,000). It follows that item d is correct. Further, items a, b, and c are incorrect because they are each inconsistent with item d.

14. b (p. 2–19; $90,000 taxable income)

In the instant case, under the capital gain and loss netting process of Cincy Corporation, Cincy's net capital gain of $10,000 [($6,000 − $8,000) + ($14,000 − $2,000)] is treated as ordinary income and is not preferentially treated. Thus, Cincy's taxable income is $90,000 ($80,000 + $10,000) and the corporate income tax on its taxable income of $90,000 is $18,850 [$13,750 + (34% × $15,000)]. It follows that item b is correct. Further, items a, c, and d are incorrect because they are each inconsistent with item b.

15. b (p. 2–27; $76,000 − $4,000 + $2,000 + $8,000 + $18,000)

Schedule M–1 reconciles Net Income per Books to Taxable Income by (a) adding deductions that are recognized for financial accounting purposes, but not for tax purposes and (b) subtracting income that is recognized for financial accounting purposes, but not for tax purposes. Thus, in the instant case, to calculate Bosse's 2002 Taxable Income of $100,000 on Schedule M–1, Bosse adjusts Bosse's 2002 Net Income per Books of $76,000 by:

- Adding deductions of $28,000 ($18,000 + $8,000 + $2,000) that are recognized for financial accounting purposes, but not for tax purposes and
- Subtracting income of $4,000 that is recognized for financial accounting purposes, but not for tax purposes.

It follows that item b is correct. Further, items a, c, and d are incorrect because they are each inconsistent with item b.

CHAPTER 3

Corporations: Organization and Capital Structure

LEARNING OBJECTIVES

After completing Chapter 3, you should be able to:

1. Identify the tax consequences of incorporating a business.
2. Understand the special rules that apply when liabilities are assumed by a corporation.
3. Recognize the basis issues relevant to the shareholder and the corporation.
4. Appreciate the tax aspects of the capital structure of a corporation.
5. Recognize the tax differences between debt and equity investments.
6. Determine the tax treatment of shareholder debt and stock losses.
7. Identify tax planning opportunities associated with organizing and financing a corporation.

KEY TERMS

Assumption of liabilities
Capital contribution
Control
Investor losses
Liabilities in excess of basis

Nonbusiness bad debt
Property
Qualified small business corporation

Qualified small business stock
Section 1244 stock
Securities
Thin capitalization

OUTLINE

I. **ORGANIZATION OF AND TRANSFERS TO CONTROLLED CORPORATIONS**
   A. In General
      1. Normally, gain or loss is recognized on a property transfer.
      2. The Internal Revenue Code (IRC) provides exceptions where:
         a. a taxpayer's economic status has not changed and
         b. the taxpayer does not have the "wherewithal to pay" tax.
      3. When a business incorporates, the owner's economic status is unchanged (only the *form* has changed).
      4. Further, Congress did not want to inhibit the incorporation of businesses.
      5. As a result, Section 351 provides nonrecognition of gain or loss when three requirements are met:
         a. property is transferred
         b. in exchange for stock and
         c. the property transferors are in control of the transferee corporation after the exchange.
      6. Section 351 is mandatory if these three requirements are met.
   B. Property Defined
      1. In general, the IRC adopts a very broad definition of property.
      2. However, the IRC specifically excludes services rendered.
   C. Stock Transferred
      1. Nonrecognition of gain occurs only when the shareholder receives "stock."
      2. All property other than transferee corporation stock received in the exchange is considered boot. Boot is taxable to the extent of any gain realized.
      3. Common and most preferred stock are included in the definition of stock.
      4. Stock rights or warrants are not "stock."
      5. Corporate debt or other securities (e.g., long-term bonds) are not "stock."
   D. Control of the Corporation
      1. The property transferors must be in control of the corporation immediately after the exchange.
      2. For "control," an 80% stock ownership test is used. 80% stock ownership defined as:
         a. 80% of the total combined voting power AND
         b. 80% of the total number of shares of all other classes of stock.
      3. Control "immediately" after the transfer
         a. Transferors may refer to one person or several persons.
         b. All transfers need not be made simultaneously.
         c. For transfers involving more than one person:
            1. the rights of the persons should be defined, in a written agreement, prior to any transfers.
            2. the transfers should occur close together in time.
      4. Transfers for property and services:
         a. persons who transfer property and perform services for stock are considered members of the transferring group; generally, the value of the property must be at least 10% of the value of the service provided.
         b. the transferor is taxed on the value of stock issued for services.
         c. if the "at least 10% test" is met, all the stock received by the transferor is counted to determine whether or not the control requirement is met.
      5. Section 351 applies whenever the three requirements are met.
   E. Assumption of Liabilities (Sec. 357)
      1. Generally, a corporation's assumption of a liability or acceptance of property subject to a liability does not result in boot to the transferor shareholder.
      2. However, liabilities assumed by the corporation are treated as boot for determining the shareholder's basis in the stock received.

3. There are two exceptions to the general rule:
   a. Liabilities in Excess of Basis: If total liabilities transferred exceeds the total adjusted bases of all property transferred, the excess is taxable gain. Without this provision, stock basis would be negative.
      1. Accounts payable of a cash-basis taxpayer are not counted as liabilities.
   b. Tax Avoidance or No Bona Fide Business Purpose: If liabilities transferred have no business purpose or were transferred to avoid taxes, all liabilities transferred trigger gain recognition.
F. Basis Determination and Related Issues
   1. Basis of stock to shareholder is determined as follows:
      a. basis held in the property transferred, plus
      b. gain recognized on the exchange, minus
      c. boot received, including any liabilities transferred.
   2. Property (other than stock) received by the shareholder has a fair market value basis.
   3. Basis of property received by the corporation is determined as follows:
      a. transferor's basis, plus
      b. gain recognized by the transferor shareholder.
   3. Holding period for shareholder's stock received
      a. If the property transferred is a capital asset or § 1231 property, the holding period of stock received includes the holding period of the property transferred.
      b. If the property transferred is inventory, the holding period of stock received begins the day after the exchange.
   4. The holding period for corporate property received includes the holding period of the transferor shareholder.

II. CAPITAL STRUCTURE OF A CORPORATION
A. Capital Contributions
   1. The basis of property received by a corporation from a shareholder as a capital contribution is the transferor's basis plus gain recognized by the transferor/shareholder.
   2. The basis of property received by a corporation from a nonshareholder as a capital contribution is zero.
   3. A special rule applies if money is received by a corporation from a nonshareholder
      a. Money received reduces the basis of any property acquired with the money during the 12 months following receipt of such contribution.
      b. Any excess over the cost of new property reduces the basis of other corporate property in proportion to the relative bases of the properties, in the following order:
         1. depreciable property.
         2. amortizable property.
         3. depletable property.
         4. all other remaining property.
B. Debt in the Capital Structure
   1. Advantages of debt
      a. Interest is deductible by the corporation; dividends are not.
      b. Shareholders are not taxed on loan repayments.
      c. A stock investment cannot be withdrawn tax-free if the corporation has earnings and profits.
   2. Reclassification of debt as equity
      a. A debt instrument having too many features of stock may be treated as a form of stock.
      b. Factors to be considered include:
         1. the form of the debt instrument.
         2. a definite maturity date and reasonable interest rate.
         3. timely payment.

4. payment contingent on earnings.
5. subordination to other liabilities.
6. whether shareholder holdings of debt and stock are proportionate.
7. the ratio of debt to equity.

III. INVESTOR LOSSES
A. Stock and security losses
1. For stocks and bonds held as capital assets, capital losses materialize as of the last day of the year in which the stocks or bonds become completely worthless.
2. No deduction is allowed for partial worthlessness.
B. Business versus nonbusiness bad debts
1. Business bad debts are deducted as ordinary losses.
2. Nonbusiness bad debts are treated as short-term capital losses and limited to noncorporate taxpayers.
3. Partial worthlessness can be deducted only for business bad debts.
4. All corporate bad debts qualify as business bad debts.
C. Section 1244 stock
1. Section 1244 allows ordinary loss treatment for losses on the sale or worthlessness of a small business corporation's stock.
2. To qualify as § 1244 stock:
   a. the total stock offered cannot exceed $1 million.
   b. more than 50% of the corporation's gross receipts must be derived from the active conduct of a trade or business.
3. The amount of loss deductible in any one year is limited to $50,000 or $100,000 for a jointly filed return.
4. Only the original holder of § 1244 stock qualifies for ordinary loss treatment.

IV. GAIN FROM QUALIFIED SMALL BUSINESS STOCK
A. A "qualified small business corporation" is a C corporation whose aggregate gross assets did not exceed $50 million on the date the stock was issued. In addition, the corporation must be actively involved in a trade or business (at least 80% of its assets were used in the active conduct of a trade or business).
B. Noncorporate shareholders may exclude 50% of the gain on a sale or exchange of qualified small business stock.
1. The taxpayer must have held the stock for more than 5 years.
2. The taxpayer must have acquired the stock as part of an original issue.
C. The 50% exclusion can apply to the greater of:
1. $10 million, $5 million for married filing separately, or
2. 10 times the shareholder's aggregate adjusted basis in the qualified stock disposed of during the year.

V. TAX PLANNING CONSIDERATIONS
A. Working with § 351
1. Does the desired tax result come from compliance with § 351? Should the taxpayer seek to avoid § 351?
2. In utilizing § 351, the transferors must ensure that:
   a. all parties transferring property have control in the aggregate.
   b. later transfers of property do not sabotage satisfying the control requirement, if gain recognition is to be avoided.
3. In some situations, avoiding § 351 may produce a more advantageous tax result (e.g., if loss property is being transferred).

- B. Determine which assets and liabilities should be transferred to the corporation.
- C. The debt to equity ratio of the corporation's capital structure raises issues of:
    1. thin capitalization and potential reclassification of debt to equity.
    2. investor losses and § 1244 attributes.

# TEST FOR SELF-EVALUATION—CHAPTER 3

True or False

Indicate which of the following statements is true or false by circling the correct answer.

T   F   1. Rene transferred money and property to Stable Corporation solely in exchange for stock in Stable. Immediately after the exchange, Rene owned 80% of the total combined voting power of all classes of stock entitled to vote and 51% of all other classes of stock. No gain or loss will be recognized by Rene or Stable. (IRS 97 3A-12)

T   F   2. If an individual transfers mortgaged property to a corporation he or she controls, the individual generally will NOT have to recognize gain as a result of the corporation's assumption of a liability unless the liability is greater than the individual's adjusted basis in the property. (IRS 97 3A-13)

T   F   3. B transfers land and building to CLJ, a newly formed corporation, in exchange for 100% of CLJ's only class of stock outstanding. The land and building have a fair market value of $250,000 and an adjusted basis to B of $100,000. Further, the land and building are subject to a mortgage of $100,000, which CLJ assumes. Immediately prior to the transfer, B refinanced the previously existing mortgage indebtedness on the land and building of $60,000 to get cash out of $40,000. B must recognize gain of $40,000. the transferors must ensure that: (IRS 96 3A-2)

T   F   4. A corporation does not recognize gain or loss if you transfer property and money to the corporation in exchange for the corporation's stock (including treasury stock). (IRS 96 3A-3)

T   F   5. If you acquire an asset in exchange for another asset and your basis for the new asset is figured, in whole or in part, by your basis in the old property, the holding period of the new property begins the day after the date of the exchange. (IRS 96 3A-5)

T   F   6. If the sole shareholder of a corporation receives no additional shares or other consideration for a contribution of property to the corporation, the basis of the property received by the corporation is the same as it was to the shareholder. (IRS 96 3A-7)

T   F   7. In order to protect her investment, Beth, an officer and principal shareholder of Turbo Corporation, guaranteed payment of a bank loan Turbo received. During 2002, Turbo defaulted on the loan and Beth made full payment. Beth is entitled to a business bad debt deduction. (IRS 95 2A-9)

T   F   8. Steve transferred his services to a corporation in exchange for 85% of all classes of the corporation's stock. Steve will NOT have to report the fair market value of the stock as taxable compensation. (IRS 95 3A-1)

T   F   9. BJ and CJ each own 50 shares of J Corporation's only class of outstanding stock. In 2002, BJ transfers equipment to J Corporation with a fair market value of $70,000 and an adjusted basis of $180,000 in exchange for 10 additional shares of J Corporation's only class of outstanding stock. If BJ and CJ are not related parties, BJ recognizes a realized loss of $110,000. (IRS 95 3A-2)

T   F   10. On January 1, 2002, Mr. Kitars transferred a capital asset he had originally acquired on July 1, 1999, to Westco Corporation in a nontaxable exchange for Westco's stock. After

STUDY GUIDE
CHAPTER 3
Corporations: Organization and Capital Structure

the transfer, Mr. Kitars had control of the corporation. On October 1, 2002, Westco Corporation sold the property for a gain. Westco's holding period does NOT include the period it was held by Mr. Kitars. (IRS 95 3A-4)

Fill in the Blanks

Complete the following statements with the appropriate word(s) or amount(s).

1. _____ in a § 351 transaction do not result in boot to the transferor shareholder.

2. For _____ of property received from a nonshareholder, the corporation's basis is zero.

3. _____ immediately after § 351 exchange requires _____ stock ownership in the transferee corporation.

4. _____ transferred, without taxable gain recognition, would cause the transferor shareholder to have a _____ basis in the stock received.

5. _____ are treated as short-term capital losses of noncorporate taxpayers.

6. Property for purposes of § 351 specifically excludes _____.

7. _____ allows ordinary loss treatment on the sale or worthlessness of a small business corporation's stock.

8. _____ are long-term debt instruments.

9. _____ situations arise when shareholder debt is high relative to shareholder equity.

Multiple Choice

Choose the best answer for each of the following questions.

_____ 1. Chip and Dale formed a corporation to which Chip transferred a patent right that had a fair market value of $25,000 and a zero adjusted basis. Dale transferred a building that had a fair market value of $100,000 and an adjusted basis to him of $75,000. In return, Chip received 200 shares and Dale 800 shares of the corporation's 1,000 outstanding shares of its only class of stock. As a result of this transaction, Dale should report: (IRS 97 3B-35)

    a. Neither a gain nor a loss.
    b. A capital gain of $25,000.
    c. A Section 1250 gain of $25,000.
    d. An ordinary gain of $25,000.

_____ 2. Laura, an attorney, performed legal services valued at $2,000 for Fine Corporation, a newly formed corporation, in exchange for 1% of the issued and outstanding stock. The fair market value of the shares received was $2,000. Laura would recognize: (IRS 97 3B-36)

    a. No income until the stock is sold.
    b. $2,000 as ordinary income ratable over 60 months.
    c. Compensation of $2,000.
    d. A short term capital gain of $2,000.

3. The basis of stock received in exchange for property transferred to a corporation is the same as the basis of the property transferred with certain adjustments. Which one of the following would NOT decrease the basis of the stock received? (IRS 97 3B-37)

   a. The fair market value of other property received.
   b. Any amount treated as a dividend.
   c. Any money received.
   d. Any loss recognized on the exchange.

4. Dylon transferred land having an adjusted basis of $35,000 and a fair market value of $47,000 to Octopus Corporation. In exchange for the land he received $5,000 cash, equipment having an adjusted basis of $3,000 and a fair market value of $5,000 and 80% of Octopus Corporation's only class of stock outstanding. The stock received by Dylon had a fair market value of $37,000. What is the amount of gain that Dylon will recognize? (IRS 97 3C-54)

   a. $0
   b. $10,000
   c. $12,000
   d. $20,000

5. Mr. Francois transferred an office building to Slim Corporation in exchange for 100% of Slim's only class of outstanding stock and $30,000 in cash. The building had an adjusted basis of $150,000 and a fair market value of $250,000. The building was subject to a mortgage of $120,000 which Slim assumed for a valid business reason. The fair market value of Slim Corporation's stock on the date of the transfer was $100,000. What is the amount of Mr. Francois' recognized gain? (IRS 97 3C-55)

   a. $100,000
   b. $70,000
   c. $30,000
   d. $0

6. Mr. Naqvi transferred a building having an adjusted basis of $18,500 and a fair market value of $23,000 to Nadir Corporation. In exchange for the building he received $3,000 cash and 90% of Nadir's only class of stock outstanding. The stock received by Mr. Naqvi had a fair market value of $20,000. What is Nadir Corporation's basis in the building received in this exchange? (IRS 97 3C-56)

   a. $25,000
   b. $21,500
   c. $20,000
   d. $18,500

7. Rod, Sydney, and Edgar decided to form Parody Corporation. Rod transferred property with an adjusted basis of $35,000 and a fair market value of $44,000 for 440 shares of stock. Sydney exchanged $33,000 cash for 330 shares of stock. Edgar performed services valued at $33,000 for 330 shares of stock. The fair market value of Parody Corporation's stock is $100 per share. What is Parody's basis in the property received from Rod? (IRS 97 3C-57)

   a. $44,000
   b. $35,000
   c. $9,000
   d. $0

CHAPTER 3
Corporations: Organization and Capital Structure

_____ 8. Which of the following factors is NOT taken into account when determining if a gain or loss should be recognized on the transfer of property to a corporation in exchange for a controlling interest in stock of the corporation? (IRS 96 3B-21)

    a. Receipt of money in addition to the stock.
    b. Fair market value of the property transferred to the corporation.
    c. Ownership of at least 80% of the total combined voting power of all stock entitled to vote.
    d. Ownership of at least 80% of the total number of shares of all other classes of stock.

_____ 9. Randy and Audra formed a corporation to which Randy transferred equipment that had a fair market value of $25,000 and zero adjusted basis. Audra transferred a building that had a fair market value of $100,000 and an adjusted basis to her of $80,000. In return, Randy received 200 shares and Audra received 800 shares of the corporation's outstanding shares of its only class of stock. As a result of this transaction, Audra should report: (IRS 96 3B-22)

    a. Neither a gain or loss.
    b. A section 1250 gain of $20,000.
    c. An ordinary gain of $20,000.
    d. A capital gain of $20,000.

_____ 10. In exchange for Thunder Corporation stock, Sydney performed legal services for Thunder valued at $7,000 and paid Thunder $18,000 cash. The stock received by Sydney had a fair market value at the time of the exchange of $25,000. What is the amount of Sydney's recognized gain from this exchange? (IRS 96 3C-46)

    a. $25,000
    b. $18,000
    c. $7,000
    d. $0

_____ 11. Shelly transferred property having an adjusted basis to her of $20,000 and a fair market value of $27,000 to DLW Corporation. In exchange for the property she received $6,000 cash and 100% of DLW's only class of stock. If the stock received by Shelly had a fair market value of $21,000 at the time of the transfer, what is the amount of her recognized gain? (IRS 96 3C-47)

    a. $0
    b. $6,000
    c. $7,000
    d. $21,000

_____ 12. Andrew transferred an office building that had an adjusted basis of $180,000 and a fair market value of $350,000 to Dickens Corporation in exchange for 80% of Dickens' only class of stock. The building was subject to a mortgage of $200,000, which Dickens assumed for valid business reasons. The fair market value of the stock on the date of the transfer was $150,000. What is the amount of Andrew's recognized gain? (IRS 96 3C-48)

    a. $0
    b. $20,000
    c. $170,000
    d. $350,000

SOLUTIONS TO CHAPTER 3 QUESTIONS

True or False

1. F (p. 3–6; 80% of all other classes required)

    The application of Section 351 to Rene's exchange of money and property for stock is mandatory if the following three requirements are satisfied: (1) *property* (as defined) is transferred, (2) in exchange for *stock*, and (3) where the property transferors are in *control* (as defined) of the corporation immediately after the exchange. Within the meaning of Section 351, control is defined as at least 80 percent of all classes of stock entitled to *vote* and at least 80 percent of the total number of shares of *all other classes of stock*. In the instant case, Rene does not have control, because she owns only 51 percent of *all other classes of stock*. Thus, Section 351 does not apply to Rene's exchange of money and property for stock.

2. T (p. 3–9)

    In general, Section 357(a) provides that when the acquiring corporation assumes a liability (or acquires property subject to a liability) within the context of a Section 351 exchange, the relief of indebtedness is not considered boot to the transferor shareholder for purposes of determining the transferor shareholder's recognized gain on the exchange. However, as an exception to this general rule under Section 357(c), if the sum of liabilities assumed (including liabilities to which transferred property is subject) exceeds the aggregate total of the adjusted bases of the properties transferred, then the excess is recognized gain. But for this provision, under the conditions of Section 357(c), the transferor shareholder would have a negative basis in the stock received within the context of a Section 351 exchange.

3. F (p. 3–10; tax avoidance purpose, all liabilities, tainted as boot)

    In general, Section 357(a) provides that when the acquiring corporation assumes a liability (or acquires property subject to a liability) within the context of a Section 351 exchange, the relief of indebtedness is not considered boot to the transferor shareholder for purposes of determining the transferor shareholder's recognized gain on the exchange. However, as an exception to this general rule under Section 357(b), all liabilities transferred are tainted as boot to the transferor if a tax avoidance motive exists as to the transfer of some liability. In the instant case, B transfers (to CLJ) land and building (with a fair market value of $250,000 and an adjusted basis of $100,000) subject to a mortgage of $100,000 for stock (with a fair market value of $150,000). Section 351 applies to this exchange, but B's' realized gain of $70,000 ($150,000 + $100,000 − $180,000) is recognized (or reported) to the extent of $100,000 boot (total liabilities transferred of $100,000 tainted as boot). B must recognize his realized gain of $70,000, because B had a tax avoidance motive in refinancing the previously existing mortgage indebtedness and transferring such refinanced mortgage indebtedness to CLJ.

4. T (p. 3–15)

    Under Section 1032, a corporation recognizes neither gain nor loss when such corporation receives money or property in exchange for capital stock (including treasury stock).

5. F (p. 3–14; includes the holding period of the asset transferred)

    Within the context of a Section 351 exchange under Section 1223(1), the shareholder's holding period for the stock received includes the holding period of the property transferred if (1) the basis of the stock received is determined by reference to the basis of the property transferred and (2) such property transferred is either a capital asset or Section 1231 property. In the instant case, within the context of a Section 351 exchange under Section 358, the basis of the stock received is determined by reference to the basis of the property transferred. Hence, the holding period of the new property (stock) does not begin on the day after the date of the exchange. Rather, it includes the holding period of the transferred property, as long as the transferred property is either a capital asset or Section 1231 property at the time of the exchange.

STUDY GUIDE
CHAPTER 3
Corporations: Organization and Capital Structure

6. T (p. 3–15; additional price paid for shares held)

    Under Section 1032, a corporation recognizes neither gain nor loss when such corporation receives money or property in exchange for capital stock (including treasury stock). Further, a corporation's gross income does not include the money or property received as a capital contribution from a shareholder. Such contribution represents an additional price paid for the shares held by the shareholder. Such contribution is treated by the corporation as adding to the operating capital of the corporation. In the instant case, the basis of the property received by a corporation from a sole shareholder as a contribution to capital is equal to the basis of the property in the hands of such shareholder increased by any gain recognized to the shareholder on the transfer. In this situation, no gain is recognized by the transferor.

7. F (p. 3–19; non-business, to protect her investment)

    A bad debt deduction may arise for those persons who have extended credit to a corporation, upon the financial demise of such corporation. As a guarantor of a corporation's debt, if the corporation fails to repay the debt, the guarantor must pay. In the instant case, the guarantor is subrogated to the rights of the creditor so that the guarantor may exercise against the debtor all the rights which the creditor, if unpaid, may have exercised against the debtor, including the right to take a bad debt deduction. There are two types of bad debt deductions—business and non-business bad debt deductions. According to the Supreme Court in *Whipple*, if Beth extends credit to a corporation in her capacity as an investor, any resulting bad debt is classified as non-business. In contrast, business bad debt deductions arise out of an extension of credit within the context of a trade or business.

8. F (p. 3–5; he must report FMV of stock as compensation)

    The non-recognition provisions of Section 351 apply to an exchange of property for stock if the following three requirements are satisfied: (1) *property* (as defined) is transferred, (2) in exchange for *stock*, and (3) where the property transferors are in *control* (as defined) of the corporation immediately after the exchange. Within the meaning of Section 351, *property* does not include services rendered. Thus, in the instant case, Section 351 does not apply to the exchange of services for stock and Steve must include in gross income under Section 61 the fair market value of the stock as taxable compensation.

9. T (p. 3–22; immediate recognition of loss)

    The non-recognition provisions of Section 351 are mandated to apply to an exchange of property for stock if the following three requirements are satisfied: (1) *property* (as defined) is transferred, (2) in exchange for *stock*, and (3) where the property transferors are in *control* (as defined) of the corporation immediately after the exchange. Within the meaning of Section 351, *control* is defined as at least 80 percent of all classes of stock entitled to *vote* and at least 80 percent of the total number of shares of all other classes of stock. In the instant case, BJ transfers (to J Corporation) equipment (with a fair market value of $70,000 and an adjusted basis of $180,000) for 10 shares of J stock (with an assumed fair market value of $70,000). BJ does not have control immediately after the exchange, because he owns only approximately 55 percent (60/110) of J's only class of stock issued and outstanding. Thus, Section 351 does not apply to BJ's exchange of equipment for stock and BJ may recognize the realized loss of $110,000 ($70,000 − $180,000). Section 267 does not disallow the loss in this instance.

10. F (p. 3–14; holding period does carry over)

    In the instant case, Section 351 applied to the original exchange, an exchange of property for Westco stock. Within the context of this Section 351 exchange under Section 1223(1) and with respect to the property transferred to Westco by Mr. Kitars, Westco's holding period includes Mr. Kitars' holding period for such property transferred if: (1) the basis of the transferred property received by Westco is determined by reference to the basis of the transferred property in the hands of Mr. Kitars and (2) such transferred property is either a capital asset or Section 1231 property in the hands of Westco. Within the context of a Section 351 exchange under Section 362, the basis of the transferred property received by Westco is determined with reference to the basis of the transferred property in the hands of Mr. Kitars. Hence, Mr. Kitars' holding period of the property transferred is *tacked on* to Westco's holding period of the transferred property, as long as the transferred property is either a capital asset or Section 1231 property at the time of the exchange.

Fill in the Blanks

1. liabilities assumed (p. 3–9)

    In general, Section 357(a) provides that when the acquiring corporation assumes a liability (or acquires property subject to a liability) within the context of a Section 351 exchange, the relief of indebtedness is not considered boot to the transferor shareholder for purposes of determining the transferor shareholder's recognized gain on the exchange.

2. capital contributions (p. 3–15)

    A corporation's gross income does not include the money or property received as a capital contribution from a nonshareholder. Such contribution is treated by the corporation as adding to the operating capital of the corporation. In this case, the basis of the property received by a corporation from a nonshareholder is zero. If a corporation receives money from a nonshareholder, the basis of any property acquired with such money (during the 12-month period beginning on the day the contribution is received) is zero. Further, upon the expiration of such 12-month period, the bases of other properties held by the corporation is reduced by the excess of such money received over the cost of property purchased with such money (during a 12-month period beginning on the day the contribution is received).

3. control, 80% (p. 3–6)

    The application of Section 351 to an exchange of money and property for stock is mandatory if the following three requirements are satisfied: (1) *property* (as defined) is transferred, (2) in exchange for *stock*, and (3) where the property transferors are in *control* (as defined) of the corporation immediately after the exchange. Within the meaning of Section 351, *control* is defined as at least 80 percent of all classes of stock entitled to *vote* and at least 80 percent of the total number of shares of *all other classes of stock.*

4. liabilities in excess of basis, negative (p. 3–10)

    In general, Section 357(a) provides that when the acquiring corporation assumes a liability (or acquires property subject to a liability) within the context of a Section 351 exchange, the relief of indebtedness is not considered boot to the transferor shareholder for purposes of determining the transferor shareholder's recognized gain on the exchange. However, as an exception to this general rule under Section 357(c), if the sum of liabilities assumed (including liabilities to which transferred property is subject) exceeds the aggregate total of the adjusted bases of the properties transferred, the excess is recognized gain. But for this provision, under the conditions of Section 357(c), the transferor shareholder would have a negative basis in the stock received within the context of a Section 351 exchange.

5. nonbusiness bad debts (p. 3–19)

    There are two types of bad debt deductions—business and nonbusiness bad debt deductions. A nonbusiness bad debt is treated as a short-term capital loss only when it becomes entirely worthless. Nonbusiness bad debt treatment is limited to noncorporate taxpayers.

6. services (p. 3–5)

    The nonrecognition provisions of Section 351 apply to an exchange of property for stock if the following three requirements are satisfied: (1) *property* (as defined) is transferred, (2) in exchange for *stock*, and (3) where the property transferors are in *control* (as defined) of the corporation immediately after the exchange. Within the meaning of Section 351, *property* does not include services rendered.

7. § 1244 (p. 3–20)

    Assuming a *small business corporation* (as defined) issues Section 1244 stock, upon the subsequent sale of such Section 1244 stock at a loss, the seller/issuee (within limits) recognizes an ordinary loss. The amount of ordinary loss deductible in any one year is $50,000 ($100,000 for spouses filing a joint return).

STUDY GUIDE
CHAPTER 3
Corporations: Organization and Capital Structure

8. bonds (p. 3–5)

The nonrecognition provisions of Section 351 apply to an exchange of property for stock if the following three requirements are satisfied: (1) *property* (as defined) is transferred, (2) in exchange for *stock*, and (3) where the property transferors are in *control* (as defined) of the corporation immediately after the exchange. Within the meaning of Section 351, *stock* does not include bonds, which are long-term debt instruments. Hence, the receipt of debt securities (within the context of a Section 351 exchange) constitutes the receipt of boot for purposes of determining a transferor shareholder's recognition of gain on such exchange.

9. thin capitalization (p. 3–17)

A corporation is thinly capitalized when the debt-to-equity ratio is relatively high. In these situations, the IRS may employ a substance-versus-form argument and find that part of the debt is, in substance, an equity interest. The effect of establishing part of the debt as an equity interest would be to deny the corporation the tax benefit of debt financing (i.e., the deductibility of interest).

Multiple Choice

1. a (p. 3–4; § 351 is mandatory, $25,000 realized gain not recognized)

    The nonrecognition provisions of Section 351 are mandated to apply to an exchange of property for stock if three requirements are satisfied. In the instant case, Chip and Dale: (1) transfer *property* (as defined), (2) in exchange for *stock*, and (3) where the property transferors (Chip and Dale) are in *control* (as defined) of the corporation immediately after the exchange. Hence, Section 351 applies to Dale's exchange of property (building with an adjusted tax basis of $75,000) for stock (with a fair market value of $100,000) and Dale's realized gain of $25,000 ($100,000 – $75,000) is not recognized (or reported). Thus, item a is correct. Further, the other items are incorrect because they each are inconsistent with the correct answer.

2. c (p. 3–5; stock for services is compensation)

    The nonrecognition provisions of Section 351 apply to an exchange of property for stock if the following three requirements are satisfied: (1) *property* (as defined) is transferred, (2) in exchange for *stock*, and (3) where the property transferors are in *control* (as defined) of the corporation immediately after the exchange. Within the meaning of Section 351, *property* does not include services rendered. Hence, in the instant case, Section 351 does not apply and Laura must include in gross income under Section 61 the fair market value of the stock ($2,000) as taxable compensation. Thus, item c is correct. Further, the other items are incorrect because they each are inconsistent with the correct answer.

3. b (p. 3–12; a dividend on the stock would be income to the shareholder)

    Within the context of a Section 351 exchange under Section 358, the basis of the stock received is determined by reference to the basis of the property transferred. Specifically, the adjusted basis of such stock is the same as the adjusted basis that the taxpayer has in the property transferred, increased by any gain recognized on the exchange and decreased by *the fair market value of boot received and any loss that is recognized on the exchange*. Thus, item b is correct, since distributions treated as dividends do not decrease stock basis. Further, choice items a, c, and d are incorrect because they each have the effect of decreasing stock basis.

4. b (p. 3–4; boot received, $5,000 cash + 5,000 FMV of equipment)

    The nonrecognition provisions of Section 351 apply to an exchange of property for stock if the following three requirements are satisfied: (1) *property* (as defined) is transferred, (2) in exchange for *stock*, and (3) where the property transferors are in *control* (as defined) of the corporation immediately after the exchange. However, if the taxpayer receives property (boot) other than stock, realized gain is recognized under Section 351(b) to the extent of the fair market value of the boot received. In the instant case, Dylon transfers land (with an adjusted tax basis of $35,000) for stock (with a fair market value of $37,000) and other property (cash and equipment having a fair market value of $5,000 and $5,000, respectively). Section 351 applies to this exchange, but Dylon's realized gain of $12,000 ($37,000 + $5,000 + $5,000 − $35,000) is recognized (or reported) to the extent of $10,000 (the fair market value of the boot received). Thus, item b is correct. Further, the other items are incorrect because they each are inconsistent with the correct answer.

5. c (p. 3–4; boot received, $30,000 cash)

The nonrecognition provisions of Section 351 apply to an exchange of property for stock if the following three requirements are satisfied: (1) *property* (as defined) is transferred, (2) in exchange for *stock*, and (3) where the property transferors are in *control* (as defined) of the corporation immediately after the exchange. However, if the taxpayer receives property (boot) other than stock, realized gain is recognized under Section 351(b) to the extent of the fair market value of the boot received. Further, Section 357(a) provides that when the acquiring corporation acquires property subject to a liability (within the context of Section 351) the relief of indebtedness is not considered boot to the transferor shareholder for purposes of determining the transferor shareholder's recognized gain on the exchange. In the instant case, Mr. Francois transfers an office building (with an adjusted basis of $150,000) subject to a mortgage of $120,000 for stock (with a fair market value of $100,000) and other property (cash having a fair market value of $30,000). Section 351 applies to this exchange, but Mr. Francois' realized gain of $100,000 ($100,000 + $120,000 + $30,000 − $150,000) is recognized (or reported) to the extent of $30,000 (the fair market value of the boot received). Recall: Section 357(a) provides that when Slim Corporation acquires the office building subject to the $120,000 mortgage (within the context of Section 351), Mr. Francois' relief of indebtedness is not considered boot to Mr. Francois for purposes of determining Mr. Francois' recognized gain on the exchange. Thus, item c is correct. Further, the other items are incorrect because they each are inconsistent with the correct answer.

6. b (p. 3–12; transferor's basis plus gain recognized, $18,500 + $3,000)

The nonrecognition provisions of Section 351 apply to an exchange of property for stock if the following three requirements are satisfied: (1) *property* (as defined) is transferred, (2) in exchange for *stock*, and (3) where the property transferors are in *control* (as defined) of the corporation immediately after the exchange. However, if the taxpayer receives property (boot) other than stock, realized gain is recognized under Section 351(b) to the extent of the fair market value of the boot received. Within the context of a Section 351 exchange under Section 362, the basis of the transferred property received by the transferee corporation is determined by reference to the basis of the transferred property in the hands of the transferor shareholder, increased by any gain recognized by the transferor shareholder. Mr. Naqvi transfers a building (with an adjusted tax basis of $18,500) for stock (with a fair market value of $20,000) and other property (cash having a fair market value of $3,000). Section 351 applies to this exchange. Mr. Naqvi's realized gain of $4,500 ($20,000 + $3,000 − $18,500) is recognized (or reported) to the extent of $3,000 (the fair market value of the boot received). Hence, within the context of a Section 351 exchange under Section 362, the adjusted basis of the building received by Nadir Corporation ($21,500) is determined by reference to the basis of the building in the hands of Mr. Naqvi ($18,500), increased by the $3,000 gain recognized by Mr. Naqvi on the exchange. Thus, item b is correct. Further, the other items are incorrect because they each are inconsistent with the correct answer.

7. a (p. 3–6, 12; fair market of property, control requirement was not met for Section 351)

The nonrecognition provisions of Section 351 apply to an exchange of property for stock if the following three requirements are satisfied: (1) *property* (as defined) is transferred, (2) in exchange for *stock*, and (3) where the property transferors are in *control* (as defined) of the corporation immediately after the exchange. Within the meaning of Section 351, control is defined as at least 80 percent of all classes of stock entitled to *vote* and at least 80 percent of the total number of shares of *all other classes of stock*. In the instant case, the control requirement is not met because Edgar's 330 shares are not counted in determining whether the property transferors have control immediately after the exchange. Theses shares are not counted because Edgar did not contribute property (services are not property). Without Edgar's shares, the property transferors hold in the aggregate only 70 percent of *all voting stock* [(440 + 330)/(440

+ 330 + 330)]. Accordingly, the exchange is a taxable event and Parody's adjusted basis in the property received from Rod equals its fair market value of $44,000. Thus, item a is correct. Further, the other items are incorrect because they each are inconsistent with the correct answer.

8. b (p. 3–4; "a" refers to boot, "c" & "d" are control requirements)

The nonrecognition provisions of Section 351 apply to an exchange of property for stock if the following three requirements are satisfied: (1) *property* (as defined) is transferred, (2) in exchange for *stock*, and (3) where the property transferors are in *control* (as defined) of the corporation immediately after the exchange. Item b (dealing with the fair market value of the property transferred) is correct because such item does not relate to a Section 351 requirement. The following items are incorrect:

- a is incorrect because it relates to boot.
- c and d are incorrect because they relate to the control requirement.

9. a (p. 3–4; § 351 is mandatory, $20,000 realized gain not recognized)

The nonrecognition provisions of Section 351 are mandated to apply to an exchange of property for stock if three requirements are satisfied. In the instant case, Randy and Audra: (1) transfer *property* (as defined), (2) in exchange for *stock*, and (3) where the property transferors (Randy and Audra) are in *control* (as defined) of the corporation immediately after the exchange. Hence, Section 351 applies to Audra's exchange of property (building with an adjusted tax basis of $80,000) for stock (with a fair market value of $100,000) and Audra's realized gain of $20,000 ($100,000 − $80,000) is not recognized (or reported). Thus, item a is correct. Further, the other items are incorrect because they each are inconsistent with the correct answer.

10. c (p. 3–5; stock for services is compensation)

The nonrecognition provisions of Section 351 apply to an exchange of property for stock if the following three requirements are satisfied: (1) *property* (as defined) is transferred, (2) in exchange for *stock*, and (3) where the property transferors are in *control* (as defined) of the corporation immediately after the exchange. Within the meaning of Section 351, *property* does not include services rendered. However, a person who receives stock (which is not insubstantial) in exchange for both services and property is treated as a member of the transferring group for purposes of the Section 351 control test. In the instant case, Section 351 only applies to part of Sydney's exchange of legal services and cash for Thunder stock. Specifically, Section 351 applies to the exchange of stock for cash, but it does not apply to the exchange of stock for legal services. As a result, Sydney must include in gross income under Section 61 the fair market value of the stock ($7,000) as taxable compensation for services rendered. Thus, item c is correct. Further, other choice items are incorrect because they each are inconsistent with the correct answer.

11. b (p. 3–4; boot received, $6,000)

The nonrecognition provisions of Section 351 apply to an exchange of property for stock if the following three requirements are satisfied: (1) *property* (as defined) is transferred, (2) in exchange for *stock*, and (3) where the property transferors are in *control* (as defined) of the corporation immediately after the exchange. However, if the taxpayer receives property (boot) other than stock, realized gain is recognized under Section 351(b) to the extent of the fair market value of the boot received. In the instant case, Shelly transfers property (with an adjusted basis of $20,000) for DWL stock (with a fair market value of $21,000) and other property (cash having a fair market value of $6,000). Section 351 applies to this exchange, but Shelly's realized gain of $7,000 ($21,000 + $6,000 − $20,000) is recognized (or reported) to the extent of $6,000 (the fair market value of the boot received). Thus, item b is correct. Further, the other items are incorrect because they each are inconsistent with the correct answer.

12. b (p. 3–10; excess of liabilities over basis, $200,000 − $180,000)

In general, Section 357(a) provides that when the acquiring corporation assumes a liability (or acquires property subject to a liability) within the context of a Section 351 exchange, the relief of indebtedness is not considered boot to the transferor shareholder for purposes of determining the transferor shareholder's recognized gain on the exchange. However, as an exception to this general rule under Section 357(c), if the sum of liabilities assumed (including liabilities to which transferred property is subject) exceeds the aggregate total of the adjusted bases of the properties transferred, the excess is recognized gain. But for this provision, under the conditions of Section 357(c), the transferor shareholder would have a negative basis in the stock received within the context of a Section 351 exchange. In the instant case, Andrew transfers an office building (with an adjusted basis of $180,000) subject to a mortgage of $200,000 for stock (with a fair market value of $150,000). Section 351 applies to this exchange, but Andrew's' realized gain of $100,000 ($150,000 + $200,000 − $180,000) is recognized (or reported) to the extent of $20,000 (the excess of the liabilities transferred of $200,000 over the adjusted basis of the office building of $180,000). Thus, item b is correct. Further, other choice items are incorrect because they each are inconsistent with the correct answer.

CHAPTER 4

Corporations: Earnings & Profits and Dividend Distributions

LEARNING OBJECTIVES

After completing Chapter 4, you should be able to:

1. Understand the role that earnings and profits play in determining the tax treatment of distributions.
2. Compute a corporation's earnings and profits.
3. Apply the rules for allocating earnings and profits to distributions.
4. Understand the tax impact of property dividends on the recipient shareholder and the corporation making the distribution.
5. Understand the nature and treatment of constructive dividends.
6. Distinguish between taxable and nontaxable stock dividends and stock rights.

KEY TERMS

Accumulated earnings and profits
Constructive dividend
Current earnings and profits
Earnings and profits
Property dividend
Stock dividend
Stock rights
Unreasonable compensation

OUTLINE

I. **TAXABLE DIVIDENDS—IN GENERAL**
   A. Distributions are presumed to be dividends unless the parties can show otherwise.
   B. Dividend income is limited to the amount of earnings and profits (E & P) of the distributing corporation.
   C. Distributions not taxed as dividends, because of insufficient E & P, are a return of capital to the extent of stock basis (the stock basis is reduced accordingly). Distributions in excess of stock basis are treated as a gain.
   D. E & P represents the corporation's economic ability to pay a dividend without impairing its capital.

II. **EARNINGS AND PROFITS**
   A. The Internal Revenue Code does not define E & P.
   B. Instead, the computation of E & P begins with taxable income
      1. E & P is increased by all book income items excluded from taxable income.
         a. Examples include municipal bond interest, life insurance proceeds, and the dividends received deduction.
      2. E & P is decreased by nondeductible expenditures. Examples include:
         a. excess capital losses.
         b. expenses to produce tax-exempt income.
         c. Federal income taxes paid.
         d. nondeductible insurance premiums, fines, and penalties.
         e. related party losses.
      3. Timing adjustments may increase or decrease taxable income. Examples include:
         a. charitable contribution carryovers.
         b. net operating loss carryovers.
         c. capital loss carryovers.
      4. Accounting method adjustments may increase or decrease taxable income. Examples include:
         a. Deferred gain on installment sales, for E & P, is recognized in year of sale.
         b. Depreciation, for E & P, must be computed using the straight-line method over the assets ADR midpoint life; § 179 expense is deducted over 5 years.
         c. Depletion, for E & P, must be computed using the cost depletion method.
         d. The percentage completion method of accounting for long-term contracts is required for E & P purposes.
         e. Intangible drilling costs, for E & P, are amortized over 60 months.
         f. Mine exploration and development costs, for E & P, are amortized over 120 months.
   C. Summary: E & P measures the earnings of the corporation that are treated as being available for distribution to shareholders as dividends.
   D. Current versus Accumulated E & P
      1. Current E & P is determined by making a series of adjustments to the corporation's taxable income in the current year.
      2. Accumulated E & P is the total of all previous years' current E & P, since February 28, 1913, as computed on the first day of each tax year, reduced by distributions made.
      3. Current E & P is allocated on a pro rata basis to distributions made during the year.
      4. Accumulated E & P is applied, to the extent necessary, in chronological order beginning with the earliest distribution.
   E. Allocating E & P To Distributions (General Rules)
      1. If current E & P is positive and accumulated E & P is positive, the distribution is a dividend.
      2. If current E & P is positive and there is a deficit in accumulated E & P, the distribution is a dividend to extent of current E & P.

3. If there is a deficit in current E & P and accumulated E & P is positive, the accounts are netted.
   a. If positive, distribution is a dividend, to the extent of the balance.
   b. If negative, distribution is a return of capital.

III. **PROPERTY DIVIDENDS—IN GENERAL**
   A. Property Dividends—Effect on the Shareholder
      1. The amount of the distribution is the fair market value of the property on the date of distribution, reduced by liabilities of the corporation assumed by the shareholder.
      2. As with a cash distribution, the portion of a property distribution covered by E & P is a dividend with any excess treated as a return of capital.
      3. The shareholder's basis in the property is the fair market value of the property on the date of distribution.
   B. Property Dividends—Effect on the Corporation
      1. All distributions of appreciated property cause gain recognition. The property is treated as sold for its fair market value.
      2. On distributions of property having a tax basis in excess of its fair market value, the corporation cannot recognize a loss.
      3. If distributed property is subject to a liability in excess of basis, the fair market value of the property for determining gain on the distribution cannot be less than that liability.
   C. Effect of Corporate Distributions on E & P
      1. E & P is reduced by the amount of money distributed.
      2. If property is distributed, E & P is reduced by the greater of the property's fair market value or adjusted basis, less the amount of any liability distributed.
      3. E & P is increased by gain recognized on appreciated property distributions.
      4. Under no circumstances can a distribution generate or add to a deficit in E & P.

IV. **CONSTRUCTIVE DIVIDENDS**
   A. A measurable economic benefit conveyed by a corporation to a shareholder (and not a dividend).
   B. Types of Constructive Dividends
      1. The most frequent constructive dividend situations are:
         a. shareholder use of corporate-owned property.
         b. bargain sale of corporate property to a shareholder.
         c. bargain rental of corporate property.
         d. payments for the benefit of a shareholder.
         e. unreasonable compensation.
         f. loans to shareholders.
         g. loans to a corporation by shareholders.
   C. Tax Treatment of Constructive Dividends
      1. Constructive distributions are, for tax purposes, treated the same as actual distributions.
      2. The constructive distribution is taxable as a dividend to the extent of the corporation's current and accumulated E & P.

V. **STOCK DIVIDENDS AND STOCK RIGHTS**
   A. Stock Dividends
      1. In general, stock dividends are not taxable if they are pro rata distributions on common stock.
      2. However, the Internal Revenue Code contains five exceptions to this general rule. In these situations, the stock dividend is taxable:
         a. distributions payable either in stock or property.
         b. distributions of property to some shareholders and an increase in the proportionate interest of other shareholders in the assets or E & P of the distributing corporation.
         c. distributions of preferred stock to some common stock shareholders and common stock to other common shareholders.

d. distributions of stock to preferred shareholders. However, changes in the conversion ratio of convertible preferred stock to account for a stock dividend or stock split are not taxable in some circumstances.
   e. distributions of convertible preferred stock, unless it can be shown that the distribution will not result in a disproportionate distribution.
3. Effect on corporate E & P:
   a. Nontaxable stock dividends have no effect on E & P.
   b. Taxable stock dividends are treated the same as any other property distribution.
4. If the stock dividend is taxable, the shareholder's basis is fair market value.
5. If the stock dividend is nontaxable, the shareholder's basis in the stock is reallocated to all the shares.
   B. Stock rights are subject to the same rules as stock dividends for determining taxability.

VI. **TAX PLANNING CONSIDERATIONS**
   A. Corporation Distributions
      1. An E & P account should be established and maintained because E & P is the measure of dividend income to shareholders.
      2. There is no statute of limitations on the computation of E & P.
   B. Constructive Dividends
      1. Shareholders should try to structure their dealings with the corporation on an arm's length basis.
      2. Dealings between shareholders and closely held corporations should be as formal as possible.

Section 301 – Property Distributions: Effect on the Shareholder

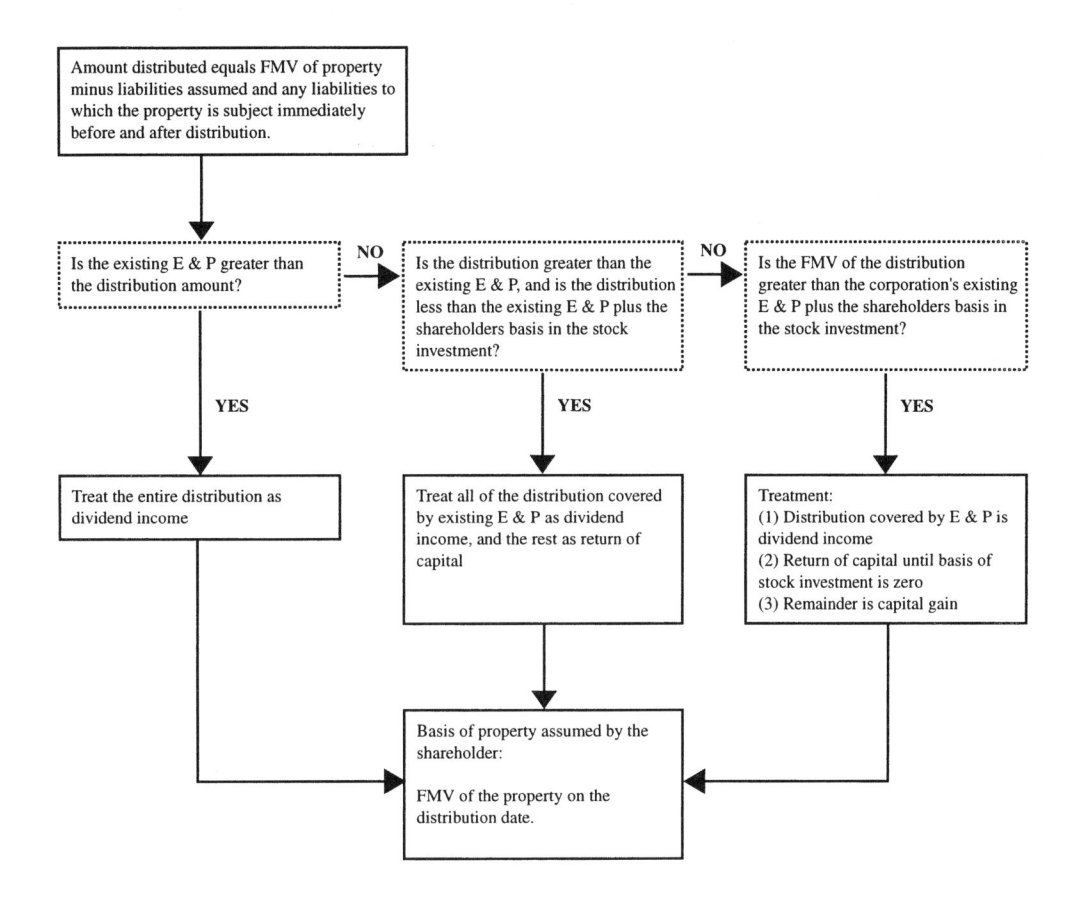

```
┌─────────────────────────────────────┐
│ Amount distributed equals FMV of    │
│ property minus liabilities assumed  │
│ and any liabilities to which the    │
│ property is subject immediately     │
│ before and after distribution.      │
└─────────────────────────────────────┘
                  │
                  ▼
┌───────────────────────┐  NO   ┌──────────────────────────┐  NO   ┌──────────────────────────┐
│ Is the existing E & P │──────▶│ Is the distribution      │──────▶│ Is the FMV of the        │
│ greater than the      │       │ greater than the         │       │ distribution greater     │
│ distribution amount?  │       │ existing E & P, and is   │       │ than the corporation's   │
└───────────────────────┘       │ the distribution less    │       │ existing E & P plus the  │
         │                      │ than the existing E & P  │       │ shareholders basis in    │
         │ YES                  │ plus the shareholders    │       │ the stock investment?    │
         ▼                      │ basis in the stock       │       └──────────────────────────┘
┌───────────────────────┐       │ investment?              │                  │
│ Treat the entire      │       └──────────────────────────┘                  │ YES
│ distribution as       │                  │ YES                              ▼
│ dividend income       │                  ▼                      ┌──────────────────────────┐
└───────────────────────┘       ┌──────────────────────────┐      │ Treatment:               │
         │                      │ Treat all of the         │      │ (1) Distribution covered │
         │                      │ distribution covered by  │      │     by E & P is dividend │
         │                      │ existing E & P as        │      │     income               │
         │                      │ dividend income, and the │      │ (2) Return of capital    │
         │                      │ rest as return of        │      │     until basis of stock │
         │                      │ capital                  │      │     investment is zero   │
         │                      └──────────────────────────┘      │ (3) Remainder is capital │
         │                                  │                     │     gain                 │
         │                                  ▼                     └──────────────────────────┘
         │                      ┌──────────────────────────┐                  │
         │                      │ Basis of property        │                  │
         └─────────────────────▶│ assumed by the           │◀─────────────────┘
                                │ shareholder:             │
                                │ FMV of the property on   │
                                │ the distribution date.   │
                                └──────────────────────────┘
```

Section 311 – Property Distributions: Effect on the Corporation

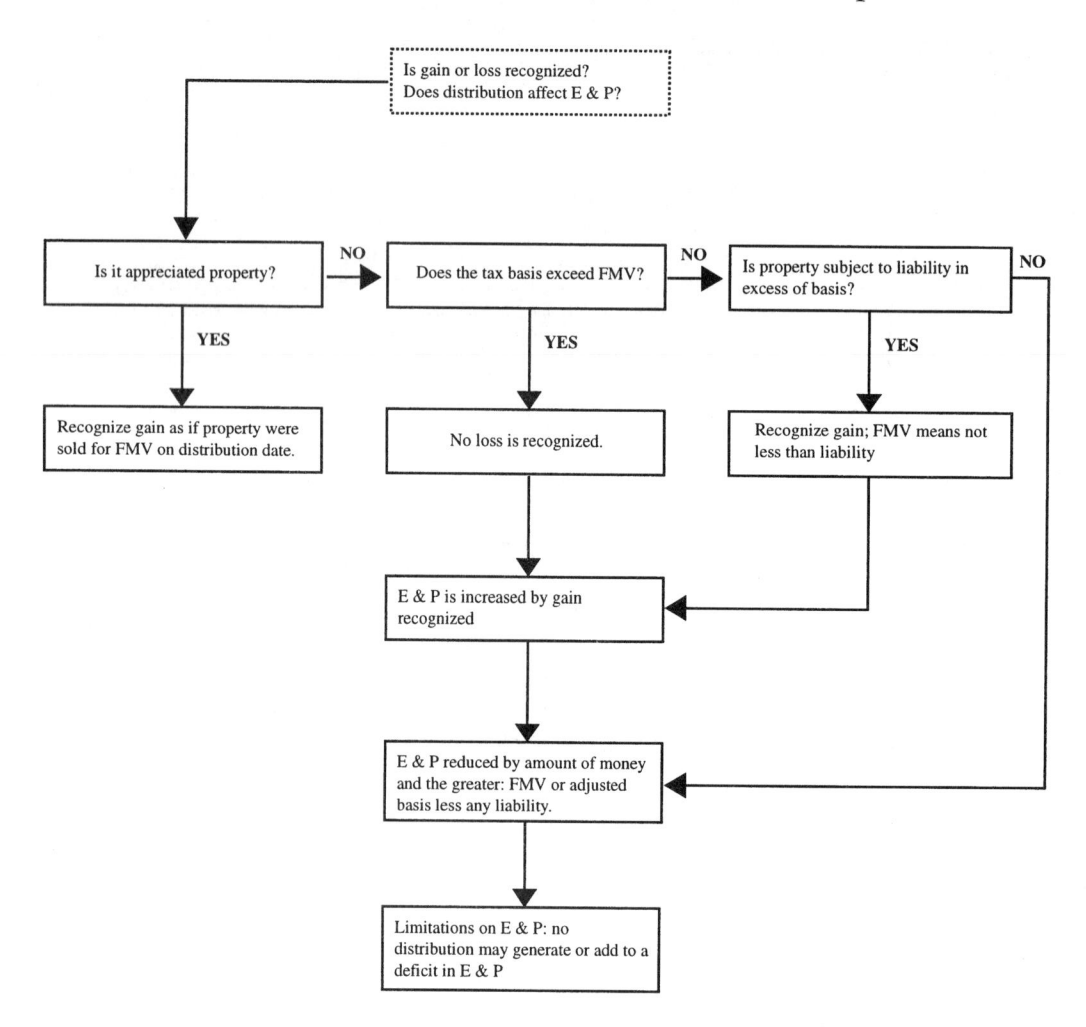

```
                    ┌─────────────────────────────┐
                    │ Is gain or loss recognized? │
                    │ Does distribution affect E & P? │
                    └─────────────────────────────┘

    ┌──────────────────┐  NO   ┌──────────────────────┐  NO   ┌────────────────────────┐  NO
    │ Is it appreciated├──────→│ Does the tax basis   ├──────→│ Is property subject to ├──────┐
    │ property?        │       │ exceed FMV?          │       │ liability in excess of │      │
    └──────────────────┘       └──────────────────────┘       │ basis?                 │      │
            │ YES                       │ YES                  └────────────────────────┘      │
            ▼                           ▼                              │ YES                   │
    ┌──────────────────┐       ┌──────────────────────┐       ┌────────────────────────┐      │
    │ Recognize gain as│       │ No loss is recognized│       │ Recognize gain; FMV    │      │
    │ if property were │       │                      │       │ means not less than    │      │
    │ sold for FMV on  │       └──────────────────────┘       │ liability              │      │
    │ distribution date│                   │                  └────────────────────────┘      │
    └──────────────────┘                   ▼                              │                   │
                               ┌──────────────────────┐                   │                   │
                               │ E & P is increased   │◄──────────────────┘                   │
                               │ by gain recognized   │                                       │
                               └──────────────────────┘                                       │
                                           │                                                  │
                                           ▼                                                  │
                               ┌──────────────────────────────┐                               │
                               │ E & P reduced by amount of   │◄──────────────────────────────┘
                               │ money and the greater: FMV   │
                               │ or adjusted basis less any   │
                               │ liability.                   │
                               └──────────────────────────────┘
                                           │
                                           ▼
                               ┌──────────────────────────────┐
                               │ Limitations on E & P: no     │
                               │ distribution may generate or │
                               │ add to a deficit in E & P    │
                               └──────────────────────────────┘
```

Section 305 – Stock Dividends

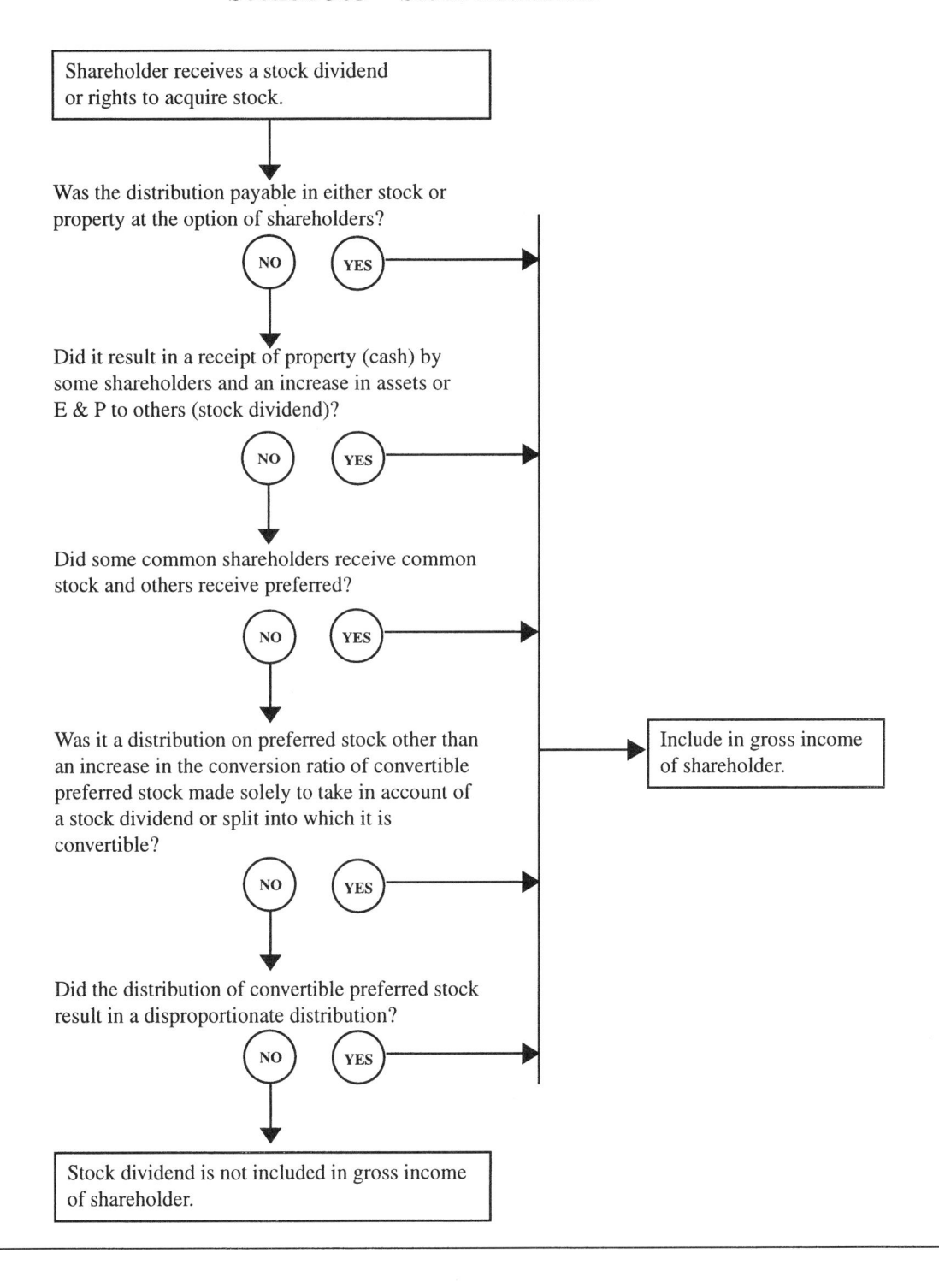

Shareholder receives a stock dividend or rights to acquire stock.

↓

Was the distribution payable in either stock or property at the option of shareholders?

- NO ↓
- YES → Include in gross income of shareholder.

Did it result in a receipt of property (cash) by some shareholders and an increase in assets or E & P to others (stock dividend)?

- NO ↓
- YES → Include in gross income of shareholder.

Did some common shareholders receive common stock and others receive preferred?

- NO ↓
- YES → Include in gross income of shareholder.

Was it a distribution on preferred stock other than an increase in the conversion ratio of convertible preferred stock made solely to take in account of a stock dividend or split into which it is convertible?

- NO ↓
- YES → Include in gross income of shareholder.

Did the distribution of convertible preferred stock result in a disproportionate distribution?

- NO ↓
- YES → Include in gross income of shareholder.

Stock dividend is not included in gross income of shareholder.

TEST FOR SELF-EVALUATION—CHAPTER 4

True or False

Indicate which of the following statements is true or false by circling the correct answer.

T F 1. Gem Corporation has two classes of stock, Class A common and Class B preferred. Class B preferred stock CANNOT be converted into Class A common stock. If Gem declares a common stock dividend on the Class A stock pro rata among the shareholders, Class A shareholders must include the dividend in gross income. (IRS 96 3A-9)

T F 2. The current earnings and profits of a corporation at the time of a distribution by the corporation, do NOT necessarily determine whether the distribution is a taxable dividend. (IRS 95 3A-9)

T F 3. Generally, a shareholder will NOT include in gross income a distribution of stock or stock rights in a corporation if it is a distribution on preferred stock. (IRS 95 3A-10)

T F 4. If a corporation distributes property subject to a liability which is greater than the property's adjusted basis, the fair market value of the property is treated as NOT less than the liability assumed or acquired by the shareholder. (IRS 95 3A-11)

T F 5. A shareholder holding solely common stock does NOT include a distribution of common stock in gross income if other common shareholders received preferred stock in the same distribution. (IRS 94 3A-4)

T F 6. Corporation Y has a dividend reinvestment plan that allows its shareholders to use its dividends to buy more shares of stock in Corporation Y rather than receiving the dividend in cash. If shareholder W uses his dividends to buy more stock at a price equal to its fair market value, he does NOT report the dividends as income. (IRS 94 1A-7)

T F 7. A shareholder does NOT include in gross income a distribution of stock or rights to acquire stock in the distributing corporation if any shareholder may elect to receive money in lieu of the stock or rights. (IRS 93 3A-9)

T F 8. Generally, additional shares of stock received from nontaxable stock dividends or stock splits results in a per share reduction in the basis of the original stock. (IRS 93 1A-10)

Fill in the Blanks

Complete the following statements with the appropriate word(s) or amount(s).

1. The key factor in determining whether a dividend has in fact been paid is the measure of _____ conveyed to the shareholder.

2. Distributions by a corporation are presumed to be _____ unless the parties can prove otherwise.

3. When stock dividends are taxable, the basis to the shareholder-distributee is the _____.

4. The rules for determining the taxability of _____ are identical to those for determining taxability of stock dividends.

STUDY GUIDE
CHAPTER 4
Corporations: Earnings & Profits and Dividend Distributions

4–9

Multiple Choice

Choose the best answer for each of the following questions.

_____ 1. Cavalier, a calendar year C corporation, had accumulated earnings and profits of $30,000 as of January 1, 2002. On April 1, 2002 Cavalier distributed $55,000 in cash to Cavalier's sole shareholder. For 2002, Cavalier had earnings and profits of $20,000. The shareholder's adjusted basis in Cavalier's stock was $12,000 before the distribution. As a result of this distribution, what is the amount of the shareholder's ordinary dividend income and return of capital? (IRS 97 3C-69)

	Dividend Income	Return of Capital
a.	$50,000	$ 5,000
b.	$55,000	$ 0
c.	$30,000	$25,000
d.	$50,000	$12,000

_____ 2. Badger Corporation had $64,000 of earnings and profits before accounting for the following distributions to its sole shareholder:

Cash	$25,000
Real estate: Adjusted Basis	70,000
Fair market value	98,000
Subject to a mortgage of	40,000

The shareholder assumes the $40,000 mortgage on the property. Without considering Federal income taxes, what is the net reduction to Badger's earnings and profits? (IRS 97 3C-70)

  a. $28,000
  b. $55,000
  c. $64,000
  d. $68,000

_____ 3. On July 1, 2002, Rose, a calendar year C corporation, distributed an auto used 100% in its business to its sole shareholder. At the time of the distribution, the auto, which originally cost $18,000, had an adjusted basis of $6,000 and a fair market value of $5,000. There were no liabilities attached to the auto. No other distributions were made during 2002. As of January 1, 2002, Rose's earnings and profits were $8,000. By what amount will Rose reduce its earnings and profits as a result of the distribution of the auto? (IRS 97 3C-71)

  a. $3,000
  b. $4,000
  c. $5,000
  d. $6,000

_____ 4. Terre Corporation distributed depreciable personal property having a fair market value of $9,500 to its shareholders. The property had an adjusted basis of $5,000 to the corporation. Terre had correctly deducted $3,000 in depreciation on the property. What is the amount of Terre's TOTAL recognized gain on the distribution and how much of this gain will be considered ordinary income? (IRS 97 3C-72)

	Total Recognized Gain	Ordinary Income
a.	$4,500	$ 0
b.	$4,500	$3,000
c.	$4,500	$4,500
d.	$9,500	$ 0

_____ 5. Noble, a calendar year accrual basis corporation, distributed shares of Reitz Corporation stock to Noble's employees in lieu of salaries. The salary expense would have been deductible as compensation if paid in cash. On the date of the payment, Noble's adjusted basis in the Reitz Corporation stock distributed was $25,000 and the stock's fair market value was $85,000. What is the tax effect to Noble Corporation? (IRS 97 3C-73)

    a. $25,000 deduction
    b. $25,000 deduction; $60,000 recognized gain
    c. $85,000 deduction
    d. $85,000 deduction; $60,000 recognized gain

_____ 6. For 2002, Roberts Corporation had a beginning balance of unappropriated retained earnings of $100,000 and net income per books of $125,000. During 2002 it paid cash dividends of $60,000, had a loss on sale of securities of $3,600, and received a refund of 2001 income taxes of $6,000. What is its ending balance of unappropriated retained earnings for 2002? (IRS 96 3C-55)

    a. $225,000
    b. $174,600
    c. $171,000
    d. $161,400

_____ 7. Camden, Inc., a calendar year C corporation that began conducting business in 1984, had accumulated earnings and profits of $20,000 as of January 1, 2002. On October 1, 2002, Camden distributed $25,000 in cash to Beaufort, Camden's sole shareholder. Camden had a $20,000 DEFICIT in earnings and profits for 2002. Beaufort had an adjusted basis of $8,000 in his stock before the distribution. What is the amount of Beaufort's ordinary dividend income and capital gain as of the date of the distribution? (IRS 96 3C-57)

	Dividend Income	Capital Gain
a.	$ 0	$25,000
b.	$25,000	$ 0
c.	$ 5,000	$12,000
d.	$ 5,000	$ 8,000

_____ 8. Elk Corporation, a calendar year C corporation, had accumulated earnings and profits of $60,000 as of January 1, 2002, the beginning of its tax year. Elk had an operating loss of $70,000 for the first 6 months of 2002, but had earnings and profits of $6,000 for the entire tax year 2002. Elk distributed $15,000 to its shareholders on July 1, 2002. What portion of the $15,000 distribution would be an ordinary dividend? (IRS 96 3C-58)

    a. $15,000
    b. $10,600
    c. $6,000
    d. $0

_____ 9. Ball, a calendar year C corporation, had accumulated earnings and profits of $50,000 as of January 1, 2002. Ball had a deficit in earnings and profits for 2002 of $65,000. Ball distributed $25,000 to its shareholders on July 1, 2002. What is Ball Corporation's accumulated earnings and profits as of December 31, 2002? (IRS 96 3C-59)

   a. $0
   b. ($15,000)
   c. ($32,500)
   d. ($40,000)

_____ 10. Which of the following statements is CORRECT? (IRS 95 1B-30)

   a. Stock dividends are distributions made by a corporation of another corporation's stock.
   b. In computing basis for new stock received as a result of a nontaxable dividend, it is immaterial whether the stock received is identical or not to the old stock.
   c. If a stock dividend is taxable, the basis of the old stock does NOT change.
   d. If you receive nontaxable stock rights and allow them to expire, you have a loss equal to the fair market value of the rights.

_____ 11. E-Z Corporation, which has a dividend reinvestment plan, paid dividends of $20 per share during 2002. Carlos, who owned 100 shares of E-Z Corporation prior to the distribution, participated in the plan by using ALL the dividends to purchase 20 additional shares of stock. He purchased the stock for $100 per share when the fair market value was $125 per share. How much dividend income must Carlos report on his 2002 income tax return? (IRS 95 1C-48)

   a. $2,500
   b. $2,000
   c. $500
   d. $0

_____ 12. In 2002, Chim purchased 100 shares of preferred stock of Donald Corporation for $5,000. In 2004, she received a stock dividend of 20 additional shares of preferred stock in Donald. On the date of the distribution, the preferred stock had a fair market value of $40 per share. What is Chim's basis in the new stock she received as a result of the stock dividend? (IRS 95 1C-60)

   a. $1,000
   b. $833
   c. $800
   d. $0

_____ 13. In 2001, Corey bought 200 shares of ABC stock at $10 a share. In 2002, Corey bought an additional 100 shares of ABC stock at $20 a share. In 2003, ABC declared a 2-for-1 stock split. How many shares of ABC stock does Corey own and what is the basis of the stock? (IRS 96 1C-58)

   a. 400 shares at $5 a share and 200 shares at $10 a share
   b. 400 shares at $10 a share and 200 shares at $20 a share
   c. 200 shares at $20 a share and 100 shares at $40 a share
   d. 600 shares at $6.67 per share

_____ 14. On January 3, 2002, Susan purchased 300 shares of common stock in Corporation Y for $120 per share. Four months later she purchased 100 additional shares at $180 per share. On December 10, 2002, Susan received a 20% nontaxable stock dividend. The new and the old stock are identical. What is the amount of Susan's basis in each share of Corporation Y stock after the stock dividend? (IRS 96 1C-59)

   a. 480 shares at $112.50 a share
   b. 360 shares at $120 a share and 120 shares at $180 a share
   c. 360 shares at $120 a share and 120 shares at $150 a share
   d. 360 shares at $100 a share and 120 shares at $150 a share

_____ 15. In 2001, Nancy bought 100 shares of Trauna, Inc. for $5,000 or $50 a share. In 2002, Nancy bought 100 shares of Trauna stock for $8,000 or $80 a share. In 2003, Trauna declared a 2-for-1 stock split. Nancy sold 50 shares of the stock she received from the stock split for $2,000. She could NOT definitely identify the shares she sold. What is the amount of Nancy's net capital gain from this sale for 2003? (IRS 96 1C-68)

  a. $0
  b. $750
  c. $1,625
  d. $2,000

Comprehensive Problem

In its financial statements for 2002, JD Corporation showed $307,000 of pre-tax accounting income. Indicate any adjustments for the following recorded transactions and determine JD Corporation's taxable income and net increase (decrease) in E & P for the year.

	Per Book	Taxable Income	E & P
Pre-tax accounting income:	$307,000		
1. Insurance Premium Expense:			
a. fire & casualty	15,000		
b. employee group life (employee named beneficiary)	20,000		
c. term life on John Doe, Pres. (JD Corp. is beneficiary)	7,000		
2. Interest Income:			
a. University City bonds	15,000		
b. CD, National Bank	10,000		
3. Dividend Income:			
a. Fuji Photo, Tokyo	3,000		
b. Sears Roebuck, Chicago	8,000		
4. Charitable Contributions:			
a. United Way	7,000		
b. bowling team shirts	350		
c. University City Park District (unimproved land, FMV $50,000; cost $35,000)	35,000		
5. Depreciation (straight-line for book, accelerated for tax)	40,000	$70,000	
6. Dividend Payments:			
a. cash $20,000			
b. common stock, 1 for 3 $12 par value			
TAXABLE INCOME		_____	
7. Federal Income Taxes:		_____	_____
NET CHANGE IN E & P			_____

SOLUTIONS TO CHAPTER 4 QUESTIONS

True or False

1. F   (p. 4–17; distribution does not change proportionate common interest)

    In general, under Section 305(a), a distribution of stock (or stock rights) received by a shareholder is excluded from the shareholder's gross income if the distribution is a pro rata distribution with respect to the common stock held by the shareholder. This general rule of nonrecognition presumes that the shareholder's ownership interest does not change as a result of the distribution. In the instant case, the pro rata distribution of Gem's Class A common stock on Gem's Class A common stock is excluded from the gross income of shareholders under Section 305(a).

2. T   (p. 4–7; current E & P determined end of tax year)

    Under Section 316(a), an amount distributed to a shareholder during a corporation's tax year is included in the gross income of a shareholder as a dividend to the extent such amount is distributed from either (1) current E & P or (2) accumulated E & P. Accumulated E & P is calculated at the beginning of a corporation's tax year. Current E & P is determined at the end of the corporation's tax year. Only by coincidence will current E & P at the time of a distribution equal current E & P at the end of the corporation's tax year.

3. F   (p. 4–17; distributions on preferred stock are generally taxable)

    In general, under Section 305(a), a distribution of stock (or stock rights) received by a shareholder is excluded from the shareholder's gross income if the distribution is a pro rata distribution with respect to the common stock held by the shareholder. This general rule of nonrecognition presumes that the shareholder's ownership interest does not change as a result of the distribution. However, in cases under Section 305(b) (where the shareholder's ownership interest is presumed to change as a result of the stock distribution), such distribution is taxable as a Section 301 distribution. For example, under Section 305(b)(4), any distribution of stock or stock rights on preferred stock is taxable as a Section 301 distribution. Thus, in the instant case, a pro rata distribution of stock (or stock rights) on preferred stock is taxable as a Section 301 distribution under Section 305(b)(4).

4. T   (p. 4–12; FMV not less than liability assumed)

    When a corporation distributes property (rather than cash) to a shareholder, the amount distributed is measured by the fair market value of the property on the date of the distribution. Further, all distributions of appreciated property generate gain to the distributing corporation under Section 311(b). In effect, a corporation that distributes gain property is treated as if it has sold the property to the shareholder for its fair market value. However, for purposes of determining such gain, the fair market value of the property is treated as being not less than the amount of the liability under Section 311(b)(2).

5. F   (p. 4–17; distribution changes proportionate common interest)

    In general, under Section 305(a), a distribution of stock (or stock rights) received by a shareholder is excluded from the shareholder's gross income if the distribution is a pro rata distribution with respect to the common stock held by the shareholder. This general rule of nonrecognition presumes that the shareholder's ownership interest does not change as a result of the distribution. However, in cases under Section 305(b) (where the shareholder's ownership interest is presumed to change as a result of the stock distribution), a distribution is taxable as a Section 301 distribution. For example, under Section 305(b)(3), a distribution of preferred stock to some common shareholders and a contemporaneous distribution of common stock to other common shareholders is taxable as a Section 301 distribution to all shareholder distributees.

6. F (p. 4–17; dividend income is used to purchase additional stock)

In general, under Section 305(a), a distribution of stock (or stock rights) received by a shareholder is excluded from the shareholder's gross income if the distribution is a pro rata distribution with respect to the common stock held by the shareholder. This general rule of nonrecognition presumes that the shareholder's ownership interest does not change as a result of the distribution. However, in cases under Section 305(b) (where the shareholder's ownership interest is presumed to change as a result of the stock distribution), a distribution is taxable as a Section 301 distribution. For example, under Section 305(b)(2), a distribution of property to some shareholders (with a corresponding increase in the proportionate interest of other shareholders in either the assets or E & P of the distributing corporation) is taxable as a Section 301 distribution to all shareholder distributees. In the instant case, W takes advantage of Y's dividend reinvestment plan and increases its proportionate interest in Y (relative to those shareholders that receive a distribution of property) by receiving additional shares in Y. Under Section 305(b)(2), Y's distribution to W is taxable as a Section 301 distribution.

7. F (p. 4–17; taxable—can alter proportionate interests)

In general, under Section 305(a), a distribution of stock (or stock rights) received by a shareholder is excluded from the shareholder's gross income if the distribution is a pro rata distribution with respect to the common stock held by the shareholder. This general rule of nonrecognition presumes that the shareholder's ownership interest does not change as a result of the distribution. However, in cases under Section 305(b) (where the shareholder's ownership interest is presumed to change as a result of the stock distribution), a distribution is taxable as a Section 301 distribution. For example, under Section 305(b)(1), a distribution of either property or stock (at the election of the shareholder) is taxable as a Section 301 distribution to all shareholder distributees.

8. T (p. 4–17; basis of old stock is allocated to old and new)

In general, under Section 305(a), a distribution of stock (or stock rights) received by a shareholder is excluded from the shareholder's gross income if the distribution is a pro rata distribution with respect to the common stock held by the shareholder. This general rule of nonrecognition presumes that the shareholder's ownership interest does not change as a result of the distribution. Within the context of a distribution of stock (or stock rights) under Section 305(a), the basis of the old stock is allocated on a pro rata basis to the old stock and the new stock (or stock rights) under Section 307(a). The effect of such allocation is to reduce the tax adjusted basis per share of the old stock.

Fill in the Blanks

1. economic benefit (p. 4–3)

To the extent that a Section 301 distribution is made from corporate earnings and profits (E & P), the distribution is a dividend, taxed as ordinary income under Section 301(c)(1). Under the tax law, corporate distributions are presumed sourced out of corporate E & P, but this presumption is rebuttable. A distribution (or a portion thereof) that is not treated as a dividend is a nontaxable return of capital under Section 301(c)(2) to the extent of the shareholder's adjusted basis in the stock on which the distribution is made. The shareholder's adjusted basis in the stock on which the distribution is made is reduced accordingly. The excess of the distribution over an amount equal to the sum of (a) the portion of the distribution treated as a dividend and (b) the portion of the distribution treated as a nontaxable return of capital is treated as a gain from the deemed sale or exchange of property under Section 301(c)(3). Accordingly, computing the amount distributed (the economic benefit conveyed) is a key element in the taxation of corporate distributions.

2. dividends (p. 4–2)

To the extent that a Section 301 distribution is made from corporate earnings and profits (E & P), the distribution is a dividend, taxed as ordinary income under Section 301(c)(1). Under the tax law, corporate distributions are presumed sourced out of corporate E & P, but this presumption is rebuttable.

3. fair market value (p. 4–17)

   In general under Section 305(a), a distribution of stock (or stock rights) received by a shareholder is excluded from the shareholder's gross income if the distribution is a pro rata distribution with respect to the common stock held by the shareholder. This general rule of nonrecognition presumes that the shareholder's ownership interest does not change as a result of the distribution. However, in cases under Section 305(b) (where the shareholder's ownership interest is presumed to change as a result of a stock distribution), the distribution is taxable as a Section 301 distribution. Under Section 301(d), in cases under Section 305(b) where the distribution is taxable as a Section 301 distribution, the shareholder's adjusted basis of the stock acquired is the stock's fair market value at the time of the distribution.

4. stock rights (p. 4–18)

   In general, under Section 305(a), a distribution of stock (or stock rights) received by a shareholder is excluded from the shareholder's gross income if the distribution is a pro rata distribution with respect to the common stock held by the shareholder. This general rule of nonrecognition presumes that the shareholder's ownership interest does not change as a result of the distribution. As noted, stock rights are included within the scope of Section 305.

Multiple Choice

1. a (p. 4–8; presumed that current E & P cover all distributions until shown otherwise)

   Under Section 316(a), an amount distributed to a shareholder during a corporation's tax year is included in the gross income of the shareholder as a dividend to the extent that such amount is sourced out of either (1) current E & P or (2) accumulated E & P. Current E & P is allocated first to distributions on a pro rata basis. Subsequently, accumulated E & P is applied in chronological order. To the extent that a Section 301 distribution is made from corporate earnings and profits (E & P), the distribution is a dividend, taxed as ordinary income under Section 301(c)(1). A distribution (or a portion thereof) that is not treated as a dividend is a nontaxable return of capital (to the extent of the shareholder's basis in the stock on which the distribution is made) under Section 301(c)(2). The shareholder's basis in the stock on which the distribution is made is reduced accordingly. The excess of the distribution over an amount equal to the sum of (a) the portion of the distribution treated as a dividend and (b) the portion of the distribution treated as a nontaxable return of capital is treated as a gain from the deemed sale or exchange of property under Section 301(c)(3). In the instant case, the aggregate amount of Cavalier's current and accumulated E & P is $50,000 ($20,000 + $30,000). Cavalier's sole shareholder has dividend income of $50,000 and a nontaxable return of capital of $5,000, which correspondingly reduces the basis of such shareholder's stock from $12,000 to $7,000 ($12,000 − $5,000). Thus, item a is correct. Further, the other items are incorrect because they are each inconsistent with the correct answer.

2. b (p. 4–12; + $28,000 gain, − $25,000 cash, − $98,000 FMV, + 40,000 mortgage)

   Corporate distributions reduce E & P by:

   - the amount of money distributed
   - the greater of (a) the fair market value and (b) the adjusted basis of property distributed, less the amount of any liability to which the property is subject.

   Further, E & P is increased by the gain recognized on appreciated property that is distributed. In the instant case, Badger's E & P is increased by $28,000 of gain ($98,000 − $70,000) and decreased by (a) $25,000 (cash distribution) and (b) $58,000 (the property distribution of $98,000 less the mortgage of $40,000). Thus, as a result of the cash and property distributions, Badger has decreased its accumulated E & P by $55,000 ($25,000 + $58,000 − $28,000) from $64,000 to $9,000. Thus, item b is correct. Further, the other items are incorrect because they are each inconsistent with the correct answer.

3. d (p. 4–12; adjusted basis > FMV, no loss recognized)

   Corporate distributions reduce E & P by:

   - the amount of money distributed
   - the greater of (a) the fair market value and (b) the adjusted basis of property disstributed, less the greater of (a) the fair market value and (b) the adjusted basis of property

   Further, E & P is increased by the gain recognized on appreciated property that is distributed. In the instant case, Rose's E & P is decreased as a result of Rose's property distribution to the extent of such property's adjusted basis of $6,000. Thus, as a result of such property distribution, Rose has decreased its accumulated E & P by $6,000 from $8,000 to $2,000. Thus, item d is correct. Further, the other items are incorrect because they are each inconsistent with the correct answer.

4. b (p. 4–12; total gain: $9,500 – $5,000 = $4,500; depreciation recap is ordinary income)

   When a corporation distributes property (rather than cash) to a shareholder, the amount distributed is measured by the fair market value of the property on the date of the distribution. Further, all distributions of appreciated property generate gain to the distributing corporation under Section 311(b). In effect, a corporation that distributes gain property is treated as if it had sold the property to the shareholder for its fair market value. The character of the gain to the distributing corporation depends upon the extent to which the gain is recaptured under either Section 1245 or Section 1250. Under Section 1245, which generally applies to personalty, the gain is ordinary to the extent of all depreciation taken. In the instant case, Terre's realized and recognized gain is $4,500 ($9,500 – $5,000), of which $3,000 (all depreciation taken) is ordinary income. Thus, item b is correct. Further, the other items are incorrect because they are each inconsistent with the correct answer.

5. d (p. 4–12; gain: $85,000 FMV – $25,000 basis; salary deduction is FMV)

   A distribution is a unilateral transfer from a corporation to its shareholders with respect to such shareholders' stock. In the instant case, the transfer to Noble employees of appreciated property in satisfaction of a corporate debt does not constitute a distribution. Instead, Noble recognizes gain of $60,000 ($85,000 – $25,000) and an ordinary salaries expense deduction of $85,000. Thus, item d is correct. Further, the other items are incorrect because they are each inconsistent with the correct answer.

6. c (p. 4–8; beginning balance + net income per books – dividends paid = $165,000; official answer, $171,000 assumes Roberts is a cash basis taxpayer and the refund arose only in 2002)

   The concept of E & P is not the same as unappropriated retained earnings. The beginning balance of unappropriated retained earnings is increased for net income per books (and certain prior period adjustments) and decreased for dividends. In the instant case, Roberts' ending balance of unappropriated retained earnings is $171,000 ($100,000 + $125,000 + $6,000 – $60,000). Thus, item c is correct. Further, the other items are incorrect because they are each inconsistent with the correct answer.

7. c (p. 4–9; accumulated, $20,000 – ¾($20,000) = $5,000 dividend; $25,000 distribution – $5,000 dividend – $8,000 basis = $12,000 capital gain)

   Under Section 316(a), the amount distributed to a shareholder during a corporation's tax year is included in the gross income of a shareholder as a dividend to the extent such distributed amount is sourced out of either (1) current E & P or (2) accumulated E & P. Current E & P is allocated first to distributions on a pro rata basis. Subsequently, accumulated E & P is applied in chronological order. Further, when there is accumulated E & P (but a deficit in current E & P) accumulated E & P is netted with an estimate of current E & P at the time of the distribution. To the extent that a Section 301 distribution is made from corporate earnings and profits (E & P), the distribution is a dividend, taxed as ordinary income under Section 301(c)(1). A distribution (or a portion thereof) that is not treated as a dividend is a nontaxable return of capital (to the extent of the shareholder's basis in the stock on which the distribution is made) under Section 301(c)(2). The shareholder's basis in the stock on which the distribution is made is reduced accordingly. The excess of the distribution over an amount equal to the sum of (a) the portion of the distribution treated as a dividend and (b) the portion of the distribution treated as a nontaxable return of capital is treated as a gain from the deemed sale or exchange of property under Section 301(c)(3). In the instant case, the estimate of Camden's deficit in current E & P on October 1, 2002 is $15,000 (¾ × $20,000). Thus, on October 1, 2002 the net of Camden's current and accumulated E & P is $5,000 ($20,000 − $15,000). Hence, Beaufort has dividend income of $5,000 and a nontaxable return of capital of $8,000, which reduces the basis of such shareholder's stock from $8,000 to $–0–. Further, the excess of the $25,000 distribution over $13,000 (an amount equal to the sum of (a) the portion of the distribution treated as a dividend ($5,000) and (b) the portion of the distribution treated as a nontaxable return of capital ($8,000)) is treated as a $12,000 gain from the deemed sale or exchange of property. Thus, item c is correct. Further, the other items are incorrect because they are each inconsistent with the correct answer.

8. a (p. 4–8; see #1)

Under Section 316(a), the amount distributed to a shareholder during a corporation's tax year is included in the gross income of a shareholder as a dividend to the extent such distributed amount is sourced out of either (1) current E & P or (2) accumulated E & P. Current E & P is allocated first to distributions on a pro rata basis. Subsequently, accumulated E & P is applied in chronological order. In the instant case, Elk has accumulated E & P of $60,000 and current E & P of $6,000. Hence, Elk's shareholders have ordinary dividend income of $15,000 as a result of Elk's $15,000 distribution. Current E & P is computed at the end of the Elk's 2002 tax year. Thus, item a is correct. Further, the other items are incorrect because they are each inconsistent with the correct answer.

9. c (p. 4–7; accumulated $50,000 − ½($65,000) = $18,500 dividend; $25,000 distribution − $18,500 dividend = $7,500 return of capital. 7/1/02 balance in E & P is zero; 12/31 balance is $32,500 or remaining ½($65,000))

Under Section 316(a), an amount distributed to a shareholder during a corporation's tax year is included in the gross income of a shareholder as a dividend to the extent such distributed amount is sourced out of either (1) current E & P or (2) accumulated E & P. Current E & P is allocated first to distributions on a pro rata basis. Subsequently, accumulated E & P is applied in chronological order. Further, when there is accumulated E & P, but a deficit in current E & P, accumulated E & P is netted with an estimate of current E & P at the time of the distribution. To the extent that a Section 301 distribution is made from corporate earnings and profits (E & P), the distribution is a dividend, taxed as ordinary income under Section 301(c)(1). Accumulated E & P is reduced by (1) distributions (but not below zero) and (2) a deficit in current E & P. In the instant case, the estimate of Ball's deficit in current E & P on July 1, 2002 is $32,500 (½ × $65,000). Thus, the net of Ball's current and accumulated E & P is $17,500 ($50,000 − $32,500), immediately before the distribution on July 1, 2002. Ball's accumulated E & P is reduced by the $25,000 distribution (but not below $–0–) from $17,500 to $–0–. Further, Ball's accumulated E & P is reduced to a deficit of $32,500 by the remaining deficit in current E & P of $32,500. Thus, item c is correct. Further, the other items are incorrect because they are each inconsistent with the correct answer.

10. c (4–11; for taxable stock dividends, basis is FMV)

Within the context of a Section 301 (taxable) distribution, the adjusted basis of property distributed is such property's fair market value at the time of the distribution under Section 301(d). Accordingly, the adjusted basis of the old stock need not be allocated to the new stock. It follows, therefore, that the adjusted basis of the old stock does not change. Thus, item c is correct. Further, the following items are incorrect:

- a is incorrect because a stock dividend is a distribution made by a corporation of its own stock.
- b is incorrect because the basis calculation for the new stock is different if the new stock is not identical to the old stock. That is, the basis of the old stock must be allocated based on relative fair market value to the new stock and the old stock.
- d is incorrect because the basis of the old stock is not allocated between the new stock rights and the old stock if the new stock rights expire.

11. a (p. 4–17; FMV of stock over actual investment is constructive dividend)

   In general under Section 305(a), a distribution of stock (or stock rights) received by a shareholder is excluded from the shareholder's gross income if the distribution is a pro rata distribution with respect to the common stock held by the shareholder. This general rule of nonrecognition presumes that the shareholder's ownership interest does not change as a result of the distribution. However, in cases under Section 305(b) (where the shareholder's ownership interest is presumed to change as a result of a stock distribution), the distribution is taxable as a Section 301 distribution. For example, under Section 305(b)(2), a distribution of property to some shareholders (with a corresponding increase in the proportionate interest of other shareholders in either the assets or E & P of the distributing corporation) is taxable as a Section 301 distribution to all shareholders. In the instant case, Carlos takes advantage of E-Z's dividend reinvestment plan and increases its proportionate interest in E-Z (relative to those shareholders that received a distribution of property) by receiving 20 additional shares in E-Z with a fair market value of $125 per share. Under Section 305(b)(2), E-Z's amount distributed of $2,500 (20 × $125) is taxable to Carlos as a Section 301 distribution. Thus, item a is correct. Further, the other items are incorrect because they are each inconsistent with the correct answer.

12. c (p. 4–17; distributions of stock to preferred shareholders are taxable, 20 shares × $40 per share)

   In general under Section 305(a), a distribution of stock (or stock rights) received by a shareholder is excluded from the shareholder's gross income if the distribution is a pro rata distribution with respect to the common stock held by the shareholder. This general rule of nonrecognition presumes that the shareholder's ownership interest does not change as a result of the distribution. However, in cases under Section 305(b) (where the shareholder's ownership interest is presumed to change as a result of the stock distribution) the distribution is taxable as a Section 301 distribution. For example, under Section 305(b)(4), any distribution of stock or stock rights on preferred stock is taxable as a Section 301 distribution. Further, the adjusted basis of property distributed is such property's fair market value at the time of the distribution under Section 301(d). In the instant case, a pro rata distribution of stock (or stock rights) on preferred stock is taxable as a Section 301 distribution under Section 305(b)(4). Here, Chim received a stock dividend of 20 additional shares of Donald preferred stock with a fair market value of $40 per share. Under Section 305(b)(4), the stock dividend is a taxable Section 301 distribution. Accordingly, Chim's adjusted basis in the 20 additional shares is their fair market value of $800 (20 × $40). Thus, item c is correct. Further, the other items are incorrect because they are each inconsistent with the correct answer.

13. a (p. 4–17; basis is reallocated: $2,000 over 400 shares plus $2,000 over 200 shares)

   In general under Section 305(a), a distribution of stock (or stock rights) received by a shareholder is excluded from the shareholder's gross income if the distribution is a pro rata distribution with respect to the common stock held by the shareholder. This general rule of nonrecognition presumes that the shareholder's ownership interest does not change as a result of the distribution. Within the context of a distribution of stock (or stock rights) under Section 305(a), the basis of the old stock is allocated on a pro rata basis to the old stock and the new stock (or stock rights) under Section 307(a). The effect of such allocation is to reduce the adjusted basis per share of the old stock. In the instant case, Corey's aggregate adjusted basis of $2,000 (200 × $10) in OLDSTOCK1 is allocated across 400 (2 × 200) shares to equal an adjusted basis per share of $5 ($2,000 ÷ 400). In addition, Corey's aggregate adjusted basis of $2,000 (100 × $20) in OLDSTOCK2 is allocated across 200 (2 × 100) shares to equal an adjusted basis per share of $10 ($2,000 ÷ 200). Thus, item a is correct. Further, the other items are incorrect because they are each inconsistent with the correct answer.

14. d (p. 4–17; basis is reallocated: $36,000 over 360 shares plus $18,000 over 120 shares)

   In general under Section 305(a), a distribution of stock (or stock rights) received by a shareholder is excluded from the shareholder's gross income if the distribution is a pro rata distribution with respect to the common stock held by the shareholder. This general rule of nonrecognition presumes that the shareholder's ownership interest does not change as a result of the distribution. Within the context of a distribution of stock (or stock rights) under Section 305(a), the basis of the old stock is allocated on a pro rata basis to the old stock and the new stock (or stock rights) under Section 307(a). The effect of such allocation is to reduce the adjusted basis per share of the old stock. In the instant case, Susan's aggregate adjusted basis of $36,000 (300 × $120) in OLDSTOCK1 is allocated across 360 (300 + 60) shares to equal an adjusted basis per share of $100 ($36,000 ÷ 360). In addition, Susan's aggregate adjusted basis of $18,000 (100 × $180) in OLDSTOCK2 is allocated across 120 (100 + 20) shares to equal an adjusted basis per share of $150 ($18,000 ÷ 120). Thus, item d is correct. Further, the other items are incorrect because they are each inconsistent with the correct answer.

15. b (p. 4–17; without specific identification, FIFO applies: 50 shares at $25 per share = $1,250 basis; $2,000 proceeds − $1,250 basis = $750 gain)

In general under Section 305(a), a distribution of stock (or stock rights) received by a shareholder is excluded from the shareholder's gross income if the distribution is a pro rata distribution with respect to the common stock held by the shareholder. This general rule of nonrecognition presumes that the shareholder's ownership interest does not change as a result of the distribution. Within the context of a distribution of stock (or stock rights) under Section 305(a), the basis of the old stock is allocated on a pro rata basis to the old stock and the new stock (or stock rights) under Section 307(a). The effect of such allocation is to reduce the adjusted basis per share of the old stock. In the instant case, Nancy's aggregate adjusted basis of $5,000 (100 × $50) in OLDSTOCK1 is allocated across 200 (2 × 100) shares to equal an adjusted basis per share of $25 ($5,000 ÷ 200). In addition, Nancy's aggregate adjusted basis of $8,000 (100 × $80) in OLDSTOCK2 is allocated across 200 (2 × 100) shares to equal an adjusted basis per share of $40 ($8,000 ÷ 200). Because Nancy sold 50 shares of Trauna stock and such stock was not specifically identifiable, Nancy must employ a First-In-First-Out approach in determining her adjusted basis for the 50 shares sold. Under this approach, Nancy's adjusted basis is $1,250 (50 × $25). With an amount realized of $2,000, Nancy's gain realized and recognized is $750 ($2,000 − $1,250). Thus, item b is correct. Further, the other items are incorrect because they are each inconsistent with the correct answer.

Comprehensive Problem

For tax:

1.	+	$7,000	expense to produce tax-exempt income (life insurance proceeds)
2.	−	$15,000	tax-exempt municipal bond interest
3.	−	$5,600	dividend received deduction, 70% $(8,000), unrelated, domestic corporation
4.	+	$4,600	contribution before limitation is $7,000 + 50,000 the 10% limitation is applied to taxable income before dividends received deduction or any charitable deduction; in this problem, $30,400 10% [$307,000 + $35,000 + $7,000 − $15,000 − $30,000]; $57,000 − $30,400 results in a $26,600 carryforward; the $350 could be deducted as a promotional expense; adjustment is + $4,600 ($35,000 − $30,400).
5.	−	$30,000	net change in depreciation

TAXABLE INCOME: $268,000

7.	$87,770;	.15($50,000) + .25($25,000) + .34($193,000) + .05($168,000)

For E & P:

4.	− $15,000	$57,000 allowable − $42,000 taken
5.	− $20,000	dividend payment
7.	− $87,770	federal income tax

NET CHANGE IN E & P: $177,230 increase

CHAPTER 5

Corporations: Redemptions and Liquidations

LEARNING OBJECTIVES

After completing Chapter 5, you should be able to:

1. Identify the stock redemptions that qualify for sale or exchange treatment.
2. Recognize the restrictions on sale or exchange treatment for certain redemption-like transactions.
3. Understand the tax consequences of complete liquidations for both the corporation and its shareholders.
4. Identify tax planning opportunities available to minimize the tax impact in stock redemptions and complete liquidations.

KEY TERMS

Attribution
Complete termination redemption
Corporate liquidation
Disproportionate redemption
Meaningful reduction test
Not essentially equivalent redemption
Partial liquidation
Preferred stock bailout
Redemption to pay death taxes
Residual method
Section 338 election
Stock redemption

OUTLINE

I. **STOCK REDEMPTIONS—IN GENERAL**
   A. In a stock redemption, a corporation distributes property in exchange for a shareholder's stock.
   B. Only a qualifying stock redemption is treated as a sale or exchange for tax purposes; other redemptions are treated as distributions.
      1. Qualifying stock redemptions are defined in the Code.
      2. Generally, a qualified stock redemption occurs when there is a substantial reduction in the shareholder's ownership interest.

II. **STOCK REDEMPTIONS—SALE OR EXCHANGE TREATMENT**
   A. Currently, five types of stock redemptions qualify for sale or exchange treatment. Distributions:
      1. not essentially equivalent to a dividend.
      2. substantially disproportionate in terms of shareholder effect.
      3. in complete termination of a shareholder's interest.
      4. to noncorporate shareholders in partial liquidation of a corporation.
      5. to pay a shareholder's death taxes.
   B. Stock Attribution Rules
      1. In determining whether a distribution qualifies as a redemption, specific stock attribution rules must be applied. These rules treat a shareholder as the owner of stock held by certain related parties, in addition to the stock owned personally.
      2. For an individual redeeming stock, the following are related parties:
         a. *family:* all stock owned by a spouse, children, grandchildren, and parents is deemed to be owned by the individual.
         b. *partnership:* a partnership's stock interest times the partner's proportionate share in the partnership is deemed owned by the individual partner.
         c. *estate or trust:* an estate or trust's stock interest times the beneficiary's proportionate interest in the estate or trust is deemed to be owned by the individual beneficiary.
         d. *corporation:* if a more than 50% shareholder, a corporation's stock interest times the shareholder's proportionate interest in the corporation is deemed to be owned by the individual shareholder.
      3. Stock attribution rules also apply to partnerships, estates, trusts, and corporations redeeming stock:
         a. *partnership:* stock owned by a partner is deemed 100% owned by the partnership.
         b. *estate or trust:* stock owned by a beneficiary is deemed 100% owned by the estate or trust.
         c. *corporation:* stock owned by a 50% or more shareholder is deemed 100% owned by the corporation.
   C. Not Essentially Equivalent Redemptions (§ 302(b)(1))
      1. There is no objective test. Each case is resolved on a facts and circumstances basis.
      2. A meaningful reduction in the shareholder's proportionate ownership must take place.
      3. A decrease in the redeeming shareholder's voting control is considered the most important factor in determining whether or not a meaningful reduction has occurred.
   D. Disproportionate Redemptions (§ 302(b)(2))
      1. An objective two-part test is used to determine whether the distribution qualifies as a redemption.
      2. After the distribution, the shareholder must own *less than* 80% of the interest owned in the corporation before the redemption.
      3. After the distribution, the shareholder must own *less than* 50% of the total combined voting power of all classes of stock entitled to vote.
   E. Complete Termination Redemptions
      1. A distribution that completely terminates a shareholder's entire stock interest will qualify for exchange treatment.

2. Family attribution rules do not apply if both of the following conditions are met:
   a. the former shareholder has no interest, other than as a creditor, in the corporation for at least 10 years after the redemption and
   b. the former shareholder files an agreement to notify the IRS of any acquisition of a prohibited interest acquired within the 10 year period.
3. The former shareholder may reacquire an interest in the corporation through a bequest or inheritance but in no other manner.

F. Redemptions in Partial Liquidation
1. A noncorporate shareholder is allowed exchange treatment when:
   a. the distribution is not essentially equivalent to a dividend or
   b. an active business is terminated.
2. The not essentially equivalent to a dividend requirement tests the effect of the distribution on the corporation, not the shareholder; there must be a genuine contraction of the business of the corporation (there is no objective test for a "genuine contraction").
3. The complete termination of a business test has objective requirements. A distribution will qualify as a partial liquidation if the following conditions are met:
   a. the corporation has two or more businesses that have been in existence for at least 5 years (a "qualified business"),
   b. the corporation terminates one qualified business while continuing another qualified business, and
   c. the terminated business was not acquired in a taxable transaction within the 5 year period.
4. Any distribution must be made within the taxable year in which the plan is adopted or within the succeeding taxable year.

G. Redemptions to Pay Death Taxes
1. A redemption which qualifies as a redemption to pay death taxes is not subject to the not essentially equivalent to a dividend or substantially disproportionate tests.
2. The value of the stock in the gross estate of a decedent must exceed 35% of the value of the adjusted gross estate.
3. The distribution is limited to the sum of death taxes, funeral, and certain estate administration expenses.

H. Effect on the Corporation Redeeming Its Stock
1. If appreciated property is distributed as part of the redemption, the corporation must recognize the gain. Losses, however, are not recognized.
2. The E & P account of a corporation is reduced by the lesser of (1) the fair market value of the property distributed or (2) the ratable share of the E & P attributable to the stock redeemed.

III. STOCK REDEMPTIONS—ADDITIONAL LIMITATIONS
A. Redemptions that do not qualify for exchange treatment as provided for in the Code are considered dividends to the extent of the corporation's E & P.
B. The Preferred Stock Bailout
1. Clever taxpayers devised a scheme to bail out corporate profits.
   a. A corporation would issue a nontaxable, nonvoting preferred stock dividend on common stock.
   b. The shareholder would assign a portion of his common stock basis to the preferred stock.
   c. The shareholder would then sell the preferred stock to a third party.
2. The sale of the preferred stock bailed out corporate profits as capital gains without reducing the shareholder's percentage ownership of the corporation.
C. The Code Solution: Section 306
1. The shareholder has ordinary income on the sale of the preferred stock to a third party.
2. The amount of ordinary income is the fair market value of the preferred stock on the date of distribution.

3. The ordinary income is *not a dividend* and, therefore, does not reduce the corporation's E & P.
4. No loss is recognized on the sale of the preferred stock by the shareholder.
5. If the shareholder does not sell the preferred stock but instead has it redeemed by the corporation, the proceeds constitute dividend income to the extent of the corporation's E & P on the date of the redemption.

D. Section 306 Stock Defined
1. Section 306 Stock is stock other than common that is either:
   a. received as a nontaxable stock dividend,
   b. received tax-free in a corporate reorganization which is substantially the same as a stock dividend or received in exchange for § 306 stock, or
   c. has a basis determined by reference to the basis of § 306 stock.
2. If a corporation has no E & P on the date of a nontaxable preferred stock dividend, the stock will not be § 306 stock.

E. Redemption Through Use of Related Corporations
1. When a shareholder controls two corporations and sells stock of one corporation to the other corporation, the sale may be treated as a redemption subject to the not essentially equivalent (§ 302(b)(1)) and disproportionate redemption (§ 302(b)(2)) rules.
   a. Control is 50% of the combined voting power or 50% of the total value of all classes of stock.
   b. Stock attribution rules apply in determining the degree of control.
2. If one of the two qualified redemption rules are NOT satisfied, the exchange is treated as a taxable dividend to the extent of the corporations' E & P.
   a. The taxable dividend first reduces the E & P of the acquiring corporation, then, if necessary, the E & P of the issuing corporation.
   b. The acquiring corporation treats the stock received as a contribution to capital, having the same basis as the transferring shareholder had.
   c. The individual's basis in the stock of the acquiring corporation is increased by his basis in the stock surrendered.
3. If one of the qualified redemption rules are satisfied, the sale is recast as a redemption of the stock of the acquiring corporation.

F. Distribution of Stock and Securities of a Controlled Corporation
1. Stock in an existing subsidiary corporation can be distributed to the shareholders of the parent tax-free, if the requirements of § 355 are met.

IV. LIQUIDATIONS
A. A corporate liquidation occurs, for tax purposes, when a corporation ceases to be a going concern.
B. Legal dissolution under state law is not required for Federal tax purposes.

V. LIQUIDATIONS—EFFECT ON THE DISTRIBUTING CORPORATION
A. A liquidating corporation recognizes gain or loss on the distribution of property.
1. The property distributed is treated as if sold at its fair market value.
2. If subject to a liability, the fair market value cannot be less than that liability.

B. Loss recognition is prohibited (or limited) in two situations:
1. When distributions are made to related parties (a shareholder owning more than 50% of the corporation's stock), or
2. When "built-in loss" property is distributed.

C. Losses are not allowed on distributions to related parties if either:
1. the distribution is NOT pro rata or
2. the property distributed is disqualified property.
   a. Pro rata means that each shareholder receives his or her share of *each* corporate asset.
   b. Disqualified property is property acquired by the corporation as a capital contribution or in a §351 exchange during the five year period before the liquidating distribution.

- D. "Built-in loss" property
  1. For property whose fair market value was less than its adjusted basis when transferred to the corporation ("built-in loss property") and held for 2 years or less, it is assumed that the property was contributed to the corporation for the purpose of providing a loss.
  2. If this property is sold or distributed, the built-in loss is not allowed.
  3. Further, note that this rule applies to a broader set of transactions (sales or distributions) and a broader set of taxpayers (related or unrelated parties).

VI. LIQUIDATIONS—EFFECT ON THE SHAREHOLDER
- A. Generally, gain or loss is recognized as though the shareholder sold his or her stock.
- B. The shareholder's gain recognition on the receipt of notes from corporate installment sales of capital assets may be deferred and recognized as cash is received.

VII. LIQUIDATIONS—PARENT SUBSIDIARY SITUATIONS
- A. If a parent corporation liquidates a subsidiary under § 332, no gain or loss is recognized by the parent or by the subsidiary for property distributed to the parent.
- B. Section 332 requires all of the following:
  1. The parent must own at least 80% of the subsidiary's voting stock and 80% of the value of the subsidiary's stock on the date the plan of liquidation is adopted and thereafter until all property is distributed.
  2. The subsidiary must distribute all its property within the taxable year or within 3 years from the close of the tax year when the plan was adopted and the first distribution was made.
  3. The subsidiary must be solvent.
- C. Minority Interests
  1. Distributions to minority shareholders cause gain, but not loss, recognition to the distributing corporation.
  2. The minority shareholder recognizes gain or loss as on a stock sale.
- D. Indebtedness of the Subsidiary to the Parent
  1. In general, the subsidiary does not recognize gain or loss on property transferred to the parent in a § 332 liquidation, even when the property is transferred to satisfy subsidiary debt held by the parent corporation.
  2. The parent corporation, however, recognizes gain or loss when property is received to satisfy a debt of the subsidiary (even if the property is received during the subsidiary's liquidation).
- E. Basis of Property Received by the Parent Corporation—The General Rule
  1. Property received by the parent retains the same basis as it had in the hands of the subsidiary.
  2. The parent's basis in the subsidiary's stock disappears.
  3. The parent acquires various tax attributes of the subsidiary including any net operating loss carryover, capital loss carryover, and E & P.
- F. Basis of Property Received by the Parent Corporation—§ 338 Election
  1. §338 permits the purchase of a controlling interest of stock to be treated as a purchase of the (new) subsidiary's assets.
  2. To qualify, all of the following requirements must be met.
     a. At least 80% of the voting power and value must be acquired by the purchasing corporation.
     b. Acquisition takes place within a 12-month period beginning with the first purchase of stock.
     c. The stock must be acquired in a taxable transaction.
     d. The § 338 election must be made by the 15th day of the 9th month after the month of the acquisition date.
  3. A § 338 election is irrevocable. Liquidation of the subsidiary is not required.

TEST FOR SELF-EVALUATION—CHAPTER 5

True or False

Indicate which of the following statements is true or false by circling the correct answer.

True or False

T F 1. Liquidating distributions are, at least in part, one form of a return of capital, assuming the distributee has at least some adjusted basis in the stock. (IRS 91 1A-5)

T F 2. A corporation will recognize a gain or loss on the distribution of its property to its shareholders in complete liquidation of the corporation, the same as if the corporation had sold the property to its shareholders at fair market value. (IRS 90 3A-17)

T F 3. A proportionate distribution to a corporate shareholder by a corporation in partial redemption of stock, pursuant to a plan of partial liquidation, is treated as a dividend to the extent of earnings and profits of the distributing corporation. (IRS 90 3A-18)

T F 4. When a corporation does not cancel redeemed stock but holds the stock in its treasury, the corporation will recognize a gain or loss on its retransfer or redistribution. (IRS 92 3A-9)

T F 5. Corporation W has 2,000 shares of its only class of stock outstanding. Mr. D owns 1,500 shares and his son, Randy, owns 500 shares. W redeemed all 1,500 shares from Mr. D for $45,000. Mr. D kept his position in W as an officer and director. This redemption qualifies for capital gain treatment by Mr. D since all of his ownership in W has been terminated. (IRS 90 3A-19)

T F 6. Corporation K distributed land use in its business to its shareholders in a qualified redemption of stock. At the time of the distribution, the land had an adjusted basis to K of $200,000, and a fair market value of $500,000. Corporation K does not recognize any gain on this distribution. (IRS 90 3A-20)

T F 7. In a complete liquidation of a corporation, the character of a shareholder's gain or loss is generally determined by the character of the asset(s) in the hands of the corporation before distribution to the shareholder. (IRS 91 3A-18)

T F 8. The gain or loss to a shareholder from a distribution in liquidation of a corporation is to be determined by comparing the amount of the distribution with the adjusted basis of the stock regardless of whether the distribution is in partial or complete liquidation of the corporation. (IRS 91 3A-19)

T F 9. After a stock redemption, if a shareholder's ownership percentage of all voting stock is less than 80% of his percentage of all voting stock held before the redemption, and the shareholder owns less than 50% of all voting stock of the corporation after the redemption, the redemption is considered substantially disproportionate. (IRS 91 3A-20)

T F 10. In May 2002, Lion Corporation distributed property in proportionate redemption of its stock in partial liquidation. Lion distributed land to Peter, a 50% shareholder. Lion distributed a building to Black Corporation, a 50% shareholder. The distribution was NOT essentially equivalent to a dividend and was made pursuant to a plan adopted in March of 2002. With respect to Peter and Black, this transaction meets the requirements of Section 302 and would be treated as a distribution of corporate assets in exchange for stock. (IRS 93 3A-10)

T F 11. Under the constructive ownership rules that apply to a stock redemption, a waiver of family attribution may qualify a redemption for exchange treatment. (IRS 92 3A-10)

Fill in the Blanks

Complete the following statements with the appropriate word(s) or amount(s).

Fill in the Blanks

1. Generally, in the application of Section 332 to the liquidation of a subsidiary by a parent corporation, the property received by the parent carries the _____ basis in the hands of the parent as it did in the hands of the subsidiary.

2. Section 332 _____ apply to an insolvent subsidiary.

3. The effect of Section 338 is to give the assets acquired by a parent corporation in the liquidation of its subsidiary the _____ basis as the stock which the parent held in the subsidiary.

4. Section 306 was enacted to preclude individuals from pulling earnings out of a corporation via the _____.

5. Stock redemptions which qualify for exchange treatment include distributions that are: _____ to a dividend, _____, in _____ of a shareholder's interest and, to pay _____.

6. A stock redemption is treated as "substantially disproportionate" if, after the distribution, the shareholder owns less than _____ of his holdings prior to the distribution and less than _____ of the combined voting power of all stock.

7. A subsidiary does not recognize gain or loss on a liquidating distribution to a parent corporation that directly owns _____ of the subsidiary's stock.

Multiple Choice

Choose the best answer for each of the following questions.

Multiple Choice

_____ 1. Under a plan of complete liquidation, Jayhawk Corporation distributed land, having an adjusted basis of $26,000, to its sole shareholder. The land was subject to a liability of $38,000 which the shareholder assumed for legitimate business purposes. The fair market value of the land on the date of distribution was $35,000. What is the amount of Jayhawk's recognized gain or loss? (IRS 97 3C-74)

    a. $9,000
    b. $12,000
    c. ($3,000)
    d. ($29,000)

_____ 2. Anne owned 1,000 shares of Oswego Corporation. Anne had purchased the stock in 1989 at $100 per share. Pursuant to Oswego's plan of complete liquidation, Anne received land with a fair market value of $75,000 and an adjusted basis to Oswego of $50,000 on December 1, 2002, and she received $50,000 cash on January 15, 2003. The distributions resulted in complete liquidation of Oswego Corporation. What is the amount of Anne's long-term capital gain for 2002 and 2003? (IRS 97 3C-75)

	2002	2003
a.	$0	$0
b.	$12,500	$12,500
c.	$0	$25,000
d.	$15,000	$10,000

_____ 3. Burke Corporation had earnings and profits of $500,000 before distributions. Due to economic conditions, Burke, in partial liquidation, distributed land having an adjusted basis to Burke of $135,000 and a fair market value of $150,000 to Mr. Ashby for 95% of his interest in Burke. Mr. Ashby's adjusted basis in the stock at the time of the distribution was $180,000. What is the amount of Burke Corporation's recognized gain or (loss)? (IRS 97 3C-76)

　　a. $0
　　b. $15,000
　　c. ($30,000)
　　d. ($45,000)

_____ 4. Two unrelated individuals, Tom and Dave, own all the stock of Huskie Corporation, which has earnings and profits of $400,000. Because of his inactivity in the business for the last several years, Tom has decided to retire from the business completely and move to Hawaii. Accordingly, Huskie Corporation will redeem all the stock owned by Tom and, in return, Tom will receive a distribution of $500,000. Tom's adjusted basis in the stock is $250,000. What will be the tax effect to Tom? (IRS 97 3C-77)

　　a. $400,000 dividend
　　b. $500,000 dividend
　　c. $100,000 capital gain
　　d. $250,000 capital gain

_____ 5. You may receive a return of capital distribution based on your stock. All of the following are true except: (IRS 96 1B-28)

　　a. A return of capital reduces the basis of your stock.
　　b. When the basis of your stock has been reduced to zero, report any additional return of capital as a capital loss.
　　c. Any liquidating distribution you receive is NOT taxable to you until you have recovered the basis of your stock.
　　d. If the total liquidating distributions you receive are less than the basis of your stock, you may have a capital loss.

_____ 6. Ranger Corporation's only class of stock is owned as follows:

Matthew	40%
Darlene, Matthew's sister	25%
Matthew's and Darlene's father	25%
Matthew's and Darlene's grandfather	10%

What is Matthew's direct and indirect stock ownership under the attribution rules for stock redemptions? (IRS 96 3B-26)

a. 65%
b. 75%
c. 90%
d. 100%

_____ 7. Heritage Corporation distributed an antique automobile to Rene, its sole shareholder. On the date of the distribution, the automobile had a fair market value of $30,000 and an adjusted basis to Heritage of $22,000. What is the amount of Heritage Corporation's recognized gain on the distribution? (IRS 96 3C-60)

a. $30,000
b. $12,000
c. $8,000
d. $0

_____ 8. Ann owned two blocks of Biddle Corporation stock which had the following characteristics:

Block	Shares	Acquired	Basis
1	200	06/01/02	$20,000
2	50	07/01/03	$12,500

Ann's two blocks of stock combined represented 10% of Biddle's only class of stock outstanding. Pursuant to Biddle's complete liquidation, Ann received a $50,000 cash distribution on December 1, 2003 in exchange for her 250 shares. Biddle's earnings and profits balance immediately before any liquidating distribution was $50,000. What is the amount and character of Ann's gain or loss? (IRS 96 3C-61)

a. $50,000 dividend income
b. $17,500 long-term capital gain
c. $20,000 long-term capital gain and $2,500 short-term capital loss
d. No gain or loss

_____ 9. In 2002 Daring Corporation, pursuant to a plan of complete liquidation, distributed land acquired in 1992 to Maria, its sole shareholder. The land had a fair market value of $120,000, an adjusted basis to Daring of $90,000, and was subject to a liability of $125,000 which was assumed by Maria. Maria owned 500 shares of Daring which she had purchased in 1990 for $50,000. Daring does NOT qualify as a small business corporation. What is the character and the amount of the gain or (loss) recognized by Maria and Daring Corporation? (IRS 96 3C-62)

	Maria	Daring
a.	$50,000 ordinary loss	$30,000 ordinary gain
b.	$50,000 long-term capital loss	$35,000 long-term capital gain
c.	$55,000 long-term capital loss	$30,000 long-term capital gain
d.	$55,000 long-term capital loss	$35,000 long-term capital gain

_____ 10. Mouse Corporation owns as an investment, 10% of the stock of Salem Corporation with an adjusted basis of $4,000 and a fair market value of $44,000. Mouse uses the Salem stock to redeem approximately 1%, or $10,000 par value, of its own outstanding stock from unrelated, noncorporate shareholders. As a result of this transaction, Mouse must report gain of: (IRS 96 3C-64)

a. $0
b. $2,000
c. $40,000
d. $44,000

____ 11. Diana, the sole shareholder of Ancient Corporation's only class of stock, owns 1,000 shares which she purchased in 1986. Diana's basis in the stock is $2,000,000. During 2002, Ancient, which had earnings and profits of $5,000,000, redeemed 900 shares for $4,500,000. What is the amount and character of Diana's gain? (IRS 96 3C-65)

    a. $4,500,000 dividend
    b. $4,500,000 capital gain
    c. $2,700,000 dividend
    d. $2,700,000 capital gain

SOLUTIONS TO CHAPTER 5 QUESTIONS

True or False

1. T (p. 5-24)

    Under Section 331(a), a distribution from a corporation to a shareholder in complete liquidation of the corporation is treated as a sale or exchange of the shareholder's stock. Within this context, at least part of the liquidating distribution constitutes a return of capital as long as the shareholder has an adjusted basis in the stock.

2. T (p. 5-20)

    Generally, under Section 336(a), a distribution of property from a corporation to a shareholder in complete liquidation of the corporation is treated by the distributing corporation as if such corporation sold the distributed property to the shareholder. Accordingly, the distributing corporation must recognize a gain or loss on the deemed sale.

3. T (p. 5-10; sale or exchange treatment in partial liquidations apply only to noncorporate shareholders)

    Generally, a proportionate (not a disproportionate) distribution of property from a corporation to a corporate shareholder in partial redemption of stock (under a plan of partial redemption) is treated under Section 302(d) by the distributing corporation as a Section 301 distribution. Thus, such distribution constitutes a dividend to the extent of the E & P of the distributing corporation. Sale or exchange treatment under Section 302(b)(4) only applies to noncorporate shareholders in partial liquidation.

4. F (p. 5-12; capital transaction)

    A distribution of a corporation's own stock is not a distribution of property since stock of the distributing corporation is not considered property. Further, under Section 1032, a corporation recognizes no gain or loss on the receipt of money or other property in exchange for stock of such corporation, including treasury stock.

5. F (p. 5-9; no interest other than as a creditor)

    In a stock redemption, a corporation redeems its stock from a shareholder. Hence, a stock redemption involves an exchange of a shareholder's stock in the corporation for property of the corporation. The exchange resembles a sale of the stock to an outsider. However, a shareholder receives sale or exchange treatment only if the stock redemption is a qualifying stock redemption. Under Section 302(b)(3), a qualifying stock redemption includes a distribution in complete termination of a shareholder's interest in the corporation. In determining whether a shareholder has completely terminated his interest, the constructive ownership rules of Section 318(a) apply. However, the family attribution rules under Section 318(a)(1) may be avoided if the shareholder has no interest in the corporation (for at least 10 years), other than that of a creditor. In the instant case, even though W redeemed all of the shares that Mr. D directly owned, Mr. D has not terminated his interest in W, since Mr. D constructively owns the 500 shares that his son directly owns. In addition, the family attribution rules cannot be avoided since Mr. D continues to be an officer and director of W. Thus, the stock redemption in the instant case does not qualify the shareholder for sale or exchange treatment.

6. F (p. 5-12; FMV – adjusted basis)

    When a corporation distributes property (rather than cash) to a shareholder in a qualified redemption of stock, distributions of appreciated property generate gain to the distributing corporation under Section 311(b). In effect, a corporation that distributes gain property is treated as if it had sold the property to the shareholder for its fair market value. In the instant case, K distributed appreciated property to its shareholders. Thus, K must recognize a gain of $300,000 ($500,000 – $200,000).

7. F (p. 5–24; in the hands of the shareholder)

   Under Section 331(a), a distribution from a corporation to a shareholder in complete liquidation of the corporation is treated as a sale or exchange of the shareholder's stock. Thus, the character of the shareholder's gain is not determined by the character of the underlying corporate assets.

8. T (p. 5–4, 24)

   Under Section 331(a) [302(a)], a distribution from a corporation to a shareholder in complete liquidation [partial redemption] of the corporation is treated as a sale or exchange of the shareholder's stock. Under Section 1001, sale or exchange treatment requires a comparison of the amount realized and the adjusted basis of the stock given up.

9. T (p. 5–8)

   In a stock redemption, a corporation redeems its stock from a shareholder. Hence, a stock redemption involves an exchange of a shareholder's stock in the corporation for property of the corporation. The exchange resembles a sale of the stock to an outsider. However, a shareholder receives sale or exchange treatment only if the stock redemption is a qualifying stock redemption. Under Section 302(b)(2), a qualifying stock redemption includes a disproportionate distribution. A disproportionate distribution requires that the shareholder's ownership interest of both (a) voting stock and (b) common stock (whether voting or nonvoting) immediately after the redemption amount to less than 80% of such shareholder's former ownership interest. In addition, a disproportionate distribution requires that the shareholder's ownership interest of voting stock immediately after the redemption amount to less than 50%. In determining a shareholder's ownership interest for purposes of these tests, the constructive ownership rules of Section 318(a) apply.

10. F (p. 5–10; only noncorporate shareholders)

    In a stock redemption, a corporation redeems its stock from a shareholder. Hence, a stock redemption involves an exchange of a shareholder's stock in the corporation for property of the corporation. The exchange resembles a sale of the stock to an outsider. However, a shareholder receives sale or exchange treatment only if the stock redemption is a qualifying stock redemption. Under Section 302(b)(2), a qualifying stock redemption includes a disproportionate distribution. But in the instant case, the distribution is proportionate. Further, sale or exchange treatment under Section 302(b)(4) only applies to noncorporate shareholders in partial liquidation. Further, one of the distributees is a corporation. Finally, under Section 302(b)(1), a qualifying stock redemption includes a distribution that is NOT essentially equivalent to a dividend. In the instant case, the facts identify the distribution as one that is NOT essentially equivalent to a dividend. However, a case law requirement for a distribution to be NOT essentially equivalent to a dividend under Section 302(b)(1) is a substantial reduction in a shareholder's voting ownership interest as a result of the redemption. In the instant case, such reduction does not exist, since the distribution was proportionate. Hence, the requirements of Section 302(b)(1) are not met. Accordingly, the stock redemption in the instant case is not a qualifying stock redemption.

11. T (p. 5–9; attribution waived only for complete termination redemptions)

    In a stock redemption, a corporation redeems its stock from a shareholder. Hence, a stock redemption involves an exchange of a shareholder's stock in the corporation for property of the corporation. The exchange resembles a sale of the stock to an outsider. However, a shareholder receives sale or exchange treatment only if the stock redemption is a qualifying stock redemption. Under Section 302(b)(3), a qualifying stock redemption includes a distribution in complete termination of a shareholder's interest in the corporation. In determining whether a shareholder has completely terminated his interest, the constructive ownership rules of Section 318(a) apply. However, the family attribution rules under Section 318(a)(1) may be avoided if the shareholder has no interest in the corporation (for at least 10 years), other than that of a creditor.

STUDY GUIDE   **CHAPTER 5**   5–13
Corporations: Redemptions and Liquidations

Fill in the Blanks

1. same (p. 5–28)

    A complete liquidation of a subsidiary corporation occurs when, under a plan of complete liquidation, the subsidiary redeems all of its stock from both the parent corporation and minority shareholders. In complete liquidation of a subsidiary under Section 332, no gain or loss is recognized by the subsidiary on any distribution of property to the parent under Section 337(a). Also, under Section 332(a), no gain or loss is recognized by the parent on the receipt of property from the subsidiary in exchange for stock of such subsidiary. A parent and subsidiary relationship exists within the meaning of Section 332 if: (1) at least 80% of the combined value of the outstanding stock of the subsidiary is owned by the parent, (2) at least 80% of the outstanding voting stock of the subsidiary is owned by the parent and (3) the subsidiary is solvent. Further, under Section 334(b), the adjusted basis of property received by the parent corporation *is equal* to such property's adjusted basis in the hands of the distributing subsidiary.

2. doesn't (p. 5–26)

    A complete liquidation of a subsidiary corporation occurs when, under a plan of complete liquidation, the subsidiary redeems all of its stock from both the parent corporation and minority shareholders. In complete liquidation of a subsidiary under Section 332 (a), no gain or loss is recognized by the parent on the receipt of property from the subsidiary in exchange for stock of such subsidiary. A parent and subsidiary relationship exists within this context when (1) at least 80% of the combined value of the outstanding stock of the subsidiary is owned by the parent, (2) at least 80% of the outstanding voting stock of the subsidiary is owned by the parent and (3) the subsidiary is solvent. Thus, in the instant case, Section 332 does not apply.

3. same (p. 5–28)

    Section 338 is an elective provision whereby a parent may elect to treat stock purchases as a purchase of the assets of a subsidiary. A parent and subsidiary relationship exists within this context when (1) at least 80% of the combined value of the outstanding stock of the subsidiary is owned by the parent, (2) at least 80% of the outstanding voting stock of the subsidiary is owned by the parent and (3) the subsidiary is solvent. The tax treatment under Section 338 with respect to certain stock purchases of an electing parent takes a two-step approach. First, the subsidiary is treated as having sold all of its assets at fair market value in a single transaction on the close of the acquisition date. Here, the subsidiary recognizes on its final return any gain or loss that is realized on the deemed sale. In addition, the fair market value of assets is determined by reference to the price that the parent corporation paid for the subsidiary's stock, appropriately adjusted for liabilities and purchases of less that 100%. Second, on the day after the acquisition date, the subsidiary is treated as a new corporation that is deemed to have purchased all of the assets of the old subsidiary at their fair market value. In the instant case, assuming the parent purchases 100% of the stock of subsidiary in one transaction, the subsidiary has no liabilities, and the parent makes a Section 338 election, the aggregate of the adjusted bases of the subsidiary's assets will equal the parent's adjusted basis in the subsidiary's stock.

4. preferred stock bail-out approach (p. 5–15)

    But for Section 306, the following scheme bails out corporate profits, where such profits are taxed at capital gain rates, rather than ordinary income rates. If a corporation declares a proportionate stock dividend of nonvoting preferred stock on common stock, such stock dividend would be nontaxable under Section 305. As a result, the adjusted basis of the common stock would be allocated between the current holdings of preferred and common stock. Then, if the shareholder sold the preferred stock to an outside party, the shareholder's voting ownership interest would not be affected and the shareholder would probably recognize a long-term capital gain, which would be preferentially treated if the shareholder were an individual. Section 306 eliminates the tax avoidance possibilities found in this preferred stock bail-out scheme by producing the following tax consequences.

- At the time of the proportionate stock dividend of nonvoting preferred stock on common stock, an amount called the Section 306 taint is determined. The amount of the taint is the fair market value of the preferred stock, but not to exceed the amount that would have been a dividend had the issuing corporation distributed cash rather than the preferred stock.
- On the sale of the preferred stock to an outside party, the shareholder has ordinary income (not a dividend) to the extent of the Section 306 taint. The excess of the amount realized over the Section 306 taint reduces the shareholder's adjusted basis in the preferred stock, but not below zero. If the amount realized exceeds the sum of (a) the Section 306 taint and (b) the shareholder's adjusted basis in the preferred stock, such excess is capital gain. However, no loss is ever recognized.

5. not essentially equivalent; substantially disproportionate; termination; shareholder's death taxes (p. 5–5)

   In a stock redemption, a corporation redeems its stock from a shareholder. Hence, a stock redemption involves an exchange of a shareholder's stock in the corporation for property of the corporation. The exchange resembles a sale of the stock to an outsider. However, a shareholder receives sale or exchange treatment only if the stock redemption is a qualifying stock redemption. Under Section 302(b)(1), a qualifying stock redemption includes a distribution that is NOT essentially equivalent to a dividend. Under Section 302(b)(2), a qualifying stock redemption includes a disproportionate distribution. Under Section 302(b)(3), a qualifying stock redemption includes a distribution in complete termination of a shareholder's interest in the corporation. Finally, under Section 303, a distribution to an estate in redemption of stock to pay death taxes, etc., is a qualifying stock redemption.

6. 80%; 50% (p. 5–8)

   In a stock redemption, a corporation redeems its stock from a shareholder. Hence, a stock redemption involves an exchange of a shareholder's stock in the corporation for property of the corporation. The exchange resembles a sale of the stock to an outsider. However, a shareholder receives sale or exchange treatment only if the stock redemption is a qualifying stock redemption. Under Section 302(b)(2), a qualifying stock redemption includes a disproportionate distribution. A disproportionate distribution requires that the shareholder's ownership interest of both (a) voting stock and (b) common stock (whether voting or nonvoting) immediately after the redemption amount to less than 80% of such shareholder's former ownership interest. In addition, a disproportionate distribution requires that the shareholder's ownership interest of voting stock immediately after the redemption amount to less than 50%. In determining a shareholder's ownership interest for this purpose, the constructive ownership rules of Section 318(a) apply.

7. 80% or more (p. 5–26)

   A complete liquidation of a subsidiary corporation occurs when, under a plan of complete liquidation, the subsidiary redeems all of its stock from both the parent corporation and minority shareholders. In complete liquidation of a subsidiary under Section 332, no gain or loss is recognized by the subsidiary on any distribution of property to the parent under Section 337(a). Also, under Section 332(a), no gain or loss is recognized by the parent on the receipt of property in exchange for stock of the subsidiary. A parent and subsidiary relationship exists within the meaning of Section 332 if: (1) at least 80% of the combined value of the outstanding stock of the subsidiary is owned by the parent, (2) at least 80% of the outstanding voting stock of the subsidiary is owned by the parent and (3) the subsidiary is solvent.

Multiple Choice

1. b   (p. 5–20; FMV not less than liability, $38,000 – $26,000)

   Generally, under Section 336(a), a distribution of property from a corporation to a shareholder in complete liquidation of the corporation is treated by the distributing corporation as if such corporation sold the distributed property to the shareholder. Accordingly, the distributing corporation must realize and recognize a gain or loss on this deemed sale. For purposes of determining such gain under Section 336(b), the fair market value of the property is treated as being not less than the amount of the liability. Under Section 1001, sale or exchange treatment requires a comparison of the amount realized and the adjusted basis of the property given up in order to compute the corporation's realized and recognized gain or loss. In the instant case, the amount realized is $38,000 (the greater of (a) the fair market value of $35,000 and (b) the liability of $38,000 to which the land was subject). Given the adjusted basis of $26,000 in the land, Jayhawk's recognized gain is $12,000 ($38,000 − $26,000). Thus, item b is correct. Further, the other items are incorrect because they each are inconsistent with the correct answer.

2. c (p. 5–24; original basis: $100,000 − $75,000 received in 2002; remaining basis $25,000 − $50,000 received in 2003)

A complete liquidation of a corporation occurs when, under a plan of complete liquidation, the corporation redeems all of its stock from its shareholders. This plan of complete liquidation may be accomplished by means of a series of liquidating distributions. In this case, until the last distribution in the series of liquidating distributions occurs, the transaction remains open (not closed). Within the context of an open transaction, the distributee shareholder accounts for the fair market value of property received as a nontaxable return of capital to the extent of the shareholder's aggregate adjusted basis in the stock to be redeemed. The shareholder's aggregate adjusted basis in the stock to be redeemed is then reduced by the fair market value of such property received (but not below zero). The excess of property received over the shareholder's aggregate adjusted basis in the stock to be redeemed is gain from the deemed sale or exchange of the stock. In the instant case, Anne's aggregate adjusted basis in the Oswego stock to be redeemed is $100,000 (1,000 × $100). Anne accounts for the fair market value of the land received on December 1, 2002 as a nontaxable return of capital. Hence, Anne's aggregate adjusted basis in the stock to be redeemed of $100,000 is then reduced by $75,000 (the fair market value of the land received) to $25,000. Subsequently, on January 15, 2003 (the date of the last distribution), the excess of the cash received of $50,000 over $25,000 (Anne's aggregate adjusted basis in the Oswego stock to be redeemed) is gain from the sale or exchange of the stock. Thus, item c is correct. Further, the other items are incorrect because they each are inconsistent with the correct answer.

3. b (p. 5–12; FMV minus adjusted basis)

In a stock redemption, a corporation redeems its stock from a shareholder. Hence, a stock redemption involves an exchange of a shareholder's stock in the corporation for property of the corporation. The exchange resembles a sale of the stock to an outsider. However, a shareholder receives sale or exchange treatment only if the stock redemption is a qualifying stock redemption. In particular, sale or exchange treatment under Section 302(b)(4) applies to noncorporate shareholders in partial liquidation of a corporation. In the instant case, the distribution is assumed to be in partial liquidation to a noncorporate shareholder. Thus, Mr. Ashby must realize and recognize a gain or loss on the qualifying stock redemption. Under Section 1001, sale or exchange treatment requires a comparison of the amount realized and the adjusted basis of the stock given up in order to compute the shareholder's realized and recognized gain or loss. In the instant case, the amount realized is $150,000 (the fair market value of the land). Given that the adjusted basis of the Burke stock given up by Mr. Ashby is $180,000, Mr. Ashby's realized and recognized loss is $30,000 ($150,000 − $180,000). In addition, Burke realizes and recognizes a $15,000 ($150,000 − $135,000) gain on the deemed sale of the land under Section 311(b). Thus, item b is correct. Further, the other items are incorrect because they each are inconsistent with the correct answer.

4. d (p. 5–9; complete termination redemption)

In a stock redemption, a corporation redeems its stock from a shareholder. Hence, a stock redemption involves an exchange of a shareholder's stock in the corporation for property of the corporation. The exchange resembles a sale of the stock to an outsider. However, a shareholder receives sale or exchange treatment only if the stock redemption is a qualifying stock redemption. Under Section 302(b)(3), a qualifying stock redemption includes a distribution in complete termination of a shareholder's interest in the corporation. In determining whether a shareholder has completely terminated his interest, the constructive ownership rules of Section 318(a) apply. In the instant case, Tom has terminated his interest in Huskie. Thus, the stock redemption qualifies Tom for sale or exchange treatment. Under Section 1001, sale or exchange treatment requires a comparison of the amount realized and the adjusted basis of the stock given up in order to compute the shareholder's realized and recognized gain or loss. In the instant case, the amount realized is $500,000. Given that the adjusted basis of Huskie stock given up by Tom is $250,000, Tom's realized and recognized gain is $250,000 ($500,000 − $250,000). Thus, item d is correct. Further, the other items are incorrect because they each are inconsistent with the correct answer.

5. b (p. 5–24; additional return of capital would be capital gain)

A complete liquidation of a corporation occurs when, under a plan of complete liquidation, the corporation redeems all of its stock from its shareholders. A plan of complete liquidation may be accomplished by means of a series of liquidating distributions. In this case, until the last distribution in the series of liquidating distributions occurs, the transaction remains open (not closed). Within the context of an open transaction, the distributee shareholder accounts for the fair market value of property received as a nontaxable return of capital to the extent of the shareholder's aggregate adjusted basis in the stock to be redeemed. The shareholder's aggregate adjusted basis in the stock to be redeemed is then reduced by the fair market value of such property received (but not below zero). The excess of property received over the shareholder's aggregate adjusted basis in the stock to be redeemed is gain from the deemed sale or exchange of the stock. In the instant case, item b is not true because any additional return (amount realized) in excess of adjusted basis is treated as a gain. The other items are true.

6. a (p. 5–6; spouse, children, grandchildren and parents, not sibling or grandparent)

The constructive ownership rules of Section 318(a) apply to a stock redemption. These rules include rules for family attribution. That is, the shareholder is deemed to own the stock directly owned by the shareholder's spouse, children, grandchildren, and parents (but not brothers, sisters and grandparents). In the instant case, Mathew owns directly and constructively 65% of Ranger (40% directly plus 25% constructively through Mathew's father). Thus, item a is correct. Further, the other items are incorrect because they each are inconsistent with the correct answer.

7. c (p. 5–12; $30,000 − $22,000)

When a corporation distributes property (rather than cash) to a shareholder, the amount distributed is measured by the fair market value of the property on the date of the distribution. Further, all distributions of appreciated property generate gain to the distributing corporation under Section 311(b). In effect, a corporation that distributes gain property is treated as if it had sold the property to the shareholder for such property's fair market value. Under Section 1001, sale or exchange treatment requires a comparison of the amount realized and the adjusted basis of the property given up in order to compute the corporation's realized and recognized gain or loss. In the instant case, the amount realized is assumed to be $30,000 (the fair market value of the automobile). Given that Heritage's adjusted basis in the automobile is $22,000, Heritage's recognized gain is $8,000 ($30,000 − $22,000). Thus, item c is correct. Further, the other items are incorrect because they each are inconsistent with the correct answer.

8. c (p. 5–24; distribution @ $200 per share, 200 shares @ $100 per share, long-term, 50 shares @ $250, short-term)

Under Section 331(a), a distribution from a corporation to a shareholder in complete liquidation of the corporation is treated as a sale or exchange of the shareholder's stock. Under Section 1001, sale or exchange treatment requires a comparison of the amount realized and the adjusted basis of the property given up in order to compute the shareholder's realized and recognized gain or loss. In the instant case, the Biddle stock is specifically identifiable. Thus, the amount realized of $50,000 must be allocated to each specifically identifiable block of shares. A total amount realized of $50,000 translates to $200 per share ($50,000/250 shares). Given that Ann's aggregate adjusted basis in block 1 of Biddle stock is $20,000, Ann's realized and recognized long-term capital gain is $20,000 ((200 × $200) − $20,000). Ann held the block 1 stock for more than 12 months. Given that Ann's aggregate adjusted basis in block 2 of Biddle stock is $12,500, Ann's realized and recognized short-term capital loss is $2,500 ((50 × $200) − $12,500). Ann held the block 2 stock for less than 12 months. Thus, item c is correct. Further, the other items are incorrect because they each are inconsistent with the correct answer.

9. b (p. 5–20; Maria: zero($125,000 FMV − $125,000 Liability) Amount realized − $50,000 Basis = $50,000 long-term capital loss; Daring: $125,000 Amount realized − $90,000 Basis = $35,000 long-term capital gain)

Generally, under Section 336(a), a distribution of property from a corporation to a shareholder in complete liquidation of the corporation is treated by the distributing corporation as if such corporation sold the distributed property to the shareholder. Accordingly, the distributing corporation must recognize a gain or loss on the deemed sale. For purposes of determining such gain under Section 336(b), the fair market value of the property is treated as being not less than the amount of the liability. Under Section 1001, sale or exchange treatment requires a comparison of the amount realized and the adjusted basis of the property given up in order to compute the corporation's realized and recognized gain or loss. In the instant case, the amount realized is $125,000 (the greater of (a) the fair market value of $120,000 and (b) the liability of $125,000 to which the land was subject). Given that Daring's adjusted basis of the land is $90,000, Daring's recognized long-term capital gain is $35,000 ($125,000 − $90,000). Daring held the land for more than 12 months. Under Section 331(a), a distribution from a corporation to a shareholder in complete liquidation of the corporation is treated as a sale or exchange of the shareholder's stock. Under Section 1001, sale or exchange treatment requires a comparison of the amount realized and the adjusted basis of the property given up in order to compute the shareholder's realized and recognized gain or loss. In the instant case, the amount realized is $–0– (the deemed fair market value of the land of $125,000 less the liability assumed of $125,000). Given that Maria's adjusted basis of the land is $50,000, Maria's realized and recognized long-term capital loss is $50,000. Maria held the Daring stock for more than 12 months. Thus, item b is correct. Further, the other items are incorrect because they each are inconsistent with the correct answer.

10. c (p. 5–12; FMV − basis)

When a corporation distributes property (rather than cash) to a shareholder in a partial redemption of its stock, the amount distributed is measured by the fair market value of the property on the date of the distribution. Further, all distributions of appreciated property generate gain to the distributing corporation under Section 311(b). In effect, a corporation that distributes gain property is treated as if it has sold the property to the shareholder for such property's fair market value. Under Section 1001, sale or exchange treatment requires a comparison of the amount realized and the adjusted basis of the property given up in order to compute the corporation's realized and recognized gain or loss. In the instant case, the amount realized is assumed to be $44,000 (the fair market value of the Salem stock). Given that Mouse's adjusted basis in the Salem stock is $4,000, Mouse's recognized gain is $40,000 ($44,000 − $4,000). In this case, the Salem stock constitutes property. Thus, item c is correct. Further, the other items are incorrect because they each are inconsistent with the correct answer.

11. a (p. 5–5; no reduction in proportionate ownership and adequate E & P)

In a stock redemption, a corporation redeems its stock from a shareholder. Hence, a stock redemption involves an exchange of a shareholder's stock in the corporation for property of the corporation. The exchange resembles a sale of the stock to an outsider. However, a shareholder receives sale or exchange treatment only if the stock redemption is a qualifying stock redemption. Under Section 302(b)(2), a qualifying stock redemption includes a disproportionate distribution. A disproportionate distribution requires that the shareholder's ownership interest of both (a) voting stock and (b) common stock (whether voting or nonvoting) immediately after the redemption amount to less than 80% of such shareholder's former ownership interest. In addition, a disproportionate distribution requires that the shareholder's ownership interest of voting stock immediately after the redemption amount to less than 50% (the 50% test). In the instant case, the 50% test is not met. Diana owns directly 100% of the voting stock immediately after the redemption. In addition, the distribution is a proportionate distribution. Thus, the stock redemption in the instant case is not a qualifying redemption and does not qualify the shareholder for sale or exchange treatment. Generally, a proportionate (not a disproportionate) distribution of property from a corporation to a shareholder in partial redemption of stock (under a plan of redemption) is treated under Section 302(d) by the distributing corporation as a Section 301 distribution. Thus, in the instant case, the distribution from Ancient to Diana constitutes a dividend to the extent of the E & P of Ancient. With Ancient having E & P of $5,000,000, the $4,500,000 constitutes a dividend to Diana. Thus, item a is correct. Further, the other items are incorrect because they each are inconsistent with the correct answer.

CHAPTER 6

Alternative Minimum Tax and Certain Penalty Taxes Imposed on Corporations

LEARNING OBJECTIVES

After completing Chapter 6, you should be able to:

1. Explain the reason for the alternative minimum tax.
2. Calculate the alternative minimum tax applicable to corporations.
3. Understand the function of the adjusted current earnings (ACE) adjustment.
4. Appreciate the purpose of the accumulated earnings tax.
5. Determine the reasonable needs of the business.
6. Compute the accumulated earnings tax.
7. Discuss the reason for the personal holding company tax.
8. Recognize the requirements for personal holding company status.
9. Compute the personal holding company tax.
10. Compare the accumulated earnings and personal holding company taxes.

KEY TERMS

Accumulated earnings credit
Accumulated earnings tax
Adjusted current earnings
Adjusted ordinary gross income
Alternative minimum tax
Alternative minimum taxable income
Bardahl formula
Consent dividend
Deficiency dividend
Dividends paid deduction
Minimum credit (AET)
Minimum tax credit (AMT)
Ordinary gross income
Personal holding company (PHC)
Reasonable needs of a business
Tax preference items

OUTLINE

I. **ALTERNATIVE MINIMUM TAX**
   A. C corporations are subject to an alternative minimum tax (AMT).
      1. Qualified 'small corporations' are exempt from the AMT.
      2. A corporation initially qualifies as a 'small corporation' if it has average gross receipts of $5 million or less, in the preceding 3 years.
         a. If the corporation did not exist for three years, this gross receipts test is applied on the basis of the period during which it did exist.
      3. A corporation that passes the $5 million average gross receipts test will continue to qualify as a small corporation as long as average gross receipts for three years preceding the tax year do not exceed $7.5 million.
   B. AMT calculation:
      Regular Taxable Income Before NOL Deduction
      ± Adjustments
      + Preferences
      = Unadjusted alternative minimum taxable income (AMTI)
      ± ACE adjustment
      = AMTI before AMT NOL deduction
      − AMT NOL deduction (limited to 90%)
      = AMTI
      − Exemption
      = Tentative minimum tax base
      × 20% rate
      = Tentative minimum tax
   C. AMT Adjustments
      1. Depreciation of property placed in service after 1986 and before 1999:
         a. real property—the excess of regular tax depreciation over straight-line, 40 year life, mid-month convention.
         b. personal property—the excess of accelerated depreciation over the amount determined using 150% DB, ADS class life, same convention as for regular tax.
      2. Depreciation of property placed in service after 1998—the depreciation adjustment for real estate is eliminated and the adjustment for personal property is applied to the difference between DDB and 150% DB over the property's MACRS recovery period.
      3. Amortization of mining and exploration costs—the difference between the costs incurred and what would have resulted if the costs were capitalized and amortized over 10 years.
      4. Adjusted gain or loss—the difference between AMT and regular tax gain or loss on asset dispositions.
      5. Long-term contracts for AMT purposes are determined under the percentage of completion method for contracts entered into after March 1, 1986.
      6. Passive activities losses of certain closely held and personal service corporations.
   D. AMT Preferences
      1. Amortization claimed on certified pollution control facilities.
      2. Accelerated depreciation on real property in excess of straight line for property placed in service before 1987.
      3. Tax-exempt interest from specified private activity bonds.
      4. Percentage depletion claimed in excess of the adjusted basis of property.
   E. Adjusted Current Earnings (ACE)
      1. ACE is a separate tax computation that requires adjustments to 'unadjusted AMTI.'
         a. The ACE adjustment (which can be positive or negative) is 75% of the difference between 'unadjusted AMTI' and ACE.

STUDY GUIDE
CHAPTER 6
Alternative Minimum Tax and Certain Penalty Taxes Imposed on Corporations

2. ACE depreciation must be computed for property placed in service prior to 1994.
3. Inclusion in ACE of items included in E & P, net of related expenses, include:
   a. tax-exempt interest income.
   b. death benefits from life insurance contracts.
   c. tax benefit exclusions.
4. Disallowance of items not deductible from E & P: 70% dividends received deduction from a less than 20% owned corporation.
5. Other adjustments based on rules for determining E & P include:
   a. intangible drilling costs.
   b. circulation expenditures.
   c. amortization of organizational expenditures.
   d. LIFO inventory adjustments.
   e. installment sales.

F. Exemption
   1. Generally the AMT is 20% of AMTI that exceeds the exemption amount ($40,000).
   2. The exemption amount is reduced by 25% of AMTI in excess of $150,000.

G. Minimum Tax Credit
   1. AMT paid in one tax year may be carried forward indefinitely and used as a credit against the corporation's future regular tax liability that exceeds its tentative minimum tax.
   2. The minimum tax credit may not be carried back and may not be offset against any future minimum tax liability.

II. PENALTY TAX ON UNREASONABLE ACCUMULATIONS

A. The tax law is designed to discourage the retention of earnings in a corporation beyond the normal business needs. A penalty tax is imposed on corporations that retain a surplus amount of earnings which, had they been distributed to the shareholder, would have been taxed, § 531.

B. The Element of Intent
   1. Application of the penalty tax is triggered when a group of shareholders control corporate policy and withhold dividends with the INTENT to avoid personal, ordinary income taxes.
   2. Tax avoidance need not be the controlling reason for retaining earnings in the corporation; it just has to be a contributing reason to result in the application of the accumulated earnings tax.

C. Imposition of the Tax and the Accumulated Earnings Credit
   1. The AET is in addition to the regular corporate tax and the alternative minimum tax.
   2. It is 38.6% (in 2002 and 2003) of accumulated taxable income (the current year's addition to the corporate accumulated earnings balance not needed for a reasonable business purpose).
   3. The computation of accumulated taxable income includes a reduction for the accumulated earnings credit. The accumulated earnings credit is the greater of:
      a. current E & P for the tax year needed to meet the reasonable needs of the business less net long-term capital gains for the year and
      b. the minimum credit: the difference between $250,000 ($150,000 for certain personal service corporations) and accumulated E & P at the close of the previous year.

D. Reasonable Needs of the Business (see Concept Summary 6–2)
   1. Must be specific, definite and feasible, anticipated needs for:
      a. working capital and
      b. noncurrent expenditures, i.e., capital expenditures and extraordinary expenses.
   2. The "Bardahl" formula is the standard method used to determine the working capital needs of a merchandising or manufacturing corporation.

         Inventory Cycle (Average inventory/Cost of goods sold)
   + Accounts Receivable Cycle (Average accounts receivable/Net sales)
   − Accounts Payable Cycle (Average accounts payable/(purchases + cash operating expenses))
   = Decimal factor

×   Operating expenses other than accrued Federal income tax, depreciation, profit sharing and charitable contributions.
=   Working Capital Needs

3. A formula to develop the working capital needs required in a service oriented corporation has not yet been resolved. It is assumed that it will follow the Bardahl formula using a human resource accounting approach.

E. Mechanics of the Penalty Tax
1. The accumulated earnings tax is applied against accumulated taxable income.
2. Accumulated taxable income is computed as follows:
   Taxable Income
   ± Certain Adjustments
   − Dividends Paid Deduction
   − Accumulated Earnings Credit
   = Accumulated taxable income
3. "Certain adjustments" that are deducted include:
   a. corporate income tax for the year.
   b. excess charitable contributions,
   c. capital loss adjustment.
   d. excess of net long-term capital gain over net short-term capital loss, minus the capital gain tax and net capital losses from prior years.
4. "Certain adjustments" that are added include:
   a. capital loss carryovers and carrybacks.
   b. net operating loss deductions.
   c. the dividends received deduction.

III. **PERSONAL HOLDING COMPANY PENALTY TAX**
A. The personal holding company (PHC) penalty tax, § 541, was imposed to discourage the sheltering of passive income in a PHC.
B. The PHC penalty tax is in addition to the regular corporate tax and is 38.6% of undistributed personal holding company income (in 2002 and 2003).
C. Definition of a PHC
1. For a company to be classified as a PHC, that company must meet both a stock ownership test and a gross income test.
   a. *Stock Ownership Test.* More than 50% of the value of the outstanding stock of the corporation must have been owned by five or fewer individuals at any time during the last half of the taxable year.
   b. *Gross Income Test.* Sixty percent or more of the corporation's adjusted ordinary gross income must be composed of certain passive income items (PHC income): dividends, interest, rents, royalties or certain personal service income.
2. For the stock ownership test, very broad rules of constructive ownership apply:
   a. Stock owned by a corporation, partnership, trust, or estate is considered to be owned proportionately by its stockholders, partners, or beneficiaries.
   b. Stock owned by members of an individual's family (brothers, sisters, spouse, ancestors, or lineal descendants) or by the individual's partner is considered to be owned by the individual.
   c. A stock option is regarded as stock.
   d. A convertible security is considered stock.
3. For the gross income test, adjusted ordinary gross income (AOGI) is computed in two steps.
   a. Gross income, less capital gains and § 1231 gains equals ordinary gross income (OGI).
   b. OGI less expenses related to income from rents and mineral royalties equals AOGI.
D. Rental income is normally classified as PHC income. However, it may be excluded if:
1. 50% or more of the corporation's AOGI is "adjusted income from rents" and

STUDY GUIDE
CHAPTER 6
Alternative Minimum Tax and Certain Penalty Taxes Imposed on Corporations

6–5

2. the dividends paid during the year are equal to or greater than the amount by which the nonrent PHC income exceeds 10% of OGI.
   a. Adjusted income from rents is gross income from rents less depreciation, property taxes, interest, and rent.
E. Adjusted income from mineral, oil, and gas royalties may be excluded from PHC income classification if the following three tests are met.
   1. 50% or more of AOGI must constitute income from royalties;
   2. Nonroyalty PHC income may not exceed 10% of OGI; and
   3. Section 162 business expenses, other than compensation paid to stockholders, must be at least 15% of AOGI.
F. Income from personal service contracts is PHC income only if:
   1. the individual who is to perform the services is designated by someone other than the corporation and
   2. the person designated to perform the services owns 25% or more of the corporation directly or indirectly at some time during the year.
G. Calculation of the PHC Tax
   1. The PHC tax rate (38.6% in 2002 and 2003) is applied against undistributed PHC income.
   2. Undistributed PHC income is computed as follows:
   Taxable income
   Plus:
   1. Dividends received deductions
   2. A net operating loss, other than from the preceding year
   3. The excess of business expenses and depreciation over the income from nonbusiness property owned by the corporation
   Minus:
   1. Federal income tax accrued
   2. Excess charitable contributions
   3. The excess of long-term capital gain over short-term capital loss (net of tax)
   Equals: Adjusted taxable income
   Minus: Dividends paid deduction
   Equals: Undistributed personal holding company income (UPHCI)
H. Dividends include the total of dividends paid during the year, dividends considered as paid on the last day of the tax year, and consent dividends.

IV. **A COMPARISON OF ACCUMULATED EARNINGS AND PHC TAXES**
   A. The imposition of the PHC tax does not require intent.
   B. The PHC tax can be applied to newly formed as well as older corporations.
   C. The PHC tax presents a more explicit threat to closely-held corporations because of the constructive stock ownership tests which are very objective. In contrast, under the AET, determination of earnings accumulated beyond the reasonable needs of the business is subjective in nature.
   D. Sufficient dividend distributions can eliminate either tax.
      1. The dividends include actual dividends, consent dividends, and distributions made during the grace period.
      2. In the case of a PHC, a deficiency dividend procedure can be used.
   E. § 541 is a self-assessed tax; § 531 is assessed by the IRS.

V. **TAX PLANNING**
   A. AMT Planning
      1. Corporate taxpayers must monitor preferences and adjustments carefully (including their amounts and when they are recognized).
      2. A corporate taxpayer subject to the AMT in a particular year should accelerate income and defer deductions—taking advantage of the rate differences between the AMT and the regular tax.

B. A corporation cannot be subjected to the AET and PHC tax simultaneously.
C. To avoid the accumulated earnings tax
   1. Justification of earnings accumulated should be:
      a. documented during the period of accumulation,
      b. sincere, and
      c. pursued to the extent feasible.
   2. Avoid the argument that loans to shareholders have no bona fide business purpose.
   3. Payments of dividends demonstrate good faith and the lack of tax avoidance motivation.
D. An S corporation election will circumvent application of the AET. The S election is prospective in nature and may not be applied retroactively.
E. Avoiding the PHC tax may be accomplished by:
   1. failing either test to avoid PHC classification by means of either:
      a. dispersion of stock ownership or
      b. decreasing the percentage relationship of PHCI to AOGI (e.g., reducing PHCI or increasing AOGI).
   2. maximizing adjusted income to exempt it from PHC treatment (where rents or royalties are involved).
   3. properly timing dividend distributions.

TEST FOR SELF-EVALUATION—CHAPTER 6

True or False

Indicate which of the following statements is true or false by circling the correct answer.

T F 1. The fact that a business is a mere holding or investment company is of no import for the purpose of finding intent to avoid federal income tax.

T F 2. A corporation may have to pay the alternative minimum tax if taxable income for regular income tax purposes, when combined with certain adjustments and preference items that apply in computing the alternative minimum tax, total more than $40,000. (IRS 90 3A-10)

T F 3. The reasonable business needs of a corporation are precisely outlined by the IRS.

T F 4. If a corporation paid an alternative minimum tax in 2001 because of adjustments or preference items that defer its tax liability rather than cause a permanent avoidance of the tax, the corporation's 2001 alternative minimum tax is available to be claimed as credit against its regular income for 2002 and later years. (IRS 90 3A-11)

T F 5. The Bardahl formula is used to determine the reasonable needs of the business to the exclusion of other significant data.

T F 6. Long-term capital gains can be accumulated by a corporation without any penalty tax.

T F 7. Accumulation of income for exotic ventures into areas not related to the business are acceptable as long as the company stays under the $250,000 accumulated earnings credit.

T F 8. Assuming a company is close to being classified as a personal holding company, due to its proximity to the 60% PHC income rule, it would be wise for the company to hold growth stocks, as opposed to high yield stocks. High growth stocks will not enter into the PHC income calculation until they are sold and consequently taxed at a capital gains rate.

T F 9. For tax years beginning after 1989, the alternative minimum tax rules require that the 150% declining balance method of depreciation be used for property placed in service after 1989. (IRS 91 3A-12)

T F 10. In determining working capital needs, it has been firmly established that all assets should be evaluated at their fair market values.

T F 11. Corporation X carries its net operating loss for 2004 back to 2002 for which X incurred a minimum tax liability. X must recompute its minimum tax liability for 2002. (IRS 87 3A-17)

Fill in the Blanks

Complete the following statements with the appropriate word(s) or amount(s).

1. The penalty tax on unreasonable accumulation of income is known as the _____ tax.

2. The tax rate on the excess accumulated income in excess of the $250,000 credit is _____%.

3. The justifiable needs of a business may be classified into two categories: _____ and _____ expenditures.

4. Average inventory, divided by the cost of goods sold, equals the _____.

5. The _____ of marketable securities should be used in determining whether a corporation has excess accumulated earnings.

6. For purposes of calculating the Accumulated Earnings Tax, Accumulated Taxable Income (ATI) is equal to taxable income, plus or minus certain adjustments, minus the dividend paid deduction and the _____.

7. The payment of dividends _____ the amount of accumulated earnings subject to the accumulated earnings tax.

8. A personal holding company (PHC) is defined as a corporation which meets _____ of the following tests:

9. More than _____% of the value of the outstanding stock must be owned by _____ or fewer individuals at any time during the _____ of the taxable year.

10. A substantial proportion, _____%, of the corporate income (AOGI) must be composed of passive type income and amounts from certain personal service contracts.

Multiple Choice

Choose the best answer for each of the following questions.

____ 1. XYZ Corporation has the following items of income and expense during the year:

Dividend income	$ 30,000
Rent income	120,000
Depreciation expense	30,000
Mortgage interest	25,000
Real estate taxes	25,000
Salaries	15,000
Dividends paid (4 shareholders)	18,000
Corporate income tax liability	?

From the above data, AOGI would be:

    a. $150,000
    b. $132,000
    c. $ 70,000
    d. $ 55,000
    e. None of the above

____ 2. From the data in #1, above, the corporate income tax liability is:

    a. 4,855
    b. 4,560
    c. 5,100
    d. 3,750
    e. None of the above

STUDY GUIDE

CHAPTER 6
Alternative Minimum Tax and Certain Penalty Taxes Imposed on Corporations

6–9

_____ 3. Referring to the data in item 1., meet the ten percent rental income test, XYZ Corporation must pay out how much in dividends?

    a. $30,000
    b. $15,000
    c. $18,000
    d. –0–
    e. None of the above

_____ 4. Taxable income is $41,500, of which $1,500 is dividend income, after the dividend exclusion. The corporate income tax (§ 11) is $6,225 and dividends paid are $2,000. The PHC tax liability would be:

    a. $8,338
    b. $14,563
    c. $14,421
    d. $15,821
    e. None of the above

_____ 5. Given the following data, determine the accumulated taxable income of Z Corporation:

Tax liability	116,280
Excess charitable contributions	15,000
Long-term capital gain, adjusted	20,000
Dividends received	80,000
Dividends paid this year	30,000
Accumulated earnings (1/1/02)	110,000
Taxable income	342,000

    a. $ 76,720
    b. $104,370
    c. $ 84,730
    d. $ 67,930
    e. None of the above

_____ 6. Assume the accumulated taxable income of the Z Corporation in Question 5 was $110,500. The accumulated earnings tax would be:

    a. $42,653
    b. $41,580
    c. $31,542
    d. $40,387
    e. None of the above

_____ 7. To avoid the classification of rental income as PHC income, adjusted income from rents must be 50% or more of AOGI. In the following problem, what is that percentage?

Interest on mortgage	$ 3,000
Real estate property taxes	2,000
Depreciation	1,500
Salaries	5,000
Rental income	14,000
AOGI	18,000

a. 61%
b. 19%
c. 42%
d. 25%
e. None of the above

_____ 8. Given the following data, the operating capital needed for one business cycle would be:

Annual revenues	$800,000
Average annual accounts receivable	80,000
Yearly expenses	700,000
Average accounts payable	60,000

a. $10,010
b. $80,000
c. $60,000
d. $70,000
e. None of the above

_____ 9. The accumulated earnings tax does not apply to corporations that are:

a. Personal service corporations
b. Personal holding companies
c. Members of an affiliated group

_____ 10. The personal holding company tax

a. Is imposed on corporations having 15 or more equal stockholders
b. Applies regardless of the extent of dividend distributions
c. Is self-assessed
d. May apply if the minimum credit of $150,000 is exceeded

_____ 11. The accumulated earnings tax can be imposed

a. Regardless of the number of stockholders of a corporation
b. On personal holding companies
c. On companies that make distributions in excess of accumulated earnings
d. Only on conglomerates

_____ 12. Ray Holding Corp. has 18 unrelated equal stockholders. Ray's reported income from the following:

Interest Income	$ 25,000
Merchandising Operations	$ 40,000
Dividends from taxable domestic corporations	$125,000

Deductible expenses totaled $20,000. Ray paid no dividends for the past three years. Ray's liability for personal holding company tax based on

a. $102,500
b. $ 12,500
c. $ 90,000
d. $ –0–

CHAPTER 6
Alternative Minimum Tax and Certain Penalty Taxes Imposed on Corporations

_____ 13. If a corporation's tentative minimum tax exceeds the regular tax, the excess amount is: (IRS 95 3B-28)

   a. payable in addition to the regular tax.
   b. carried back to the third preceding tax year.
   c. carried back to the first preceding tax year.
   d. subtracted from the regular tax.

_____ 14. Given the following facts, what is Wood Corporation's alternative minimum tax? (IRS 95 3C-59)

Taxable income before net operating loss deductions	$85,000
Total adjustments to taxable income	(2,000)
Total tax preference items	45,000
Regular income tax	17,150

   a. $1,250
   b. $850
   c. $450
   d. $–0–

_____ 15. Barrett Corporation's alternative minimum taxable income was $200,000. The exempt portion of Barrett's alternative minimum taxable income was: (IRS 95 3C-60)

   a. $0
   b. $12,500
   c. $27,500
   d. $40,000

SOLUTIONS TO CHAPTER 6 QUESTIONS

True or False

1. **F** (p. 6–13; prima facie evidence of tax avoidance).

    In our system of double taxation, income that is recognized at the corporate level is again taxed at the shareholder level (as a dividend). The corporation may mitigate the detrimental effects of this system of double taxation by accumulating corporate earnings. In this manner, the second level of tax is avoided (or deferred at least for the moment). However, the tax law is framed with the intent to discourage the accumulation of corporate earnings. In particular, the accumulated earnings tax (AET) imposes a penalty tax of 38.6% (in 2002 and 2003) on the current year's addition to the accumulated earnings balance that is not needed for a reasonable business purpose. Often, the penalty tax is applied against closely held corporations, but being closely held is not determinative. Instead, whether or not a shareholder group controls corporate policy is a determining factor. Such a condition is presumed to exist within the context of a holding or investment company.

2. **T** (p. 6–10).

    It is (and has been) the opinion and perception of many that some large corporations do not pay their fair share of taxes. As a political reaction to this sentiment, Congress passed the corporate version of the Alternative Minimum Tax (AMT). This provision represents a tax system within a tax system with a quasi-flat tax rate structure. Its mechanics ensure that a corporation with substantial economic income will pay a minimum level of corporate income tax. With the enactment of the corporate AMT, corporations are less able to utilize exclusions, deductions and credits to eliminate all Federal income tax. In general, the AMT is applied each year to a corporation's economic income (Alternative Minimum Taxable Income). If the tentative alternative minimum tax is greater than the corporation's regular tax, the corporation effectively pays this tentative alternative minimum tax.

    With an exemption amount of at most $40,000, a corporation with more than $40,000 of Tentative Minimum Tax Base may have an AMT to pay.

3. **F** (p. 6–14; reasonable business needs difficult to determine).

    In our system of double taxation, income that is recognized at the corporate level is again taxed at the shareholder level (as a dividend). The corporation may mitigate the detrimental effects of this system of double taxation by accumulating corporate earnings. In this manner, the second level of tax is avoided (or deferred at least for the moment). However, the tax law is framed with the intent to discourage the accumulation of corporate earnings. In particular, the accumulated earnings tax (AET) imposes a penalty tax of 38.6% (in 2002 and 2003) on the current year's addition to the accumulated earnings balance that is not needed for a reasonable business purpose. However, assessing the reasonable needs of the business is difficult for the taxpayer as well as for the IRS.

4. **T** (p. 6–11).

    A Minimum Tax Credit is available to corporate taxpayers that have paid an AMT. The amount of the Minimum Tax Credit is the excess of the corporation's regular tax liability over its tentative minimum tax, to the extent of AMT paid. In the instant case, the fact that the corporation's regular tax liability is greater that its tentative minimum tax (for 1989 or a later year) implies that previously accounted for adjustments or preference items were temporary in nature and have reversed. Thus, a Minimum Tax Credit for AMT paid is allowed against future tax liabilities to eliminate the possibility of taxing the same income twice.

STUDY GUIDE
CHAPTER 6
Alternative Minimum Tax and Certain Penalty Taxes Imposed on Corporations

6-13

5. F (p. 6–15; merely an objective estimate of working capital needs).

   To determine the extent to which a corporation has excess liquid assets that may be used to pay dividends, the Bardahl formula may be applied to objectively determine the working capital needs of the business. But such formula is not a precise tool and is subject to many interpretations. Thus, other relevant information is considered in appropriately modifying the results obtained in a mechanical application of the Bardahl formula.

6. T (p. 6–19).

   In our system of double taxation, income that is recognized at the corporate level is again taxed at the shareholder level (as a dividend). The corporation may mitigate the detrimental effects of this system of double taxation by accumulating corporate earnings. In this manner, the second level of tax is avoided (or deferred at least for the moment). However, the tax law is framed with the intent to discourage the accumulation of corporate earnings by identifying conditions under which the corporation may be found to be intentionally retaining its earnings so that its shareholders may avoid the tax on dividends. In particular, the accumulated earnings tax (AET) imposes a penalty tax of 38.6% (in 2002 and 2003) on the current year's addition to the accumulated earnings balance that is not needed for a reasonable business purpose. For the purpose of calculating the current year's addition to the accumulated earnings balance, corporate taxable income is reduced by modified net capital gain. This reduction is made to produce an amount that more closely represents the dividend-paying capacity of the corporation.

7. T (p. 6–13).

   The tax law is framed with the intent to discourage the accumulation of corporate earnings by identifying conditions under which the corporation may be found to be intentionally retaining its earnings so that its shareholders may avoid the tax on dividends. In particular, the accumulated earnings tax (AET) imposes a penalty tax of 38.6% (in 2002 and 2003) on the current year's addition to the accumulated earnings balance that is not needed for a reasonable business purpose. However, most corporations are allowed a minimum amount of accumulated earnings ($250,000) without exposure to the AET. Accordingly, if (1) earnings are being accumulated for purposes of an exotic venture (unrelated to the current business of the corporation) and (2) the amount of corporate accumulated earnings is less than $250,000, the AET does not generally apply.

8. T (p. 6–27).

   The highest marginal tax bracket for individuals is 38.6% (in 2002 and 2003). In contrast, the highest marginal tax bracket for corporations is 35%. Under these conditions, high bracket individuals may opt to shelter unearned income by holding the underlying income producing property in corporate form. However, the tax law is framed with the intent to discourage the sheltering of certain types of passive income in corporations by identifying conditions under which the corporation may be found to be intentionally retaining its earnings so that its shareholders may avoid the tax on dividends. In particular, the Personal Holding Company tax (PHC tax) imposes a penalty tax of 38.6% (in 2002 and 2003) on undistributed PHC income of a PHC. A PHC is a corporation that satisfies 2 tests: (1) a 50% stock test and (2) a 60% passive income test. Under the 60% passive income test, at least 60% of adjusted ordinary gross income must be either passive income or personal service income. One tax effect of converting investments from high yield stocks to growth stocks may be to reduce the percentage of adjusted ordinary gross income that passive income represents.

9. F (p. 6–5; after 1986).

   The corporate version of the Alternative Minimum Tax (AMT) mechanics ensure that a corporation with substantial economic income will pay a minimum level of corporate income tax. With the enactment of the corporate AMT, corporations are less able to utilize exclusions, deductions and credits to eliminate all Federal income tax. In general, the AMT is applied each year to a corporation's economic income (Alternative Minimum Taxable Income). If the tentative alternative minimum tax is greater than the corporation's regular tax, the corporation effectively pays this tentative alternative minimum tax. More specifically, Regular Taxable Income (RTI) before any Net Operating Loss (NOL) deduction is modified for (1) AMT adjustments (other than the ACE adjustment) and (2) tax preferences to equal Alternative Minimum Taxable Income (AMTI) before the AMT NOL deduction and Adjusted Current Earnings (ACE) adjustment. One AMT adjustment to RTI is a portion of depreciation on property placed in service after 1986. For personalty placed in service before 1999, the adjustment is the excess of accelerated depreciation over the amount determined using the 150 percent declining-balance method switching to straight-line.

10. F (p. 6–19; FMV of marketable securities).

To determine the extent to which a corporation has excess liquid assets that may be used to pay dividends, the Bardahl formula may be applied to objectively determine the working capital needs of the business. Once such needs have been determined, the amount representing these needs is compared against the corporation's current working capital position. In determining this position, the Supreme Court in *Ivan Allen Co. v. U.S.* held that a corporation's marketable securities should be measured at their fair value. It is unknown as to whether a corporation's other assets and liabilities should be measured at their fair value for purposes of determining such corporation's current working capital position.

11. T (p. 6–4; AMT NOL deduction cannot exceed 90% of AMTI).

With the enactment of the corporate AMT, corporations are less able to utilize exclusions, deductions and credits to eliminate all Federal income tax. In general, the AMT is applied each year to a corporation's economic income (Alternative Minimum Taxable Income). If the tentative alternative minimum tax is greater than the corporation's regular tax, the corporation effectively pays this tentative alternative minimum tax. More specifically, AMTI is calculated as follows.

- Regular Taxable Income (RTI) before any Net Operating Loss (NOL) deduction
- Modified for (1) AMT adjustments (other than the Adjusted Current Earnings (ACE) adjustment) and (2) tax preferences EQUALS Alternative Minimum Taxable Income (AMTI) before the AMT NOL deduction and the ACE adjustment
- Less the ACE adjustment EQUALS AMTI before the AMT NOL deduction
- Less the AMT NOL deduction (limited to 90%) EQUALS AMTI.

The corporation's NOL deduction is the aggregate of all NOL carryovers and NOL carrybacks. Accordingly, a corporation's AMTI is recomputed in any carryback year (e.g., 2002) to which a NOL is carried back.

Fill in the Blanks

1. accumulated earnings (p. 6–11).

In our system of double taxation, income that is recognized at the corporate level is again taxed at the shareholder level (as a dividend). The corporation may mitigate the detrimental effects of this system of double taxation by accumulating corporate earnings. In this manner, the second level of tax is avoided (or deferred at least for the moment). However, the tax law is framed with the intent to discourage the accumulation of corporate earnings by identifying conditions under which the corporation may be found to be intentionally retaining its earnings so that its shareholders may avoid the tax on dividends. In particular, the accumulated earnings tax (AET) imposes a penalty tax of 38.6% (in 2002 and 2003) on the current year's addition to the accumulated earnings balance that is not needed for a reasonable business purpose.

2. 38.6% (in 2002 and 2003) (p. 6–11).

The accumulated earnings tax (AET) imposes a penalty tax of 38.6% (in 2002 and 2003) on the current year's addition to the accumulated earnings balance that is not needed for a reasonable business purpose. Generally, the AET applies if a corporation accumulates funds beyond its reasonable business needs that exceed the $250,000 accumulated earnings credit.

3. working capital; extraordinary (p. 6–14).

To determine the extent to which a corporation has excess liquid assets that may be used to pay dividends, the Bardahl formula may be applied to objectively determine the working capital needs of the business. If the statistically computed working capital needs plus any extraordinary expenses are more than the current year's net working capital, no penalty tax is imposed. However, if working capital needs plus any extraordinary expenses are less than the current year's net working capital, the AET may be imposed.

4. inventory cycle (p. 6–15).

The accumulated earnings tax (AET) imposes a penalty tax of 38.6% (in 2002 and 2003) on the current year's addition to the accumulated earnings balance that is not needed for a reasonable business purpose. Accordingly, the AET generally applies if a corporation accumulates funds beyond its business needs. However, assessing the reasonable needs of the business is difficult for the taxpayer as well as for the IRS. To determine the extent to which a corporation has excess liquid assets that may be used to pay dividends, the Bardahl formula may be applied to objectively determine the working capital needs of the business. Within this context, Average inventory, divided by Cost of Goods Sold, equals Inventory Cycle.

5. fair market value (p. 6–19).

To determine the extent to which a corporation has excess liquid assets that may be used to pay dividends, the Bardahl formula may be applied to objectively determine the working capital needs of the business. Once such needs have been determined, the amount representing these needs is compared against the corporation's current working capital position. In determining this position, the Supreme Court in *Ivan Allen Co. v. U.S.* held that a corporation's marketable securities should be measured at their fair value.

6. accumulated earnings credit (p. 6–19).

In our system of double taxation, income that is recognized at the corporate level is again taxed at the shareholder level (as a dividend). The corporation may mitigate the detrimental effects of this system of double taxation by accumulating corporate earnings. In this manner, the second level of tax is avoided (or deferred at least for the moment). However, the tax law is framed with the intent to discourage the accumulation of corporate earnings by identifying conditions under which the corporation may be found to be intentionally retaining its earnings so that its shareholders may avoid the tax on dividends. In particular, the accumulated earnings tax (AET) imposes a penalty tax of 38.6% (in 2002 and 2003) on the current year's addition to the accumulated earnings balance that is not needed for a reasonable business purpose. Mechanically, AET is calculated by applying the applicable percentage of 38.6% (in 2002 and 2003) against Accumulated Taxable Income (ATI). ATI is equal to modified taxable income less dividends paid and less the accumulated earnings credit.

7. reduces (p. 6–19).

In our system of double taxation, income that is recognized at the corporate level is again taxed at the shareholder level as a dividend. The corporation may mitigate the detrimental effects of this system of double taxation by accumulating corporate earnings. In this manner, the second level of tax is avoided (or deferred at least for the moment). However, the tax law is framed with the intent to discourage the accumulation of corporate earnings by identifying conditions under which the corporation may be found to be intentionally retaining its earnings so that its shareholders may avoid the tax on dividends. In particular, the accumulated earnings tax (AET) imposes a penalty tax of 38.6% (in 2002 and 2003) on the current year's addition to the accumulated earnings balance that is not needed for a reasonable business purpose. Mechanically, AET is calculated by applying the applicable percentage of 38.6% (in 2002 and 2003) against Accumulated Taxable Income (ATI). ATI is equal to modified taxable income less dividends paid and less the accumulated earnings credit. Accordingly, dividends that are paid reduce the tax base subject to the AET.

8. both (p. 6–21).

The highest marginal tax bracket for individuals is 38.6% (in 2002 and 2003). In contrast, the highest marginal tax bracket for corporations is 35%. Under these conditions, high bracket individuals may opt to shelter unearned income by holding the underlying income producing property in corporate form. However, the tax law is framed with the intent to discourage the sheltering of certain types of passive income in corporations by identifying conditions under which the corporation may be found to be intentionally retaining its earnings so that its shareholders may avoid the tax on dividends. In particular, the Personal Holding Company (PHC) tax imposes a penalty tax of 38.6% (in 2002 and 2003) on the undistributed PHC income of a PHC. A PHC is a corporation that satisfies 2 tests: (1) a 50% stock test and (2) a 60% passive income test. Under the 60% passive income test, at least 60% of Adjusted Ordinary Gross Income (AOGI) must be either passive income or personal service income.

9. 50%; five; last half (p. 6–22).

The highest marginal tax bracket for individuals is 38.6% (in 2002 and 2003). In contrast, the highest marginal tax bracket for corporations is 35%. Under these conditions, high bracket individuals opt to shelter unearned income by holding the underlying income producing property in corporate form. However, the tax law is framed with the intent to discourage the sheltering of certain types of passive income in corporations by identifying conditions under which the corporation may be found to be intentionally retaining its earnings so that its shareholders may avoid the tax on dividends. In particular, the Personal Holding Company (PHC) tax imposes a penalty tax of 38.6% (in 2002 and 2003) on the undistributed PHC income of a PHC. A PHC is a corporation that satisfies 2 tests: (1) a 50% stock test and (2) a 60% passive income test. Under the 60% passive income test, at least 60% of Adjusted Ordinary Gross Income (AOGI) must be either passive income or personal service income. With respect to the 50% stock test, 50% of the value of the outstanding stock must be owned by 5 or fewer individuals at any time during the last half of the taxable year.

10. 60% (p. 6–22).

The highest marginal tax bracket for individuals is 38.6% (in 2002 and 2003). In contrast, the highest marginal tax bracket for corporations is 35%. Under these conditions, high bracket individuals opt to shelter unearned income by holding the underlying income producing property in corporate form. However, the tax law is framed with the intent to discourage the sheltering of certain types of passive income in corporations by identifying conditions under which the corporation may be found to be intentionally retaining its earnings so that its shareholders may avoid the tax on dividends. In particular, the Personal Holding Company (PHC) tax imposes a penalty tax of 38.6% (in 2002 and 2003) on the undistributed PHC income of a PHC. A PHC is a corporation that satisfies 2 tests: (1) a 50% stock test and (2) a 60% passive income test. Under the 60% passive income test, at least 60% of Adjusted Ordinary Gross Income (AOGI) must be either passive income or personal service income.

Multiple Choice

1. c (p. 6–24) Example 28 ($30,000 + 120,000) − ($30,000 + $25,000 + $25,000) = $70,000

AOGI is $70,000 [gross income $150,000 ($30,000 + $120,000) less expenses directly related to rental income (not to exceed 100% of rental income) of $80,000 ($30,000 + $25,000 + $25,000)].

The highest marginal tax bracket for individuals is 38.6% (in 2002 and 2003). In contrast, the highest marginal tax bracket for corporations is 35%. Under these conditions, high bracket individuals may opt to shelter unearned income by holding the underlying income producing property in corporate form. However, the tax law is framed with the intent to discourage the sheltering of certain types of passive income in corporations by identifying conditions under which the corporation may be found to be intentionally retaining its earnings so that its shareholders may avoid the tax on dividends. In particular, the Personal Holding Company (PHC) tax imposes a penalty tax of 38.6% (in 2002 and 2003) on the undistributed PHC income of a PHC. A PHC is a corporation that satisfies 2 tests: (1) a 50% stock test and (2) a 60% passive income test. Under the 60% passive income test, at least 60% of Adjusted Ordinary Gross Income (AOGI) must be either passive income or personal service income. AOGI is equal to gross income less the sum of (1) capital and 1231 gains and (2) expenses directly related to passive income (not to exceed 100% of passive income). Thus, item c is correct. Further, choice items a,b,d&e are incorrect because they each are inconsistent with item c.

2. c (p. 6–27)

Dividend income	$ 30,000	
Rental income	120,000	$150,000
Less: Depreciation	$ 30,000	
Mortgage interest	25,000	
Real estate taxes	25,000	
Salaries	15,000	95,000
		$ 55,000
Less dividend received deduction		21,000
Taxable income		$ 34,000
Tax: 15%(34,000)		$ 5,100

The highest marginal tax bracket for individuals is 38.6% (in 2002 and 2003). In contrast, the highest marginal tax bracket for corporations is 35%. Under these conditions, high bracket individuals may opt to shelter unearned income by holding the underlying income producing property in corporate form. However, the tax law is framed with the intent to discourage the sheltering of certain types of passive income in corporations by identifying conditions under which the corporation may be found to be intentionally retaining its earnings so that its shareholders may avoid the tax on dividends. In particular, the Personal Holding Company (PHC) tax imposes a penalty tax of 38.6% (in 2002 and 2003) on the undistributed PHC income of a PHC. Undistributed PHC income is equal to Taxable Income (TI):

- Plus the sum of (1) the Dividends Received Deduction (DRD), (2) modified Net Operating Loss (NOL) deduction and (3) certain excess business expenses attributable to non-business property;
- Less the sum of (1) accrued federal income tax (without the PHC tax and the AET), (2) excess charitable contributions and (3) net capital gain (net of tax); and
- Less the dividends paid deduction.

In the instant case, accrued federal income tax (without the PHC tax and the AET) is equal to $5,100 [15% of TI of $34,000 (gross income of $150,000 ($30,000 + $120,000) less the sum of (1) ordinary and necessary expenses of $95,000 ($30,000 + $25,000 + $25,000 + $15,000) and (2) DRD of $21,000 (70% of $30,000))]. Thus, item c is correct. Further, choice items a, b, d & e are incorrect because they are inconsistent with item c.

3. b (p. 6–24)

Nonrental PHC income	$30,000
Less 10% of OGI	15,000
	$15,000

The highest marginal tax bracket for individuals is 38.6% (in 2002 and 2003). In contrast, the highest marginal tax bracket for corporations is 35%. Under these conditions, high bracket individuals may opt to shelter unearned income by holding the underlying income producing property in corporate form. However, the tax law is framed with the intent to discourage the sheltering of certain types of passive income in corporations by identifying conditions under which the corporation may be found to be intentionally retaining its earnings so that its shareholders may avoid the tax on dividends. In particular, the Personal Holding Company (PHC) tax imposes a penalty tax of 38.6% (in 2002 and 2003) on the undistributed PHC income of a PHC. A PHC is a corporation that satisfies the following 2 tests: (1) a 50% stock value test and (2) a 60% passive income test. Under the 60% passive income test, at least 60% of Adjusted Ordinary Gross Income (AOGI) must be either passive income or personal service income. AOGI is equal to gross income less capital and 1231 gains to equal Ordinary Gross Income (OGI), less expenses directly related to passive income (not to exceed 100% of passive income). Rental income is normally classified as PHC income. However, rental income is not passive income if the following 2 tests are met: (1) modified rental income is at least equal to 50% of AOGI and (2) total dividends is at least equal to the excess of non-rent PHC income over 10% of OGI. In the instant case, since OGI is equal to $150,000, 10% of OGI is $15,000 and the excess of non-rent PHC income of $30,000 over 10% of OGI is $15,000. Thus, to meet the second test XYZ must pay at least $15,000 in dividends and item b is correct. Further, choice items a,c,d&e are incorrect because they each are inconsistent with item b.

4. e (p. 6–27)

Taxable income	$ 41,500
Plus dividend received deduction ($1,500/.30) – ($1,500)	3,500
	$ 45,000
Less Section 11 tax	6,225
Less dividends paid	2,000
	$ 36,775
	× 38.6%
PHC tax liability	$ 14,195

5. a (p. 6–19)

Taxable income	$342,000
Plus 70% dividend deduction	56,000
	$398,000
Less: Tax liability	116,280
Excess charitable contributions	15,000
Net long-term capital gain	20,000
Dividends paid	30,000
Accumulated earnings credit carryover	140,000
Accumulated taxable income	$ 76,720

The accumulated earnings tax (AET) imposes a penalty tax of 38.6% (in 2002 and 2003) on the current year's addition to the accumulated earnings balance that is not needed for a reasonable business purpose. Mechanically, AET is calculated by applying the applicable percentage of 38.6% (in 2002 and 2003) against Accumulated Taxable Income (ATI). ATI is equal to modified taxable income less dividends paid and less the accumulated earnings credit. In the instant case, the dividends received deduction is $56,000 (dividends received of $80,000 multiplied by the applicable dividends received deduction rate of 70%). Further, modified taxable income is equal to $246,720 (taxable income of $342,000 plus the dividends received deduction of $56,000, less the sum of (1) the corporate income tax for the year of $116,280, (2) charitable contributions in excess of 10% of ATI of $15,000 and (3) net capital gain (adjusted for the capital gains tax) of $20,000). ATI is equal to $76,720 (modified taxable income of $246,720 less dividends paid of $30,000 and less the accumulated earnings credit of $140,000).

6. a (p. 6–19) 38.6% (110,500).

The tax law is framed with the intent to discourage the accumulation of corporate earnings by identifying conditions under which the corporation may be found to be intentionally retaining its earnings so that its shareholders may avoid the tax on dividends. In particular, the accumulated earnings tax (AET) imposes a penalty tax of 38.6% (in 2002 and 2003) on the current year's addition to the accumulated earnings balance that is not needed for a reasonable business purpose. Mechanically, AET is calculated by applying the applicable percentage of 38.6% against Accumulated Taxable Income (ATI). In the instant case, if ATI is $110,500, AET is $42,653 (38.6% × $110,500). Thus, item a is correct. Further, choice items b,c,d&e are incorrect because they each are inconsistent with item a.

7. c (p. 6–24) $14,000 − ($3,000 + $2,000 + 1,500) = $7,500 adjusted income from rents. $7,500/$18,000 = 42%

The Personal Holding Company (PHC) tax imposes a penalty tax of 38.6% (in 2002 and 2003) on the undistributed PHC income of a PHC. A PHC is a corporation that satisfies the following 2 tests: (1) a 50% stock test and (2) a 60% passive income test. Under the 60% passive income test, at least 60% of Adjusted Ordinary Gross Income (AOGI) must be either passive income or personal service income. AOGI is equal to gross income less capital and 1231 gains to equal Ordinary Gross Income (OGI), less expenses directly related to passive income (not to exceed 100% of passive income). Rental income is normally classified as passive PHC income. However, rental income is not passive income if the following 2 tests are met: (1) modified rental income is at least equal to 50% of AOGI and (2) total dividends is at least equal to the excess of non-rent PHC income over 10% of OGI. In the instant case, since AOGI is equal to $18,000, 50% of AOGI is $9,000. Further, modified rental income is $7,500 ($14,000 − $3,000 − $2,000 − $1,500). Since $7,500 is not at least equal to $9,000, the first rental income test is not met. In fact, the ratio of modified rental income to AOGI is equal to 41.67% ($7,500/$18,000). Hence, such rental income is passive income for purposes of the PHC tax. Thus, item c is correct. Further, the other choice items are incorrect because they each are inconsistent with the correct answer.

8. a (p. 6–15) (($80,000/$800,000) − ($60,000/$700,000)) × $700,000 = (.1−.0857) × $700,000 = $10,010

To determine the extent to which a corporation has excess liquid assets that may be used to pay dividends, the Bardahl formula may be applied to objectively determine the working capital needs of the business. Under the Bardahl formula, a derived decimal percentage is multiplied against the sum of (1) cost of goods sold and (2) general, selling & administrative expenses. The derived decimal percentage is calculated by adding (1) the inventory cycle (if applicable) and (2) the accounts receivable cycle and subtracting the accounts payable cycle. The accounts receivable cycle is calculated by dividing net sales into average accounts receivable. The accounts payable cycle is calculated by dividing the sum of (1) purchases plus (2) cash operating expenses into average accounts payable. In the instant case, the accounts receivable cycle is .1000 (calculated by dividing net sales of $800,000 into the accounts receivable average of $80,000). The accounts payable cycle is .0857 (calculated by dividing the sum of (1) purchases plus (2) cash operating expenses of $700,000 into average accounts payable of $60,000). Thus, the derived decimal percentage is .0143 (.1000 − .0857) and the working capital needs of the business under the Bardahl formula is $10,010 [the derived decimal percentage of .0143 multiplied by $700,000 (the sum of (1) cost of goods sold and (2) general, selling & administrative expenses)]. Thus, item a is correct. Further, the other choice items are incorrect because they each are inconsistent with the correct answer.

9. b (p. 6–13).

The accumulated earnings tax (AET) imposes a penalty tax of 38.6% (in 2002 and 2003) on the current year's addition to the accumulated earnings balance that is not needed for a reasonable business purpose. The AET is not imposed upon S corporations and personal holding companies. Thus, item b is correct. Choice items a & c are incorrect because the AET may apply to a personal service corporation or to a group of affiliated companies.

10. c (p. 6–33).

The Personal Holding Company (PHC) tax imposes a penalty tax of 38.6% (in 2002 and 2003) on the undistributed PHC income of a PHC. Undistributed PHC income is equal to Taxable Income (TI):

- Plus the sum of (1) the Dividends Received Deduction (DRD), (2) modified Net Operating Loss (NOL) deduction and (3) certain excess business expenses attributable to non-business property;

- Less the sum of (1) accrued federal income tax (without the PHC tax and the AET), (2) excess charitable contributions and (3) net capital gain (net of tax); and
- Less the dividends paid deduction. Item c is correct because the application of the PHC tax for a particular tax year requires the corporation to follow certain reporting procedures. That is, the corporation must file a Schedule PH along with its Form 1120. Failure to file the Schedule PH may result in additional interest and penalties. The following choice items are incorrect:
- a is incorrect because the PHC tax is generally imposed on closely held corporations. The number of shareholders or their ownership interest percentages is determinative of PHC status, where a 50% stock value test must be satisfied to attain PHC status.
- b is incorrect because sufficient dividend distributions may eliminate the PHC tax.
- d is incorrect because there is no minimum credit in the computation of the PHC tax.

11. a (p. 6–12).

The AET generally applies if a corporation accumulates funds beyond its reasonable business needs. Item a is correct because the application of the AET depends upon whether a particular shareholder group controls corporate policy. The number of shareholders is not necessarily determinative. The following choice items are incorrect:

- b is incorrect because the AET does not apply to personal holding companies under Section 532(b)(1).
- c is incorrect because the AET applies to companies that do not make sufficient distributions.
- d is incorrect because application of the AET is not limited to conglomerates.

12. d (p. 6–22; definition, 5 or fewer owning 50% or more).

The Personal Holding Company (PHC) tax imposes a penalty tax of 38.6% (in 2002 and 2003) on the undistributed PHC income of a PHC. A PHC is a corporation that satisfies the following 2 tests: (1) a 50% stock value test and (2) a 60% passive income test. Under the 50% stock value test, 50% of the value of the outstanding stock must be owned by 5 or fewer individuals. In the instant case, there are 18 unrelated equal stockholders. The 50% stock value test is not met and Ray Holding is not a PHC and is not subject to the PHC tax. Thus, item d is correct. Further, choice items a,b&d are incorrect because they each are inconsistent with item d.

13. a (p. 6–2).

With the enactment of the corporate AMT, corporations are less able to utilize exclusions, deductions and credits to eliminate all Federal income tax. In general, the AMT is applied each year to a corporation's economic income (Alternative Minimum Taxable Income). If the tentative alternative minimum tax is greater than the corporation's regular tax, the corporation effectively pays this tentative alternative minimum tax by adding to the regular tax the amount of the excess of the tentative alternative minimum tax over the regular tax. Thus, item a is correct. Choice items b,c&d are incorrect because they each are inconsistent with item a.

14. c (p. 6–4)

Taxable income before NOL	$85,000
Minus adjustments	2,000
Plus preferences	45,000
Minus exemption	40,000
AMTI	$88,000
Times 20%	17,600
Less Regular tax	$17,150

If they are subject to the AMT, corporations are less able to utilize exclusions, deductions and credits to eliminate all Federal income tax. In general, the AMT is applied each year to a corporation's economic income (Alternative Minimum Taxable Income). If the tentative alternative minimum tax is greater than the corporation's regular tax, the corporation effectively pays this tentative alternative minimum tax. More specifically, Regular Taxable Income (RTI) before any Net Operating Loss (NOL) deduction:

- Modified for (1) AMT adjustments (other than the Adjusted Current Earnings (ACE) adjustment) and (2) tax preferences EQUALS Alternative Minimum Taxable Income (AMTI) before the AMT NOL deduction and ACE adjustment
- Less the ACE adjustment EQUALS AMTI before the AMT NOL deduction
- Less the AMT NOL deduction (limited to 90%) EQUALS AMTI
- Less the exemption amount EQUALS Tentative Minimum Tax Base
- Multiplied by 20% EQUALS Tentative Minimum Tax before AMT foreign tax credit
- Less the AMT foreign tax credit EQUALS Tentative Minimum Tax
- Less the Regular Tax Liability before credits (other than the AMT foreign tax credit) EQUALS AMT

With an exemption amount of at most $40,000, a corporation with more than $40,000 of Tentative Minimum Tax Base may have an AMT to pay. In the instant case, Wood's RTI before any NOL deduction is $85,000 and Wood's exemption is assumed to amount to $40,000 ($40,000 reduced by 25% of the amount by which AMTI exceeds $150,000). Thus, Wood's AMTI is $128,000 ($85,000 + $45,000 − $2,000) and Wood's Tentative Minimum Tax Base is $88,000 ($128,000 − $40,000). Hence, Wood's Tentative Minimum Tax is $17,600 (20% × $88,000) and Wood's AMT is $450 ($17,600 − $17,150) and item c is correct. Further, choice items a,b&d are incorrect because they each are inconsistent with item c.

15. c   (p. 6–10; $40,000 reduced by 25% of ATMI in excess of $150,000; 40,000 − 25%(50,000))

If they are subject to the AMT, corporations are less able to utilize exclusions, deductions and credits to eliminate all Federal income tax. In general, the AMT is applied each year to a corporation's economic income (Alternative Minimum Taxable Income). If the tentative alternative minimum tax is greater than the corporation's regular tax, the corporation effectively pays this tentative alternative minimum tax. More specifically, Regular Taxable Income (RTI) before any Net Operating Loss (NOL) deduction:

- Modified for (1) AMT adjustments (other than the Adjusted Current Earnings (ACE) adjustment) and (2) tax preferences EQUALS Alternative Minimum Taxable Income (AMTI) before the AMT NOL deduction and ACE adjustment
- Less the ACE adjustment EQUALS AMTI before the AMT NOL deduction
- Less the AMT NOL deduction (limited to 90%) EQUALS AMTI
- Less the exemption amount EQUALS Tentative Minimum Tax Base
- Multiplied by 20% EQUALS Tentative Minimum Tax before AMT foreign tax credit
- Less the AMT foreign tax credit EQUALS Tentative Minimum Tax
- Less the Regular Tax Liability before credits (other than the AMT foreign tax credit) EQUALS AMT

With an exemption amount of at most $40,000 ($40,000 reduced by 25% of the amount by which AMTI exceeds $150,000), a corporation with more than $40,000 of Tentative Minimum Tax Base may have an AMT to pay. In the instant case, Barrett's AMTI is $200,000. Thus, Barrett's exemption amount is $27,500 [$40,000 less 25% of $50,000 ($200,000 − $150,000)] and item c is correct. Further, choice items a,b&d are incorrect because they each are inconsistent with item c.

CHAPTER 7

Corporations: Reorganizations

LEARNING OBJECTIVES

After completing Chapter 7, you should be able to:

1. Understand the general requirements of corporate reorganizations.
2. Determine the tax consequences of a corporate reorganization.
3. Explain the statutory requirements for the different types of reorganizations.
4. Delineate the judicial and administrative conditions for a nontaxable corporate reorganization.
5. Apply the rules pertaining to the carryover of tax attributes in a corporate reorganization.
6. Structure corporate reorganizations to obtain the desired tax consequences.

KEY TERMS

Business purpose
Consolidation
Continuity of business enterprise
Continuity of interest test
Control
Equity structure shift

Long-term tax-exempt rate
Merger
Owner shift
Ownership change
Recapitalization
Reorganization

Section 382 limitation
Spin-off
Split-off
Split-up
Step transaction

OUTLINE

I. **REORGANIZATIONS—IN GENERAL**
   A. Types of Reorganizations under Section 368 include:
      1. Type A: a statutory merger or consolidation;
      2. Type B: an exchange of stock for voting stock;
      3. Type C: an exchange of assets for voting stock;
      4. Type D: a divisive reorganization (a spin-off, split-off, or split-up);
      5. Type E: a recapitalization;
      6. Type F: a mere change in identity, form, or place of organization;
      7. Type G: an insolvent corporation reorganization.
   B. Summary of Tax Consequences in a Tax-Free Reorganization
      1. The tax treatment virtually parallels the like-kind exchange provisions of Section 1031.
      2. Gain or Loss
         a. Generally, no gain or loss is recognized unless consideration other than stock or securities is received.
         b. If the target corporation receives *other property* along with stock or securities, it may recognize gain (but not loss) if it fails to distribute the *other property*. The recognized gain is the lesser of the fair market value of the property received or gain realized.
            1. If it distributes the *other property* to its shareholders, it will not recognize a gain.
            2. The target corporation may also recognize a gain if it distributes its own appreciated property to its shareholders.
         c. If the shareholders of the corporations involved receive cash or other property in addition to stock, the other property is considered boot; the recognized gain is the lesser of boot received or the realized gain.
         d. Any gain is treated as a dividend, to the extent of the shareholder's pro rata share of the corporation's E & P. Any remaining gain is generally a capital gain.
         e. Losses are not recognized.
         f. Debt security (debenture) holders have treatment similar to shareholders. Gain is recognized only when the principal amount of the debentures received is more than the debt securities given up.
      3. Basis
         a. The basis of property received by the acquiring corporation is the same basis as in the hands of the target increased by the amount of gain recognized by the target on the transfer.
         b. The basis of stock and securities surrendered carries over to the stock and securities received, decreased by the fair market value of boot received, and increased by the gain and dividend income recognized, if any.

II. **TYPES OF TAX-FREE REORGANIZATIONS**
   A. Type A
      1. Type A reorganizations include statutory mergers and consolidations.
         a. A merger is the union of two or more corporations.
         b. A consolidation occurs when a new corporation is created to take the place of two or more corporations.
      2. Advantages
         a. Type A reorganizations permit the greatest flexibility of any of the tax-free reorganizations, because the use of voting stock is not required.
         b. The use of money or property will constitute "boot," which may require the recognition of a gain. However, this will not destroy the tax-free treatment if the continuity of interest test is satisfied: at least 50% of the consideration must be stock.

c. There is no requirement that "substantially all" of the target's assets be transferred to the acquiring corporation (as in a Type C reorganization).
   3. Disadvantages
      a. The reorganization requires a majority approval of all shareholders; dissenting shareholders have the right to have their shares appraised and bought (which can prove cumbersome and expensive).
      b. The acquiring corporation must assume all liabilities of the acquired corporation.
      c. The use of a subsidiary to acquire the stock of the target company may reduce these problems, since:
         1. only the board of directors' approval is required (because the parent corporation is the majority stockholder).
         2. the parent's assets will be protected from target's creditors.
B. Type B
   1. Type B reorganizations require the exchange of stock for voting stock.
      a. The acquiring corporation must give up only voting stock ("solely stock").
      b. After the exchange the acquiring corporation must own at least 80% of all classes of the target corporation's stock ("control").
   2. Voting stock must be the sole consideration; this requirement is strictly construed by the courts.
C. Type C
   1. Type C reorganizations require the exchange of substantially all the assets of the target corporation for the voting stock of the acquiring corporation. A limited amount of other property is also allowed.
   2. The target corporation must distribute the stock, securities, and other properties it receives in the reorganization, as well as its own properties to its shareholders. It then liquidates.
   3. Type C reorganizations have almost the same effect as Type A reorganizations (although the requirements for consideration are more restrictive with Type C). However, the acquiring corporation in a Type C reorganization may choose which liabilities of the target corporation to assume.
D. Type D
   1. Acquisitive D reorganization
      a. The acquiring corporation transfers assets to the target corporation in exchange for control, 50%, of the target.
      b. All stock and property received by the acquiring corporation must be distributed to the acquiring corporation's shareholders.
      c. The acquiring corporation is then liquidated.
   2. Divisive D reorganization
      a. The acquiring corporation transfers assets to the target corporation in exchange for control, 80%, of the target.
      b. All stock received by the acquiring corporation must be distributed to the acquiring corporation's shareholders as:
         1. *a spin-off:* the shareholders do not give up any stock in the distributing corporation.
         2. *a split-off:* the shareholders exchange stock in the distributing corporation for stock in the new corporation.
      c. In a *split-up*, the assets of one corporation are transferred to two or more new corporations, where:
         1. the stock of the new corporations is distributed to the transferor corporation's shareholders.
         2. the transferor corporation is then liquidated.
E. Type E
   1. E reorganizations are recapitalizations, an exchange of:
      a. bonds for stock.
      b. stock for stock.
      c. bonds for bonds.

2. Potential tax consequences affect the shareholders, who exchange stock or securities, not the corporation.
F. Type F
1. F reorganizations merely change the identity, form or place of organization.
2. Because the surviving corporation is the same corporation as its predecessor, tax attributes carry over.
3. F reorganizations are restricted to single operating corporations.
4. An F reorganization does not jeopardize a valid S election or § 1244 stock status.
G. Type G
1. All or part of the assets of a debtor corporation are transferred to an acquiring corporation in a bankruptcy proceeding.
2. The debtor corporation's creditors must receive voting stock of the acquiring corporation in exchange for debt representing 80% or more of the fair market value of the debt of the debtor corporation.

III. **JUDICIAL DOCTRINES**
A. Various judicially-created doctrines have become basic requirements of a tax-free corporate reorganization.
B. Sound business purpose: the transaction must have economic consequences germane to the businesses that go beyond tax avoidance.
C. Continuity of interest: a shareholder must have substantially the same investment after the restructuring as before.
1. This element is satisfied if shareholders of the target corporation receive stock in the purchasing corporation equal in value to at least 50% of all formerly outstanding stock of the target corporation.
D. Continuity of business enterprise: the acquiring corporation must either continue the target corporation's business or use a significant portion of the target's assets in its businesses,
E. Step transaction: a series of transactions will be collapsed into a single step if they are interdependent.

IV. **CARRYOVER OF CORPORATE TAX ATTRIBUTES**
A. Assumption of Liabilities
1. The acquiring corporation's assumption of target corporation liabilities does not constitute "boot" when determining gain recognition by corporations that are parties to the restructuring.
2. Generally, liabilities are only problematic in Type C reorganizations.
B. Allowance of Carryovers
1. Section 381(c) lists specific tax attributes of an acquired corporation which can be carried over to a successor corporation.
2. Only the A, C, acquisitive D, F, and G reorganizations are subject to the carryover limitation rules.
C. Net Operating Loss Carryovers
1. An NOL carryover is permitted as a deduction of the successor corporation.
2. The NOL cannot be carried back; it can only be used prospectively.
3. Ownership Changes. If there has been an "ownership change," Section 382 limits the amount of NOL that can be utilized each year by the successor corporation.
D. Earnings and Profits
1. E & P of an acquired corporation carries over to the successor corporation as of the date of the transfer.
2. A deficit can only offset E & P accumulated after the date of the transfer.

STUDY GUIDE | **CHAPTER 7** | 7–5
Corporations: Reorganizations

TEST FOR SELF-EVALUATION—CHAPTER 7

True or False

Indicate which of the following statements is true or false by circling the correct answer.

T F 1. Generally, if a reorganization consists of only stocks and/or securities, there will no tax consequences to the security holders.

T F 2. The recognition of gain realized on a § 368 reorganization is limited to the amount of cash received and the fair market value of other property.

T F 3. Even though a corporation distributes all the cash and securities it receives to its shareholders in a tax-free reorganization, it still must pay a tax to the Federal government.

T F 4. The Type B reorganization is restricted to the exchange of stock for assets.

T F 5. The effective control level which must be reached by the acquiring corporation in a Type B reorganization is at least 80% of the total combined voting power of all classes of stock entitled to vote, and at least 80% of the total number of shares of all other classes of stock of the corporation.

T F 6. A Type D reorganization is a mechanism through which a corporation can divide itself—that is, effect a spin-off, split-off, or split-up.

T F 7. The Type E reorganization is of significance to the shareholders only, and is of no consequence to the corporation.

T F 8. The IRS has ruled that if a reorganization qualifies as an A, C, or D reorganization, and at the same time as an F reorganization, Type F will prevail.

T F 9. A split-up involves three corporations, none of which are liquidated.

T F 10. In a Type B reorganization, the assumption of a liability will not violate the "solely for voting stock" requirement.

Fill in the Blanks

Complete the following statements with the appropriate word(s) or amount(s).

1. Section 382 limitations on NOL carryovers are triggered only if there is an _____ or _____.

2. The §382 limitations apply if there has been a change of more than _____% in the ownership of the loss corporation.

3. Earnings and profits and deficits carry over, but deficits reduce E & P only after _____.

4. In order to substantiate a reorganization as having a bona fide business purpose, it is practically mandatory to have a _____ of _____.

5. In an A-type reorganization, the use of a subsidiary to acquire another corporation requires compliance with _____.

Multiple Choice

Choose the best answer for each of the following questions.

_____ 1. Green Corporation exchanges voting stock in Blue Corporation, its parent, for 91% of the stock in Yellow Corporation. This is an example of which type of reorganization?

    a. Type A
    b. Type B
    c. Type C
    d. Type D
    e. None of the above

_____ 2. Jots Corporation is acquired in a merger with Tons Corporation. Tons, the surviving corporation, has a $40,000 deficit in E & P, while Jots has a $150,000 positive E & P. After the merger, Tons distributes $75,000 to its shareholders. The distribution will be treated as:

    a. $35,000 ordinary dividend
    b. $75,000 ordinary dividend
    c. $35,000 ordinary income and $40,000 long-term capital gain
    d. $75,000 long-term capital gain
    e. None of the above

_____ 3. Taos Corporation, a Texas corporation, organizes Chilton Corporation in Oklahoma. It transfers all of its assets to Chilton and distributes the Chilton stock to its shareholders, who turn in their Taos stock. Consequently, Taos is liquidated. This is an example of which type of reorganization?

    a. Type A
    b. Type C
    c. Type D
    d. Type F
    e. None of the above

_____ 4. Which one of the following is not a corporate reorganization as defined in § 368?

    a. Stock redemption
    b. Recapitalization
    c. Change in identity
    d. Split off

_____ 5. Thomas and Bond each own a 50% interest in TomBoy Corporation. TomBoy is merged into Gunnison Corporation. Thomas receives cash for his stock, while Bond receives stock in Gunnison. As a result:

    a. Both Thomas and Bond are not taxed
    b. Thomas is taxed but Bond is not
    c. Bond is taxed but Thomas is not
    d. Both Thomas and Bond are taxed
    e. None of the above

_____ 6. The transactions described in item 5. are an example of:

    a. "Continuity of business purpose"
    b. A step transaction
    c. "Continuity of interest"
    d. All of the above
    e. None of the above

_____ 7. To take full tax advantage of a net operating loss carry-over between two corporations, one of which is the acquired corporation, the change in ownership of the acquired corporation cannot exceed:

   a. 40%
   b. 33⅓%
   c. 60%
   d. 50%
   e. None of the above

_____ 8. Carter Corporation merges with Dutch Corporation, which has a $140,000 net operating loss. Carter acquires Dutch to obtain the $140,000 loss. Carter reports on a calendar year basis and had a profit of $200,000 for the year. Carter acquired Dutch on September 1. Carter currently can deduct Dutch's loss of:

   a. –0–
   b. $66,667
   c. $46,667
   d. $140,000
   e. $200,000

_____ 9. Would your answer to Question 8 be any different if both firms had other business reasons for the merger?

   a. Yes
   b. No

_____ 10. Tums Corporation has been engaged in two businesses over the last 12 years. It decides to transfer the assets from one of its businesses to a new corporation, and distributes the stock to the shareholders of Tums. This is an example of a:

   a. Spin-off
   b. Split-off
   c. Split-up
   d. Type A reorganization
   e. None of the above

_____ 11. Following a plan of corporate reorganization Mike exchanged 5,000 shares of Cable Corporation common stock for 900 shares of Wire Corporation common stock. Mike had paid $18,750 for the Cable stock. The fair market value of the Wire stock was $21,500 on the date of the exchange. How much was Mike's recognized gain?

   a. $2,050
   b. $4,100
   c. $2,750
   d. $–0–

_____ 12. With regard to corporate reorganizations, which one of the following statements is not correct?

   a. A mere change in identity, form, or place of organization of one corporation qualifies as reorganization.
   b. The reorganization provisions can be used to provide tax-free treatment for corporate transactions.
   c. A plan of reorganization is not required.
   d. A Letter Ruling should be requested when planning a corporate reorganization.

13. Following a plan of corporate reorganization adopted in February 1998, Lori exchanged 10 shares of Green Corp. common stock that she had purchased in March 1988 at a cost of $1,000 for 15 shares of Brown Corp. common stock having a fair market value of $1,200. Lori's recognized gain on this exchange was:

   a. $–0–
   b. $200 ordinary income
   c. $200 short-term capital gain
   d. $200 long-term capital gain

STUDY GUIDE
CHAPTER 7
Corporations: Reorganizations

SOLUTIONS TO CHAPTER 7 QUESTIONS

True or False

1. T (p. 7–5)

    For tax purposes, the term "reorganization" refers to a corporate restructuring under Section 368 in which non-recognition sections of gain or loss generally apply. The underlying rationale for such non-recognition treatment is similar to the rationale underlying the non-recognition provisions of Section 351. Under Section 351, the new property (stock) is substantially a continuation of the old investment (property). Within the context of a reorganization under Section 368, the new enterprise, the new corporate structure, and the new property are substantially continuations of the old. Even though the reorganization falls outside the scope of Section 1031 (dealing with like-kind exchanges), the tax treatment of the parties involved in a reorganization under Section 368 parallel the non-recognition provisions under Section 1031. Under these provisions, when boot is received, gain is recognized to the extent of the lesser of (a) boot received or (b) gain realized. Under Section 1031, boot is non-like-kind property. Within the context of a reorganization under Section 368 (where boot is property other than stock or securities of the acquiring corporation):

    - In general, under Section 361(a), no gain or loss is recognized by a corporation (acquired corporation) who is a *party* to a reorganization and pursuant to a plan of reorganization who transfers property in exchange for stock or securities. However, under Section 361(b), if the acquired corporation receives boot and if such corporation either (1) fails to distribute to shareholders the boot it receives from the acquiring corporation or (2) distributes to shareholders its own property, the acquired corporation may recognize gain.
    - In general, under Section 354(a)(1), a *stockholder* recognizes no gain or loss if stock or securities of a corporation (who is a *party* to the reorganization) are transferred (pursuant to a plan of reorganization) in exchange for stock or securities of such corporation or another corporation (who is a *party* to the reorganization). However, under Section 356(a)(1), if the stockholder receives boot [cash or other property (including securities)], the stockholder recognizes gain only to the extent of the lesser of (a) boot received or (b) gain realized. Further, under Section 356(a)(2), such gain is treated as a dividend to the extent of such stockholder's proportionate share of the corporation's earnings and profits, where the excess of gain over the amount treated as a dividend is capital gain.
    - In general, under Section 354(a)(1), a *security holder* recognizes no gain or loss if stock or securities of a corporation (who is a *party* to the reorganization) are transferred (pursuant to a plan of reorganization) in exchange for stock or securities of such corporation or another corporation (who is a *party* to the reorganization). However, under Section 356(a)(1), if the security holder receives boot (cash or other property), the security holder recognizes gain only to the extent of the lesser of (a) boot received or (b) gain realized. In this case, under Section 356(d), boot includes the aggregate amount of securities principal received in excess of the principal amount of securities given up.

    Thus, in a reorganization under Section 368 that consists solely of stock or securities, given the right combination of stock or securities, securities may be boot, which may result in gain being recognized by either the stockholder or security holder.

2. T (p. 7–5)

    See introductory part of Answer #1.

    In a reorganization under Section 368, when boot is received, gain is recognized to the extent of the lesser of (a) the fair market value of boot (cash and other property) received or (b) gain realized.

3. **F** (p. 7–15; tax free)

   Several types of corporate restructurings that constitute reorganizations under Section 368 can be classified as either acquisitive or divisive reorganizations.

   The Type D reorganization under Section 368(a)(1)(D) can either be divisive or acquisitive. Other acquisitive reorganizations include:

   - The Type A reorganization (statutory merger or consolidation) under Section 368(a)(1)(A).
   - The Type B reorganization (stock for stock acquisition) under Section 368(a)(1)(B).
   - The Type C reorganization (stock for asset acquisition) under Section 368(a)(1)(C).

   Parties to acquisitive reorganizations include acquired corporations, acquiring corporations and shareholders. These acquisitive reorganizations generally produce nontaxable treatment for parties to such reorganizations.

4. **F** (p. 7–13; stock for voting stock)

   Specifically, in a Type B acquisitive reorganization, the acquiring corporation receives stock of the acquired corporation in exchange for solely voting stock, where immediately after the exchange the acquiring corporation has control of the acquired corporation (at least 80% of all classes of stock of the acquired corporation).

5. **T** (p. 7–14; 80% of all classes of stock).

   In a Type B acquisitive reorganization, the acquiring corporation receives stock of the acquired corporation in exchange for solely voting stock, where immediately after the exchange the acquiring corporation has control of the acquired corporation. Under Section 368(c), control is defined as stock possessing at least 80% of the total combined voting power of all classes of stock entitled to vote and at least 80% of the total number of shares of all other classes of stock.

6. **T** (p. 7–18)

   The Type D reorganization under Section 368(a)(1)(D) can either be divisive or acquisitive. The two-step Type D divisive reorganization under Section 368(a)(1)(D) and Section 355 is described as follows.

   - In the first step, assets of the transferor corporation are transferred to one or more transferee corporations, in exchange for stock representing 80% control of each of the transferee corporations.
   - In the second step, stock representing 80% control of each of the transferee corporations is distributed by the transferor corporation to its shareholders as follows:
     - Spin-off. Stock of the transferee corporations is distributed pro rata across all shareholders, where no stock of the transferor is redeemed.
     - Split-off. Stock of the transferee corporations is distributed to shareholders in redemption of part or all of their stock.
     - Split-up. Stock of the transferee corporations is distributed to shareholders in complete liquidation of the transferor corporation.

7. **T** (p. 7–22)

   For tax purposes, the term "reorganization" refers to a corporate restructuring under Section 368 in which non-recognition sections of gain or loss generally apply. The underlying rationale for such non-recognition treatment is similar to the rationale underlying the non-recognition provisions of Section 351. Under Section 351, the new property (stock) is substantially a continuation of the old investment (property). Within the context of a reorganization under Section 368, the new enterprise, the new corporate structure and the new property are substantially continuations of the old. Even though the reorganization falls outside the scope of Section 1031 (dealing with like-kind exchanges), the tax treatment of the parties involved in a reorganization under Section 368 parallel the non-recognition provisions under Section 1031.

   Specifically, under Section 368(a)(1)(E), a Type E reorganization is a recapitalization (i.e., an exchange of stock or securities for stock or securities). This reorganization has tax implications only for shareholders that exchange stock or securities. Further, the income tax effects on the corporation are minimal because the corporation neither transfers nor receives property. Within this context, property does not include stocks and bonds of the issuing corporation.

8. T (p. 7–23)

Under Section 368(a)(1)(F), a Type F reorganization is a mere change in identity (i.e., a change in identity, form, or place of organization). Within the context of a Type F reorganization, there is only one operating corporation, where the successor and predecessor corporations are the same corporation. Under Rev. Rul. 57-276, if a reorganization simultaneously satisfies the requirements under (a) Section 368(a)(1)(F) and (b) either Section 368(a)(1)(A), Section 368(a)(1)(C), or Section 368(a)(1)(D), the reorganization is treated as a Type F reorganization.

9. F (p. 7–18; original corporation is liquidated).

Several types of corporate restructurings that constitute reorganizations under Section 368 can be classified as either acquisitive or divisive reorganizations.

The Type D reorganization under Section 368(a)(1)(D) can either be divisive or acquisitive. The two-step Type D divisive reorganization under Section 368(a)(1)(D) and Section 355 is described as follows.

- In the first step, assets of the transferor corporation are transferred to one or more transferee corporations, in exchange for stock representing 80% control of each of the transferee corporations.
- In the second step, stock representing 80% control of each of the transferee corporations is distributed by the transferor corporation to its shareholders as follows:
  - Spin-off. Stock of the transferee corporations is distributed pro rata across all shareholders, where no stock of the transferor is redeemed.
  - Split-off. Stock of the transferee corporations is distributed to shareholders in redemption of part or all of their stock.
  - Split-up. Stock of the transferee corporations is distributed to shareholders in complete liquidation of the transferor corporation.

10. F (p. 7–13; would be considered 'boot').

In a Type B acquisitive reorganization, the acquiring corporation receives stock of the acquired corporation in exchange solely for voting stock, where immediately after the exchange the acquiring corporation has control of the acquired corporation. Under Section 368(c), control is defined as stock possessing at least 80% of the total combined voting power of all classes of stock entitled to vote and at least 80% of the total number of shares of all other classes of stock. Moreover, the "solely for voting stock" requirement is strictly construed.

In the instant case, voting stock must be the sole consideration given by the acquiring corporation. Since the "solely for voting stock" requirement is strictly construed, the acquiring corporation's assumption of an acquired corporation liability violates the "solely for voting stock" requirement of a Type B reorganization.

Fill in the Blanks

1. owner shift, equity structure shift (p. 7–29)

For tax purposes, the term "reorganization" refers to a corporate restructuring under Section 368 in which non-recognition sections of gain or loss generally apply. The underlying rationale for such non-recognition treatment is similar to the rationale underlying the non-recognition provisions of Section 351. Under Section 351, the new property (stock) is substantially a continuation of the old investment (property). Within the context of a reorganization under Section 368, the new enterprise, the new corporate structure and the new property are substantially continuations of the old. Even though the reorganization falls outside the scope of Section 1031 (dealing with like-kind exchanges), the tax treatment of the parties involved in a reorganization under Section 368 parallel the non-recognition provisions under Section 1031.

Another issue that arises within the context of a reorganization is the carryover of corporate tax attributes [e.g., net operating losses (NOL)] from the acquired/transferor corporation. Under Section 382, the extent an NOL of an acquired/transferor corporation can be utilized by a successor corporation in a reorganization under Section 368 is limited if there is an ownership change. Under Section 382(g), there is an ownership change if the combined effects of (a) owner shifts with respect to 5-percent shareholders and (b) an equity structure shift result in more than a 50% change in the ownership of the acquired/transferor corporation. Section 382 effectively limits the annual tax benefit arising from the successor corporation recognizing an NOL generated by the acquired/transferor corporation. Section 382 does not disallow any portion of this NOL.

2. 50% (p. 7–29)

Under Section 382(g), there is an ownership change if the combined effects of (a) owner shifts with respect to 5-percent shareholders and (b) an equity structure shift result in more than a 50% change in the ownership of the acquired/transferor corporation. Section 382 effectively limits the annual tax benefit arising from the successor corporation recognizing an NOL generated by the acquired/transferor corporation. Section 382 does not disallow any portion of this NOL.

3. the date of transfer (p. 7–29)

One of the issues that arises within the context of a reorganization is the carryover of corporate tax attributes [e.g., accumulated earnings and profits (AE & P)] from the transferor/distributing corporation to a successor corporation. Under Section 381(c)(2), the AE & P of a transferor/distributing corporation is carried over to the successor corporation as of the date of the transfer/distribution. However, a deficit in AE & P of a transferor/distributing corporation may only offset positive E &P of the successor corporation accumulated after the transfer/distribution date.

4. written plan, reorganization (p. 7–4)

For tax purposes, the term "reorganization" refers to a corporate restructuring under Section 368 in which non-recognition sections of gain or loss generally apply. Under Treas. Reg. Sec. 1.368–3(a)(1), a party to a reorganization must file with the tax return for the year within which the reorganization occurs:

- A copy of the plan of reorganization.
- A statement setting forth:
  - The purposes of the plan.
  - The transactions incident to, or pursuant to, the consummation of the plan.

However, when a party to a reorganization has not complied with this treasury regulation, the IRS has argued (although unsuccessfully) that non-compliance with such regulation causes such party not to be availed of the tax treatment of parties involved in a tax-free reorganization under Section 368.

5. state law (p. 7–10)

A Type A acquisitive reorganization under Section 368 is described either as a statutory merger or consolidation. In a statutory merger, the acquired corporation ceases to exist by operation of law, whereas the acquiring corporation survives. The terms "statutory" and "by operation of law" refer to state law. Thus, in a Type A reorganization, parties to such reorganization must necessarily comply with the requirements of state law regarding mergers or consolidations. If these requirements are not met, the reorganization is not a Type A under Section 368.

One of the disadvantages of the Type A statutory merger is the statutorily mandated assumption of acquired corporation's liabilities (unknown and contingent) by the acquiring corporation. The acquiring corporation can mitigate this risk of loss by using the triangular form of the Type A reorganization under Section 368(a)(2)(D). However, the triangular form of the Type A reorganization under Section 368(a)(2)(D) can never be used unless allowable under state law.

Multiple Choice

1. **b** (Figure 7–3; stock for stock acquisition)

   Specifically, in a Type B acquisitive reorganization, the acquiring corporation receives stock of the acquired corporation in exchange solely for voting stock of the acquiring corporation, where immediately after the exchange the acquiring corporation has control of the acquired corporation. Under Section 368(c), control is defined as stock possessing at least 80% of the total combined voting power of all classes of stock entitled to vote and at least 80% of the total number of shares of all other classes of stock. Moreover, the "solely for voting stock" requirement is strictly construed. Thus, no boot may be given in exchange for acquired corporation stock. However, under Section 368(a)(2)(C), in a triangular form of the Type B reorganization the acquiring corporation may give up voting stock of its parent.

   In the instant case, item b is the correct answer, since in exchange for stock possessing control of Yellow, Green issues voting stock of Blue, Green's parent. Thus, the reorganization constitutes the triangular form of the Type B reorganization (stock for stock acquisition) under Section 368(a)(1)(B). Further, items a, c, d and e are incorrect because they each are inconsistent with item b.

2. **b** (p. 7–32; positive E & P of acquired, $150,000 cannot offset deficit of successor)

   One issue that arises within the context of a reorganization under 368 is the carryover of corporate tax attributes [e.g., accumulated earnings and profits (AE&P)] from the transferor/distributing corporation to a successor corporation. Under Section 381(c)(2), the AE&P of a transferor/distributing corporation is carried over to the successor corporation as of the date of the transfer/distribution.

   In the instant case, Jots merges into Tons and ceases to exist. On the date the assets of Jots are effectively transferred to Tons, the AE&P of Jots and Tons combine to equal $110,000 ($150,000 – $40,000). Thus, item b is correct since a post-merger distribution of $75,000 by Tons to its shareholders is a Section 301 distribution, which is treated as ordinary dividend income to the shareholders (to the extent of Tons AE&P of $110,000). Further, items a, c, d and e are incorrect because they each are inconsistent with item b.

3. **d** (p. 7–23; mere change in identity)

   A Type F reorganization is a mere change in identity (i.e., a change in identity, form, or place of organization). Within the context of a Type F reorganization, there is only one operating corporation, where the successor and predecessor corporations are the same corporation. Under Rev. Rul. 57-276, if a reorganization simultaneously satisfies the requirements under (a) Section 368(a)(1)(F) and (b) either Section 368(a)(1)(A), Section 368(a)(1)(C), or Section 368(a)(1)(D), the reorganization is treated as a Type F.

   In the instant case, the reorganization constitutes a two-step Type D divisive reorganization under Section 368(a)(1)(D) and Section 355. In the first step, Taos transfers all of its assets to Chilton in exchange for stock representing control of Chilton. In the second step, Stock of Chilton is distributed to Taos shareholders in complete liquidation of Taos. In addition, the reorganization constitutes a Type F reorganization as a mere change in identity (a change in identity and place of organization). Thus, the reorganization is treated as a Type F, since such reorganization simultaneously satisfies the requirements under (a) Section 368(a)(1)(F) and (b) Section 368(a)(1)(D) and item d is correct. Items a, b, c and e are incorrect because they each are inconsistent with item d.

4. **a** (p. 7–4; may constitute but one step in a reorganization)

   A mere stock redemption is not a reorganization, although it does constitute one step in a split-off or split-up within the context of a Type D reorganization. Thus, item a is correct. Items b, c and d are incorrect because they each constitute a reorganization under Section 368.

5. **b** (p. 7–25; statutory merger with Thomas cashed out)

   The following narrative relates to both Question #5 and Question #6.

For tax purposes, the term "reorganization" refers to a corporate restructuring under Section 368 in which non-recognition sections of gain or loss generally apply. The underlying rationale for such non-recognition treatment is similar to the rationale underlying the non-recognition provisions of Section 351. Under Section 351, the new property (stock) is substantially a continuation of the old investment (property). Within the context of a reorganization under Section 368, the new enterprise, the new corporate structure, and the new property are substantially continuations of the old. Even though the reorganization falls outside the scope of Section 1031 (dealing with like-kind exchanges), the tax treatment of the parties involved in a reorganization under Section 368 parallel the non-recognition provisions under Section 1031. Under these provisions, when boot is received, gain is recognized to the extent of the lesser of (a) boot received or (b) gain realized.

Several types of corporate restructurings that constitute reorganizations under Section 368 can be classified as either acquisitive or divisive reorganizations.

The Type D reorganization under Section 368(a)(1)(D) can either be divisive or acquisitive. Other acquisitive reorganizations include:

- The Type A reorganization (statutory merger or consolidation) under Section 368(a)(1)(A).
- The Type B reorganization (stock for stock acquisition) under Section 368(a)(1)(B).
- The Type C reorganization (stock for asset acquisition) under Section 368(a)(1)(C).

Parties to acquisitive reorganizations include acquired corporations, acquiring corporations and shareholders. These reorganizations generally produce nontaxable treatment for such parties to an acquisitive reorganization. However, for parties to avail themselves of such nontaxable treatment, the reorganization must not only satisfy certain requirements under Section 368 but also must not violate certain doctrines enumerated under the common law.

For example, within the context of a Type A reorganization (statutory merger) under Section 368(a)(1)(A), such reorganization must also not violate the common law's continuity of interest test. The purpose of this reorganization common law requirement is to ensure that the new enterprise, the new corporate structure and the new property are substantially continuations of the old. Under Rev. Proc. 74-26, the IRS deems this test met if shareholders in the aggregate receive acquiring corporation stock that has a fair market value that is at least equal to 50% of the value of the acquired corporation stock given up.

With regard to Question #5, the reorganization constitutes a Type A reorganization (statutory merger) under Section 368(a)(1)(A). In addition, the continuity of interest test is met since Thomas and Bond in the aggregate receive Gunnison stock that is at least equal to 50% of the value of the TomBoy stock given up. Thus, item b is correct. Bond receives nontaxable treatment. Thomas, however, is taxed since Thomas was cashed out of his interest in TomBoy.

6. c (p. 7–25; Thomas and Bond receive in the aggregate at least 50%)

With regard to Question #6, the reorganization constitutes a Type A reorganization (statutory merger) under Section 368(a)(1)(A). In addition, the continuity of interest test is met since Thomas and Bond in the aggregate receive Gunnison stock that has a fair market value that is at least equal to 50% of the value of the TomBoy stock given up. Thus, item c is correct.

7. d (p. 7–29)

An issue that arises within the context of a reorganization is the carryover of corporate tax attributes [e.g., a net operating losses (NOL)] from the acquired/transferor corporation to a successor corporation. Under Section 382, if there is an ownership change, the extent an NOL of an acquired/transferor corporation can be utilized by a successor corporation is limited. Under Section 382(g), there is an ownership change if the combined effects of (a) owner shifts with respect to 5-percent shareholders and (b) an equity structure shift result in more than a 50% change in the ownership of the acquired/transferor corporation. Section

382 effectively limits the annual tax benefit arising from the successor corporation recognizing an NOL generated by the acquired/transferor corporation. Section 382 does not disallow any portion of this NOL. Thus, item d is correct.

8. a (p. 7–24; tax avoidance scheme)

The statutory merger of Dutch into Carter is assumed to meet the statutory requirements of a Type A reorganization (statutory merger) under Section 368(a)(1)(A). However, the assumed sole purpose of such merger is the avoidance of federal income tax. Thus, the sound business purpose test is not satisfied and accordingly, the reorganization does not constitute a Type A reorganization under Section 368. Thus, item a is correct. Since Dutch's corporate tax attributes do not carry over for use by Carter, Carter will not be able to use Dutch's NOL as a tax write-off.

9. a (p. 7–28; sound business purpose test satisfied, corporate tax attributes carryover)

Since the sound business purpose test is assumed satisfied, the statutory merger of Dutch into Carter does constitutes a Type A reorganization under Section 368(a)(1)(A). As a result, Dutch's corporate tax attributes do carry over for use by Carter. Thus, Carter is able to use Dutch's NOL as a tax write-off. Specifically, the amount of Dutch's NOL that can be used by Carter in the tax year of the reorganization is subject to a ceiling limitation. Such limitation equals $16,530 [(121/365) × $200,000] and is calculated by applying a percentage (121/365) against the taxable income of Carter ($200,000). Such percentage is calculated by dividing the total number of days in the taxable year (365) by the total number of days in the taxable year remaining after the effective date of asset transfer (121). Hence, item a is correct. Given the change in the facts (an exhibition of a sound business purpose for the reorganization), the answer in Question #9 is different from Question #8.

10. a (Figure 7–6; stock of New is distributed pro rata without redemption)

Under Section 368(a)(1)(D) and Section 355, the two-step Type D divisive reorganization is described as follows.

- In the first step, assets of the transferor corporation are transferred to one or more transferee corporations, in exchange for stock representing 80% control of each of the transferee corporations.
- In the second step, stock representing 80% control of each of the transferee corporations is distributed by the transferor corporation to its shareholders as follows:
  - Spin-off. Stock of the transferee corporations is distributed pro rata across all shareholders, where no stock of the transferor is redeemed.
  - Split-off. Stock of the transferee corporations is distributed to shareholders in redemption of part or all of their stock.
  - Split-up. Stock of the transferee corporations is distributed to shareholders in complete liquidation of the transferor corporation.

In the instant case, the assets of Tums are transferred to new corporation, in exchange for stock representing 80% control of new corporation. Then, the stock of the new corporation is distributed pro rata across all shareholders of Tums, where no stock of Tums is redeemed. Thus, item a is correct. The reorganization is a divisive Type D (Spin-off) under Section 368(a)(1)(D).

11. d (p. 7–7; no consideration other than stock was received)

In a Type B acquisitive reorganization, the acquiring corporation receives stock of the acquired corporation in exchange solely for voting stock, where immediately after the exchange the acquiring corporation has control of the acquired corporation. Under Section 368(c), control is defined as stock possessing at least 80% of the total combined voting power of all classes of stock entitled to vote and at least 80% of the total number of shares of all other classes of stock.

In the instant case, Mike's realized gain is $2,750 [Mike's amount realized of $21,500 (the fair market value of the 900 shares of Wire stock) less Mike's adjusted basis of $18,750 in the 5,000 shares of Cable stock]. However, since the reorganization is assumed to be a Type B reorganization (stock for stock acquisition) under Section 368(a)(1)(B), Mike's realized gain is recognized to the extent of the lesser of (a) boot received of zero or (b) gain realized of $2,750. Thus, item d is correct.

12. a   (p. 7–4; general requirement)

For tax purposes, the term "reorganization" refers to a corporate restructuring under Section 368 in which non-recognition sections of gain or loss generally apply. The underlying rationale for such non-recognition treatment is similar to the rationale underlying the non-recognition provisions of Section 351. Under Section 351, the new property (stock) is substantially a continuation of the old investment (property). Within the context of a reorganization under Section 368, the new enterprise, the new corporate structure and the new property are substantially continuations of the old. Even though the reorganization falls outside the scope of Section 1031 (dealing with like-kind exchanges), the tax treatment of the parties involved in a reorganization under Section 368 parallel the non-recognition provisions under Section 1031. Under these provisions, when boot is received, gain is recognized to the extent of the lesser of (a) boot received or (b) gain realized.

Under Treas. Reg. Sec. 1.368–3(a)(1), a party to a reorganization must file with the tax return for the year within which the reorganization occurs:

- A copy of the plan of reorganization.
- A statement setting forth:
  - The purposes of the plan.
  - The transactions incident to, or pursuant to, the consummation of the plan.

However, when a party to a reorganization has not complied with such regulation, the IRS has argued (although unsuccessfully) that non-compliance with this treasury regulation causes such party not to be availed of the tax treatment of parties involved in a tax-free reorganization under Section 368. Given the occasional antagonistic position of the IRS, in situations where the economic implications are significant, parties contemplating a reorganization should obtain a favorable letter ruling concerning the tax treatment of the proposed reorganization. Such ruling commits the IRS to a position with regard to the tax treatment of the proposed reorganization, as long as the parties accomplish the reorganization as set forth in the ruling.

Specifically, under Section 368(a)(1)(F), a Type F reorganization is a mere change in identity (i.e., a change in identity, form, or place of organization). In the instant case, item a is correct because a plan of reorganization is requisite for a finding of a reorganization under Section 368. Items b, c and d are incorrect because each item is true.

13. a   (p. 7–7; no consideration other than stock was received)

Lori's realized gain is $200 [Lori's amount realized of $1,200 (the fair market value of the 15 shares of Brown stock) less Lori's adjusted basis of $1,000 in the 10 shares of Green stock]. However, since the reorganization is assumed to be a Type B reorganization (stock for stock acquisition) under Section 368(a)(1)(B), Lori's realized gain is recognized to the extent of the lesser of (a) boot received of zero or (b) gain realized of $200. Thus, item a is correct. Items b, c and d are incorrect because they each are inconsistent with item a.

CHAPTER 8

Consolidated Tax Returns

LEARNING OBJECTIVES

After completing Chapter 8, you should be able to:

1. Apply the fundamental concepts of consolidated tax returns.
2. Identify the sources of the rules for consolidated taxable income.
3. Recognize the major advantages and disadvantages of filing consolidated tax returns.
4. Describe the corporations that are eligible to file on a consolidated basis.
5. Explain the compliance aspects of consolidated income tax returns.
6. Compute a parent's investment basis in a subsidiary.
7. Account for intercompany transactions of a consolidated group.
8. Identify limitations that restrict the use of losses and credits of group members that are derived in separate return years.
9. Derive deductions and credits on a consolidated basis.
10. Demonstrate tax planning opportunities available to consolidated groups.

KEY TERMS

Affiliated group
Consolidated return
Excess loss account
Restoration event
Separate return limitation year (SRLY)

OUTLINE

I. **CONTEXT OF THE CONSOLIDATED RETURN RULES**
   A. Motivations to Consolidate
      1. A desire to isolate assets of other group members from the liabilities of specific operating divisions.
      2. A need to carry out specific estate planning objectives.
      3. A wish to isolate the group's exposure to losses and liabilities incurred in joint ventures with "outside" entities.
      4. A perception that separate divisions/group members will be worth more on the market if they maintain unique identities.
   B. Source and Philosophy of Consolidated Return Rules
      1. Initially, the consolidated return rules were an effort by the IRS to limit tax benefits available to multiple corporations.
      2. Today, the underlying purpose of the consolidated return rules is one of organizational neutrality.
      3. A group of closely related corporations should have neither a tax advantage nor a disadvantage compared to taxpayers who file separate corporate returns.

II. **ASSESSING CONSOLIDATED RETURN STATUS**
   A. Potential Advantages
      1. Operating and capital loss carryovers of one group member may be used to shelter income of other group members.
      2. Taxation of intercompany dividends may be eliminated.
      3. Deferral of gain recognition on some intercompany transactions.
      4. Optimization of certain deductions and credits by using consolidated amounts to compute pertinent limitations.
      5. The tax basis of investments in the stock of subsidiaries increases as the members contribute to consolidated taxable income.
   B. Potential Disadvantages
      1. The consolidated return election is binding on all subsequent years until an eligible group no longer exists or the IRS consents to revocation of the election.
      2. Capital and operating loss carryover to separate return year(s) may provide a greater tax benefit than applying the loss to consolidated income.
      3. Deferral of loss recognition on some intercompany transactions.
      4. Return elections made by the parent are binding on all members of the filing group for that year.
      5. The tax basis of investments in the stock of subsidiaries decreases when the members generate operating losses and by distributions from members' E & P.
      6. All group members must use the parent's tax year. This may create short tax years for the subsidiaries and cause income bunching.
      7. Incurring additional administrative costs to comply with consolidated return regulations.

III. **ELECTING CONSOLIDATED RETURN STATUS**
   A. All members of a corporate group must meet three requirements.
      1. The stock ownership criteria of an affiliated group must be satisfied.
         a. The identifiable parent must own 80% of the voting power and 80% of the value of each subsidiary.
         b. This ownership test must be satisfied on every day of the tax year.

2. Each member must be statutorily eligible to make the consolidated election.
   a. Noncorporate entities such as partnerships, trusts and estates are ineligible.
   b. Foreign corporations, tax-exempt charitable corporations and insurance companies may be statutorily ineligible.
3. Each member must satisfy the compliance requirements in making and maintaining the election.
   a. The Initial Consolidated Return. The first Form 1120 must include the taxable results of all consolidated group members.
      1. In addition, a consolidated return election must be made on Form 1122 (for each subsidiary) and attached to the Form 1120.
      2. The election must be made no later than the extended due date of the parent's return for the year.
   b. Subsequent Consolidated Returns. Subsequent consolidated returns must include Form 851, Affiliations Schedule.
      1. Form 851 identifies members of the consolidated group.
      2. The group continues to file consolidated returns until an eligible group no longer exists or the parent applies for and is granted permission to terminate the consolidated election.
B. Liability for consolidated taxes is born by the members, jointly and severally.
   1. Consolidated tax liability is allocated in proportion to each group member's contribution to consolidated taxable income unless an election to use some other allocation method is made.
C. Tax Accounting Periods and Methods
   1. All consolidated group members must use the parent's tax year.
   2. Consolidated group members may use different tax accounting methods. However, a cash-basis member may need to change to accrual basis reporting because the $5 million gross receipts test is applied on a consolidated basis.

IV. STOCK BASIS OF SUBSIDIARY
A. Upon acquiring a subsidiary, the parent's basis is the acquisition price. At each consolidated year-end, stock basis adjustments are required to prevent overlapping recognition of gains and losses.
   1. Positive adjustments include:
      a. an allocable share of consolidated taxable income for the year.
      b. an allocable share of consolidated operating or capital losses of a subsidiary that could not be used through a carryback.
   2. Negative adjustments include:
      a. an allocable share of consolidated taxable loss for the year.
      b. an allocable share of any carryover operating or capital losses that are deducted on the consolidated return and have not previously reduced stock basis.
      c. dividends paid by the subsidiary to the parent out of E & P.
B. An "excess loss account" is created when accumulated post-acquisition taxable losses of the subsidiary exceed the acquisition price.
   1. The losses of the subsidiary are recognized in the current year's consolidated return.
   2. The stock basis account is not negative.
   3. If the subsidiary stock is redeemed or sold to a nongroup member, this account represents capital gain on disposition.
C. In a chain of subsidiaries, computation of stock basis amounts starts with the lowest-level subsidiary and proceeds up the ownership structure to the parent's holdings.

V. COMPUTING CONSOLIDATED TAXABLE INCOME
A. Computational Procedure
   1. Each group member first computes its taxable income as though such member is a separate entity.
   2. Each member's taxable income is then split to eliminate some intercompany items, to remove certain transactions which must be accounted for as a group and to isolate certain transactions which receive deferral/restoration treatment.

3. Consolidated taxable income is a combination of the revised separate taxable incomes and the resulting income/loss from group items and deferral/restoration events.
B. Typical Intercompany Transactions
1. Transactions which generate income to one member and a deductible expense to another member are left in consolidated income as direct offsets.
2. Adjustments may be required if all members do not use the same accounting method.
3. Dividends received from other group members are removed from separate taxable incomes, these dividends are not considered in the computation of a dividends received deduction.
C. Members' Net Operating Losses
1. The usual coporate NOL computations are available for the losses of the consolidated group (2 year carryback; 20 year carryforward).
2. Where members of a consolidated group change over time, the taxpayer must apportion the consolidated NOL among the group members.
3. Special "separate return limitation year" rules apply when an NOL is carried forward from a separate return year to a consolidated return year.
D. Computation of Group Items
1. A number of income and deduction items are derived on a consolidated-group basis. Therefore, statutory limitations and allowances are applied to the group as though it were a single corporation. Group items include:
   a. net capital gain/loss.
   b. § 1231 gain/loss.
   c. casualty/theft gain/loss.
   d. charitable contributions.
   e. dividends received deduction.
   f. net operating loss.
   g. the general business and research credits.
   h. any recapture of those credits.
   i. the foreign tax credit.
   j. the percentage depletion deduction.
   k. alternative minimum tax elements.
2. The statutory limitations of group items are applied to consolidated taxable income after adjusting for intercompany transactions.
E. Deferral and Restoration Events
1. Deferral/restoration treatment applies to sales of assets or the performance of services among group members.
2. Gain or loss is deferred until a "restoration event" occurs (e.g., the asset is sold to a party outside the group).
3. Under the "acceleration rule," the entire deferred gain or loss is restored to consolidated income when the transferor leaves the group or the consolidation election is terminated.
4. An election may be made to include or deduct all intercompany gain or loss immediately; this election remains in effect until IRS permission for revocation is received.

VI. TAX PLANNING CONSIDERATIONS
A. Taxpayers should optimize their overall tax benefits when choosing consolidated partners. Attributes of potential target corporations might include some of the following:
1. Loss and credit carryovers.
2. Passive activity income, loss, or credits.
3. Gains that can be deferred through intercompany sales.
4. Contributions to consolidated ACE adjustments.
5. Excess limitation amounts.
6. Section 1231 gains, losses, and look-back profiles.
B. The 100% dividends received deduction is an alternative to filing consolidated returns.

STUDY GUIDE
CHAPTER 8
Consolidated Tax Returns

8–5

TEST FOR SELF-EVALUATION—CHAPTER 8

True or False

Indicate which of the following statements is true or false by circling the correct answer.

T F 1. The Code describes the various elements of consolidated tax return rules.

T F 2. All members of the consolidated group must have the same tax year.

T F 3. All members of the consolidated group must use the same accounting method.

T F 4. Financial accounting consolidated income is the same as tax-basis consolidated income.

T F 5. The most commonly encountered intercompany transactions are removed from member's separate taxable incomes for consolidated tax purposes.

T F 6. Members of an affiliated group must file consolidated income tax returns.

T F 7. Only the parent corporation is responsible for consolidated tax liabilities.

Fill in the Blanks

Complete the following statements with the appropriate word(s) or amount(s).

1. The general function of the consolidated return rules is _____.

2. Controlled groups of corporations include _____ and _____ groups.

3. An _____ group requires an identifiable parent having control of _____% of the voting stock or _____% of the value of the subsidiary.

4. The three basic requirements for consolidated return rules are: _____, _____, _____.

5. To qualify as a parent-subsidiary controlled group, the parent must own _____% of the voting stock or _____% of the value of the subsidiary.

6. Upon acquiring a subsidiary, the parent corporation records a stock basis on its tax balance sheet equal to _____.

7. Adjustments to the parent's stock basis in the subsidiary are made on _____ of the consolidated return year, or _____.

8. An _____ is created when accumulated deficits in the subsidiary's post-acquisition E & P exceed the acquisition price.

Multiple Choice

Choose the best answer for each of the following questions.

_____ 1. Sub sold a building to Parent for $400,000. Sub had originally paid $300,000 for the building and had accumulated depreciation of $100,000. Parent, after six years, sold the building to an unrelated third party for $500,000. Sub's realized gain on the sale to parent was:

   a. $100,000
   b. $200,000
   c. $300,000
   d. $400,000

_____ 2. Sub's recognized gain on the sale to parent was:

   a. $–0–
   b. $100,000
   c. $200,000
   d. $300,000

_____ 3. Parent's realized gain on the sale to the third party was:

   a. $–0–
   b. $100,000
   c. $100,000 plus accumulated depreciation
   d. $100,000 minus accumulated depreciation

_____ 4. Parent Corporation acquired 100% of the stock of Sub Corporation on July 5. Both corporations intend to file a consolidated return immediately upon acquisition. Parent's tax year ends March 31; Sub's tax year ends July 30. The first consolidated return is due:

   a. October 15
   b. September 15
   c. June 15
   d. March 15

_____ 5. A parent corporation's adjustments to its stock basis in a consolidated subsidiary includes:

   a. an allocable share of the subsidiary's E & P
   b. dividends paid by the subsidiary
   c. both a and b
   d. neither a nor b

_____ 6. In the current year Parent Corporation provided services to its 100% owned subsidiary valued at $75,000. Sub will pay Parent next year. Sub uses the cash method of accounting, Parent uses the accrual method. Is any adjustment required in computing consolidated taxable income?

   a. No
   b. Yes

_____ 7. The filing of consolidated tax returns is available only to:

   a. parent-subsidiary controlled groups
   b. brother-sister controlled groups
   c. affiliated groups
   d. all of the above

_____ 8. With regard to a controlled corporate group, all of the following statements are correct except: (IRS 94 3B-26)

    a. The controlled group is allowed only ONE set of graduated income tax brackets.
    b. Controlled groups are allowed ONE $80,000 exemption amount for alternative minimum tax purposes.
    c. The controlled group is allowed ONE $250,000 accumulated earnings credit.
    d. The tax benefits of the graduated rate schedule are to be allocated equally among the members of the group unless they all consent to a different apportionment.

SOLUTIONS TO CHAPTER 8 QUESTIONS

True or False

1. F (p. 8-5; most are found in the Regulations under Section 1502)

    The computational and compliance rules for filing a consolidated income tax return (consolidated tax return rules) are promulgated under the authority of Section 1502. Section 1502 mandates that Treasury prescribe regulations (under Section 1502) to determine the manner in which the tax (associated with a consolidated income tax return) is determined, computed, assessed collected, and adjusted. In formulating these regulations, Treasury has been guided by the principle of organizational neutrality. That is, an affiliated group of corporations that files a consolidated income tax return should have neither benefited nor suffered merely by reason of filing a consolidated income tax return. Treasury Regulations under Section 1502:

    - Are categorized as legislative regulations because of Congress' specific delegation of authority to Treasury to write such regulations.
    - Are highly complex.
    - Allow a certain type of corporate group to be treated as a single entity for tax purposes, thereby permitting:
        - The sheltering of the taxable income of some members with the taxable losses of other members.
        - The application of tax exemptions and brackets in the most optimal manner.

2. T (p. 8-15)

    Under Section 1501, only affiliated groups can file consolidated income tax returns. Under Section 1504, an affiliated group of corporations includes one or more chains of includible (not ineligible) corporations connected through a common parent if:

    (a) The parent DIRECTLY owns stock of at least one corporation in each chain where such stock ownership possesses 80% of the voting power AND stock value of such corporation and
    (b) At least 80% of the voting power AND stock value of each member of a chain (other than the parent) is owned DIRECTLY by other members of the affiliated group.

    Under Treas. Reg. Sec. 1.1502-76, an affiliated group of corporations files a consolidated income tax return based on the parent's tax year. Thus, each member of an affiliated group filing a consolidated income tax return must use the parent's tax year as its tax year.

3. F (p. 8-16; generally, can use tax accounting method in place prior to consolidation)

    Under Section 1501, only affiliated groups can file consolidated income tax returns. Under Section 1504, an affiliated group of corporations includes one or more chains of includible (not ineligible) corporations connected through a common parent if:

    (a) The parent DIRECTLY owns stock of at least one corporation in each chain where such stock ownership possesses 80% of the voting power AND stock value of such corporation and
    (b) At least 80% of the voting power AND stock value of each member of a chain (other than the parent) is owned DIRECTLY by other members of the affiliated group.

    Under Treas. Reg. Sec. 1.1502-76, an affiliated group of corporations files a consolidated income tax return based on the parent's tax year. Thus, each member of an affiliated group filing a consolidated income tax return must use the parent's tax year as its tax year. However, in reporting items of income, deduction, gain and loss, different accounting methods can be used across members of an affiliated group filing a consolidated income tax return. But for purposes of determining whether such member of an affiliated group can use the cash method under the $5 million gross-receipts test, gross receipts is calculated on a consolidated basis. This rule implies that a member of an affiliated group filing with a consolidated group for the first time may have to change its method of accounting from cash to accrual if it no longer meets the $5 million gross-receipts test.

4. F   (p. 8–6; income measures correspond only slightly)

Financial accounting consolidated net income and consolidated taxable income are different statistics, where the derivation of each statistic is based upon a different set of rules that have different objectives. Financial accounting consolidated net income is based on Generally Accepted Accounting Principles (GAAP) whose main objective is the fair presentation of accounting information. In contrast, consolidated taxable income is based on the tax law (including promulgated Treasury Regulations under Section 1502) whose primary objective is revenue collection.

5. F   (p. 8–19; generally, remain and cancel each other on consolidated basis)

An affiliated group of corporations filing a consolidated income tax return calculates consolidated taxable income by applying the following four-step approach.

(a) First, the taxable income of each member of such affiliated group is calculated.
(b) Second, each taxable income calculation is adjusted by eliminating the effects of group and intercompany items.
(c) Third, group and intercompany items are treated in a manner consistent with the computational rules under Section 1502.
(d) Fourth, the adjusted taxable income of each member of the affiliated group is cumulated along with the cumulative effect of post-treated group and intercompany items.

Through this process, Treasury intends:

- To separately group certain items of income, deduction, gain and loss (e.g., charitable contribution deduction, short-term capital gains/losses, long-term capital gains/losses, and Section 1231 gains/losses) that are required to be reported on a consolidated basis.
- To eliminate the effects of certain intercompany transactions so that the affiliated group filing a consolidated income tax return is treated as a single entity for tax purposes. However, the most commonly encountered type of intercompany transaction (income from providing services to another member of the affiliated group) is NOT eliminated from the taxable income of each member of an affiliated group filing a consolidated income tax return. In this case, Treasury found no need for elimination, since the net effect on consolidated taxable income is equal to zero (gross income from services provided less an ordinary and necessary business deduction for the same amount). Further, elimination of all intercompany items may cause the disallowance rules under Section 267 for losses/deductions arising from transactions between related parties to become ineffective.

6. F   (p. 8–9; may file separately and claim 100% dividend received deduction)

In general, a corporation is a single taxpaying entity. Section 11(a) imposes a tax on the taxable income of a corporation. However, every corporation is not treated as separate entity for tax purposes. By employing a substance over form argument to mitigate the advantages of multiple incorporation, related corporations are treated differently in cases where one business enterprise is artificially divided into more than one related corporate enterprise. In particular, members of a controlled group of corporations (as defined under Section 1563) must share certain tax benefits, as if such group constitutes a single taxpaying entity. Under Section 1563, types of a controlled group include a parent-subsidiary controlled group and a brother-sister controlled group.

Under Section 1501, only affiliated groups can file consolidated income tax returns. An affiliated group (defined under Section 1504) is necessarily a controlled group. In particular, an affiliated group is necessarily a parent-subsidiary controlled group. However, not all parent-subsidiary controlled groups are affiliated groups, which means that not all parent-subsidiary controlled groups can file consolidated returns.

Members of an affiliated group can file tax returns in one of two ways. All members must file either:

(a) Separate tax returns (where a 100% dividend received deduction is allowable for intra-member Section 301 distributions) or
(b) One consolidated return (where Section 301 distributions between members are eliminated).

If members of an affiliated group file separate tax returns, each member is a member of a parent-subsidiary controlled group. As a result, each member must share certain tax benefits with other members.

7. F (p. 8–13; members are jointly and severally liable)

Similar to individual taxpayer liability within the context of filing a joint return, each member of an affiliated group filing a consolidated income tax return is joint and severally liable for the consolidated return tax liability.

Fill in the Blanks

1. organizational neutrality (p. 8–5).

The computational and compliance rules for filing a consolidated income tax return (consolidated tax return rules) are promulgated under the authority of Section 1502. Section 1502 mandates that Treasury prescribe regulations (under Section 1502) to determine the manner in which the tax (associated with a consolidated income tax return) is determined, computed, assessed collected, and adjusted. In formulating these regulations, Treasury has been guided by the principle of organizational neutrality. That is, an affiliated group of corporations that files a consolidated income tax return should have neither benefited nor suffered merely by reason of filing a consolidated income tax return.

2. parent-subsidiary, brother-sister (p. 8–9).

Under Section 1563, types of a controlled group include a parent-subsidiary controlled group and a brother-sister controlled group. A brother-sister controlled group is defined as 2 or more corporations if (ON DECEMBER 31) 5 or fewer persons (individuals, estates, trusts) own (DIRECTLY and CONSTRUCTIVELY) of each corporation in the aggregate stock possessing:

(a) At least 80% of the voting power OR stock value of such corporation and
(b) More than 50% of the voting power OR stock value where, for purposes of determining such aggregate voting power OR stock value, each person's stock ownership interest (in terms of voting power OR stock value) is not greater than the smallest respective ownership interest of any of the members of the brother-sister controlled group.

A parent-subsidiary controlled group is defined as one or more chains of corporations connected through a common parent if (ON DECEMBER 31):

(a) The parent owns (DIRECTLY and CONSTRUCTIVELY) stock of at least one corporation in each chain possessing 80% of the voting power OR stock value of such corporation and
(b) At least 80% of the voting power OR stock value of each member of the chain (other than the parent) is owned (DIRECTLY and CONSTRUCTIVELY) by other members of the parent-subsidiary controlled group.

3. affiliated, 80%, 80% (p. 8–9).

Under Section 1504, an affiliated group of corporations includes one or more chains of includible (not ineligible) corporations connected through a common parent if:

(a) The parent DIRECTLY owns stock of at least one corporation in each chain where such stock ownership possesses 80% of the voting power AND stock value of such corporation and
(b) At least 80% of the voting power AND stock value of each member of the chain (other than the parent) is owned DIRECTLY by other members of the affiliated group.

4. stock ownership, statutory eligibility, compliance (p. 8–6).

Thus, a group of corporations can file a consolidated income tax return (in lieu of separate returns) for a taxable year only if each member of such group:

- Meets the stock ownership and eligibility requirements under the affiliated group definition in Section 1504 during any part of such taxable year.
- Consents to the compliance requirements under Treasury Regulation Section 1.1502. For example, under Treas. Reg. Sec. 1.1502-76, an affiliated group of corporations files a consolidated income tax return based on the parent's tax year. Thus, each member of an affiliated group filing a consolidated income tax return must use the parent's tax year as its tax year.

5. 80%, or 80% (p. 8–10).

A parent-subsidiary controlled group is defined as one or more chains of includible (not ineligible) corporations connected through a common parent if (ON DECEMBER 31):

(a) The parent owns (DIRECTLY and CONSTRUCTIVELY) stock of at least one corporation in each chain possessing 80% of the voting power OR stock value of such corporation and

(b) At least 80% of the voting power OR stock value of each member of the chain (other than the parent) is owned (DIRECTLY and CONSTRUCTIVELY) by other members of the parent-subsidiary controlled group.

6. the acquisition price (p. 8–16).

Within the context of an affiliated group of corporations filing a consolidated income tax return, the parent's tax adjusted basis in the stock of a subsidiary is modified in a manner similar to the equity method of accounting for an investment in stock over which the parent has significant influence. This adjustment process treats the parent and subsidiary as a single entity and prevents an overlapping of tax effects (income/gain or deduction/loss) when the investment in the subsidiary is ultimately sold or otherwise disposed. Within the context of an affiliated group of corporations filing a consolidated income tax return, under Treas. Reg. Sec. 1.1502-32, the process of modifying a subsidiary's stock basis is described as follows.

- The initial basis of stock of a subsidiary acquired by purchase is such stock's acquisition price.
- On the last day of the parent's tax year (the consolidated group's tax year) or the date of disposition, whichever is earlier, the parent:
  - Positively adjusts stock basis for such parent's allocable share of:
    - Consolidated taxable income.
    - Tax-exempt income.
  - Negatively adjusts stock basis (but not below zero) for:
    - Such parents allocable share of:
      - Consolidated taxable loss.
      - Non-deductible loss.
      - Dividends received by the parent.

In a case where negative adjustments exceed acquisition price, an excess loss account is created to allow the consolidated group to take account of losses, without application of a stock basis ceiling limitation. If the stock that is associated with the excess loss account is sold or is otherwise disposed, the parent either:

- Recognizes the balance in the excess loss account as capital gain or
- Reduces the adjusted basis of other stock of the subsidiary that it holds by the balance in the excess loss account.

7. the last day, the date of disposition (p. 8–16).

Within the context of an affiliated group of corporations filing a consolidated income tax return, under Treas. Reg. Sec. 1.1502-32, the process of modifying a subsidiary's stock basis is described as follows.

- The initial basis of stock of a subsidiary acquired by purchase is such stock's acquisition price.
- On the last day of the parent's tax year (the consolidated group's tax year) or the date of disposition, whichever is earlier, the parent:
  - Positively adjusts stock basis for such parent's allocable share of:
    - Consolidated taxable income.
    - Tax-exempt income.
  - Negatively adjusts stock basis (but not below zero) for:
    - Such parents allocable share of:
      - Consolidated taxable loss.
      - Non-deductible loss.
    - Dividends received by the parent.

In a case where negative adjustments exceed acquisition price, an excess loss account is created to allow the consolidated group to take account of losses, without application of a stock basis ceiling limitation. If the stock that is associated with the excess loss account is sold or is otherwise disposed, the parent either:

- Recognizes the balance in the excess loss account as capital gain or
- Reduces the adjusted basis of other stock of the subsidiary that it holds by the balance in the excess loss account.

8. excess loss account (p. 8–17).

Within the context of an affiliated group of corporations filing a consolidated income tax return, the parent's adjusted basis in the stock of a subsidiary is modified in a manner similar to the equity method of accounting for an investment in stock over which the parent has significant influence. This adjustment process treats the parent and subsidiary as a single entity and prevents an overlapping of tax effects (income/gain or deduction/loss) when the investment in the subsidiary is ultimately sold or otherwise disposed.

In a case where negative adjustments exceed acquisition price, an excess loss account is created to allow the consolidated group to take account of losses, without application of a stock basis ceiling limitation. If the stock that is associated with the excess loss account is sold or is otherwise disposed, the parent either:

- Recognizes the balance in the excess loss account as capital gain or
- Reduces the adjusted basis of other stock of the subsidiary that it holds by the balance in the excess loss account.

Multiple Choice

1. b (p. 8–27; $400,000 sale price − (300,000 − 100,000) basis)

    Gain or loss realized on sales of property between affiliated group members is deferred until a restoration event occurs. Events constituting restoration events include the following:

- The subject property is transferred outside the affiliated group by means of a sale.
- The transferor/affiliated group member no longer is a member of the affiliated group.
- The consolidation election is terminated.
- The transferee/affiliated group member recovers a portion of its cost of the subject (depreciable) property through application of a cost recovery system (e.g. MACRS).
- The transferee/affiliated group member writes down inventory (the subject property) from cost to market by applying the lower of cost or market rule.

The process by which gain or loss realized is deferred and subsequently recognized when a restoration event occurs is described as follows.

(a) Gain or loss realized on sales of property between affiliated group members is deferred.
(b) The transferee's asset basis and holding period start anew.
(c) Upon the happening of a restoration event, the deferred gain (or loss) realized is restored.

Sub's realized gain is $200,000 [Sub's amount realized of $400,000 less Sub's adjusted basis of $200,000 ($300,000 − $100,000)]. Thus, item b is the correct answer.

2. a (p. 8–29; deferral event).

The sale of property at a gain by Sub to Parent is an intercompany transaction. Thus, the gain is deferred until a restoration event occurs and item a is the correct answer.

3. c (p. 8–29; $500,000 sale price − basis).

Parent's realized gain on the subsequent sale of the property is $100,000 (Parent's amount realized of $500,000 less Parent's adjusted basis of $400,000) plus accumulated depreciation. Thus, item c is the correct answer.

4. c (p. 8–12; two and one-half months after parent's tax year ends).

An affiliated group of corporations files a consolidated income tax return based on the parent's tax year. Thus, each member of an affiliated group filing a consolidated income tax return must use the parent's tax year as its tax year. An affiliated group elects to file a consolidated return when each member of the group consents to the filing of a consolidated return. Such consent is accomplished as follows.

- On the first filing of a consolidated return, the combined operations of consolidated group members are reported on Form 1120 and filed no later than the extended due date for the parent's return.
- Each member consents to being a consolidated group member by preparing Form 1122 and filing such form with the first consolidated return.
- The affiliated group continues to file a consolidated return until a terminating event occurs.

In the instant case, the affiliated group (Parent/Sub) filing a consolidated return has the same tax year as Parent (March 31). Thus, item c is the correct answer. The due date of the consolidated return is two and one-half months after Parent's year-end (June 15).

5. c (p. 8–16; basis is modified in a manner similar to equity method).

Within the context of an affiliated group of corporations filing a consolidated income tax return, the parent's adjusted basis in the stock of a subsidiary is modified in a manner similar to the equity method of accounting for an investment in stock over which the parent has significant influence. This adjustment process treats the parent and subsidiary as a single entity and prevents an overlapping tax effects (income/ gain or deduction/loss) when the investment in the subsidiary is ultimately sold or otherwise disposed. Within the context of an affiliated group of corporations filing a consolidated income tax return, under Treas. Reg. Sec. 1.1502–32, the process of modifying a subsidiary's stock basis is described as follows.

- The initial basis of stock of a subsidiary acquired by purchase is such stock's acquisition price.
- On the last day of the parent's tax year (the consolidated group's tax year) or the date of disposition, whichever is earlier, the parent:
  - Positively adjusts stock basis for such parent's allocable share of the subsidiary's:
    - Consolidated taxable income.
    - Tax-exempt income.
  - Negatively adjusts stock basis (but not below zero) for the subsidiary's:
    - Such parents allocable share of:
      - Consolidated taxable loss.
      - Non-deductible loss.
    - Dividends received by the parent.

In a case where negative adjustments exceed acquisition price, an excess loss account is created to allow the consolidated group to take account of losses, without application of a stock basis ceiling limitation.

If the stock that is associated with the excess loss account is sold or is otherwise disposed, the parent either:

- Recognizes the balance in the excess loss account as capital gain or
- Reduces the adjusted basis of other stock of the subsidiary that it holds by the balance in the excess loss account.

In the instant case, the parent's allocable share of the subsidiary's earnings and profits takes account of the parent's allocable share of (a) taxable income/loss and (b) nontaxable income/loss. Further, the parent's allocable share of dividends paid by the subsidiary are dividends received by the parent. Thus, item c is the correct answer.

6. b (p. 8–19; different methods of accounting requires adjustment to match income and expense).

Parent and sub are within the same consolidated group and transact with each other. Parent and Sub account for the deduction of $75,000/income of $75,000 differently such that the deduction of $75,000 would have been accounted for first, but for Section 267. Thus, item b is the correct answer because a matching of the Sub deduction of $75,000 and the Parent income of $75,000 is required under Treas. Reg. Sec. 1.1502–13(b)(2), where both the income of $75,000 and the deduction of $75,000 are recognized in the later year.

7. c (p. 8–9).

Under Section 1501, only affiliated groups can file consolidated income tax returns. Under Section 1504, an affiliated group of corporations includes one or more chains of includible (not ineligible) corporations connected through a common parent if:

(a) The parent DIRECTLY owns stock of at least one corporation in each chain where such stock ownership possesses 80% of the voting power AND stock value of such corporation and
(b) At least 80% of the voting power AND stock value of each member of a chain (other than the parent) is owned DIRECTLY by other members of the affiliated group.

Thus, in the instant case, item c is correct.

8. b (p. 8–15; the exemption for computing AMTI is $40,000).

In general, a corporation is a single taxpaying entity. Section 11(a) imposes a tax on the taxable income of a corporation. However, every corporation is not treated as separate entity for tax purposes. By employing a substance over form argument to mitigate the advantages of multiple incorporation, related corporations are treated differently in cases where one business enterprise is artificially divided into more than one related corporate enterprise. In particular, members of a controlled group of corporations (as defined under Section 1563) must share in certain tax benefits, as if such group was a single taxpaying entity. Such tax benefits include:

- Application of lower rates (below 35%) to lower taxable income brackets (e.g., 20% applies to the first $25,000 of taxable income, 25% applies to the next $50,000 of taxable income, 34% applies to the next $25,000 of taxable income).
- For purposes of calculating the accumulated earnings tax, the $250,000 allowance in computing the accumulated earnings credit.
- For purposes of calculating the alternative minimum tax, the $40,000 exemption.
- The ceiling limitations with respect to various credits.
- The ceiling limitations with respect to the Section 179 expense deduction.

In the instant case, item b is correct because in calculating the alternative minimum tax, the exemption is $40,000, rather than $80,000. Items a, c and d are incorrect because each item is true.

CHAPTER 9

Taxation of International Transactions

LEARNING OBJECTIVES

After completing Chapter 9, you should be able to:

1. Understand the framework underlying the U.S. taxation of cross-border transactions.
2. Understand the interaction between the Internal Revenue Code provisions and tax treaties.
3. Apply the rules for sourcing income and deductions into U.S. and foreign categories.
4. Explain how foreign currency exchange affects the tax consequences of international transactions.
5. Work with the U.S. tax provisions affecting U.S. persons earning foreign-source income, including the rules relating to export property tax incentives, cross-border asset transfers, antideferral provisions, and the foreign tax credit.
6. Apply the U.S. tax provisions concerning nonresident alien individuals and foreign corporations.

KEY TERMS

Branch profits tax
CFC (controlled foreign corporation)
Dividend equivalent amount (DEA)
Effectively connected income
Extraterritorial income
FIRPTA
Foreign tax credit
Functional currency
Inbound taxation
Nonresident alien (NRA)
Outbound taxation
Qualified business unit (QBU)
Subpart F
Tax haven
Tax treaty
Treaty shopping
U.S. shareholder
U.S. trade or business

OUTLINE

I. **OVERVIEW OF INTERNATIONAL TAXATION**
   A. Global trade creates the need for special tax considerations. From a U.S. perspective, international tax laws should promote the global competitiveness of U.S. enterprises while protecting the U.S. tax revenue base.
   B. U.S. international tax provisions are primarily concerned with two types of potential taxpayers:
      1. U.S. persons earning foreign-source income, and
      2. Foreign persons earning U.S. source income.
   C. The United States taxes the worldwide income of its citizens ("outbound taxation").
      1. Because foreign governments may also tax some of this income, these taxpayers may be subject to double-taxation.
      2. The U.S. mitigates this problem via the foreign tax credit.
   D. For foreign taxpayers, the U.S. generally taxes only income earned within its borders ("inbound taxation").

II. **Tax Treaties**
   A. The U.S. international tax rules are based on both the Internal Revenue Code and tax treaties.
   B. Tax treaties are bilateral agreements between countries that define how its citizens will be taxed when they have income within both countries ("taxing rights").
      1. Income tax treaties generally provide taxing rights with regard to the taxable income of residents of one treaty country who have income sourced in the other treaty country.
      2. Treaties generally provide for primary taxing rights which require the other treaty partner to allow a credit for the taxes paid on the twice-taxed income.
      3. Primary taxing rights are usually determined by the residence of the taxpayer or the presence of a permanent establishment in a treaty country to which the income is attributable.
   C. The U.S. maintains tax treaties with more than 50 other countries.

III. **SOURCING OF INCOME AND DEDUCTIONS**
   A. Income sourced within the United States:
      1. Interest received from the U.S. government, District of Columbia, noncorporate U.S. residents and domestic corporations
      2. Dividends received from domestic corporations
      3. Income from personal services performed within the U.S.
      4. Income from rental of tangible property located within the U.S.
      5. Income from royalties on intangible property used in the U.S.
      6. Income from the sale or exchange of real property located in the U.S.
      7. Income from the sale or exchange of personal property by U.S. residents
      8. Income from transportation beginning *and* ending in the U.S.
      9. 50% of income from transportation beginning *or* ending in the U.S.
      10. Space and ocean activities conducted by U.S. residents
      11. 50% of income from international communications between the U.S. and a foreign country
      12. Income from the sale or license of software is sourced using the royalty rules (in the case of a right to use the software) or the personal property sales rules (in the case of a right to use a copy of the software).
   B. Income sourced outside the United States is all remaining income.
   C. Allocation and Apportionment of Deductions
      1. Deductions directly related to an activity or property are allocated to those classes of income. This is followed by apportionment between foreign and domestic groups using some reasonable basis.
      2. Specific rules apply to the allocation and apportionment of interest expense, research and development expenditures, certain stewardship expenses, legal and accounting fees, income taxes, and losses.

3. Deductions not definitely related to any class of gross income are ratably allocated to all classes of gross income and apportioned between sources.
D. The Internal Revenue Service can use Internal Revenue Code Section 482 to reallocate gross income, deductions, credits, or allowances as necessary to prevent the evasion of taxes or to reflect income more clearly.
1. The reach of Section 482 is very broad.
2. In applying Section 482, an arm's length price must be determined to assign the correct profits to related entities.
3. The IRS has an Advance Pricing Agreement program that, with IRS approval, provides a safe-harbor for the company proposed transfer pricing method.

IV. **Foreign Currency Transactions**
A. Tax Concepts When Dealing with Foreign Currency Exchange
1. Foreign currency is treated as property other than money.
2. Gain or loss on the exchange of foreign currency is considered separate from the underlying transaction.
3. No gain or loss is recognized until a transaction is closed.
B. Tax Issues When Dealing with Foreign Currency Exchange
1. The date of recognition of any gain or loss (see Concept Summary 9-1).
2. The source (U.S. or foreign) of the foreign currency gain or loss.
3. The character of the gain or loss (ordinary or capital).
C. The Code generally adopted SFAS 52 which introduced the functional currency approach to foreign currency translation.
D. Where a Qualified Business Unit (QBU), e.g., foreign branch, uses foreign currency as its functional currency, profit or loss is computed in the foreign currency and translated using a weighted average exchange rate for the year.
E. Dividend distributions from a foreign corporation are included in income at the exchange rate in effect on the distribution date. Deemed dividend distributions under Subpart F are translated at the average exchange rate for the corporation's taxable year.
F. For purposes of the foreign tax credit, foreign taxes accrued are generally translated at the average exchange rate for the tax year to which the taxes relate.
G. Section 988 governs the disposition of nonfunctional currencies (with exchange gain or loss generally treated as ordinary income).

V. **U.S. Persons with Foreign Income**
A. U.S. taxpayers often "internationalize" gradually over time.
B. Exporting U.S.-produced goods is the easiest way for a U.S. enterprise to engage in global commerce.
1. All such income is taxed in the U.S. to the U.S. taxpayer.
2. The U.S. has provided incentives to promote the exporting of U.S. goods (e.g., the Domestic International Sales Corporation (DISC)).
3. The World Trade Organization found one of these incentives illegal (the foreign sales corporation (FSC)). In 2000, the Congress repealed the FSC provisions and replaced it with a benefit that excludes "extraterritorial income" (ETI) from U.S. taxation (a benefit similar to the FSC rules).
a. The WTO is now challenging the ETI provisions.
C. A U.S. taxpayer may decide to transfer assets outside the U.S. so that any foreign business will be conducted outside the U.S. tax jurisdiction. This will require a transfer of assets to the foreign entity.
1. Certain "outbound" capital transactions may qualify for U.S. income tax deferral (e.g., when a U.S. corporation starts up a new corporation outside the U.S).
a. However, certain "tainted" assets will trigger gain (but not loss) when transferred. These assets include inventory, installment obligations and receivables, foreign currency, and property leased by the transferor (unless the transferee is the lessee).
b. The transfer of intangibles is subject to separate rules.

2. Inbound and offshore transfers involving a controlled foreign corporation generally recognize dividend income to the extent of their pro rata share of previously untaxed E & P of the foreign corporation.
D. Tax havens provide an opportunity to avoid taxation. A tax haven is a country where either locally sourced income or residents are subject to no or low internal taxation. A foreign corporation located in such a country can provide tax relief.
E. Certain types of income generated by a Controlled Foreign Corporation (CFC) must be included in current tax year gross income by U.S. shareholders.
   1. A U.S. shareholder is a U.S. person who owns, or is considered to own, 10% or more of the total combined voting power of the CFC.
   2. Stock owned directly, indirectly or constructively is counted.
   3. A CFC is any foreign corporation in which more than 50% of the combined voting power of all classes of voting stock or the total value of the stock of the corporation is owned by U.S. shareholders on any day during the taxable year.
   4. For Subpart F to apply, the foreign corporation must have been a CFC for an uninterrupted period of 30 days or more during the taxable year.
   5. U.S. shareholders must include their pro rata share of Subpart F income in their gross income to the extent of their ownership. Subpart F income consists of:
      a. insurance income.
      b. foreign base company income:
         (1) foreign personal holding company income.
         (2) foreign base company sales income.
         (3) foreign base company service income.
         (4) foreign base company shipping income.
         (5) foreign base company oil-related income.
      c. international boycott factor income.
      d. illegal bribes.
      e. income derived from a § 901(j) foreign country.
F. The Foreign Tax Credit
   1. The U.S. retains the right to tax its citizens on their world-wide taxable income. The foreign tax credit (FTC) was enacted to reduce the possibility of double taxation that can result.
   2. The FTC is elective for any particular tax year. If the taxpayer does not choose to take the FTC, a deduction for foreign taxes is allowed in computing taxable income.
   3. The direct credit is available only to the taxpayer who bears the legal incidence of the foreign tax.
   4. The indirect credit is available to corporate taxpayers who receive actual or constructive dividends from foreign corporations that have paid a foreign tax on earnings.
      a. These foreign taxes are deemed paid by the corporate shareholders in the same proportion as the dividends received bear to the corporation's post-1986 E & P.
      b. Specific ownership requirements must be met before the indirect credit is available to a domestic corporation.
   5. The FTC for any taxable year cannot exceed the lesser of:
      a. the actual foreign taxes paid or accrued or
      b. U.S. taxes, before the FTC, on foreign-sourced taxable income:

$$\text{U.S. Tax before FTC} \times \frac{\text{Foreign-source taxable income}}{\text{Worldwide taxable income}}$$

   6. To prevent cross-crediting, separate limitations apply to certain categories of foreign-source taxable income and the related foreign income taxes (see Concept Summary 9–3).
   7. A two-year carryback and a five-year carryover of excess foreign taxes are allowed. The carryback/carryover provision is available only within the separate baskets.

8. Foreign losses must be recaptured as U.S.-source income for FTC purposes. This is accomplished by reducing the numerator of the FTC limitation formula by the lesser of:
   a. Any unrecaptured overall foreign loss, or
   b. 50% of foreign-source taxable income for the taxable year.
9. If the taxpayer incurs the Alternative Minimum Tax (AMT), the FTC is limited to the lesser of the credit for regular tax purposes or 90% of the tentative minimum tax (TMT) before the credit. For AMT purposes, the general FTC limitation is calculated by using alternative minimum taxable income (AMTI) rather than taxable income and the TMT rather than the regular tax.
   a. Thus, the AMT FTC limitation formula is:

$$\text{TMT before FTC} \times \frac{\text{AMTI from foreign sources}}{\text{Worldwide AMTI}}$$

   b. The taxpayer may elect to use foreign-source regular taxable income in the numerator to the extent it does not exceed total AMTI.
G. Domestic corporations may elect to receive a § 936 credit against U.S. taxes generally equal to 35% of possession-source taxable income and qualified investment income whether any tax is paid or due to the possession.
   1. 1996 tax legislation repealed the credit except for existing credit claimants. The credit will be eliminated by January 1, 2006.
   2. The credit is allowed against the U.S. tax attributable to foreign-source taxable income from the active conduct of a trade or business in a U.S. possession. It is also allowed on the sale or exchange of substantially all the assets used by the domestic corporation in that active trade or business.
   3. Income received in the United States does not qualify for the credit unless it is possession-source income received from an unrelated person and is attributable to an active trade or business conducted in a possession.
   4. The credit is not available for intangible property income.

VI. **U.S. TAXATION OF NONRESIDENT ALIENS AND FOREIGN CORPORATIONS**
A. A nonresident alien (NRA) is an individual who is not a citizen or resident of the U.S.
B. NRAs with U.S.-source income that is *not* effectively connected with the conduct of a U.S. trade or business is subject to a flat 30% tax.
   1. This income includes dividends, interest, rents, royalties, certain compensation, premiums, annuities, and other fixed, determinable, annual or periodic (FDAP) income.
   2. The tax is generally levied via withholding.
C. NRAs having U.S. source income effectively connected with a U.S. trade or business are taxed at the same rate as U.S. residents.
   1. A U.S. trade or business is a prerequisite to having effectively connected income.
   2. Effectively connected income is determined under either:
      a. *the asset-use test:* income derived from assets used in, or held for use in, the trade or business or
      b. *the business-activities test:* if the activities of the trade or business were a material factor in the production of the income.
D. Foreign Corporations
   1. A foreign corporation is not a domestic corporation; a domestic corporation is created or organized in the U.S.
   2. U.S. source fixed, determinable, annual or periodic income of foreign corporations is taxed at a flat 30% rate.
   3. Effectively connected income of foreign corporations conducting a trade or business in the U.S. are subject to the same tax rates as domestic corporations. Any U.S. source income attributable to a U.S. office of a foreign corporation is deemed to be effectively connected.
   4. The branch profits tax may impose a 30% tax on the dividend equivalent amount for the taxable year on any foreign corporation operating through a U.S. subsidiary.

E. The Foreign Investment in Real Property Tax Act (FIRPTA)
1. FIRPTA treats gains and losses realized by NRAs and foreign corporations from the sale or disposition of U.S. real property as effectively connected income.
2. NRA individuals must pay a tax equal to the lesser of 26, or 28, percent of their AMTI, or regular U.S. rates on the net U.S. real property realized and recognized gain for the taxable year.
3. Any direct interest in real property located in the U.S. and any equity interest in a domestic corporation are U.S. real property interests.
4. Stock regularly traded on an established securities market is not treated as a U.S. Real Property Interest (USRPI), where a person holds no more than 5% of the stock.
5. Anyone acquiring a USRPI from a foreign person must withhold 10% of the amount realized on the disposition.
F. Section 877 provides for U.S. taxation of U.S. source income earned by persons who relinquished their U.S. citizenship within 10 years of deriving such income if one of the principal purposes of terminating U.S. citizenship was to avoid U.S. taxation.
1. Under § 877, taxes must be paid on U.S. source income under the provisions pertaining to citizens of the United States.
2. The expatriate tax will not apply if U.S. taxation of the NRA under normal provisions applicable to NRAs results in a greater tax liability.
3. The expatriate provisions also can apply for estate and gift tax purposes.

VII. REPORTING REQUIREMENTS
A. A domestic corporation that is 25% or more foreign owned must file an informational return and maintain certain records where they will be accessible to the IRS.
B. Any foreign corporation carrying on a trade or business in the U.S. must file an informational return and maintain certain records where they will be accessible to the IRS.
C. U.S. partners of a controlled foreign partnership must file an information return.
D. A foreign partnership with U.S. source or effectively connected income associated with a U.S. trade or business must file a partnership return.
E. Changes in 10% or more ownership of interests in a foreign partnership must be reported.
F. Creation of, or a property transfer to, a foreign trust by a U.S. person requires the filing of Form 3520.
G. Information returns are required in connection with foreign investment in U.S. real property interests.

STUDY GUIDE
CHAPTER 9
Taxation of International Transactions

9–7

TEST FOR SELF-EVALUATION—CHAPTER 9

True or False

Indicate which of the following statements is true or false by circling the correct answer.

T   F   1. With respect to foreign corporations, one of the factors that can be considered in establishing whether fixed or determinable annual or periodic income and similar amounts from U.S. sources are effectively connected with a U.S. trade or business, is whether the business activities were a material factor in the realization of the income. (IRS 97 3A-9)

T   F   2. A domestic corporation must withhold tax on cash distributions made on its stock in the ordinary course of its business to foreign shareholders. (IRS 97 3A-10)

T   F   3. For a foreign tax levy to qualify for the foreign tax credit, it must resemble U.S. income tax.

T   F   4. Unused excess foreign taxes can be carried back 2 years and carried over 5 years subject to limitations in the same basket for the carryover year.

T   F   5. One of the factors that is considered in establishing whether a foreign corporation's fixed or determinable annual or periodic income from U.S. sources is effectively connected with a U.S. trade or business is whether the income is from assets used in the conduct of that trade or business. (IRS 94 3A-18)

T   F   6. A purchaser of U.S. real property is required to withhold 10% of the amount realized on purchases from foreign persons.

T   F   7. The Foreign Personal Holding Company Tax is levied on the corporation's U.S. shareholders rather than the corporation.

T   F   8. The de minimis rule applies to all Subpart F income.

T   F   9. The foreign earned income exclusion is more beneficial than the foreign tax credit if the foreign country's tax rate is higher than the U.S. income tax rate.

T   F   10. Interest expense must always be apportioned and allocated between U.S. and foreign sourced income components.

Fill in the Blanks

Complete the following statements with the appropriate word(s) or amount(s).

1. The Foreign Tax Credit is _____ for any particular year.

2. Issuance of a _____ and physical presence in the U.S. establishes residency for U.S. income taxes.

3. Foreign currency is treated as property other than _____.

4. For FTC purposes, foreign taxes are translated at the exchange rate in effect when _____.

5. Functional currency is translated at _____ exchange rate for the _____.

6. An _____ is an individual who is not a citizen or resident of the U.S.

7. A foreign corporation is a FPHC if _____% or more of gross income is FPHC income and, more than _____% of the total voting power or the total value of the stock is held by _____ or fewer U.S. persons.

Multiple Choice

Choose the best answer for each of the following questions.

_____ 1. Which one of the following factors is most important in establishing whether fixed or determinable annual or periodic income and similar amounts from U.S. sources are effectively connected with a U.S. trade or business? (IRS 92 3B-44)

    a. Whether the income is from assets used in, or held for use in, the conduct of that trade or business.
    b. Whether the activities in the U.S. were a material factor in the realization of income and whether a certain percent of its employees were U.S. citizens.
    c. Whether the trade or business sold a majority of its products to other businesses in the United States.
    d. Whether a majority of the principal suppliers to the trade or business were in the United States.

_____ 2. Foreign tax credits are:

    a. elective
    b. subject to multiple ceiling limitations that are applied across separate income categories
    c. based on an average exchange rate under certain circumstances
    d. all of the above
    e. none of the above

_____ 3. Eric, a nonresident alien, employed by a foreign manufacturing company, spent 5 weeks in the U.S. arranging equipment purchases. His salary for the 5 weeks was $4,000.

    a. This will be considered U.S. source income.
    b. This will not be considered U.S. source income.

_____ 4. Which of the following statements is not correct in respect to withholding on nonresident aliens and foreign corporations? (IRS 92 3B-45)

    a. Generally, fixed or determinable annual or periodic income from within the United States is subject to withholding unless specifically exempted under the Internal Revenue Code or a tax treaty.
    b. Generally, income is from United States sources if it is paid by any domestic or foreign businesses located in the United States.
    c. Income effectively connected with the conduct of a trade or business in the United States is generally not subject to withholding if certain conditions are met.
    d. Winnings from wagers or blackjack, baccarat, craps, roulette, or big-6 wheel are not subject to income tax withholding or 30 percent withholding tax.

_____ 5. The foreign earned income exclusion is:

    a. elective
    b. limited in amount
    c. available to self-employed individuals
    d. all of the above
    e. a and b only

6. For this year, Bill, a U.S. resident, has worldwide taxable income of $180,000, $150,000 in salary from a U.S. employer and $30,000 from investments in foreign securities. Foreign tax authorities withheld $9,000 of tax on the dividend income. If Bill's U.S. income tax before FTC is $48,540, his FTC is:

   a. $9,000
   b. $8,090
   c. $8,292
   d. $7,200

7. A, a U.S. corporation, incurred $100,000 of interest expense during the year. None of this interest expense can be attributed to a specific purpose. Based on the following information, how should this interest be allocated and apportioned?

Asset Value:	Fair Market	Tax/Book
U.S. Source Income	$3,500,000	$2,300,000
Foreign Source Income	2,000,000	1,500,000

   a. $63,636, U.S. sourced
   b. $60,526, foreign sourced
   c. $52,632, foreign sourced
   d. $41,818, U.S. sourced

8. D, a domestic corporation, began operation of a QBU in 2000 with an initial capitalization of 900K, (1K:$1). Determine the income taxed to D in each year based on the following:

	Income in Ks	Exchange Rate
2000	200K	1K = $1
2001	200K	1.25K = $1
2002	200K	1.6K = $1

   a. 125, 160, 200
   b. 200, 160, 125
   c. 200, 125, 160
   d. 160, 125, 200

9. In 2002 the QBU from question 8 above distributes 300 K to D when the exchange rate is 1.6K to $1. Does D have a foreign currency loss and if so, how much?

   a. No, –0–
   b. Yes, $55.50
   c. Yes, $77.50
   d. Yes, $89.50

10. Corporation R, a domestic corporation, distributed the following dividends to its shareholders.

    $5,000 to Shareholder A, a foreign partnership
    $4,000 to Shareholder B, an unrelated foreign corporation
    $3,000 to Shareholder C, a resident alien
    $2,000 to Shareholder D, a nonresident alien

All of the income of Corporation R was from sources within the U.S. On what amount of dividends must R withhold tax? (IRS 90 3B-43)

    a. $–0–
    b. $7,000
    c. $9,000
    d. $11,000

11. All of the following items of gross income earned by a foreign corporation in the United States are subject to 30% withholding except: (IRS 90 3B-55)

    a.   Rents
    b.   Sale of real property
    c.   Interest
    d.   Dividends

SOLUTIONS TO CHAPTER 9 QUESTIONS

True or False

1. T (p. 9–37).

    Under Section 864, there are 2 requirements for income to be effectively connected with the conduct of a U.S. trade or business.

    (a) First, a U.S. trade or business must exist, a finding which depends on factors such as the location of critical business functions (e.g., management, production, distribution, etc.).
    (b) Second, the income must be effectively connected with a U.S. trade or business, a finding that is met if either one of the two following tests is satisfied with respect to such income.

        (1) Asset-Use Test. This test is satisfied if such income is derived from the assets used in (or held for use in) the trade or business.
        (2) Business-Activities Test. This test is satisfied if the business activities are material to such income production.

    Other types of U.S.-source income [e.g., fixed, determinable, annual or periodic (FDAP) income] that are NOT effectively connected with the conduct of a U.S. trade or business are subject to a flat 30% tax. FDAP income includes dividends, interest, rent and annuities. Such flat tax is generally collected through a withholding requirement that is imposed at the source of the income.

    In the instant case, a domestic corporation makes a dividend distribution to a nonresident alien shareholder. Thus, the dividend paid to the nonresident alien is U.S.-source, FDAP income, which is subject to a 30% withholding tax that must be withheld and remitted to the federal government by the U.S. distributing corporation.

2. T (p. 9–37).

    A domestic corporation makes a dividend distribution to a nonresident alien shareholder. Thus, the dividend paid to the nonresident alien is U.S.-source, FDAP income, which is subject to a 30% withholding tax that must be withheld and remitted to the federal government by the U.S. distributing corporation.

3. T (p. 9–34).

    In general, U.S. taxpayers are allowed a direct foreign tax credit (FTC) for foreign income taxes paid or accrued on foreign-source income subject to U.S. taxation. Thus, no direct FTC is available for foreign taxes assessed and paid in a year in which a U.S. tax return includes no foreign-source income. The purpose of the direct FTC is to mitigate the double taxation of foreign-source income. Under the FTC regime, the direct FTC is analogous to a down payment on the domestic taxpayer's U.S. tax liability with respect to such income. Thus, only foreign taxes that resemble the U.S. income tax qualify for the FTC.

4. T (p. 9–32).

    In general, U.S. taxpayers are allowed a direct foreign tax credit (FTC) for foreign income taxes paid or accrued on foreign-source income subject to U.S. taxation. Thus, no direct FTC is available for foreign taxes assessed and paid in a year in which a U.S. tax return includes no foreign-source income. The purpose of the direct FTC is to mitigate the double taxation of foreign-source income. Under the FTC regime, the direct FTC is analogous to a down payment on the domestic taxpayer's U.S. tax liability with respect to such income.

    A two-year carry-back and a five-year carry-forward are allowed with respect to currently unused foreign tax credits (because of the application of the ceiling limitation). Though, this rule is of little benefit if the effective foreign tax rate forever exceeds the effective U.S. rate.

- The ceiling limit of the FTC is calculated as follows:

$$\text{Tentative U.S. Tax} \times \frac{\text{Taxable Income from foreign sources}}{\text{Total taxable income}} = \text{Maximum total credit}$$

5. F (p. 9–38).

In general, a foreign corporation is subject to U.S. taxation to the extent such foreign corporation has either (a) U.S.- source income (Section 881) or (b) income that is effectively connected with the conduct of a U.S. trade or business (Section 882).

Under Section 864, there are 2 requirements for income to be effectively connected with the conduct of a U.S. trade or business.

(a) First, a U.S. trade or business must exist, a finding which depends on factors such as the location of critical business functions (e.g., management, production, distribution, etc.).

(b) Second, the income must be effectively connected with a U.S. trade or business, a finding that is met if either one of the two following tests is satisfied with respect to such income.
   (1) Asset-Use Test. This test is satisfied if such income is derived from the assets used in (or held for use in) the trade or business.
   (2) Business-Activities Test. This test is satisfied if the business activities are material to such income production.

In the instant case, if the Business-Activities Test is satisfied, there is no need to consider the Asset-Use Test.

6. T (p. 9–40).

Under the Foreign Investment in Real Property Tax Act, a gain or loss realized from the sale of a U.S. Real Property Interest by a nonresident alien or foreign corporation is treated as U.S. source income that is effectively connected with the conduct of a U.S. trade or business. Accordingly, under Section 1445, withholding provisions apply to require the purchaser within this context to withhold 10% of the amount realized. As with other withholding provisions, such provisions insure that a foreign person will not receive 100% of the amount realized, where because of jurisdictional issues the federal government lacks the authority to collect the lawfully imposed income tax. Failure to withhold subjects the purchaser to liability for:

- The unpaid portion of the amount realized that should have been withheld.
- Interest on such unpaid portion under Section 6601.
- A failure to pay penalty under Section 6651.
- Either (a) a civil penalty of 100% of such unpaid portion under Section 6672 or (b) a criminal penalty of up to $10,000 or 5 years in prison under Section 7202.

7. T (p. 9–26).

The objective of the FPHC tax regime is to mitigate the tax avoidance effect of having a foreign corporation hold income-producing property, thereby deferring the U.S. tax until the foreign corporation repatriates such income to the U.S. shareholder. The FPHC tax regime accomplishes this objective by creating the following fiction:

(a) A constructive dividend is attributed to each U.S. shareholder in the amount of such shareholder's pro rata share of undistributed FPHC income (but not to exceed such shareholder's pro rata share of current earnings and profits).

(b) Such shareholder is deemed to contribute the amount of the constructive dividend to the capital of the FPHC, which increases the adjusted basis of such shareholder's stock.

Accordingly, each U.S. shareholder of a FPHC is subject to U.S. tax on the amount of constructive dividend attributed to such shareholder.

8. F (p. 9–23; De minimus rule applies only to Foreign Base Company Income).

   Another way in which the tax law mitigates the tax avoidance effect of having a foreign corporation hold income-producing property, thereby deferring the U.S. tax until the foreign corporation repatriates such income to the U.S., is described as follows. Assuming, for example, the foreign operation of a domestic person is conducted through a locally incorporated foreign subsidiary, the U.S. tax on the earnings of the foreign subsidiary is generally deferred until the earnings are actually repatriated to the U.S. However, under Section 951(a), as an exception to this actual repatriation rule, the Controlled Foreign Corporation (CFC) look-through rules provide for immediate Subpart F income inclusion with respect to qualifying U.S. shareholders of a CFC that earns Subpart F income, notwithstanding whether actual distributions are made.

   In the instant case, the de minimis rule applies to only FBCI, not to all types of Subpart F income.

9. F (p. 9–44; Electing the credit may be more beneficial).

   The relative tax benefit of electing the foreign earned income exclusion versus the foreign tax credit depends on the relative tax rates of the foreign country and the U.S. If the tax rate of the foreign country is lower than the U.S., the tax benefit from electing the foreign earned income exclusion is greater than such benefit from electing the foreign tax credit. However, if the tax rate of the foreign country is higher than the U.S., as in the instant case, the tax benefit from electing the foreign tax credit may be greater (not lower) than such benefit from electing the foreign earned income exclusion.

10. F (p. 9–9; Interest expense allocated across all assets, then apportioned).

    In general, U.S. taxpayers are allowed a direct foreign tax credit (FTC) for foreign income taxes paid or accrued on foreign-source income subject to U.S. taxation. Thus, no direct FTC is available for foreign taxes assessed and paid in a year in which a U.S. tax return includes no foreign-source income. The purpose of the direct FTC is to mitigate the double taxation of foreign-source income. Under the FTC regime, the direct FTC is analogous to a down payment on the domestic taxpayer's U.S. tax liability with respect to such income.

    Under the FTC regime and for each separate category of income, Taxable Income from Foreign Sources must be computed. This calculation requires that deductions must be apportioned in an orderly manner, as follows.

    (a) First, a deduction directly related to an activity (or property) is allocated to a class of income.
    (b) Second, such allocated amount is then apportioned between U.S.-source and foreign-source income.
    (c) Third, a deduction not directly related to an activity (or property) is allocated and apportioned in some rationale manner. For example, with respect to interest expense, interest is fungible. Therefore, interest expense may be allocated to all properties, irrespective of the use of the loan proceeds. Within this context, interest is allocated across all assets based on either
        (1) the fair market value or
        (2) the tax adjusted basis of those assets.

    In the instant case, under the FTC regime, interest expense is not first allocated to classes of income (i.e., income components). Instead, it is allocated across all assets and then apportioned between U.S.-source and foreign-source income.

Fill in the Blanks

1. elective (p. 9–28)

   - The direct FTC is elective in nature. Alternatively, a deduction is allowed. In general, taking a credit is more advantageous than claiming a deduction. The credit can be used to offset a taxpayer's U.S. income tax liability on a dollar-for-dollar basis, whereas a deduction merely reduces taxable income.

2. green card (p. 9–36)

In general, a nonresident alien is subject to U.S. taxation to the extent such nonresident alien has either (a) *U.S.-source income* [Section 871(a)] or (b) income that is *effectively connected with the conduct of a U.S. trade or business* [Section 871(b)].

A nonresident alien is a foreign citizen that is not a resident alien. An alien is a resident alien for a particular calendar year under Section 7701(b) if one of the two following tests is satisfied.

(a) Green Card Test. Under this test, an alien that acquires a green card (Immigration Form I–551) is a resident when such alien is physically present in the U.S. after issuance. The alien remains a resident until either:
(1) the green card is revoked or
(2) such alien is no longer a permanent resident of the U.S.
(b) Substantial Presence Test. Under this test, for example, an alien is a resident for a particular calendar year after such alien is physically present in the U.S. for 183 days during such year.

3. money (p. 9–11)

Underlying the taxation of foreign currency exchange (i.e., the recognition of gain or loss associated with a foreign currency exchange), there are three precepts that build upon each other.

(a) Foreign currency is treated as property other than money.
(b) Because foreign currency is treated as property (rather than a currency), the taxation of a foreign currency exchange (i.e., the recognition of gain or loss associated with a foreign currency exchange) is treated separately and distinctly from the underlying transaction.
(c) Consistent with the view that foreign currency is property, the incidence of taxation of a foreign currency exchange (e.g., the recognition of gain or loss associated with a foreign currency exchange) occurs when such transaction closes.

4. foreign taxes are paid (p. 9–13)

In reporting the results of foreign activities for tax purposes, Section 985 requires the use of the functional currency approach, where functional currency is defined as the currency used within a particular economic environment to measure assets, liabilities, gains, losses, and credits. Under this approach:

For purposes of computing the Foreign Tax Credit (FTC), the manner in which foreign income taxes are translated depends (in part) on the taxpayer's method of accounting.

- If the taxpayer accrues foreign income taxes, foreign income taxes are translated into U.S. dollars using the average exchange rate for the taxable year in which such taxes relate. However, this rule applies only if such taxes are paid on or before the end of the second taxable year after the taxable year in which such taxes relate (but not before the taxable year in which such taxes relate).
  - OTHERWISE, foreign income taxes are translated into U.S. dollars at the exchange rate when such taxes are paid.
- If the taxpayer accrues foreign income taxes and translates such taxes into U.S. dollars using the average exchange rate for the taxable year in which such taxes relate, the FTC is computed by using such translated dollar amount. If there is a difference between the translated dollar amount and the actual amount paid, a re-determination of the FTC is not necessary if such difference is merely due to currency exchange fluctuation.
  - OTHERWISE, a re-determination is required.

5. weighted average; taxable year (p. 9–12)

In reporting the results of foreign activities for tax purposes, the tax law under Section 985 the functional currency approach, where functional currency is defined as the currency used in a particular economic environment to measure assets, liabilities, gains, losses, and credits. Under this approach:

STUDY GUIDE   CHAPTER 9   9–15
                                Taxation of International Transactions

- Foreign activities are combined into Qualified Business Units (QBUs). Each QBU represents a separately delineated set of foreign undertakings of a taxpayer's trade or business activities (e.g., the production facilities of a foreign branch). In most cases, a QBU's functional currency is a foreign currency. For U.S. income tax purposes, the assets, liabilities, gains, losses, and credits of a QBU that are denominated in a foreign currency must be translated into U.S. dollars.
  - For example, the QBU's profit or loss is translated into U.S. dollars using the average exchange rate for the taxable year in which such profit or loss occurred.

6. NRA nonresident alien (p. 9–35)

   In general, a nonresident alien is subject to U.S. taxation to the extent such nonresident alien has either (a) *U.S.-source income* [Section 871(a)] or (b) income that is *effectively connected with the conduct of a U.S. trade or business* [Section 871(b)].

   A nonresident alien is a foreign citizen that is not a resident alien. An alien is a resident alien for a particular calendar year under Section 7701(b) if one of the two following tests is satisfied.

   (a) Green Card Test. Under this test, an alien that acquires a green card (Immigration Form I-551) is a resident when such alien is physically present in the U.S. after issuance. The alien remains a resident until either:
       (1) the green card is revoked or
       (2) such alien is no longer a permanent resident of the U.S.
   (b) Substantial Presence Test. Under this test, for example, an alien is a resident for a particular calendar year after such alien is physically present in the U.S. for 183 days during such year.

7. 60 (p. 9–26)

   A Foreign Personal Holding Company (FPHC), which is subject to the FPHC tax, is a foreign corporation that satisfies both of the following requirements.

   (a) At any time during the taxable year, more than 50% of either stock value OR power is owned (directly or indirectly) by 5 or fewer individuals who are U.S. persons.
   (b) For the first taxable year under consideration, an amount equal to at least 60% of such corporation's gross income constitutes FPHC income. For succeeding years, the applicable percentage is 50% until either:
       (1) Such 50% gross income test is not met for 3 consecutive years or
       (2) The 50% stock ownership requirement is not met for the entire year.

8. 50, 5 (p. 9–26)

   A Foreign Personal Holding Company (FPHC), which is subject to the FPHC tax, is a foreign corporation that satisfies both of the following requirements.

   (a) At any time during the taxable year, more than 50% of either stock value OR power is owned (directly or indirectly) by 5 or fewer individuals who are U.S. persons.
   (b) For the first taxable under consideration, an amount equal to at least 60% of such corporation's gross income constitutes FPHC income. For succeeding years, the applicable percentage is 50% until either:
       (1) Such 50% test is not met for 3 consecutive years or
       (2) The 50% stock ownership requirement is not met for the entire year.

Multiple Choice

1. a   (p. 9–39; Asset use test is an alternative test in establishing income effectively connected).

   Item a is correct because it illustrates the Asset-Use Test, one of the two alternative tests of the second requirement for income to be effectively connected with the conduct of a U.S. trade or business. Items b, c and d are incorrect because each of these items is not a factor to be considered in establishing whether

Fixed or Determinable Annual or Periodic (FDAP) U.S-source income is effectively connected with the conduct of a U.S. trade or business.

2. d (p. 9–27; All are characteristics of the foreign tax credit regime).

In general, U.S. taxpayers are allowed a direct foreign tax credit (FTC) for foreign income taxes paid or accrued on foreign-source income subject to U.S. taxation. Thus, no direct FTC is available for foreign taxes assessed and paid in a year in which a U.S. tax return includes no foreign-source income. The purpose of the direct FTC is to mitigate the double taxation of foreign-source income. Under the FTC regime, the direct FTC is analogous to a down payment on the domestic taxpayer's U.S. tax liability with respect to such income.

- The direct FTC is elective in nature.
- The FTC is determined on a worldwide (rather than on a country-by-country) basis. Income earned and taxes incurred (in all foreign countries in which the U.S. taxpayer has operations) are aggregated. In effect, foreign taxes are "mixed" (or "blended") under the FTC regime.
- Moreover, the FTC has a ceiling limit so that application of the FTC rules generally results in the taxpayer effectively paying the larger of the U.S. or foreign tax.
  - However, a two-year carry-back and a five-year carry-forward are allowed with respect to currently unused foreign tax credits (because of the application of the ceiling limitation). This rule is of little benefit if the effective foreign tax rate forever exceeds the effective U.S. rate.
- The ceiling limit of the FTC is calculated as follows:

$$\text{Tentative U.S. Tax} \times \frac{\text{Taxable Income from foreign sources}}{\text{Total taxable income}} = \text{Maximum total credit}$$

- The FTC ceiling limitation is applied separately across a specified set of income categories. Thus, the total allowable FTC equals the cumulative sum of the separate FTC determinations across the specified set of foreign income categories.
- For purposes of computing the Foreign Tax Credit (FTC), the manner in which foreign income taxes are translated depends (in part) on the taxpayer's method of accounting.
  - If the taxpayer accrues foreign income taxes, foreign income taxes are translated into U.S. dollars using the average exchange rate for the taxable year in which such taxes relate. However, this rule applies only if such taxes are paid on or before the end of the second taxable year after the taxable year in which such taxes relate (but not before the taxable year in which such taxes relate).
    - OTHERWISE, foreign income taxes are translated into U.S. dollars at the exchange rate when such taxes are paid.
  - If the taxpayer accrues foreign income taxes and translates such taxes into U.S. dollars using the average exchange rate for the taxable year in which such taxes relate, the FTC is computed by using such translated dollar amount. If there is a difference between the translated dollar amount and the actual amount paid, a re-determination of the FTC is not necessary if such difference is merely due to currency exchange fluctuation.
    - OTHERWISE, a re-determination is required.

In the instant case, item a is correct. Items b, c, d and e are either incomplete or incorrect.

3. a (p. 9–7; commercial traveler exception not met, compensation over $3,000).

Under Section 861(a)(3), personal service income is U.S.-source income if the services are performed in the U.S.

- However, as an exception, the commercial traveler does NOT have U.S.-source income from rendering personal services inside the U.S. if all of the following requirements are met.
  - Such traveler is a nonresident alien inside the U.S. for not more than 90 days.
  - Compensation from such personal services does not exceed $3,000.
  - Such services are performed on behalf of either (a) a foreign person not engaged in a U.S. trade or business or (b) a Qualified Business Unit (QBU) maintained by a U.S. person.

In the instant case, Eric's compensation of $4,000 is U.S.-source income because he does not meet the commercial traveler exception (the compensation of $4,000 is greater than the $3,000 exception ceiling limitation). Thus, item a is correct.

4. b (p. 9–35; type of income is determinative of source, not where paid).

In general, a nonresident alien is subject to U.S. taxation to the extent such nonresident alien has either (a) *U.S.-source income* [Section 871(a)] or (b) income that is *effectively connected with the conduct of a U.S. trade or business* [Section 871(b)].

Under Section 861, the rules determining the source of an item of income vary across types of income. Thus, the classification of an item of income (as to type) is in part determinative of its source.

Under Section 864, there are 2 requirements for income to be effectively connected with the conduct of a U.S. trade or business.

(a) First, a U.S. trade or business must exist, a finding which depends on factors such as the location of critical business functions (e.g., management, production, distribution, etc.).
(b) Second, the income must be effectively connected with a U.S. trade or business, a finding that is met if either one of the two following tests is satisfied with respect to such income.
 (1) Asset-Use Test. This test is satisfied if such income is derived from the assets used in (or held for use in) the trade or business.
 (2) Business-Activities Test. This test is satisfied if the business activities are material to such income production.

Other types of U.S.-source income [e.g., fixed, determinable, annual or periodic (FDAP) income] that are NOT effectively connected with the conduct of a U.S. trade or business are subject to a flat 30% tax. FDAP income includes dividends, interest, rent and annuities. Such flat tax is generally collected through a withholding requirement that is imposed at the source of the income.

Under Section 1441, a withholding of tax on nonresident aliens and foreign partnerships is required.

Under Section 1442, such withholding of tax on foreign corporations is required.

However, treaties and special provisions of the tax law decrease or eliminate these withholding requirements.

- For nonresident aliens and foreign partnerships under Section 1441(c)(1), US source income that is effectively connected with the conduct of a U.S. trade or business (other than compensation) is exempt from the withholding requirement under Section 1441(a).
- For foreign corporations under Section 1442(b), US source income that is effectively connected with the conduct of a U.S. trade or business (other than compensation) is exempt from the withholding requirement under Section 1442(a) if the following requirements are met.
  - The withholding requirement imposes an undue administrative burden.
  - The collection of the tax is not jeopardized.
- In addition, the following income items of the nonresident alien are not taxed, and accordingly, are exempt from the withholding requirement.
  - Interest earned from (a) certain portfolio debt investments under Section 871(h) or (b) deposits with banking institutions under Section 871(i).
  - Under Section 871(a)(2), a capital gain as long as such gain was realized by a nonresident alien who was in the U.S. for a period during the taxable year of less than 183 days.
  - Under Section 871(j), winnings from wagers, blackjack, baccarat, craps, roulette, and the big-6 wheel.

In the instant case, item b is the only incorrect answer. It is incorrect because the classification of an item of income (as to type) is determinative of its source. The mere fact that the income is paid by a domestic or foreign business located in the U.S. is not determinative of income source.

5. d (p. 9–14; All are characteristics of the foreign earned income exclusion).

Citizens and residents of the U.S. are subject to federal income taxation on their worldwide income. Many objectives of the Internal Revenue Code enacted by Congress serve purposes other than revenue collection. By enacting the foreign earned income exclusion under Section 911, Congress intended to benefit *employees and self-employed persons* for the purpose of assisting domestic businesses in becoming more competitive within the global economy. Under Section 911, a qualified individual may elect to exclude qualified foreign earned income from gross income. A qualified individual makes this election by filing Form 2555.

- A qualified individual is an individual who:
  - Has a tax home that is a foreign country. The foreign country is NOT the individual's tax home if such individual is temporarily living outside the U.S.
  - Is either (a) a U.S. citizen and resident of a foreign country or (b) a citizen or resident of the U.S. and physically present in a foreign country (or countries) for at least 330 days during a 12 month period.
- Qualified foreign earned income is earned income that does not exceed the lesser of:
  - $78,000 (for 2001). Such amount must be proportionately reduced if the taxpayer only qualifies for the exclusion during a portion of such taxpayer's tax year.
  - The amount of foreign earned income less the exclusion for housing costs.
    - The exclusion for housing costs is allowable only for employees and is equal to the excess of qualified housing expenses over a base amount, calculated as 16% of the salary of a U.S. government employee that is a Grade GS-14, Step 1.

In the instant case, item d is correct because items a, b, and c are correct.

6. b (p. 9–29; $48,540 × 30,000/180,000)

In general, U.S. taxpayers are allowed a direct foreign tax credit (FTC) for foreign income taxes paid or accrued on foreign-source income subject to U.S. taxation. Thus, no direct FTC is available for foreign taxes assessed and paid in a year in which a U.S. tax return includes no foreign-source income. The purpose of the direct FTC is to mitigate the double taxation of foreign-source income. Under the FTC regime, the direct FTC is analogous to a down payment on the domestic taxpayer's U.S. tax liability with respect to such income.

- The ceiling limit of the FTC is calculated as follows:

$$\text{Tentative U.S. Tax} \times \frac{\text{Taxable Income from foreign sources}}{\text{Total taxable income}} = \text{Maximum total credit}$$

In the instant case:

- Foreign tax paid is equal to $9,000.
- Tentative U.S. tax is equal to $48,540.
- Taxable income from foreign sources is equal to $30,000.
- Total taxable income is equal to $180,000.
- The maximum total credit is $8,090 [$48,540 × ($30,000/$180,000)].

Thus, item d is correct because the FTC is $8,090 (the lesser of (a) the maximum total credit of $8,090 and (b) the foreign tax paid of $9,000).

7. a (p. 9–10; using fair market: US = 63636, foreign = 36364; using tax book: US = 60526, foreign = 39474).

For purposes of calculating Taxable Income from Foreign Sources, interest expense is allocated to all assets based on either (1) the fair market value of each asset or (2) the tax adjusted basis of each asset. Then, interest expense is apportioned between U.S.-source and foreign-source income based on each asset's affiliation with either U.S.-source or foreign-source income. Assuming that interest expense may be allocated based on either (1) fair market value or (2) adjusted basis, the only correct answer is item a.

STUDY GUIDE	**CHAPTER 9** Taxation of International Transactions	9–19

In this case, interest expense of $100,000 is first allocated across each asset based upon its fair market value. Then, it is apportioned to U.S. Source Income in the amount of $63,636 [$100,000 × ($3,500,000/$5,500,000)].

8. b (p. 9–13; 200K × 1, 200K × .8, 200K × .625)

The following narrative relates to both Question #8 and Question #9.

In reporting the results of foreign activities for tax purposes, the tax law under Section 985 the functional currency approach, where functional currency is defined as the currency used in a particular economic environment to measure assets, liabilities, gains, losses, and credits. Under this approach:

- Foreign activities are combined into Qualified Business Units (QBUs). Each QBU represents a separately delineated set of foreign undertakings of a taxpayer's trade or business activities (e.g., the production facilities of a foreign branch). In most cases, a QBU's functional currency is a foreign currency. For U.S. income tax purposes, the assets, liabilities, gains, losses, and credits of a QBU that are denominated in a foreign currency must be translated into U.S. dollars. For example:
  - In the case where the QBU is a foreign branch:
  - The QBU's profit or loss is translated into U.S. dollars using the average exchange rate for the taxable year in which such profit or loss occurred.
  - A remittance from the QBU to the domestic corporation is translated into U.S. dollars using the exchange rate in effect on the date of the remittance. Exchange gain or loss is realized recognized on a remittance. Such gain (loss) is calculated by subtracting the $ value of the remittance from the $ value of the equity pool attributable to the remittance.
- An amount actually distributed from a foreign corporation to a U.S. shareholder that is sourced out of earnings and profits is translated into U.S. dollars using the exchange rate in effect on the date of distribution.

In the instant case, the direct exchange rate of K into $ for the years 2000, 2001, and 2002 is 1.0 (1/1), 0.8 (1/1.25), and .625 (1/1.6), respectively. Thus, taxable income of D's QBU for years 2000, 2001, and 2002 is $200 (200K × 1), $160 (200K × .8), and $125 (200K × .625), respectively. Accordingly, item b is correct.

9. d (p. 9–13; equity in K's: 900 + 200 + 200 + 200 = 1500; basis in $s: 900 + 200 + 160 + 125 = 1385 distribution 300K of 1500K total equity = 20%; 20% of 1385 basis = 277; 277 – (300K@1.6) or $187.50 = $89.50 loss).

In the instant case, the direct exchange rate of K into $ in effect on the date of remittance is equal to .625 (1/1.6). The $ value of the remittance is equal to $187.5 (300K × .625), The K value equity pool is equal to 1500K (900K + 200K + 200K + 200K). The $ value of the basis pool is equal to $1,385 ($900 + $200 + $160 + $125) and the $ value of the basis pool attributable to the remittance is equal to $277 (20% × $1,385). Thus, D has a foreign currency exchange loss of $89.50 [the $ value of the remittance of $187.50 less the $ value of the basis pool attributable to the remittance of $277] and item d is correct.

10. d (p. 9–6; $5,000 (A) + $4,000 (B) + $2,000 (C)).

Under Section 861, the rules determining the source of an item of income vary across types of income. Thus, the classification of an item of income (as to type) is in part determinative of its source.

Other types of U.S.-source income [e.g., fixed, determinable, annual or periodic (FDAP) income] that are NOT effectively connected with the conduct of a U.S. trade or business are subject to a flat 30% tax. FDAP income includes dividends, interest, rent and annuities. Such flat tax is generally collected through a withholding requirement that is imposed at the source of the income.

Under Section 1441, a withholding of tax on nonresident aliens and foreign partnerships is required.

Under Section 1442, such withholding of tax on foreign corporations is required.

However, treaties and special provisions of the tax law decrease or eliminate these withholding requirements.

In the instant case, domestic Corporation R is required to withhold a tax on the distribution of its earnings (U.S. source income) to the following shareholders.

To A (a foreign partnership) under Section 1441	$ 5,000
To B (a foreign corporation) under Section 1442	$ 4,000
To D (a nonresident alien) under Section 1441	$ 2,000
	$11,000

Thus, item d is correct.

11. b (p. 9–38; treated as US-Source income effectively connected).

Other types of U.S.-source income [e.g., fixed, determinable, annual or periodic (FDAP) income] that are NOT effectively connected with the conduct of a U.S. trade or business are subject to a flat 30% tax. FDAP income includes dividends, interest, rent and annuities. Such flat tax is generally collected through a withholding requirement that is imposed at the source of the income.

Under Section 1442, a 30% withholding of tax on foreign corporations is required.

Under the Foreign Investment in Real Property Tax Act, a gain or loss realized from the sale of a U.S. Real Property Interest by a nonresident alien or foreign corporation is treated as US source income that is effectively connected with the conduct of a U.S. trade or business. Accordingly, under Section 1445, withholding provisions apply to require the purchaser within this context to withhold 10% of the amount realized. As with other withholding provisions, such provisions insure that a foreign person will not receive 100% of the amount realized from the sale of U.S. real property, where because of jurisdictional issues the federal government lacks the authority to collect the lawfully imposed income tax.

In the instant case, sales of real property by a foreign corporation are treated as U.S.-source income that is effectively connected with the conduct of a U.S. trade or business. Thus, item b is correct. Further, items a, c and d are incorrect because rents, interest and dividends earned in the U.S. each constitutes an item of Gross Income (assumed) that is U.S.-source Income, which is Fixed, Determinable, Annual or Periodic (FDAP) income that is generally NOT effectively connected with the conduct of a U.S. trade or business and, accordingly, is subject to a flat 30% tax.

CHAPTER 10

Partnerships: Formation, Operations, and Basis

LEARNING OBJECTIVES

After completing Chapter 10, you should be able to:

1. Discuss governing principles and theories of partnership taxation.
2. Describe the tax effects of forming a partnership with cash and property contributions.
3. Identify elections available to a partnership, and specify the tax treatment of expenditures of a newly formed partnership.
4. Specify the accounting methods available to a partnership and the methods of determining a partnership's tax year.
5. Calculate partnership taxable income and describe how partnership items affect a partner's income tax return.
6. Determine a partner's basis in the partnership interest.
7. Explain how liabilities affect a partner's basis.
8. Describe the limitations on a partner's deducting his/her/its distributive share of partnership losses.
9. Describe the treatment of transactions between a partner and the partnership.
10. Provide insights regarding advantageous use of a partnership.

KEY TERMS

Aggregate concept
Basis in partnership interest
Capital account
Capital interest
Capital sharing ratio
Constructive liquidation scenario
Disguised sale
Economic effect test
Electing large partnership

Entity concept
General partnership
Guaranteed payment
Inside basis
Least aggregate deferral rule
Limited liability company (LLC)
Limited liability partnership (LLP)
Limited partnership
Nonrecourse debt

Outside basis
Precontribution gain or loss
Profit and loss sharing ratios
Profits (loss) interest
Qualified nonrecourse debt
Recourse debt
Separately stated items
Special allocation
Syndication costs

OUTLINE

I. **OVERVIEW OF PARTNERSHIP TAXATION**
   A. What is a Partnership?
      1. A partnership is an association of two or more persons organized to carry on a trade or business, with each contributing money, property, labor, or skill and with all expecting to share in profits and losses.
      2. For Federal tax purposes, a partnership includes a syndicate, group, pool, joint venture, or other unincorporated organization through which any business, financial operation, or venture is carried on, and which is not classified as a corporation, trust, or estate.
      3. Four types of entities taxed as partnerships are:
         a. general partnerships.
         b. limited partnerships.
         c. limited liability partnerships (LLPs).
         d. limited liability companies (LLCs).
      4. Liability of partners
         a. General partners are personally liable for partnership debt.
         b. Limited partners are liable for partnership debt only to the extent of their investment in the partnership.
         c. Limited liability partners are not liable for malpractice committed by their partner(s).
         d. Limited liability company members are generally provided liability protection similar to corporate shareholders.
      5. Elections Related to Partnership Status
         a. The "check-the-box" Regulations allow most unincorporated business entities to select their federal tax status.
         b. Entities with two or more owners can generally choose to be taxed as either a partnership or a C corporation.
         c. A partnership may elect out of the partnership taxation rules if it is involved in one of the following activities:
            1. Investment (rather than the active conduct of a business).
            2. Joint production, extraction, or use of property.
            3. Underwriting, selling, or distributing a specific security issue.
         d. If a partnership elects out, the partnership is disregarded for Federal tax purposes, and its operations are reported directly on the owners' tax returns.
   B. Partnership Taxation
      1. Partnerships are not taxable entities; the taxable income or loss of the partnership flows through to the partners.
      2. Partners report their allocable share of partnership income or loss on their personal tax returns.
      3. Separately stated items are partnership income, expense, gain, or loss that retains its identity when it flows through to the partners. This reporting is required because such items might affect any two partners' tax liabilities in different ways.
   C. Partnership Reporting
      1. A partnership must report the results of its activities on Form 1065.
      2. Each partner receives a Form 1065, Schedule K–1 which shows that partner's share of partnership items.
   D. Partner's Ownership Interest in a Partnership
      1. Each partner typically owns a capital interest and a profits (loss) interest.
      2. A capital interest is measured by the partner's capital sharing ratio (the percentage ownership of partnership capital). It is usually measured as the percentage of net assets a partner would receive on immediate liquidation of the partnership.
      3. A profits (loss) interest is the partner's percentage allocation of current partnership operating results.

4. The partnership agreement may provide for a special allocation of certain items to specified partners.
5. A partner has a basis in the partnership interest. When income (loss) flows through to a partner from the partnership, the partner's basis in the partnership interest increases (decreases) accordingly.

E. Conceptual Basis for Partnership Taxation
1. The aggregate (conduit) concept treats the partnership as a channel through which income, credits, deductions, and other items flow to the partners.
2. The entity concept treats partners and the partnership as distinct, separate units. The nature and amount of entity gains and losses are determined at the partnership level.

II. **FORMATION OF A PARTNERSHIP: TAX EFFECTS**
A. Gain or Loss on Contributions to the Partnership
1. The formation of a partnership involves a contribution of assets to the partnership by the partners. Section 721 permits these contributions to generally be tax free; gain or loss recognition is deferred.
2. Gain/Loss recognition is not deferred when:
a. appreciated stocks are contributed to an investment partnership.
b. the transaction is essentially a taxable exchange of properties.
c. the transaction is a disguised sale of properties.
d. the partner interest is received in the partnership in exchange for services rendered to the partnership by the partner.

B. Tax Issues Relative to Contributed Property
1. Basis
a. The partnership uses a carryover basis (the contributing partner's basis in the property becomes the partnership's basis in that property).
b. The partner uses a substituted basis (the basis of the property contributed becomes the basis of that partner's partnership interest).
2. Holding Period
a. The holding period of an interest acquired by a cash contribution begins on the day the interest is acquired.
b. The holding period of an interest acquired by a contribution of property, which was a § 1231 or capital asset, carries over to the holding period of the partnership interest.
c. The partnership's holding period for contributions of property includes the period during which the partner owned the property individually.
3. The transferring partner's method and remaining recovery period of depreciable property contributed to the partnership carries over (the partnership continues the same cost recovery calculations).
4. Gain or loss is treated as ordinary when the partnership disposes of either:
a. contributed receivables.
b. contributed inventory, if disposed of within 5 years of the contribution.
5. A loss is treated as a capital loss if the property had a "built-in" capital loss on the contribution date and the partnership disposes of the property within 5 years of the contribution. The capital loss is limited to the "built-in" loss amount on the contribution date.

C. Inside and Outside Basis
1. Inside basis refers to the adjusted basis of each partnership asset, as determined from the partnership's tax accounts.
2. Outside basis represents each partner's basis in the partnership interest.

D. Tax Accounting Elections
1. Most tax elections are made by the partnership; these elections dictate how particular transactions and tax attributes will be handled. Elections include inventory method, accounting method, tax year, cost recovery methods and assumptions, Section 179 deductions, and amortization of organization costs and start-up expenditures (and related amortization period).

      2. Each partner is bound by the elections made by the partnership.
      3. The only elections made by individual partners concern:
         a. whether to reduce the basis of depreciable property first when excluding income from discharge of indebtedness.
         b. whether to claim cost or percentage depletion for oil and gas wells.
         c. whether to take a deduction or a credit for foreign taxes paid.
  E. Initial Costs of a Partnership
      1. Organization costs are costs incident to the creation of the partnership.
         a. Examples include accounting and legal fees connected to the partnership formation.
         b. These costs may be amortized over a period of 60 months or more.
      2. Start up costs are operating costs incurred after formation but before the entity begins business.
         a. These costs may be amortized over a period of 60 months or more.
      3. Acquisition costs of depreciable assets are added to the partnership's basis in the assets.
      4. Intangible assets (e.g., goodwill, licenses, customer lists, trademarks) are generally amortized over a period of 15 years.
      5. Syndication costs are costs incurred in promoting and marketing partnership interests.
         a. These costs are capitalized with no amortization allowed.
  F. Method of Accounting
      1. A newly formed partnership generally may adopt either the cash or the accrual method of accounting, or a hybrid of these two methods.
      2. If one of the partners is a C corporation, the cash method may only be used if:
         a. the partnership meets a $5 million gross receipts test,
         b. the corporation is a qualified personal service corporation, or
         c. the partnership is in the farming business.
  G. Taxable Year of the Partnership
      1. A partnership's tax year is, generally, determined in the following order:
         a. the tax year of the majority partners having the same tax year,
         b. the tax year of all the principal partners,
         c. the least aggregate deferral year.
      2. Exceptions are allowed:
         a. if the existence of a business purpose can be established to the satisfaction of the IRS, (e.g., if a partnership recognizes 25% or more of its gross receipts in the last two months of a 12 month period).
         b. if taxes are deferred for not more than 3 months from the required year and deposits of estimated deferred taxes are made.

III. **OPERATION OF THE PARTNERSHIP**
  A. Measuring and Reporting Income
      1. Form 1065 is an informational return which organizes and reports the year's activities.
      2. A partnership must file its return by the 15th day of the fourth month following the close of the partnership's tax year.
      3. Income measurement:
         a. First, under the conduit concept of partnership taxation, items which affect income, exclusions, deductions, and credits at the partner level are reported separately.
         b. Second, under the entity concept of partnership taxation, all items not required to be stated separately are netted at the partnership level to determine the partnership's ordinary income or loss.
  B. Partnership Allocations
      1. The partnership agreement can provide for any partner to share capital, profits and losses in different ratios.
      2. Special allocations must follow the rules and Regulations of § 704(b). One of these is the economic effect test.

3. The economic effect test requires that:
   a. income allocations increase a partner's capital account balance.
   b. deduction or loss allocations decrease a partner's capital account balance.
   c. when a partner's interest is liquidated such partner must:
      1. receive assets having a FMV equal to his capital account or
      2. restore his capital account if it is negative.
4. Precontribution gain or loss
   a. Precontribution gain or loss must be allocated among the partners taking into account variations between the basis and the FMV of the property on the contribution date.
   b. Built-in gain or loss is allocated to the contributing partner when the partnership disposes of nondepreciable property.
   c. Regulations describe allowable methods of allocating depreciation deductions if the property is depreciable.

C. Basis of Partnership Interest
   1. The original basis of a contributing partner's interest is:
      FMV of any services performed
      + money contributed
      + adjusted basis of property contributed
      − liabilities transferred
      + share of partnership debt.
   2. For partnership interests acquired after the partnership has been formed, the method of acquisition determines how the partner's adjusted basis is computed.
      a. If purchased from another partner, basis equals the amount paid (cost basis).
      b. If acquired by gift, basis equals the donor's basis plus some, or all, of the gift tax paid by the donor.
      c. If acquired by inheritance, basis equals the FMV on date of partner's death.
   3. Basis can never be less than zero.
   4. A partner's basis in the partnership interest is subject to continuous fluctuations. Events and transactions which will have an effect on the basis of the partnership interest are:
      a. Increases:
         1. additional contributions and debt increases.
         2. taxable income of the partnership, including capital gains.
         3. tax-exempt income of the partnership.
      b. Decreases:
         1. distributions of partnership property and debt decreases.
         2. partnership expenditures, which are not deductible in computing taxable income or loss and which are not capital expenditures.
         3. partnership losses, including capital losses.
   5. Liability Sharing
      a. A partner's basis is affected by the partner's share of partnership debt. Two types of partnership debt exist—recourse debt and nonrecourse debt.
      b. Recourse debt is partnership debt for which the partnership or at least one partner is personally liable.
      c. Nonrecourse debt is debt for which no partner is personally liable.
      d. How liabilities are shared among the partners depends on whether the debt is recourse or nonrecourse and when the liability was incurred.
      e. Debts created before January 29, 1989:
         1. recourse debt is shared according to the partners' loss sharing ratio.
         2. nonrecourse debt is shared according to the partners' profit sharing ratio.
      f. Debts created after January 29, 1989:
         1. Recourse debt is shared according to a constructive liquidation scenario.
         2. Nonrecourse debt is allocated in three stages:
            a. minimum gain (liability in excess of book basis).
            b. remaining precontribution gain.

    c. remainder is allocated according to profit sharing or the manner in which future nonrecourse deductions are expected to be shared.
  D. Loss Limitations
    1. Three different limitations may apply to partnership losses that are passed through to a partner.
    2. The overall limitation allows losses only to the extent of the partner's adjusted basis in the partnership interest.
    3. The at-risk limitation allows losses only to the extent of the partner's economic investment basis. Economic investment includes the adjusted basis of cash and property contributed by the partner and the partner's share of earnings that has not been withdrawn.
    4. Passive loss limitations, generally, allow losses only to the extent of passive income.
    5. These three loss limitations are applied in the order listed: (1) overall, (2) at-risk, and (3) passive.

IV. **TRANSACTIONS BETWEEN PARTNER AND PARTNERSHIP**
  A. Fixed or guaranteed payments made by the partnership to a partner for services rendered or use of the partner's capital are deductible by the partnership as ordinary business expenses, as long as the payments are not based on the income of the partnership.
    1. Guaranteed payments resemble salary or interest payments of other businesses.
    2. Guaranteed payments are always treated as ordinary income to the recipient partner.
  B. When a partner engages in certain transactions with the partnership, he or she can be treated as a nonpartner, thus recognizing any gain or loss that may be realized. Two exceptions to this rule follow.
    1. No loss is recognized on the sale of property between a person and the partnership if the person owns (directly or indirectly) more than 50% of partnership capital or profits.
    2. Any gain on a sale or exchange of property between a partner and the partnership is treated as ordinary income if the partner controls a capital or profit interest of more than 50%. Capital gain treatment is allowed if the asset is a capital asset to both the seller and the purchaser.

TEST FOR SELF-EVALUATION—CHAPTER 10

True or False

Indicate which of the following statements is true or false by circling the correct answer.

T   F   1. A partner in a partnership can be an individual, a corporation, an estate, a trust, or another partnership. (IRS 96 2A-13)

T   F   2. A partnership liability affects a partner's basis in a cash basis partnership if, and to the extent that, the liability increases the partnership's basis in any of its assets. (IRS 96 2A-14)

T   F   3. The partnership agreement can be modified for a particular tax year after the close of the year, but NOT later than the date for filing the partnership return for that year, not including extensions. (IRS 97 2A-9)

T   F   4. Syndication fees for issuing and marketing interests in the partnership, such as commissions and professional fees, can be deducted as a current expense. (IRS 97 2A-11)

T   F   5. A joint undertaking merely to share expenses or a mere co-ownership of property that is maintained and rented is NOT a partnership. But, if the co-owners provide services to the tenants, a partnership exists. (IRS 97 2A-10)

T   F   6. A partnership is the relationship between two or more persons who join together to carry on a trade or business. Persons, when used to describe a partner, means only an individual. (IRS 92 2A-14)

T   F   7. In determining a partner's income tax for the year, a partner must take into account separately his or her distributive share of all of the following partnership items whether or not they are actually distributed. (IRS 92 3A-15)

   1. Net income from rental real estate
   2. Charitable contributions
   3. Gains and losses from sales or exchanges of capital assets
   4. Ordinary income or loss from trade or business activities

T   F   8. On March 10, 2001, Daniel contributed land in exchange for a partnership interest in Parr Company. The fair market value of the land at that time was $40,000 and Daniel's adjusted basis was $25,000. On December 2, 2002, Parr distributed that land to another partner. The fair market value at that time was $40,000. These transactions would not require a gain to be recognized by Daniel. (IRS 92 2A-16)

T   F   9. Dr. Diaz and Dr. Garcia are both dentists who maintain separate practices, but they share the same office space. They equally divide the expenses, such as receptionist salary, rent, and utilities. This arrangement is a partnership for federal income tax purposes. (IRS 92 2A-13)

T   F   10. The character of a partner's distributive share of a partnership item of income, gain, loss, credit or deduction that the partner must take into account separately, is determined as if the partner had realized it directly from the same source or incurred it in the same manner as it was realized or incurred by the partnership. (IRS 90 2A-23)

Fill in the Blanks

Complete the following statements with the appropriate word(s) or amount(s).

1. Two legal concepts which have had a significant influence on the tax treatment of partners and partnerships are known as the _____ concept and the _____ concept.

2. According to Section 704(a), a partner's share of any partnership item is to be determined by _____.

3. Under Section 707(b) a loss from the sale or exchange of property will be disallowed if the partner has _____ percent interest in the partnership.

4. The measurement and reporting of partnership income requires a two step approach: the first step is the _____ and _____ of specific items on the partnership return; the second step is the measurement and reporting of the partnership's _____ income or loss.

5. The partnership return is filed on Form _____.

6. The individual's copy of the partnership return is known as Schedule _____.

7. A partner's share of a distributive loss in the partnership is limited to his _____ in the partnership.

Multiple Choice

Choose the best answer for each of the following questions.

_____ 1. DCS Partnership, formed on September 15, 2002, elected to use a fiscal year ending November 30. DCS is required to file its return by which of the following dates? (IRS 97 2B-21)

    a. December 31, 2002
    b. January 15, 2003
    c. March 15, 2003
    d. April 15, 2003

_____ 2. Tri-State Partnership has a fiscal year ending June 30. The partnership's four partners have the following fiscal years:

Boulder	40% Owner	March 31
Granite	30% Owner	June 30
Shale	20% Owner	September 30
Slate	10% Owner	December 31

Assuming the partnership does NOT make a Section 444 election and does NOT establish a business purpose for a different period, what tax year must Tri-State use to file its tax return? (IRS 97 2B-31)

    a. March 31
    b. June 30
    c. September 30
    d. December 31

CHAPTER 10
Partnerships: Formation, Operations, and Basis

_____ 3. With regard to a partnership computing its income, which of the following is determined by the individual partners and NOT by the partnership? (IRS 97 2B-32)

    a. Accounting methods.
    b. Amortization of certain organization fees and start-up costs.
    c. Income from cancellation of debt.
    d. Depreciation methods.

_____ 4. In which one of the following ownership combinations of Prescott Partnership would Pete be treated as owning more than 50% of the partnership? (IRS 97 2B-33)

    a.
       Pete   30 percent
       Wife   10 percent
       Pete's Aunt   60 percent

    b.
       Pete   45 percent
       His Uncle's trust   55 percent

    c.
       Pete   10 percent
       Pete's wife's corporation 90 percent

    d.
       Pete   30 percent
       Pete's Father   10 percent
       Pete's Nephew   60 percent

_____ 5. Ken and Liz each have a 50% interest in KeLi Partnership. The partnership and the individuals file on a calendar year basis. For its 2002 tax year, KeLi had a $30,000 loss. Ken's adjusted basis in his partnership interest on January 1, 2002 was $8,000. In 2003, KeLi Partnership had a profit of $28,000. Assuming there were NO other adjustments to Ken's basis in the partnership in 2002 and 2003, what amount of partnership income (loss) would Ken show on his 2002 and 2003 individual income tax returns? (IRS 97 2C-62)

	2002	2003
a.	($ 8,000)	$ 0
b.	($ 8,000)	$ 7,000
c.	($15,000)	$ 7,000
d.	($15,000)	$14,000

_____ 6. The DKC Partnership, which is NOT a publicly traded partnership or a rental real estate partnership, was formed on January 1, 2002. DKC incurred a $24,000 loss for the year ending December 31, 2002 and had no income. The three partners share profits and losses equally. Ms. K is a passive investor in DKC. She contributed $3,000 to the partnership on January 1, 2002, and an additional $5,000 during 2002. Ms. K had draws totaling $1,000 during 2002. What is Ms. K's deductible loss from DKC for 2002, if she had $4,500 in income from other passive investments? (IRS 97 2C-63)

    a. $8,000
    b. $7,000
    c. $6,000
    d. $4,500

_____ 7. Gerard has a 60% interest in the capital and profits of Sly Partnership. He also owns a 65% interest in the capital and profits of Brice Partnership. On February 5, 2002, Sly Partnership sold land to Brice Partnership for $35,000. At the time of the sale, the land had an adjusted basis to Sly Partnership of $40,000. What is the amount of loss that Sly Partnership can recognize in 2002? (IRS 97 2C-64)

    a. $6,500
    b. $5,000
    c. $3,250
    d. $0

_____ 8. Under the terms of a partnership agreement, Annabelle is entitled to a fixed annual payment of $10,000 without regard to the income of the partnership. Her distributive share of the partnership income is 10 percent. The partnership has $50,000 of ordinary income after deducting the guaranteed payment. Which of the following states the amount and character of Annabelle's income from the partnership? (IRS 97 2C-65)

    a. $15,000 of ordinary income.
    b. $10,000 capital gain and $5,000 of ordinary income.
    c. $15,000 of capital gain.
    d. $10,000 of ordinary income and $5,000 capital gain.

_____ 9. At-risk rules apply to most trade or business activities, including activities conducted through a partnership. The at-risk rules limit a partner's deductible loss to the amounts for which that partner is considered at risk in the activity. Select the statement below that is INCORRECT. A partner is considered at risk for (IRS 97 2C-66):

    a.   The money and adjusted basis of any property he or she contributed to the activity.
    b.   The partner's share of net income retained by the partnership.
    c.   Certain amounts borrowed by the partnership for use in the activity if the partner is personally liable for repayment or the amounts borrowed are secured by the partner's property (other than property used in the activity).
    d.   90% of the total expected tax for the current year.

_____ 10. Josephine acquired a 20 percent interest in a partnership by contributing property that had an adjusted basis to her of $8,000 and a $4,000 mortgage. The partnership assumed payment of the mortgage. What is the basis of Josephine's interest? (IRS 97 2C-71)

    a. $1,600
    b. $2,400
    c. $3,600
    d. $4,800

# SOLUTIONS TO CHAPTER 10 QUESTIONS

True or False

1. T (p. 10-4)

    Who may be a partner for tax purposes is discussed as follows. Under Section 761(b), a partner is defined as a member of a partnership. A member is a person who has an interest in a partnership. A person includes an individual, trust, estate, partnership, association, company or corporation under Section 7701(a)(1).

2. T (p. 10-27)

    The effect of a change in a partner's share of partnership liabilities on the basis of a partner's interest in a partnership is discussed as follows. Under Section 752(a), after a partnership begins its activities or after a partner is admitted, any increase in a partner's share of the liabilities of a partnership is treated as a contribution of money. Under Section 722, the basis of a partner's interest in a partnership (outside basis) is increased for a contribution of money. Thus, a partner's adjusted basis in his partnership interest is increased (decreased) for the partner's proportionate share of any increase (decrease) in partnership debt. Partnership debt includes any partnership obligation that (1) creates an asset, (2) results in a deductible expense, or (3) results in either a nondeductible or noncapitalizable item at the partnership level. However, for purposes of determining a partner's basis in his partnership interest, partnership debt does not include accounts payable with respect to a cash basis partnership.

3. T (p. 10-4)

    The partnership agreement is discussed as follows. Under Section 761(c), the partnership agreement associated with a particular tax year includes any modification of such partnership agreement, which is (1) made prior to (or at) the time prescribed by law for the filing of the partnership income tax return for such tax year (not including extensions) and (2) agreed to by all partners (or adopted in such other manner as may be provided by such partnership agreement).

4. F (p. 10-17; syndication fees capitalizable, not amortizable)

    Organizational costs are discussed as follows. Under Section 709, the partnership may elect to amortize capitalized organizational costs ratably over a period of 60 months or more (starting with the month business begins). Organizational costs include costs that are (1) incident to the creation of the partnership, (2) chargeable to a capital account and (3) of a character that would be amortized over the life of the partnership, if the partnership had an ascertainable life. However, syndication costs incurred for promoting and marketing interests in partnerships are not organizational costs. Thus, syndication costs must be capitalized because they are incurred incident to the creation of the partnership. Such costs are not amortizable.

5. T (p. 10-4; service is active conduct of trade or business)

    The definition of a partnership is discussed as follows. Under Treas. Reg. Sec. 1.761-1(a), the term "partnership" is broader in scope than the common law meaning of partnership and may include groups not commonly called partnerships. However, a joint undertaking merely to share expenses is not a partnership. For example, mere co-ownership of property that is maintained, kept in repair and leased does not constitute a partnership. However, tenants in common may be partners if they actively carry on a trade or business.

6. F (p. 10-4, 20; definition of partner is broader).

    Who may be a partner for tax purposes is discussed as follows. Under Section 761(b), a partner is defined as a member of a partnership. A member is a person who has an interest in a partnership. A person includes an individual, trust, estate, partnership, association, company or corporation under Section 7701(a)(1).

7. T (p. 10–21)

The Federal income taxation of a partner is discussed as follows. Under Section 702(a), in determining his tax, each partner shall take into account separately his distributive share of the partnership's (1) net long-term capital gain or loss, (2) net short-term capital gain or loss, (3) net Section 1231 gain or loss, (4) aggregate amount of charitable contributions, (5) aggregate amount of dividends, (6) aggregate amount of any other item that must be separately stated, and (7) other ordinary income or ordinary loss. Other items that must be separately stated include net income or loss from a passive activity (e.g., the rental of real estate). The reason for separately stating certain items may be found within an application of the aggregate concept. Separately stated items affect various exclusions and deductions at the partner level. These items must pass through without loss of identity so that the proper tax for each partner is determined.

8. F (p. 10–24; recognition of precontribution appreciation as gain)

The tax consequences of a distribution by a partnership to a partner are discussed as follows. Under Section 721, no gain or loss shall be recognized to the partnership (or to any of its partners), in the case of a contribution of property to the partnership in exchange for an interest in the partnership. Under Section 731, in the case of a distribution by a partnership to a partner, gain shall not be recognized to such partner, except to the extent that any money distributed exceeds the adjusted basis of such partner's interest in the partnership immediately before the distribution. However, under Section 704(c)(1)(B), if (1) property is contributed by a partner to a partnership and (2) on the date of contribution the property's fair value does not equal such property's adjusted basis, then if such property is subsequently distributed to another partner within 7 years (beginning on the date of contribution), the contributing partner will recognize (on the date of distribution) the difference between such property's fair value and adjusted basis on the date of contribution. In the instant case, Daniel contributed appreciated land to Parr on March 10, 2001. On that date, the land's fair value of $40,000 exceeded Daniel's adjusted basis in the land of $25,000 by $15,000. On December 2, 2002, the land contributed by Daniel was distributed to another partner. As a result, Daniel must recognize gain of $15,000 under Section 704(c)(1)(B).

9. F (p. 10–4; mere sharing of expenses, no division of profits)

The definition of a partnership is discussed as follows. Under Treas. Reg. Sec. 1.761–1(a), the term "partnership" is broader in scope than the common law meaning of partnership, and may include groups not commonly called partnerships. However, a joint undertaking merely to share expenses is not a partnership. In the instant case, Dr. Diaz and Dr. Garcia equally divide certain expenses. They do not divide profits. Thus, such an arrangement is not a partnership for federal income tax purposes.

10. T (p. 10–21)

The Federal income taxation of a partner is discussed as follows. Under Section 702(a), in determining his tax, each partner shall take into account separately his distributive share of the partnership's (1) net long-term capital gain or loss, (2) net short-term capital gain or loss, (3) net Section 1231 gain or loss, (4) aggregate amount of charitable contributions, (5) aggregate amount of dividends, (6) aggregate amount of any other item that must be separately stated, and (7) other ordinary income or ordinary loss. Further, under Section 702(b), the character of any item of income, gain, loss, or deduction included in a partner's distributive share under Section 702(a) shall be determined as if such item were realized directly from the source from which realized by the partnership (or incurred in the same manner as incurred by the partnership).

Fill in the Blanks

1. entity; conduit (p. 10–9)

Two concepts provide the underlying rationale for many provisions of Subchapter K. They are (1) the aggregate concept and (2) the entity concept. Application of the aggregate concept treats the partnership as a conduit through which income, deductions, gains, and losses flow to the partners. Within this context, the partnership is regarded as a collection of taxpayers joined in an agency relation with one another. In contrast, the entity concept treats partners and the partnership as separate and distinct units.

2. the partnership agreement (p. 10–7)

The Federal income taxation of a partner is discussed as follows. Under Section 702(a), in determining his tax, each partner shall take into account separately his distributive share of the partnership's (1) net long-term capital gain or loss, (2) net short-term capital gain or loss, (3) net Section 1231 gain or loss, (4) aggregate amount of charitable contributions, (5) aggregate amount of dividends, (6) aggregate amount of any other item that must be separately stated, and (7) other ordinary income or ordinary loss. Further, under Section 704(a), a partner's distributive share of partnership income, deduction, gain, or loss is determined by the partnership agreement. However, under Section 704(b), if either (1) the partnership does not provide for such partner's distributive share or (2) the allocation to such partner under the partnership agreement does not have substantial economic effect, such partner's distributive share must be determined in accordance with such partner's interest in the partnership (determined by taking into account all facts and circumstances).

3. more than 50% (p. 10–39)

The disallowance of a realized loss on a sale between related parties is discussed as follows. Underlying Section 707 is the entity concept, whereby a transaction between a partner and his partnership is treated as between the partnership and one who is not a partner. Section 707 deals with transactions between a partner and his partnership. In particular, Section 707(b)(1) deals with certain sales or exchanges of property to controlled partnerships. It states that no deduction shall be allowed for any loss realized on the sale or exchange of property between a partnership and a person owning more than 50% of the capital interest (or profits interest) in such partnership. For purposes of determining whether a person owns more than 50% of the capital interest (or profits interest) in a partnership, the constructive ownership rules of Section 267 apply.

4. segregation; reporting; ordinary (p. 10–21)

The Federal income taxation of a partner is discussed as follows. Under Section 702(a), in determining his tax, each partner shall take into account separately his distributive share of the partnership's (1) net long-term capital gain or loss, (2) net short-term capital gain or loss, (3) net Section 1231 gain or loss, (4) aggregate amount of charitable contributions, (5) aggregate amount of dividends, (6) aggregate amount of any other item that must be separately stated, and (7) other ordinary income or ordinary loss. Thus, in reporting partnership items of income, deduction, gain and loss, the partnership must follow a two-step approach in satisfying the mandate of Section 702. First, it must segregate and report on items that must be separately stated. Second, all other items are netted together at the partnership level to produce an amount of ordinary income or loss.

5. 1065 (p. 10–6)

The partnership income tax return is discussed as follows. Even though it is not a taxpaying entity, a partnership taxed under Subchapter K must file a partnership informational income tax return, Form 1065. Underlying this requirement is the entity concept. In particular, Schedule K of Form 1065 accumulates all items that must be separately reported to the partners.

6. K–1 (p. 10–6)

Even though it is not a taxpaying entity, a partnership taxed under Subchapter K must file a partnership informational income tax return, Form 1065. In particular, Schedule K of Form 1065 accumulates all items that must be separately reported to the partners. Under Section 702(a), in determining his tax, each partner shall take into account separately his distributive share of the partnership's (1) net long-term capital gain or loss, (2) net short-term capital gain or loss, (3) net Section 1231 gain or loss, (4) aggregate amount of charitable contributions, (5) aggregate amount of dividends, (6) aggregate amount of any other item that must be separately stated, and (7) other ordinary income or ordinary loss. Thus, the amounts on Schedule

K are allocated to the partners based upon the mandate of Section 702. Such allocated amounts are communicated to the partners by means of Schedule K–1, where each partner receives a Schedule K–1 that identifies such partner's distributive share of partnership items of income, deduction, gain and loss.

7. adjusted basis (p. 10–32)

The Federal income taxation of a partner is discussed as follows. Under Section 702(a), in determining his tax, each partner shall take into account separately his distributive share of the partnership's (1) net long-term capital gain or loss, (2) net short-term capital gain or loss, (3) net Section 1231 gain or loss, (4) aggregate amount of charitable contributions, (5) aggregate amount of dividends, (6) aggregate amount of any other item that must be separately stated, and (7) other ordinary income or ordinary loss. Further, under Section 704(a), a partner's distributive share of partnership income, deduction, gain, or loss is determined by the partnership agreement. However, under Section 704(d), a partner's distributive share of partnership loss (including capital loss) shall be allowed only to the extent of the adjusted basis of such partner's interest in the partnership at the end of the partnership year in which such loss occurred. Further, the excess of such loss over such basis may be allowed as a deduction in a subsequent year.

Multiple Choice

1. c (p. 10–21; 15th day of fourth month)

Even though it is not a taxpaying entity, a partnership taxed under Subchapter K must file a partnership informational return, Form 1065. Form 1065 is due on the fifteenth day of the fourth month following the close of the partnership's tax year. In the instant case, the first tax year of DCS is the fiscal year ending November 30, 2002. Thus, DCS is required to file its first return by March 15, 2003.

2. d (p. 10–19; least aggregate deferral)

Under Section 706(b)(1)(B), the taxable year of a partnership is determined by reference to the partners of such partnership, as follows. A partnership shall not have a taxable year other than (1) the majority interest taxable year, (2) the taxable year of all the principal partners (if there is no majority interest taxable year) and (3) the calendar year if neither (1) nor (2) applies. Within the meaning of Section 706(b)(1)(B), the majority interest taxable year is the tax year of partners that have in the aggregate more than a 50% capital (and profits) interest in the partnership. Further, a principal partner is a partner who has at least a 5% capital (or profits) interest in the partnership. In the instant case, Tri-State partnership has neither a majority interest taxable year nor a principal partners' tax year. Thus, Tri-State's tax year is the calendar year and item d is correct.

Further, under Treas. Reg. Sec. 1.706–1T, if there is neither a majority interest taxable year nor a taxable year of all of the principal partners, the taxable year of the partnership under Section 706(b)(1)(B)(iii) is the taxable year that results in the least aggregate deferral of income to the partners. Under Treas. Reg. Sec. 1.706–1T(a)(2), the aggregate deferral for a particular year is equal to the sum of the products determined by multiplying (1) the months of deferral for each partner that would be generated by that year against (2) the respective partner's partnership interest in partnership profits. The partnership taxable year that results in the least aggregate deferral of income to partners is the partner's taxable year that produces the lowest sum when compared to the other partner's taxable years.

In the instant case, the taxable year that results in the least aggregate deferral of income to the partners is March 31 and is determined as follows.

Partner	Year End	Partnership Interest	Months of Deferral 3/31	12/31	6/30	Aggregate Deferral 3/31	12/31	6/30
Boulder	3/31	40%	0	3	9	0%	120%	360%
Granite	6/30	30%	3	6	0	90%	180%	0%
Shale	9/30	20%	6	9	3	120%	180%	60%
Slate	12/31	10%	9	0	6	90%	0%	60%
					TOTAL	300%	480%	480%

3. c (p. 10–15; in general, elections made by partnership, but there are exceptions)

Under Section 703(b), any election affecting the computation of partnership taxable income shall be made by the partnership, except for areas dealing with (1) cancellation of indebtedness, (2) mining exploration, and (3) foreign taxes. Thus, item c is correct. Items a, b, and d are incorrect, respectively, because decisions involving (1) accounting methods, (2) amortization of certain organization fees and start-up costs, and (3) depreciation methods are made at the partnership level.

4. c (p. 10–39; a. = 40%, b. = 45%, c. = 100%, d. = 40%)

The disallowance of a realized loss on a sale between related parties is discussed as follows. Underlying Section 707 is the entity concept, whereby a transaction between a partner and his partnership is treated as between the partnership and one who is not a partner. Section 707 deals with transactions between a partner and his partnership. In particular, Section 707(b)(1) deals with certain sales or exchanges of property to controlled partnerships. It states that no deduction shall be allowed for any loss realized on the sale or exchange of property between a partnership and a person owning more than 50% of the capital interest (or profits interest) in such partnership. For purposes of determining whether a person owns more than 50% of the capital interest (or profits interest) in a partnership, the constructive ownership rules of Section 267 apply. Under Section 267(c), (1) entity attribution: stock owned by a corporation (trust) shall be considered as being owned proportionately by its shareholders (beneficiaries) and (2) family attribution: an individual is considered as owning the stock owned by his family. Within the meaning of Section 267, family includes brothers, sisters, spouse, ancestors and lineal descendants. Further, stock constructively owned by a person by reason of entity attribution shall be treated as actually owned by such person for purposes of applying either entity attribution or family attribution. Also, stock constructively owned by a person by reason of family attribution shall be treated as actually owned by such person for purposes of applying entity attribution. In the instant case, item c is correct because under c Pete owns 100% of Prescott [10% directly and 90% constructively, through his wife (family attribution) and her 100% owned corporation (entity attribution)]. The following choice items are incorrect:

- Item a is incorrect because under a Pete owns only 40% of Prescott [30% directly and 10% constructively, through his wife (family attribution)]. Pete's aunt is not considered family under Section 267.
- Item b is incorrect because under b Pete owns only 45% of Prescott [45% directly]. Pete's uncle is not considered family under Section 267.
- Item d is incorrect because under d Pete owns only 40% of Prescott [30% directly and 10% constructively, through his father (family attribution)]. Pete's nephew is not considered family under Section 267.

5. b (p. 10–33; 2002, limited to basis, 2003, $14,000 − $7,000 loss carryover)

The Federal income taxation of a partner is discussed as follows. Under Section 702(a), in determining his tax, each partner shall take into account separately his distributive share of the partnership's (1) net long-term capital gain or loss, (2) net short-term capital gain or loss, (3) net Section 1231 gain or loss, (4) aggregate amount of charitable contributions, (5) aggregate amount of dividends, (6) aggregate amount of any other item that must be separately stated, and (7) other ordinary income or ordinary loss. However, under Section 704(d), a partner's distributive share of partnership loss (including capital loss) shall be allowed as a deduction only to the extent of the adjusted basis of such partner's interest in the partnership at the end of the partnership year in which such loss occurred, where any excess of such loss over such basis may be allowed as a deduction in a subsequent year. Further, under Section 705, the adjusted basis of a partner's interest in a partnership is adjusted as follows. Basis is increased for (1) subsequent contributions, (2) an increase in such partner's share of partnership debt, (3) income and gain items (whether taxable or exempt). In the following order, basis is decreased (but not below zero) for (1) a decrease in such partner's share of partnership debt, (2) subsequent distributions, (3) loss and expense items (whether deductible or nondeductible). In the instant case, Ken's 2002 distributive share of KeLi loss is $15,000 ($30,000/2), which reduces his adjusted basis in his partnership interest from $8,000 to zero. Ken is only able to deduct $8,000 of this loss on his 2002 individual income tax return ($15,000 loss to the extent of $8,000 basis). The balance of $7,000 ($15,000 − $8,000) is carried over to a future year. Ken's 2003 distributive share of KeLi income is $14,000 ($28,000/2), which increases his adjusted basis in his partnership interest from zero to $14,000. Further, Ken is able to deduct on his 2003 individual income tax return the carryover portion ($7,000) of his 2002 distributive share of KeLi loss, which reduces his adjusted basis in his partnership interest from $14,000 to $7,000. Thus, item b is correct.

6. d (p. 10–35; passive income limitation)

The Federal income taxation of a partner is discussed as follows. Under Section 702(a), in determining his tax, each partner shall take into account separately his distributive share of the partnership's (1) net long-term capital gain or loss, (2) net short-term capital gain or loss, (3) net Section 1231 gain or loss, (4) aggregate amount of charitable contributions, (5) aggregate amount of dividends, (6) aggregate amount of any other item that must be separately stated, and (7) other ordinary income or ordinary loss. However, under Section 704(d), a partner's distributive share of partnership loss (including capital loss) shall be allowed as a deduction only to the extent of the adjusted basis of such partner's interest in the partnership at the end of the partnership year in which such loss occurred, where any excess of such loss over such basis may be allowed as a deduction in a subsequent year. Also under Section 469, for a partnership activity that is also a passive activity with respect to a partner, such partner's distributive share of partnership loss (including capital loss) shall be allowed as a deduction only to the extent that such partner has income from other passive activities. Further, under Section 705, the adjusted basis of a partner's interest in a partnership is adjusted as follows. Basis is increased for (1) subsequent contributions, (2) an increase in such partner's share of partnership debt, (3) income and gain items (whether taxable or exempt). In the following order, basis is decreased (but not below zero) for (1) a decrease in such partner's share of partnership debt, (2) subsequent distributions (where a withdrawal is considered to be distribution of cash on the last day of the partnership tax year), (3) loss and expense items (whether deductible or non-deductible). In the instant case in 2002, Ms. K has made total contributions of $8,000 ($3,000 + $5,000) and has received a withdrawal/distribution of cash of $1,000, which adjusts her adjusted basis in her partnership interest from zero to $8,000 to $7,000. Ms. K's 2002 distributive share of DKC loss is $8,000 ($24,000/3), which reduces her adjusted basis in her partnership interest from $7,000 to zero. Ms. K is only able to deduct $7,000 of this loss on her 2002 individual income tax return ($8,000 loss to the extent of $7,000 basis), subject to the passive activity loss rules. Because K only has $4,500 in income from other passive activities, K is only able to deduct $4,500 under the passive activity loss rules. Thus, item d is correct.

7. d (p. 10–39; Gerard is a more than 50% owner, related party loss is disallowed)

The disallowance of a realized loss on a sale between related parties is discussed as follows. Underlying Section 707 is the entity concept. Section 707 deals with transactions between members of a controlled group of partnerships. In particular, Section 707(b)(1) deals with certain sales or exchanges of property to controlled partnerships. It states that no deduction shall be allowed for any loss realized on the sale or exchange of property between members of a controlled group of partnerships. A controlled group of partnerships is a group of 2 or more partnerships in which the same person owns more than 50% of the capital interest and profits interest of each member of such controlled group. For purposes of determining whether a person owns more than 50% of the capital interest (or profits interest) in a partnership, the constructive ownership rules of Section 267 apply. In the instant case, Gerard owns more than 50% of the capital interest and profits interest of Sly and Brice. Thus, in 2002 when Sly sells depreciated land to Brice, Sly's realized loss of $5,000 ($35,000 − $40,000) is not recognized. Thus, item d is correct.

STUDY GUIDE

CHAPTER 10
Partnerships: Formation, Operations, and Basis

8. a (p. 10–37; guaranteed payment, $10,000 + 10%($50,000))

   Guaranteed payments to a partner are discussed as follows. If a partnership makes a payment of cash to a partner, the payment may be treated as (1) a draw against the partner's share of partnership income, (2) a nontaxable return of capital or (3) a guaranteed payment. A guaranteed payment under Section 707(c) is a payment (1) for services performed by the partner or (2) for the use of the partner's capital. Such payment may not be determined by reference to partnership income. Guaranteed payments are usually expressed as a fixed-dollar amount or as a percentage of capital contribution. The partnership may either deduct or capitalize the payment, depending upon the nature of the payment. However, the recipient partner must always recognize ordinary income as if such payment were received on the last day of the partnership tax year. In the instant case, Annabelle's distributive share of partnership ordinary income is $5,000 (10%×$50,000). In addition, Annabelle must recognize $10,000 of ordinary income arising from her receipt of the guaranteed payment income as if such payment were received on the last day of the partnership tax year. Thus, item a is correct.

9. d (p. 10–34)

   The Federal income taxation of a partner is discussed as follows. Under Section 702(a), in determining his tax, each partner shall take into account separately his distributive share of the partnership's (1) net long-term capital gain or loss, (2) net short-term capital gain or loss, (3) net Section 1231 gain or loss, (4) aggregate amount of charitable contributions, (5) aggregate amount of dividends, (6) aggregate amount of any other item that must be separately stated, and (7) other ordinary income or ordinary loss. However, under Section 704(d), a partner's distributive share of partnership loss (including capital loss) shall be allowed as a deduction only to the extent of the adjusted basis of such partner's interest in the partnership at the end of the partnership year in which such loss occurred, where any excess of such loss over such basis may be allowed as a deduction in a subsequent year. Also, under Section 465, a partner's distributive share of partnership loss (including capital loss) shall be allowed as a deduction only to the extent that the partner is at risk. In general, a partner is at risk to the extent that amounts are economically invested. Economically invested amounts include (1) cash contributed, (2) the adjusted basis of property contributed, (3) the partner's share of partnership income that has not been withdrawn and (4) the partner's share of partnership recourse indebtedness, for which the partner is personally liable. Item d makes no sense and is the only incorrect answer. Items a, b, and c are all correct answers.

10. d (p. 10–27; $8,000 − $4,000 + 20%($4,000))

   The determination of the adjusted basis of a partner's interest in a partnership is discussed as follows. Given that a partner has transferred property in exchange for a capital and profits interest in a partnership:

   - Under Section 721(a), no gain or loss is recognized either by a partnership or by a partner upon the contribution of property by a partner to a partnership.
   - Under Section 752(a), after a partnership begins its activities or after a partner is admitted, any increase in a partner's share of the liabilities of a partnership is treated as a contribution of money.
   - Under Section 722, the basis of an interest in a partnership (outside basis) acquired by a contribution of property is calculated by using a substituted basis approach and is equal to the sum of (1) money contributed and (2) the aggregate amount of adjusted bases of properties contributed.
   - Under Section 752(b), any assumption of a partner' debt by the partnership is treated as a distribution of money from the partnership to the partner.
   - Under Section 731(a), in the case of a distribution by a partnership to a partner, gain shall not be recognized to such partner, except to the extent that any money distributed exceeds the adjusted basis of such partner's interest in the partnership immediately before the distribution.
   - Under Section 733, the adjusted basis of a distributee partner's interest in the partnership is reduced (but not below zero) by the amount of money distributed.

   In the instant case, Josephine contributed property with a mortgage of $4,000 (assumed by the partnership) and an adjusted basis to Josephine of $8,000. Accordingly, the basis of Josephine's interest in the partnership (outside basis) acquired by a contribution of property is initially $8,000 (the adjusted basis of the property contributed) under Section 722. In addition, under Section 752(b) and Section 722, Josephine's adjusted basis in her partnership interest is increased by $800 for her proportionate share (20%) of the increase in partnership debt arising the partnership's assumption of the mortgage of $4,000. Further, under Section 752(b), the partnership's assumption of the mortgage of $4,000 is treated as a distribution of money (in the amount of $4,000) from the partnership to Josephine. Within this context, Josephine shall not recognize gain under 731(a), because the $4,000 distribution does not exceed the $8,800 adjusted basis. Finally, under Section 733, Josephine's adjusted basis of her interest in the partnership is reduced (but not below zero) by the amount of money distributed ($4,000) from $8,800 to $4,800. Thus, item d is correct.

CHAPTER 11

Partnerships: Distributions, Transfer of Interests, and Terminations

LEARNING OBJECTIVES

After completing Chapter 11, you should be able to:

1. Determine the tax treatment of proportionate nonliquidating distributions from a partnership to a partner.
2. Determine the tax treatment of proportionate distributions that liquidate a partnership.
3. Describe the tax treatment that applies to distributions treated as disguised sales and distributions of marketable securities and precontribution gain property.
4. Describe the general concepts governing tax treatment of disproportionate distributions.
5. Determine the tax treatment under § 736 of payments from a partnership to a retiring or deceased partner.
6. Calculate the selling partner's amount and character of gain or loss recognized on the sale or exchange of a partnership interest.
7. Describe tax issues related to other dispositions of partnership interests.
8. Calculate the optional adjustments to basis under § 754.
9. Outline the methods of terminating a partnership.
10. Describe the special considerations of a family partnership.
11. Describe the application of partnership provisions to limited liability companies (LLCs) and limited liability partnerships (LLPs).

KEY TERMS

Appreciated inventory
Disproportionate distribution
Hot assets
Liquidating distribution

Nonliquidating distribution
Optional adjustment election
Proportionate distribution
Section 754 election

Technical termination of partnership
Unrealized receivables

OUTLINE

I. **DISTRIBUTIONS FROM A PARTNERSHIP**
   A. All distributions from a partnership fall into two distinct categories:
      1. Liquidating distributions,
      2. Nonliquidating distributions.
   B. A *liquidating distribution* occurs when either the partnership liquidates and distributes all property to its partners, or when an ongoing partnership redeems the interest of one of its partners.
   C. A *nonliquidating distribution* is any distribution from a partnership to a continuing partner. The two types of nonliquidating distributions are draws or partial liquidations.
      1. Draws are distributions of a partner's share of partnership profits that have been taxed to that partner.
      2. Partial liquidations reduce the partner's interest in partnership capital and are a return of investment in a partnership interest.
   D. In general, if a nonliquidating distribution is proportionate, no gain or loss is recognized by either the partnership or partner.
      1. The partner takes a carryover basis in the assets distributed.
      2. The partner's outside basis is reduced (but not below zero) by the amount of cash and the adjusted basis of property distributed.
      3. If the cash distributed exceeds the partner's outside basis, the partner recognizes capital gain.
      4. Losses are not recognized on nonliquidating distributions.
      5. When the inside basis of the assets distributed exceeds the partner's outside basis, the Code requires that the assets be deemed distributed in the following order:
         a. first, cash.
         b. second, unrealized receivables and inventory (ordinary income producing property).
         c. third, other property.
      6. If the partner's outside basis cannot absorb the second and/or third order of distributions, the partner's basis, after the cash distribution, is to be allocated first within the second class, and then to the other property.
   E. Proportionate Liquidating Distributions
      1. The general ordering and gain recognition rules are as follows:
         a. Cash is distributed first and reduces the partner's outside basis dollar for dollar. A capital gain is recognized if the cash distributed exceeds the partner's basis.
         b. The partner's remaining outside basis is then allocated to unrealized receivables and inventory up to the amount equal to the partnership's basis (inside basis).
         c. If any outside basis remains, it is allocated to the other assets received.
      2. Special rules apply when more than one asset in a particular class is distributed.
      3. No gain or loss is recognized by the partnership.
      4. The partner recognizes a loss if:
         a. the partner receives *only* money, unrealized receivables or inventory, and
         b. the partner's outside basis exceeds the aggregate amount of the inside basis of the assets distributed.
      5. If any other property is received, loss recognition is postponed.
   F. Property Distributions with Special Tax Treatment
      1. In a "disguised sale", the partner is treated as having sold the property and must report a gain on the sale. The partnership takes a cost basis in the property purchased.
      2. Marketable securities are generally treated as cash distributions. As a result, if the value of the securities exceeds the partner's outside basis, the partner must recognize a taxable gain. Marketable securities are not treated as cash if:

a. they were originally contributed by the partner to whom they are now distributed,
b. the property was not a marketable security when acquired by the partnership, or
c. the partner is an eligible partner of an investment partnership.
3. Precontribution Gain
   a. If a partner contributes appreciated property to a partnership, that partner recognizes gain if:
      1. the contributed property is distributed to another partner within seven years of the contribution date, or
      2. the partnership distributes any property other than cash to that partner within seven years after the partner contributed the appreciated property.
   b. The partner's basis in the partnership interest is increased by the amount of gain recognized.
      1. For property distributed to another partner, the basis of the distributed property is increased by the amount of gain recognized.
      2. For property other than cash distributed to the contributing partner, the partnership increases its basis in the precontribution gain property remaining in the partnership.
G. Disproportionate Distributions
   1. A disproportionate distribution occurs when a partnership makes a distribution that increases or decreases a partner's proportionate interest in certain ordinary income producing property (known as "hot assets"—substantially appreciated inventory and unrealized receivables).
      a. "Inventory" includes all assets that are not cash, capital or §1231 assets. Substantially appreciated inventory is inventory that has a FMV in excess of 120 percent of the partnership's adjusted basis for the inventory.
      b. Unrealized receivables are rights to receive future amounts that will result in ordinary income when the income is recognized.
   2. The transaction is recast so that each partner recognizes and reports his proportionate share of ordinary income based on his proportionate share of the underlying assets of the partnership.

II. **LIQUIDATING DISTRIBUTIONS TO RETIRING OR DECEASED PARTNER**
   A. Payments made by an ongoing partnership in complete liquidation of a partner's interest are classified as either property payments (for partnership assets) or income payments (for the partnership's going-concern value).
   B. Property payments are made in exchange for the partner's pro rata share of each partnership asset, § 736(b).
      1. In general, § 736(b) payments are considered a return of the partner's outside basis in the partnership.
      2. Cash payments in excess of that outside basis will be taxed as a capital gain.
      3. Cash payments insufficient to cover the outside basis will be taxed as a capital loss.
   C. If part of the property payment is for the partner's share of "hot assets," the payment is allocated between the hot and non-hot assets. The portion of the payment related to the hot assets is treated as a disproportionate distribution (see above).
   D. Income payments, § 736(a), are all payments not classified as § 736(b) payments.
   E. Income payments are classified as guaranteed payments or distributive shares.
      1. Guaranteed payments are NOT determined by reference to partnership income and are fully deductible by the partnership; they are taxed as ordinary income to the recipient partner.
      2. Distributive share payments are determined by reference to partnership income and retain their character when distributed to the recipient partner.
   F. Series of Payments
      1. If the partners have specifically agreed to the allocation and timing of property and income payments, the agreement normally controls.
      2. If no agreement is made, regulations specify the classification rules for each payment.

III. **SALE OF A PARTNERSHIP INTEREST**
   A. As a general rule, capital gain or loss results from the sale or exchange of a partnership interest. The gain or loss recognized is the difference between the amount realized and the partner's adjusted basis, including any liabilities.
   B. When a partner sells an entire interest in the partnership, income for the partnership interest for the tax year is allocated between the buying partner and selling partner, and the partnership's tax year "closes" with respect to the selling partner.
      1. The selling partner's basis is adjusted for the allocated income or loss before the partner calculates gain or loss on disposition.
      2. There are several acceptable methods of determining the partner's share of income (e.g., proration; interim closing of the books).
   C. Major exceptions to the general rule arise when a partner sells his or her interest in a partnership and there are unrealized receivables or appreciated inventory (hot assets). Under Section 751, these items, when accounted for in the sale of a partnership interest, generate ordinary income.
      1. "Unrealized receivables" include:
         a. accounts receivable of a cash basis partnership and
         b. for sale or exchange purposes, depreciation recapture potential.
      2. "Appreciated inventory" includes essentially all partnership property except money, capital assets and § 1231 property. Unrealized receivables are included in this definition.
      3. Inventory is appreciated when aggregate FMV of receivables exceeds the aggregate adjusted basis to the partnership of such receivables.

IV. **OTHER DISPOSITIONS OF PARTNERSHIP INTERESTS**
   A. The transfer of a partnership interest to a controlled corporation will be treated as a nontaxable exchange if the conditions of Section 351 are satisfied.
      1. If the partnership interest transferred represents 50 percent or more of the total interest in capital or profits, the partnership is terminated.
      2. The incorporation method used should be carefully chosen as the method chosen may lead to different inside and outside basis amounts.
   B. Like-kind exchange rules do not apply to the exchange of different partnerships' interests but can apply to exchanges of interests in the same partnership.
   C. If a partner dies, the taxable year of the partnership closes for that partner on the date of death.
   D. Generally, the donor of a partnership interest does not recognize gain or loss.

V. **OPTIONAL ADJUSTMENTS TO PROPERTY BASIS**
   A. A partnership may elect to adjust the basis of its property when a partner's interest is sold or exchanged, a partner dies, or property (including cash) is distributed.
      1. The purpose of this optional adjustment is to equalize the inside and outside bases of the partner's interest.
      2. Once made, the election remains in effect until the IRS consents to its revocation.
   B. If a partner's interest is sold to a third party, or a partner dies, the adjustment to partnership property is the transferee's outside basis in the partnership minus the transferee's share of the inside basis of the property.
      1. The adjustment can be either positive or negative.
      2. If a step-up of depreciable property is involved, the optional adjustment is depreciated by the transferee partner, as if a newly acquired asset.
      3. The adjustment affects the basis of partnership property with respect to the transferee partner only.
   C. Optional adjustments to basis are also available to the partnership when property is distributed.
      1. The basis of partnership property is *increased* by:
         a. Any gain recognized by the distributee partner.
         b. The excess of the partnership's adjusted basis of any distributed property over the distributee partner's adjusted basis of that property.

2. The basis of partnership property is *decreased* by:
   a. Any loss recognized by the distributee partner.
   b. In the case of a liquidating distribution, the excess of the distributee partner's adjusted basis of any distributed property over the partnership's basis of that property.

VI. TERMINATION OF A PARTNERSHIP
A. The partnership terminates and its tax year closes when:
   1. The partnership incorporates.
   2. In a two-party partnership, when one partner buys out the other, creating a sole proprietorship.
   3. The partnership ceases operations and liquidates—a sale or exchange of partnership interest(s) result.
B. The partnership taxable year usually does not close when a partner dies or when a partner's interest is liquidated. However, the partnership year does close for the deceased or liquidated partner.
C. A technical termination occurs if more than 50% of the partnership's capital and profits interests are transferred within a 12 month period.

VII. OTHER ISSUES
A. Family partnerships require special consideration. Because of the close relationship between family members, channeling income from high tax-bracket members to low tax-bracket members may be found abusive.
   1. A family member will be recognized as a partner only in the following cases:
      a. If capital is a material income-producing factor and the family member's capital interest is acquired in a bona fide transaction in which ownership and control are received.
      b. If capital is not a material income-producing factor and the family member performs substantial or vital services to the partnership.
   2. When capital is a material income-producing factor and the partner is a child under 14 years of age, a substantial portion of the child's distributive income may be taxed at the parent/partner's marginal tax rate unless the income share constitutes earned income (the "kiddie tax"). If the minor child is 14 or older, these taxing restrictions are avoided.
   3. If a family member acquires a capital interest by gift in a family partnership, only part of the income may be allocated to this interest.
B. Limited Liability Companies (LLC)
   1. An LLC with two or more owners is taxed as a partnership.
   2. Since none of the LLC members is personally liable for LLC debt, the LLC is effectively treated as a limited partnership with no general partners.
   3. All owners can participate in management of the LLC.
   4. Transfers of property to the LLC in exchange for an ownership interest are generally governed by partnership tax provisions.
      a. Contributed property with built-in gains or losses is subject to the partnership allocation rules (discussed above).
      b. An LLC member contributing built-in gain property can be subject to tax on certain distributions within seven years of the contribution.
   5. All LLC liabilities are treated as nonrecourse (because of limited liability).
   6. Special allocations under § 704(b) are generally permitted.
   7. Optional adjustments to basis election can generally be made.
   8. A partnership can easily convert to an LLC. However, a corporation (either C or S) that reorganizes as an LLC is treated as having liquidated (a taxable transaction to both shareholders and the corporation) and formed as a partnership (a nontaxable event).
C. Limited Liability Partnerships (LLP)
   1. Partners in a registered LLP are jointly and severally liable for contractual liability.
   2. Partners are liable for their own malpractice or other torts, but are not liable for their partners' malpractice or torts.
D. Regulations have been issued which allow the IRS to ignore the partnership form if it believes that a transaction (or series of transactions) is abusive.

TEST FOR SELF-EVALUATION—CHAPTER 11

True or False

Indicate which of the following statements is true or false by circling the correct answer.

T F 1. Joanie received a gift from her father of a capital interest in a family partnership. There are NO limits on the amount that can be allocated Joanie as a distributive share of partnership income because capital is a material income producing factor. (IRS 97 2A-4)

T F 2. Payments made in liquidation of the interest of a retiring or deceased partner in exchange for his or her interest in partnership property are considered a distribution, not a distributive share or guaranteed payment that could give rise to a deduction (or its equivalent) for the partnership. (IRS 97 2A-20)

T F 3. During 2002, Sergio contributed property to his partnership. Sergio must recognize gain or loss on the distribution of the property to another partner within 7 years of the contribution. (IRS 96 2A-15)

T F 4. When there is a sale or liquidation of a partner's interest in a partnership, the adjusted basis of the partner's partnership interest is determined on the date of the sale or liquidation. (IRS 96 2A-16)

T F 5. Mr. Clysdale is a partner in Clysdale and Associates Partnership. The other two partners are his sister and his 17-year old son, Gregory. The partnership's income consists mostly of compensation for services performed by Mr. Clysdale and his sister. Gregory is a high school student and acquired his one-third interest by gift. Gregory is recognized as a partner in the firm for tax purposes. (IRS 95 2A-14)

T F 6. On December 31, 2002, Kay-Ann's adjusted basis in GEM Partnership was zero and her share of partnership liabilities was $30,000. The partnership had no unrealized receivables or substantially appreciated inventory items. Kay-Ann withdrew from the partnership on December 31, 2002, and was relieved of any partnership liabilities. As a result she has a $30,000 capital LOSS. (IRS 95 2A-15)

T F 7. Chad's interest in BCD Partnership had an adjusted basis of $80,000. In complete liquidation of his interest, he received $30,000 cash, inventory items having a basis to the partnership of $44,000, and a company automobile having an adjusted basis to the partnership of $12,000. The basis of the automobile in Chad's hands is $12,000. (IRS 95 2A-17)

T F 8. In a liquidating distribution a loss is recognized if the sum of the cash received plus the basis of distributed unrealized receivables and inventory is less than the adjusted basis of the partner's interest prior to the liquidating distribution and no other property is distributed.

T F 9. Recognition of gain will not occur in the liquidating distribution of property unless cash is received in excess of interest.

T F 10. The Code permits a partnership to increase or decrease the basis of partnership assets in the event of a death of one of the partners or if a partner's interest is sold or exchanged.

T F 11. An optional basis adjustment is binding only for the year in which it is made unless consent is received from the IRS to make it continuous.

Fill in the Blanks

Complete the following statements with the appropriate word(s) or amount(s).

1. Under the general rule of section 741, a partnership interest is a _____ asset, the sale or exchange of which will result in the recognition of _____.

2. Section 751 provides that amount realized from the sale of a partnership interest which are attributable to _____ or _____ must be treated as the sale of a noncapital asset.

3. Partnership liabilities forgiven or assumed by another partner are treated as _____ distributions.

Multiple Choice

Choose the best answer for each of the following questions.

_____ 1. All of the following statements with respect to property contributed to a partnership are correct except: (IRS 97 2B-34)

   a. Usually, neither the partners nor the partnership recognizes a gain or loss when property is contributed to the partnership in exchange for a partnership interest.
   b. The contributing partner must recognize gain or loss on a distribution of the property to another partner within 5 years of the contribution.
   c. Exchanges of partnership interests generally qualify for nontaxable treatment as exchanges of like-kind property.
   d. The exchange of limited partnership interests in one partnership for limited partnership interests in another partnership may qualify as a tax-free contribution of property to the second partnership if the transaction is made for business purposes.

_____ 2. All of the following statements with respect to a partner's sale or exchange of a partnership interest are correct except: (IRS 97 2B-35)

   a. The sale or exchange of a partner's interest in a partnership usually results in a capital gain or loss.
   b. Gain or loss recognized by the selling partner is the difference between the amount realized and the adjusted basis of the partner's interest in the partnership.
   c. The selling partner must include as part of the amount realized, any partnership liability he or she is relieved of.
   d. The installment method of reporting cannot be used by the partner who sells a partnership interest at a gain.

_____ 3. A partnership terminates when: (IRS 97 2C-61)

   (1) All of its operations are discontinued and no part of any business, financial operations, or venture is continued by any of its partners in a partnership or a limited liability company classified as a partnership, or
   (2) At least 50% of the total interest in partnership capital and profits is sold or exchanged within a 12 month period, including a sale or exchange to another partner.

   a. The above statement is true in its entirety.
   b. The above statement is false in its entirety.
   c. Only item (1) above is true.
   d. Only item (2) above is true.

4. Walter is a limited partner in Cat Partnership. He contributed $30,000 in cash on the formation of the partnership. His adjusted basis in the partnership is $40,000, which includes his share of partnership liabilities of $10,000. In 2002, Walter sold his interest in the partnership for $60,000 in cash. He had been paid his share of partnership income for the tax year. The partnership has no other liabilities or receivables or substantially appreciated inventory. What is the amount and character of Walter's gain? (IRS 97 2C-67)

   a. $20,000 capital gain
   b. $20,000 ordinary gain
   c. $30,000 capital gain
   d. $30,000 ordinary gain

5. The adjusted basis of Ted's partnership interest is $30,000. In complete liquidation of his interest, he receives $10,000 in cash, his share of the inventory items having a basis to the partnership of $12,000, and two parcels of land having adjusted bases to the partnership of $12,000 and $4,000. What is Ted's basis in the two parcels of land? (IRS 97 2C-68)

   a. $8,000 and $4,000
   b. $5,000 and $3,000
   c. $6,000 and $2,000
   d. $8,000 and $0

6. Rick's interest in ATP Partnership has an adjusted basis of $300,000. In a complete liquidation of his interest, he received the following:

	ATP's Adjusted Basis	Fair Market Value
Cash	$140,000	$140,000
Building	160,000	180,000
Computer	40,000	20,000
Inventory	60,000	60,000

   What is Rick's basis in the building and computer, respectively? (IRS 97 2C-69)

	Building	Computer
a.	$ 80,000	$20,000
b.	$ 90,000	$10,000
c.	$120,000	$30,000
d.	$135,000	$30,000
e.	none of the above	

7. Fred became a limited partner in the Happy Partnership by contributing $10,000 in cash on the formation of the partnership. The adjusted basis of his partnership interest at the end of the current year is $20,000, which includes his $15,000 share of partnership liabilities. The partnership has no unrealized receivables or substantially appreciated inventory items. Fred sells his interest in the partnership for $10,000 in cash. He had been paid his share of the partnership income for the tax year.

8. Fred realized $25,000 from the sale of partnership interest ($10,000 cash payment plus $15,000 liability relief). How much should he report as a capital gain? (IRS 97 2C-70)

a. $2,500
b. $5,000
c. $7,500
d. $10,000

_____ 9. Cynthia is a partner in CF Partnership. The adjusted basis of her partnership interest is $19,000, of which $15,000 represents her share of partnership liabilities. Cynthia's share of the partnership's unrealized receivables is $6,000. The partnership has no substantially appreciated inventory items. Cynthia sold her partnership interest for $28,000 cash. What is the amount and character of her gain? (IRS 97 2C-72)

a. $6,000 capital gain
b. $6,000 ordinary income; $18,000 capital gain
c. $18,000 capital gain
d. $18,000 ordinary income; $6,000 capital gain

_____ 10. You are a partner in ABC Partnership. The adjusted basis of your partnership interest at the end of the current year is zero. Your share of potential ordinary income from partnership depreciable property is $5,000. The partnership has no other unrealized receivables or substantially appreciated inventory items. You sell your interest in the partnership for $11,000 in cash. Which of the following statements is accurate: (IRS 97 2C-73)

(1) You report the entire amount as a gain since your adjusted basis in the partnership is zero.
(2) You report $5,000 as ordinary income from the partnership's depreciable property.
(3) You report the remaining $6,000 gain as capital gain.

a. 2 and 3 are correct, but 1 is incorrect.
b. All of the statements are incorrect.
c. All of the statements are correct.
d. 1 is correct, but 2 and 3 are incorrect.

SOLUTIONS TO CHAPTER 11 QUESTIONS

True or False

1. **F** (p. 11–36; father is allocated reasonable compensation first)

    Family partnerships are owned and controlled by members of the same family. Underlying the taxation of family partnerships is a basic tenet: Income is recognized by the person who performs the services or who owns the capital that generates such income. Thus, under Section 704(e), to prevent tax avoidance within the context of a family partnership, a family member shall be recognized as a partner for tax purposes only if the family member acquires (1) a capital interest in a partnership (where capital is a material income-producing factor) in a bona fide transaction (i.e., a transaction where ownership and control are substantively transferred) or (2) a capital interest in a partnership where capital is not a material income-producing factor, but where the family member provides substantial services to the partnership.

    As a special limitation to the amount of income allocable to a family member, if a family member acquires a capital interest in a partnership (where capital is a material income-producing factor) by gift, the family member shall be recognized as a partner for tax purposes only if (1) the donor/partner is allocated an amount of partnership income that represents reasonable compensation for the services that such donor/partner provided to the partnership and (2) there are no special allocations of income to the donee/partner (i.e., the remaining income is allocated pro rata based on each partner's relative capital interest). Further, if a child (who may be claimed as a dependent of a parent/partner and who is under age 14) acquires a capital interest in a partnership (where capital is a material income-producing factor), the kiddie tax may apply.

    Under the kiddie tax rules, some of the child's distributive share of partnership income may be taxed at the parents marginal tax rate. In the instant case, within the context of a family partnership, there are limits on the amount that can be specifically allocated to Joanie as a distributive share of partnership income (in the case where capital is a material income-producing factor).

2. **T** (p. 11–19; property payments)

    The tax consequences of a retiring partner's complete liquidation of his partnership interest are discussed as follows. Payments made by an ongoing partnership in complete liquidation of a retiring partner's interest are classified as either income payments under Section 736(a) or property payments under Section 736(b). Section 736(b) payments are property distributions made to a retiring partner in exchange for the partner's interest in partnership assets. Because Section 736(b) payments are characterized as distributions, the partnership is not allowed a deduction for any of these payments. In contrast, Section 736(a) payments are income payments and are treated as either (1) a partner's distributive share of partnership ordinary income or (2) a guaranteed payment to the retiring partner. In either case, the retiring partner recognizes ordinary income. Further, as a necessary consequence, the remaining partners recognize either (1) the undistributed balance of partnership ordinary income or (2) partnership ordinary income after deducting the retiring partner's guaranteed payment.

3. **T** (p. 11–14; pre-contribution gain)

    The tax consequences of a distribution (not in complete liquidation) from a partnership to a partner are discussed as follows. Under Section 721, no gain or loss shall be recognized to the partnership (or to any of its partners), in the case of a contribution of property to the partnership in exchange for an interest in the partnership. Under Section 731, in the case of a distribution by a partnership to a partner, gain shall not be recognized to such partner, except to the extent that any money distributed exceeds the adjusted basis of such partner's interest in the partnership immediately before the distribution. However, under Section 704(c)(1)(B), if (1) property is contributed by a partner to a partnership and (2) on the date of contribution the property's fair value does not equal such property's adjusted basis, then if such property is subsequently distributed to another partner within 7 years (beginning on the date of contribution), the contributing partner will recognize (on the date of distribution) the difference between such property's fair value and adjusted basis on the date of contribution. In the instant case, Sergio recognizes gain or loss on the distribution of property (originally contributed by Sergio) to another partner within seven years of such contribution.

4. T (p. 11-23; partnership tax year closes for that partner)

   Determination of a retiring partner's adjusted basis in his partnership interest is discussed as follows. Under Section 706(c)(2)(A), when a partner disposes of his entire interest in the partnership, the partnership's tax year closes with respect to such partner on the sale date. When a partnership's tax year closes with respect to a partner, such partner's distributive share of partnership items of income, deduction, gain and loss must be determined for the period during which such person was a partner. Such partner's distributive share of partnership items of income, deduction, gain and loss must be taken into account in determining not only such partner's taxable income, but also such partner's adjusted basis in his partnership interest for purposes of determining gain or loss on the sale. Under Section 706(d)(1), within the context of a partner's disposition of his entire interest in the partnership, there are several acceptable methods of determining such partner's distributive share of partnership items of income, deduction, gain and loss as of the date of sale. Under one method, the partnership allocates to the retiring partner (based upon the number of days that such partner held such interest) a prorated amount of annual measures of a partner's distributive share of partnership items of income, deduction, gain and loss. Alternatively, under an interim closing of the books method, a retiring partner's distributive share of partnership items of income, deduction, gain and loss as of the date of sale is determined from the actual measures of partnership items of income, deduction, gain and loss through the date of such sale.

5. F (p. 11-35; Gregory would need to provide services)

   Family partnerships are owned and controlled by members of the same family. Underlying the taxation of family partnerships is a basic tenet: Income is recognized by the person who performs the services or who owns the capital that generates such income. Thus, under Section 704(e), to prevent tax avoidance within the context of a family partnership, a family member shall be recognized as a partner for tax purposes only if the family member acquires (1) a capital interest in a partnership (where capital is a material income-producing factor) in a bona fide transaction (i.e., a transaction where ownership and control are substantively transferred) or (2) a capital interest in a partnership where capital is not a material income-producing factor, but where the family member provides substantial services to the partnership.

   In the instant case, Clysdale and Associates is a partnership (1) where capital is not a material income-producing factor, (2) where the other two partners (Mr. Clysdale and his sister) perform most of the services that substantially constitute the income of the partnership, but (3) where Gregory does not provide substantial services to the partnership. Thus, Gregory will not be recognized as a partner of Clysdale and Associates for tax purposes.

6. F (p. 11-5; reduction in share of debt in excess of basis is capital gain)

   The tax consequences of a partner withdrawing from his partnership are discussed as follows. Given that a partner withdraws from his partnership and does not receive a disproportionate distribution (a distribution that increases or decreases the distributee partner's interest in certain ordinary income-producing assets):

   - Under Section 731(a)(1), in the case of a distribution by a partnership to a partner, gain shall not be recognized to such partner, except to the extent that any money distributed exceeds the adjusted basis of such partner's interest in the partnership immediately before the distribution.
   - Under Section 731(a)(2), in the case of a distribution by a partnership to a partner, loss shall not be recognized to such partner, unless no property other than money, inventory and receivables is distributed and except to the extent that the sum of money distributed and the adjusted bases of inventory and receivables distributed is less than the adjusted basis of such partner's interest in the partnership immediately before the distribution.

- Under Section 752(b), any decrease in a partner's share of the liabilities of the partnership is treated as a distribution of money from the partnership to the partner.

In the instant case, when Kay-Ann withdrew from Gem, her share of partnership liabilities decreased by $30,000, which is treated as a distribution of money from the partnership to Kay-Ann. Kay-Ann's gain realized and recognized is $30,000 (the excess of money deemed distributed of $30,000 over $–0–, the adjusted basis of Kay-Ann's partnership interest immediately before the distribution).

7. F (p. 11–9; Chad's basis in the auto would be 6,000)

The tax consequences of a distribution (in complete liquidation of a partner's interest in a partnership) are discussed as follows. Given that a partnership completely liquidates a partner's interest and that the withdrawing partner does not receive a disproportionate distribution (a distribution that increases or decreases the distributee partner's interest in certain ordinary income-producing assets):

In the instant case, Chad's adjusted basis in his partnership interest of $80,000 reduced by $30,000 distributed in the same transaction is allocated to properties in the following order:

(1) $44,000 to inventory.
(2) $6,000 ($50,000 – $44,000) to the company automobile.

8. T (p. 11–11)

The tax consequences of a distribution (in complete liquidation of a partner's interest in a partnership) are discussed as follows. Given that a partner withdraws from a partnership and does not receive a disproportionate distribution (a distribution that increases or decreases the distributee partner's interest in certain ordinary income-producing assets):

- Under Section 731(a)(1), in the case of a distribution by a partnership to a partner, gain shall not be recognized to such partner, except to the extent that any money distributed exceeds the adjusted basis of such partner's interest in the partnership immediately before the distribution.
- Under Section 731(a)(2), in the case of a distribution by a partnership to a partner, loss shall not be recognized to such partner, unless no property other than money, inventory and receivables is distributed and except to the extent that the sum of money distributed and the adjusted bases of inventory and receivables distributed is less than the adjusted basis of such partner's interest in the partnership immediately before the distribution.

9. T (p. 11–9)

The tax consequences of a distribution (in complete liquidation of a partner's interest in a partnership) are discussed as follows. Given that a partner withdraws from a partnership and does not receive a disproportionate distribution (a distribution that increases or decreases the distributee partner's interest in certain ordinary income-producing assets):

- Under Section 731(a)(1), in the case of a distribution by a partnership to a partner, gain shall not be recognized to such partner, except to the extent that any money distributed exceeds the adjusted basis of such partner's interest in the partnership immediately before the distribution.

10. T (p. 11–30)

Under Section 743(a), the basis of partnership property shall not be adjusted as a result of a transfer of an interest in a partnership by sale or exchange or on the death of a partner, unless the election provided by Section 754 (relating to optional adjustment to basis of partnership property) is in effect with respect to such partnership.

11. F (p. 11–30; election is binding for all subsequent tax years)

Under Section 743(a), the basis of partnership property shall not be adjusted as a result of a transfer of an interest in a partnership by sale or exchange or on the death of a partner, unless the election provided by Section 754 (relating to optional adjustment to basis of partnership property) is in effect with respect to such partnership. Under Section 754, if a partnership files an election, the basis of partnership property shall be adjusted:

- In the case of a distribution of property, in the manner provided in Section 734.
- In the case of a transfer of a partnership interest, in the manner provided in Section 743.

Such an election shall apply with respect to (1) all distributions of property by the partnership and (2) all transfers of interests in the partnership that occur during the taxable year with respect to which an election is filed *and all subsequent taxable years*. Such election may be revoked by the partnership.

Fill in the Blanks

1. capital; capital gain or loss (p. 11-23)

    The character of a recognized gain or loss upon the sale (or deemed sale) of a partner's interest in a partnership is discussed as follows. Under Section 741, in the case of a sale or exchange of an interest in a partnership, gain or loss shall be recognized to the transferor partner. Under Section 1001, gain or loss is measured by the difference between the amount realized and the selling partner's adjusted basis in the partnership interest. Such gain or loss shall be considered as gain or loss from the sale or exchange of a capital asset (except to the extent that Section 751 applies).

2. unrealized receivables; inventory (p. 11-25)

    In the case where a partnership has HOT assets, the tax consequences of a partner's sale or exchange of his partnership interest are discussed as follows. Under Section 741, in the case of a sale or exchange of an interest in a partnership, gain or loss shall be recognized to the transferor partner. Such gain or loss shall be considered as gain or loss from the sale or exchange of a capital asset (except to the extent that Section 751 applies). As noted, Section 751 constitutes an exception to a partner characterizing realized and recognized gain or loss on the sale or exchange of a partnership interest as capital gain or loss. Specifically, Section 751 applies to the sale or exchange of a partnership interest if the partnership has HOT assets. HOT assets are assets the value of which when realized by the partnership results in ordinary income to the partnership (e.g., *unrealized receivables and substantially appreciated inventory*). In effect, under the aggregate theory as applied in Section 751, when a partner sells his partnership interest, he is deemed as selling his interest in the HOT assets, thereby realizing and recognizing ordinary income.

3. cash (p. 11-5)

    Under Section 752(b), any decrease in a partner's share of the liabilities of the partnership is treated as a distribution of money (cash) from the partnership to the partner. For example, this situation may occur to one partner if (1) another partner guarantees a partnership debt, (2) the partnership pays down its debt, or (3) the partnership distributes property (subject to a debt) to another partner.

Multiple Choice

1. c (p. 11-29; exchanges of partnership interests do not qualify under Section 1031)

    Section 1031 does not apply to a partner who has transferred property (a capital or profits interest in a partnership) in exchange for a capital and profits interest in another partnership. Section 1031 does not apply within this context because such properties are NOT properties of a like kind within the meaning of Section 1031(a)(2)(D). Thus, item c is incorrect. Further, the following choice items are correct:

    - Item a is correct because under Section 721(a), no gain or loss is recognized either by a partnership or by a partner upon the contribution of property by a partner to a partnership.
    - Item b is correct because under Section 704(c)(1)(B), if (1) property is contributed by a partner to a partnership and (2) on the date of contribution the property's fair value does not equal such property's adjusted basis, then if such property is subsequently distributed to another partner within 7 years

(beginning on the date of contribution), the contributing partner will recognize (on the date of distribution) the difference between such property's fair value and adjusted basis on the date of contribution.
- Item d is correct because, under Section 721(a), no gain or loss is recognized either by a partnership or by a partner upon the contribution of property by a partner to a partnership. Within the meaning of Section 721, *property* includes the capital or profits interest in another partnership.

2. d (p. 11–22; installment method may apply to sale of partnership interest)

Under Section 741, in the case of a sale or exchange of an interest in a partnership, gain or loss shall be recognized to the transferor partner. Under Section 1001, gain or loss is measured by the difference between the amount realized and the selling partner's adjusted basis in the partnership interest. Such gain or loss shall be considered as gain or loss from the sale or exchange of a capital asset (except to the extent that Section 751 applies). As noted, Section 751 constitutes an exception to a partner characterizing realized and recognized gain or loss on the sale or exchange of a partnership interest as capital gain or loss. Section 751 applies to the sale or exchange of a partnership interest if the partnership has HOT assets. HOT assets are assets the value of which when realized by the partnership results in ordinary income to the partnership (e.g., *unrealized receivables and substantially appreciated inventory*). In effect, under the aggregate theory as applied in Section 751, when a partner sells his partnership interest, he is deemed as selling his interest in the HOT assets, thereby realizing and recognizing ordinary income. Further, in the case of a sale or exchange of an interest in a partnership that constitutes an installment sale, income from such installment sale may be taken into account under the installment method (except to the extent that Section 751 relates to depreciation recapture under Section 1245 or Section 1250). Thus, item d is incorrect. Further, the following choice items are correct:

- Item a is correct under Section 741.
- Item b is correct under Section 1001.
- Item c is correct because, under Treas. Reg. Sec. 1001–2(a), the amount realized from a sale or other disposition of property includes the amount of liabilities from which the transferor is discharged as a result of the sale or disposition.

3. a (p. 11–33)

Under Section 708(b), a partnership shall be considered as terminated only if (1) no part of any business, financial operation or venture of the partnership continues or (2) within a 12-month period, there is a sale or exchange of 50% or more of the total interest in partnership capital and profits. Under Treas. Reg. Sec. 301.7701, relating to the check-the-box entity classification scheme, a limited liability company (LLC), unless otherwise elected, is treated as a partnership for federal income tax purposes. Thus, item a is correct in that each of the two statements is true.

4. c (p. 11–22; 60,000 + 10,000 – 40,000)

Given that a partner has transferred property in exchange for a capital and profits interest in a partnership and subsequently sells such interest:

Under Section 722, the adjusted basis of Walter's interest in Cat partnership (outside basis) acquired by a contribution of property is equal to the sum of money contributed of $40,000 ($30,000 cash contributed + $10,000 under Section 752(a)). Walter's adjusted basis is reduced from $40,000 to $30,000 under Section 752(b) and Section 733 when Walter's share of partnership liabilities are paid or otherwise satisfied. In addition, Walter's adjusted basis in his partnership interest is adjusted upwards from $30,000 as Walter recognizes his distributive share of partnership income under Section 705. Correspondingly, Walter's adjusted basis in his partnership interest is adjusted downwards under Section 733, for the same amount, when he receives his distributive share of partnership income in the form of a cash distribution. Thus, at the time of sale, the adjusted basis of Walter's interest in Cat partnership (outside basis) is $30,000. His capital gain realized and recognized is $30,000 (amount realized of $60,000 less adjusted basis of $30,000) under Section 1001 and Section 741.

5. c (p. 11-9; 30,000 − 10,000 − 12,000 = 8,000 to allocate; 8,000(12,000/16,000) + 8,000(4,000/16,000)

   Given that a partnership completely liquidates a partner's interest and that the withdrawing partner does not receive a disproportionate distribution (a distribution that increases or decreases the distributee partner's interest in certain ordinary income-producing assets):

   Ted's adjusted basis in his partnership interest of $30,000 reduced by $10,000 distributed in the same transaction is allocated to properties in the following order:

   (1) $12,000 to inventory.
   (2) $8,000 ($30,000 − $10,000 − $12,000) to the 2 parcels of land, allocated as follows (assuming no unrealized depreciation) based upon relative adjusted bases:
       (a) $6,000 ($12,000/$16,000) × $8,000] to land #1.
       (b) $2,000 [($4,000/$16,000) × $8,000] to land #2.

   Thus, item c is correct.

6. e (p. 11-9; 300,000 − 140,000 − 60,000 = 100,000 to allocate; 160,000 − (80,000 × (160/185)) + 40,000 − 20,000 − (80,000 × 20/180)

   Given that a partnership completely liquidates a partner's interest and that the withdrawing partner does not receive a disproportionate distribution (a distribution that increases or decreases the distributee partner's interest in certain ordinary income-producing assets):

   - Under Section 731(a)(1), in the case of a distribution by a partnership to a partner, gain shall not be recognized to such partner, except to the extent that any money distributed exceeds the adjusted basis of such partner's interest in the partnership immediately before the distribution.
   - Under Section 732(b), the basis of property (other than money) distributed by a partnership to a partner in liquidation of a partner's interest is the adjusted basis of such partner's interest in the partnership reduced by any money distributed in the same transaction.
   - Under Section 732(c), the adjusted basis of such partner's interest in the partnership reduced by any money distributed in the same transaction is allocated to properties in the following order:
     - To any unrealized receivables and inventory items in an amount equal to the adjusted basis of each such property to the partnership.
     - To any other distributed properties in an amount equal to the adjusted basis of each such property to the partnership.

   Ted's adjusted basis in his partnership interest of $300,000 reduced by $140,000 distributed in the same transaction is allocated to properties in the following order:

   (1) $60,000 to inventory.
   (2) $100,000 ($300,000 − $140,000 − $60,000) to the building and the computer, allocated as follows (assuming unrealized depreciation of $20,000 associated with the computer):
       (a) $88,889 [$160,000 − (($160,000/$180,000) × $80,000)] to the building.
       (b) $11,111 [$40,000 − $20,000 − (($20,000/$180,000) × $80,000)] to the computer.

   Thus, item e is correct.

7. b (p. 11-22; 25,000 realized − 20,000 basis)

   Given that a partner has transferred property in exchange for a capital and profits interest in a partnership and subsequently sells such interest:

   - Under Section 722, the basis of an interest in a partnership (outside basis) acquired by a contribution of property is calculated by using a substituted basis approach and is equal to the sum of (1) money contributed and (2) the aggregate amount of adjusted bases of properties contributed.

- Under Section 705, the adjusted basis of a partner's interest in a partnership is adjusted as follows. Basis is increased for (1) subsequent contributions, (2) an increase in such partner's share of partnership debt, (3) income and gain items (whether taxable or exempt). In the following order, basis is decreased (but not below zero) for (1) a decrease in such partner's share of partnership debt, (2) subsequent distributions, (3) loss and expense items (whether deductible or non-deductible).

    In the instant case, under § 722, the adjusted basis of Fred's interest in Happy partnership (outside basis) acquired by a contribution of property is equal to the sum of money contributed of $10,000. Such adjusted basis has been modified under § 752(a) and § 705. At the time of the sale, Fred's adjusted basis in his partnership interest is $20,000. Thus, his capital gain realized and recognized is $5,000 [amount realized of $25,000 ($10,000 cash + $15,000 relief of liabilities) less adjusted basis of $20,000] under § 1001 and § 741. Thus, item b is correct.

8. b   (p. 11-25; 15,000 + 28,000 realized – 6,000 ordinary – 19,000 basis = 18,000 capital gain)

    In the instant case, at the time of the sale, Cynthia's adjusted basis in her partnership interest is $19,000. Thus, her capital gain realized and recognized would be $24,000 [amount realized of $43,000 ($28,000 cash + $15,000 relief of liabilities) less adjusted basis of $19,000] under Section 1001 and Section 741, but for § 751. But, in the instant case, there are HOT assets (e.g., unrealized receivables) so that Section 751 applies to bifurcate this transaction into 2 parts. First, the amount realized of $6,000 and adjusted basis of zero is separately stated with respect to the deemed sale of hot assets to yield ordinary income of $6,000 ($6,000 – 0). Second, the balance of the amount realized of $37,000 ($43,000 – $6,000) and adjusted basis of $19,000 ($19,000 – 0) is separately stated with respect to the sale of Cynthia's partnership interest to yield capital gain of $18,000 ($37,000 – $19,000). Thus, in the instant case, because of the application of § 751, Cynthia realizes and recognizes ordinary income of $6,000 and capital gain of $18,000, rather than capital gain of $24,000. Thus, item b is correct.

9. c   (p. 11-25; § 751 applies to recapture potential associated with depreciable property)

    In the instant case, at the time of the sale, a partner's adjusted basis in ABC partnership interest is $–0–. Thus, his capital gain realized and recognized would be $11,000 (amount realized of $11,000 less adjusted basis of $–0–) under § 1001 and § 741, but for § 751. But, in the instant case, there are HOT assets (e.g., depreciation recapture potential of $5,000, which falls within the scope of unrealized receivables) so that § 751 applies to bifurcate this transaction into 2 parts. First, the amount realized of $5,000 and adjusted basis of zero is separately stated with respect to the deemed sale of hot assets to yield ordinary income of $5,000 ($5,000 – $–0–). Second, the balance of the amount realized of $6,000 ($11,000 – $5,000) and adjusted basis of $–0– ($–0– – $–0–) is separately stated with respect to the sale of the partnership interest to yield capital gain of $6,000 ($6,000 – $–0–). Thus, in the instant case, because of the application of § 751, the partner realizes and recognizes ordinary income of $5,000 and capital gain of $6,000, rather than capital gain of $11,000. Thus, item c is correct.

CHAPTER 12

S Corporations

LEARNING OBJECTIVES

After completing Chapter 12, you should be able to:
1. Explain the tax effects that S corporation status has on shareholders.
2. Identify corporations that qualify for the S election.
3. Understand how to make an S election.
4. Explain how an S election can be terminated.
5. Compute nonseparately stated income and identify separately stated items.
6. Allocate income, deductions, and credits to shareholders.
7. Understand how distributions to S corporation shareholders are taxed.
8. Calculate a shareholder's basis in S corporation stock.
9. Explain the tax effects that losses have on shareholders.
10. Compute the built-in gains tax.
11. Compute the passive investment income penalty tax.

KEY TERMS

Accumulated adjustments account (AAA)
Accumulated earnings and profits (AEP)
Built-in gains tax
Bypass election
Other adjustments account (OAA)
Passive investment income
Previously taxed income (PTI)
S corporation
Small business corporation
Subchapter S
Voluntary revocation

OUTLINE

I. **INTRODUCTION**
   A. The S corporation rules were enacted to minimize entity choice tax considerations for small businesses.
   B. The S election allows the corporation to avoid double taxation and loss limitations inherent with regular corporations while still enjoying many of the nontax benefits available to regular corporations.

II. **QUALIFYING FOR S CORPORATION STATUS**
   A. Definition of a Small Business Corporation
      1. For S corporation status, a small business corporation:
         a. is a domestic corporation.
         b. is an eligible corporation:
            1. certain banks and insurance companies are ineligible.
            2. Puerto Rico or possessions corporations are ineligible.
            3. foreign corporations are ineligible.
         c. issues only one class of stock:
            1. differences in voting rights are allowed.
            2. distribution or liquidation rights must be identical.
            3. debt may be reclassified as a separate class of stock unless it meets the "straight debt" safe harbor.
         d. has no more than 75 shareholders:
            1. a husband and wife are considered one shareholder.
            2. a widower (or widow) and the decedent spouse's estate are considered one shareholder.
         e. has as its shareholders only individuals, estates, certain trusts, and certain tax-exempt organizations.
         f. has no nonresident alien shareholder.
   B. Making the Election
      1. A small business corporation must file Form 2553 to make the S election.
      2. All shareholders must consent to the election in writing.
      3. In order to be effective for the current year, the election must be made on or before the 15th day of the 3rd month of the current year.
      4. The election may be made at any time during the current year to be effective for the following year.
      5. No election can be made for a corporation not yet in existence; the first month of a newly created corporation is the earliest of:
         a. when the corporation has shareholders,
         b. when the corporation acquires assets, or
         c. when the corporation begins doing business.
      6. The IRS can grant relief from the various requirements.
   C. Loss of the Election
      1. An S election remains in force until it is revoked or lost.
      2. Violation of one of the eligibility rules causes termination of the S election as of the date on which the disqualifying event occurs. Disqualifying events include:
         a. the number of shareholders exceeds the maximum allowed.
         b. a nonresident alien becomes a shareholder.
         c. another class of stock is created.
      3. Voluntary revocation may be made by shareholders owning a majority of shares (voting and nonvoting). A revocation made by the 15th day of the 3rd month is effective for the entire year unless a later date is specified.
      4. Failing to qualify as a small business corporation (e.g., issuing a second class of stock) immediately terminates the S corporation election.

5. Failing the passive investment income (PII) limitation causes termination of the S election as of the beginning of the fourth year.
   a. This limitation applies only to S corporations having accumulated E & P from years in which the corporation was a C corporation.
   b. Further, the limitation only applies if the corporation has passive income in excess of 25% of its gross receipts for three consecutive years.
   c. PII includes dividends, interest, rents, gains and losses from sale of securities, and royalties. Rents may be excluded if significant personal services are provided to the tenant.

D. Reelection After Termination
   1. Generally, five years must pass before a new election can be made.
   2. This five year waiting period is waived when:
      a. there is a more than 50% change in ownership or
      b. the event which caused disqualification was not reasonably within the control of the S corporation or its majority shareholders.

III. OPERATIONAL RULES

A. Computation of Taxable Income
   1. S corporations are treated much like partnerships for tax purposes. Differences include:
      a. S corporations can amortize organizational expenditures.
      b. S corporations must recognize gains (but not losses) on distributions of appreciated property to shareholders.
   2. In general, S corporation items are divided into (1) nonseparately stated income or loss and (2) separately stated income, losses, deductions and credits.
      a. Separately stated income, losses, deductions, and credits are items which could uniquely affect the tax liability of a shareholder.
      b. An S corporation's separately stated items are the same as for a partnership (see text for a detailed listing).
   3. Nonseparately stated income or loss and all separately stated items are allocated pro rata to each shareholder for *each day* the stock is owned.

B. Tax Treatment of Distributions to Shareholders
   1. The amount of any distribution to an S corporation shareholder is the cash plus the fair market value of any other property distributed.
   2. How the distribution is treated depends on whether the S corporation has accumulated earnings and profits (AEP) from previous C corporation years.
      a. If the S corporation was never a C corporation or there is no AEP from C corporation years, the distribution is a tax-free recovery of capital to the extent of shareholder basis in the S corporation stock.
      b. If the S corporation has AEP, the distribution is classified according to a specific statutory procedure that treats pre-S election AEP distributions as dividends and post-S election earnings differently.
   3. An accumulated adjustments account (AAA) is used to track undistributed earnings of an S corporation that have been previously taxed to shareholders.
      a. AAA is a cumulative total of undistributed nonseparately and separately stated items. It is meant to parallel the calculation of C corporation AEP.
      b. Exhibit 12–1 demonstrates the AAA computation. AAA is determined at the end of each year (not when distributions are made).
      c. In calculating AAA for distribution purposes, the net negative adjustments (e.g., the excess of losses and deductions over income) for the tax year are ignored.
      d. The AAA can have a negative balance. However, distributions cannot make the AAA negative or increase a negative balance.
   4. A shareholder has a proportionate interest in the AAA.

5. For an S corporation with accumulated E & P, a cash distribution is (see Concept Summary 12–1):
   a. tax-free up to the shareholder's interest in AAA, limited to stock basis,
   b. tax-free up to the amount of PTI (previously taxed income),
   c. a taxable dividend to the extent of AEP,
   d. return of capital, limited to remaining stock basis, and
   e. capital gain to the extent of any remaining amount distributed.
6. S corporations report changes in the AAA on Schedule M-2 of Form 1120S.
7. Special rules cover cash distributions during the one-year period after an S election termination.

C. Tax Treatment of Property Distributions by the Corporation (see Concept Summary 12-2)
   1. An S corporation recognizes a gain on any distribution of appreciated property.
   2. The corporate gain is passed through to the shareholders.
   3. The S corporation does not recognize a loss when depreciated property is distributed.
   4. The shareholder's basis in the property is its FMV.

D. Shareholder's Basis
   1. Initial stock basis is determined similar to that of stock basis in a C corporation.
   2. Basis is increased by further stock purchases and capital contributions.
   3. Next, corporate operations during the year increase stock basis.
      a. Nonseparately computed income,
      b. Separately stated income items,
      c. Depletion in excess of the property's basis increase.
   4. Basis is then reduced by distributions of AAA or PTI.
   5. Next, nondeductible expenses and nonseparately stated and separately stated loss and deduction items decrease shareholder basis.
   6. A shareholder's basis can never be negative.
      a. Once stock basis is zero, any additional basis reductions from losses or deductions, but NOT distributions, decrease the shareholder's basis in loans made to the S corporation.
      b. Any excess of losses or deductions is suspended until there are subsequent bases.
      c. Subsequent increases (e.g., income) adjust debt back to its original basis before any increase is made to stock basis.
   7. A distribution in excess of stock basis does not reduce any debt basis. If a loss and a distribution occur in the same year, distributions reduce basis first.

E. Treatment of Losses
   1. Net operating losses (NOL) are passed through to the shareholders and are deductible to the extent of stock and loan bases.
   2. An NOL which exceeds the shareholder's basis may be carried forward and deducted by the same shareholder, if and when, basis is restored.
   3. Passive activity losses and credits flow through to shareholders and decrease the shareholder's basis, whether or not deductible under the passive activity loss rules.
   4. S corporation shareholders may only deduct an NOL if they are "at-risk" for the loss.

F. Tax on Pre-Election Built-In Gain
   1. A C corporation electing S status after 1986, may incur a corporate level tax on gains attributable to asset appreciation during C corporation years.
   2. The total amount of gain recognized is limited to the aggregate, net built-in gains at the time of conversion to S status.
   3. The tax applies when the S corporation disposes of a built-in gain asset in a taxable disposition within 10 years of the conversion to S status.
   4. Any unrealized gain on appreciated assets (e.g., real estate, cash basis receivables, and goodwill) on the day the corporation elects S status is subject to this tax.
      a. The highest corporate tax rate (currently 35 percent) is applied to the gain when the asset is sold.
      b. The maximum amount of gain that can be recognized is limited to the aggregate net built-in gain on the date it converted to S status.

5. For purposes of the tax on built-in gains, certain C corporation carryovers are allowed as offsets, including:
   a. unexpired NOLs or capital losses.
   b. business credit carryovers.
6. If a corporation is using FIFO, any built-in gain is recognized as the inventory is sold. A LIFO-basis corporation does not recognize this gain unless the corporation invades the LIFO layer during the 10-year recognition period.

G. Passive Investment Income Penalty Tax
   1. An S corporation having AEP from C corporation years is taxed on its excess net passive income.
   2. Excess Net Passive Income is:

   $$\frac{\text{passive investment income} - 25\% \text{ of gross receipts}}{\text{total passive investment for the year}} \times \frac{\text{net passive investment income}}{\text{for the year}}$$

   3. The amount subject to tax cannot exceed the corporation's taxable income for the year.
   4. The applicable tax rate is the highest corporate tax rate for the year (currently 35 percent).

H. Other Operational Rules
   1. S corporations must make estimated tax payments for any recognized built-in gains and excess passive investment income.
   2. An S corporation may own stock in another corporation but, is not eligible for a dividends received deduction.
   3. An S corporation is not subject to the 10 percent of taxable income limitation applicable to charitable contributions made by a C corporation.
   4. Any family member who renders services or furnishes capital to the electing corporation must be reasonably compensated to avoid adjustments by the IRS to reflect the value of such services or capital.
   5. A shareholder's portion of S income is not self-employment income. Compensation for services rendered to an S corporation is subject to FICA taxes.

IV. **TAX PLANNING CONSIDERATIONS**
   A. In determining when the S election is advisable, it is necessary to consider all of the provisions that will affect the owners.
   B. Because Subchapter S is elective, strict compliance with the Code is required in making and preserving the election and operating the corporation. Shareholders and management should be made aware of the various transactions that could cause involuntary termination of the S election.

Section 1361 – Definition of a Small Business Corporation

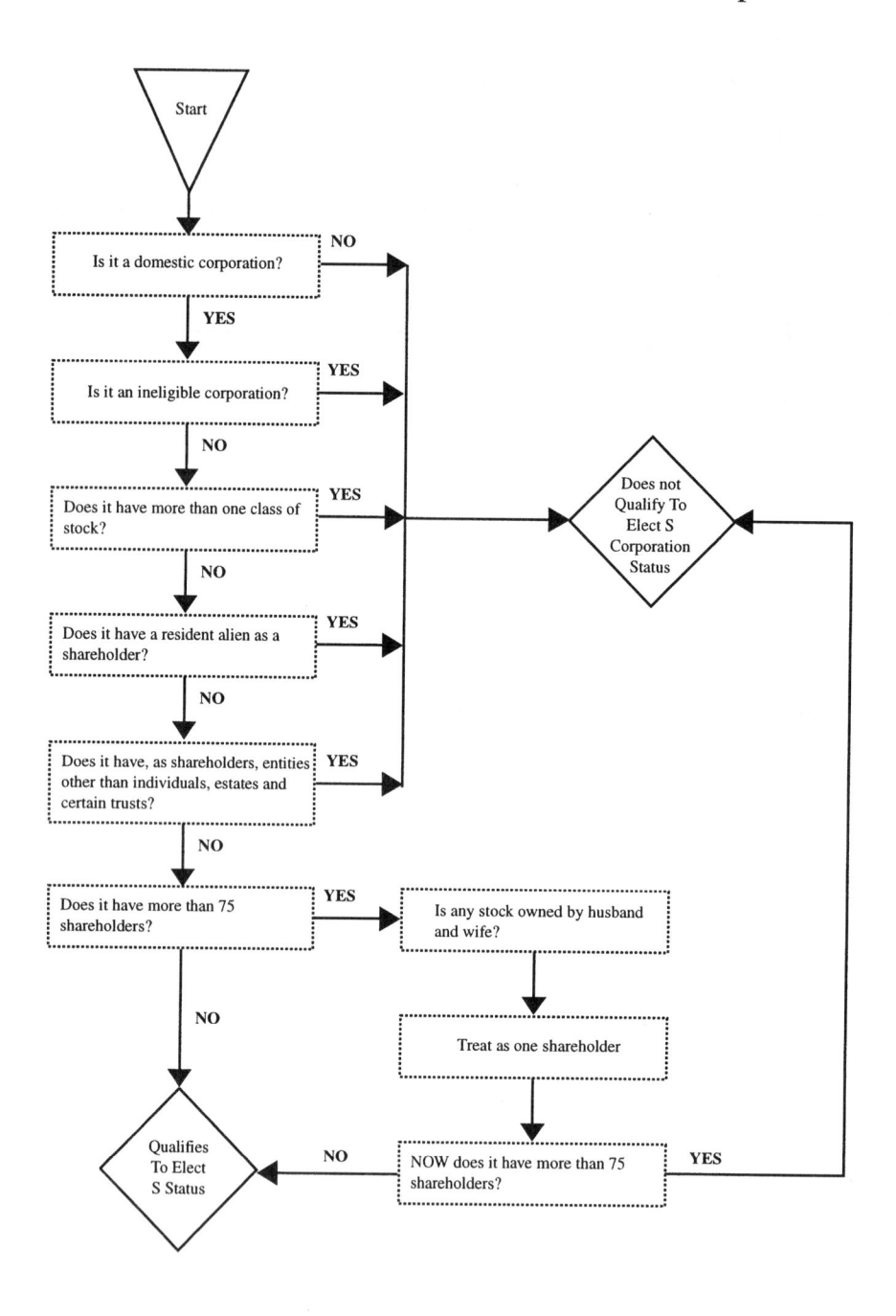

```
                        Start
                          |
                          v
              Is it a domestic corporation? ---NO--->
                          |                          |
                         YES                         |
                          v                          |
              Is it an ineligible corporation? ---YES--->
                          |                          |
                         NO                          |
                          v                          |
              Does it have more than one class       |
              of stock? ---YES--->                   |
                          |                          v
                         NO                   Does not Qualify
                          v                   To Elect S
              Does it have a resident alien   Corporation Status
              as a shareholder? ---YES--->           ^
                          |                          |
                         NO                          |
                          v                          |
              Does it have, as shareholders,         |
              entities other than individuals,       |
              estates and certain trusts? ---YES--->
                          |                          |
                         NO                          |
                          v                          |
              Does it have more than 75              |
              shareholders? ---YES---> Is any stock owned by
                          |             husband and wife?
                         NO                    |
                          v                    v
                                        Treat as one shareholder
                                               |
                                               v
              Qualifies    <---NO--- NOW does it have more than
              To Elect                75 shareholders? ---YES--->
              S Status
```

S Corporation Distributions to Shareholders

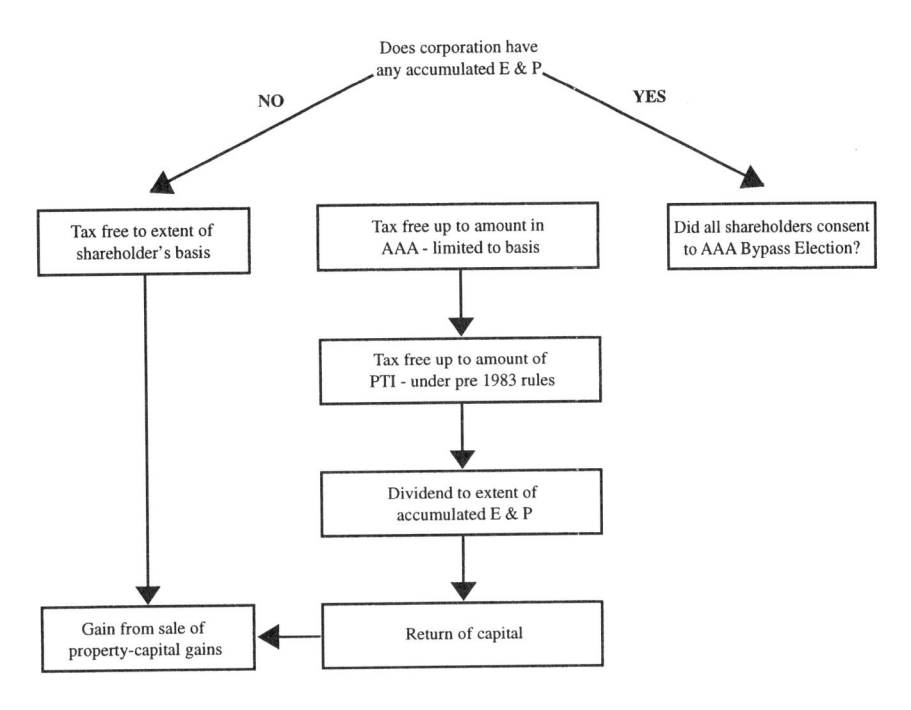

Does corporation have any accumulated E & P

NO → Tax free to extent of shareholder's basis → Gain from sale of property-capital gains

YES → Did all shareholders consent to AAA Bypass Election?

Tax free up to amount in AAA - limited to basis → Tax free up to amount of PTI - under pre 1983 rules → Dividend to extent of accumulated E & P → Return of capital → Gain from sale of property-capital gains

Shareholder's basis cannot be less than zero

TEST FOR SELF-EVALUATION—CHAPTER 12

True or False

Indicate which of the following statements is true or false by circling the correct answer.

T F 1. A corporation's election of S corporation status is valid if a majority of its shareholders consent to the election. (IRS 97 3A-18)

T F 2. Both separately stated items and the nonseparately stated income or loss are passed through to the shareholders of an S corporation in proportion to their shareholdings. (IRS 97 3A-19)

T F 3. Blue, an S Corporation, has no earnings and profits. In 2002, Blue distributed cash of $40,000 to Sunny, its sole shareholder. Sunny's basis in Blue's stock on December 31, 2002 (before considering the distribution) was $35,000. On January 1, 2003, Sunny's basis in Blue's stock would be ($5,000). (IRS 97 3A-20)

T F 4. A loss on the sale or exchange of property is NOT deductible if the transaction is directly or indirectly between two S corporations and the same persons own more than 50% in value of the outstanding stock of each corporation. (IRS 96 3A-7)

T F 5. If an S corporation is subject to the tax on excess net passive investment income, it must reduce the items of passive income passed through to the shareholders. (IRS 96 3A-10)

T F 6. If an S corporation's passive investment income is more than 25% of gross receipts for two consecutive tax years and the corporation has pre-S corporation earnings and profits at the end of each of those years, the corporation's S corporation status will be terminated. (IRS 95 3A-13)

T F 7. Omega Corporation, an S corporation, has 10 shareholders on January 1, 2002. During the year, 8 of the existing shareholders, owning 51% of the stock, sold their interests to one new individual shareholder. Omega will automatically terminate its S corporation status on the day over 50% of Omega's stock was transferred. (IRS 94 3A-9)

T F 8. Exodus Corporation, a calendar year corporation, has 75 shareholders on January 1, 2002. On June 30, 2002, a shareholder sold her stock to Interferon Corporation. On July 1, 2002, Interferon sold the stock to its sole shareholder, Anthony. Exodus Corporation will file two short period returns for 2002. (IRS 94 3A-10)

T F 9. For any tax year, an S corporation can elect its distributions as coming first from earnings and profits if all shareholders who receive a distribution during the tax year consent to the election. This election remains in effect for all tax years thereafter. (IRS 93 3A-12)

T F 10. For 2002, the books and records of Clover, Inc., a cash basis S corporation, reflected the following: (IRS 92 3A-11)

Salary to Dad Clover, President and 50% shareholder	$22,000
Salary to Son Clover, Janitor and 50% shareholder	$60,000
Loans to Dad Clover during 2002, no repayments	$30,000

Dad Clover worked 40 hour weeks for the entire year but said that the business could not afford to pay him a salary more than $22,000. The IRS could reclassify the $30,000 and/or part of the son's salary to Dad Clover, and assess income tax withholding as well as employment taxes on those amounts.

Fill in the Blanks

Complete the following statements with the appropriate word(s) or amount(s).

1. Generally an S corporation is a tax _____ rather than a tax _____ entity.

2. A distribution by an S corporation having no earnings and profits is _____ in gross income to the extent that it does not exceed the shareholder's adjusted basis in stock.

3. An S corporation's net operating loss pass through cannot exceed a shareholder's adjusted basis in the _____ plus the basis of any _____ made to the corporation.

4. The term "small" for purposes of the S election refers to the _____.

5. The long-term capital gain from the sale of securities would generally be treated as _____ investment income for the purpose of calculating the tax on Excess Net Passive Income.

6. Distributions that exceed the shareholder's tax basis for the stock are taxable as _____.

7. The _____ of stock in an S corporation is calculated similarly to the basis of stock in a regular corporation.

8. Net operating losses which exceed the shareholder's stock basis are used to reduce _____ the shareholder.

Multiple Choice

Choose the best answer for each of the following questions.

_____ 1. All of the following factors serve to determine whether an S corporation may be subject to the tax on excess net passive income except: (IRS 97 3B-45)

   a. The S corporation has been an S corporation from the date of its incorporation.
   b. The S corporation has Subchapter C earnings and profits at the end of the year.
   c. Passive investment income is more than 25% of its gross receipts.
   d. More than 50% of loans payable are not at-risk.

_____ 2. What is the nonseparately stated income amount of an accrual basis, calendar year S corporation with the following items? (IRS 97 3C-78)

Gross receipts	$200,000
Interest income	12,000
Rental income	25,000
Cost of goods sold and commissions	127,000
Net long-term capital gain	17,000
Compensation paid to shareholder	10,000

   a. $63,000
   b. $73,000
   c. $117,000
   d. $127,000

_____ 3. Twister, an S corporation, has no earnings and profits. In 2002, Twister distributed property with a fair market value of $65,000 and an adjusted basis of $52,000 to Carlos, its sole shareholder.

After recognizing his share of any corporate gain or loss, his adjusted basis in Twister's stock at year end was $50,000. How should the distribution be handled by Carlos? (IRS 97 3C-79)

    a. $50,000 as return of capital and $15,000 as nontaxable distribution.
    b. $50,000 as return of capital and $15,000 as taxable capital gain.
    c. $50,000 as return of capital and $2,000 as taxable capital gain.
    d. $50,000 as nontaxable distribution.

_____ 4.   On January 1, 2002, Jon purchased 50% of Waite, an S corporation, for $75,000. At the end of 2002, Waite incurred an ordinary loss of $160,000. How much of the loss can Jon deduct on his personal income tax return for 2002? (IRS 97 3C-80)

    a. $37,500
    b. $75,000
    c. $80,000
    d. $160,000

_____ 5.   To qualify for S corporation status, a corporation must meet all of the following requirements except: (IRS 96 3B-27)

    a.   Must be a domestic corporation.
    b.   Must have no more than 75 shareholders.
    c.   Must have as shareholders only individuals, certain trusts or other corporations.
    d.   Must have shareholders who are citizens or residents of the U.S.

_____ 6.   All of the following would reduce the basis of a shareholder's stock in an S corporation except: (IRS 96 3B-28)

    a.   A shareholder's pro rata share of nontaxable distributions by the S corporation to its shareholders.
    b.   A shareholder's pro rata share of all loss and deduction items of the S corporation that are separately stated and passed through to the shareholder.
    c.   A shareholder's pro rata share of any nonseparately stated loss of the S corporation.
    d.   A shareholder's pro rata share of any nonseparately stated income of the S corporation.

_____ 7.   On December 31, 2002, Valor, a calendar year S corporation since 1981, made a $100,000 distribution to its sole shareholder, Bryant. Valor's books and records reflect the following for 2002.

Accumulated adjustments account—1/1/02	$ 5,000
Ordinary income for 2002	50,000
Previously taxed income account at the time of the distribution	10,000
Accumulated earnings and profits at the time of the distribution	5,000

Bryant's basis in Valor's stock on January 1, 2002 was $40,000. How much income will Bryant report from this S corporation investment in 2002 and what is its character? (IRS 96 3C-67)

	Ordinary Income	Capital Gain
a.	$50,000	$10,000
b.	$55,000	$ 5,000
c.	$60,000	$ -0-
d.	$50,000	$60,000

_____ 8.   Magnolia Corporation, a calendar year S corporation, was formed on January 1, 2001. Kathy owns 25 percent of Magnolia's outstanding stock which she purchased for $20,000. In 2001, Kathy guaranteed a corporate loan for $40,000. In 2002, Kathy made payments on the loan totaling $10,000. Magnolia had losses of $90,000 and $60,000 in 2001 and 2002 respectively. What is the amount of the loss that Kathy can carry over to 2003? (IRS 96 3C-68)

    a. $0
    b. $7,500
    c. $10,000
    d. $17,500

_____ 9. On January 1, 2002, Mr. Wise purchased 50 percent of S Corporation Cobra's only class of stock outstanding for $150,000. On December 1, 2002, he purchased the other 50% of Cobra's stock for $150,000. For 2002 Cobra incurred a net operating loss of $237,250. How much of the loss can Mr. Wise deduct on his individual income tax return for 2002? (IRS 96 3C-69)

    a. $118,625
    b. $128,348
    c. $150,000
    d. $237,250

_____ 10. In 2001, Lisa acquired 100% of the stock of newly-formed Computers Inc. for $50,000 cash. Computers incurred a loss of $15,600 for 2001. On January 1, 2002, Computers properly elected S corporation status. Its net income for 2002 was $20,000. A dividend of $5,000 was declared and paid in 2002. What is Lisa's basis in Computers Inc. as of December 31, 2002? (IRS 96 3C-70)

    a. $70,000
    b. $65,000
    c. $51,000
    d. $50,000

_____ 11. In the context of the tax on excess net passive income paid by S corporations, net passive income does not include: (IRS 95 3B-33)

    a.   interest and dividends.
    b.   annuities.
    c.   net operating losses.
    d.   sales or exchanges of stock.

_____ 12. Mr. Oliver received a distribution from an S corporation that was in excess of the basis of his stock in the corporation. The S corporation had no earnings and profits. Mr. Oliver should treat the distribution in excess of his basis as (IRS 95 3B-34)

    a.   a return of capital.
    b.   previously taxed income.
    c.   a capital gain.
    d.   a reduction in the basis of his stock.

_____ 13. With regard to an S corporation and its shareholders, the at-risk rules applicable to losses (IRS 95 3B-35)

    a.   take into consideration the S corporation's ratio of debt to equity.
    b.   apply at the shareholder level rather than at the corporate level.
    c.   are subject to the elections made by the S corporation's shareholders.
    d.   depend on the type of income reported by the S corporation.

_____ 14. All of the following would reduce the basis of a shareholder's stock in an S corporation except: (IRS 95 3B-36)

a. A shareholder's pro rata share of any nonseparately stated loss of the S corporation.
b. A shareholder's pro rata share of all loss and deduction items of the S corporation that are separately stated.
c. A shareholder's pro rata share of any nondeductible expenses of the S corporation that are not properly chargeable to capital account.
d. A shareholder's pro rata share of any nonseparately stated income of the S corporation.

_____ 15. Which of the following events would cause an S corporation to cease to qualify as an S corporation: (IRS 95 3B-37)

a. A 25% shareholder sells her shares to an individual who wants to revoke the S corporation status.
b. The corporation is liable for tax on excess net passive investment income for two consecutive years.
c. A shareholder has zero basis in his stock.
d. The S corporation issues its stock to another corporation.

_____ 16. The books and records of May Inc., a calendar year S corporation since 1982, reflect the following information for 2002:

Accumulated adjustments account 1/1/02	$ 60,000
Accumulated earnings & profits 1/1/02	150,000
Ordinary income for 2002	204,000

May Inc. has one shareholder, Paula, whose basis in May's stock was $100,000 on January 1, 2002. During 2002, May distributed $300,000 to Paula. What is the amount of the distribution that would be treated as a dividend by Paula? (IRS 95 3C-73)

a. $0
b. $36,000
c. $264,000
d. $300,000

SOLUTIONS TO CHAPTER 12 QUESTIONS

True or False

1. F (p. 12–9; all shareholders must consent)

    S corporations are small business corporations (as defined under Section 1361(b)) that have made a valid election under Section 1362. Under Section 1362(a)(2), the election is valid only if ALL persons (who are shareholders on the day such election is made) consent to the election.

2. T (p. 12–15)

    Under Section 1366, in determining the federal income tax of an S corporation shareholder for a particular tax year within which the S corporation tax year ends, such shareholder must take into account such shareholder's pro rata share (determined on a per share per day basis) of S corporation (1) separately stated items of income, deduction, gain, loss and credit and (2) non-separately stated income or loss.

3. F (p. 12–23; stock basis cannot go below zero)

    The tax treatment of a current distribution from an S corporation to a shareholder depends upon the interactive effects of (1) corporate Accumulated Earnings and Profits (AE & P), (2) the corporate Accumulated Adjustments Account (AAA), and (3) the shareholder's stock basis. If the S corporation has no AE & P at the end of a taxable year, the shareholder's stock basis at the end of the S corporation's tax year exclusively determines the tax treatment of the current distribution. Under Section 1368(b), the distribution is treated as a tax-free return of capital to the extent that the amount distributed does not exceed the shareholder's stock basis. An amount distributed in excess of such shareholder's stock basis is treated as gain from the deemed sale or exchange of stock.

    Further, stock basis is generally determined only at the end of the S corporation's tax year. At that time, under Section 1367, stock basis is determined based upon a three-tiered analytical approach, as follows.

    (a) Stock basis is increased by the sum of the following items:
    - Separately stated income or gain items.
    - Nonseparately computed income.
    - Tax-exempt income.

    (b) Stock basis is decreased by:
    - Corporate distributions that constitute a return of capital.

    (c) Stock basis is decreased by the sum of the following items:
    - Nondeductible expenses that are not properly charged to a capital account.
    - Separately stated loss or deduction items.
    - Nonseparately computed loss

    In the instant case, Blue has no AE & P. Accordingly, Blue's 2002 distribution of $40,000 to Sunny is treated by Sunny as a tax-free return of capital to the extent of $35,000 (Sunny's stock basis) and a gain from the deemed sale or exchange of stock to the extent of $5,000 ($40,000 – $35,000). Further, Sunny's stock basis is $–0– ($35,000 – $35,000) as of January 1, 2003.

4. T (p. 12–23; related party)

    Regular C corporation provisions apply to S corporations as long as such provisions are not inconsistent with a provision of Subchapter S. For example, under Section 267(b)(12), an S corporation and another S corporation are related parties if the same persons own more that 50% in value of the outstanding stock of each corporation. Accordingly, under Section 267(a), if one S corporation sells depreciated property to another S corporation (where the two S corporations are related parties), the realized loss of the first S corporation is not recognized. Instead, the realized loss is suspended until the second S corporation sells the property to an unrelated party, where the suspended loss may be used to offset any gain realized and recognized by the second S corporation.

5. T (p. 12-31; passive income reported by each shareholder is reduced by their allocable portion of the tax)

Consistent with the application of the aggregate theory, the incidence of taxation of an S corporation generally occurs at the shareholder level, rather than at the corporate level. However, there are exceptions, as follows.

- Under Section 1374, a tax is imposed at the corporate level on certain built-in gains.
- Under Section 1375, a tax is imposed at the corporate level on Excess Net Passive Income (ENPI) if the following two conditions are satisfied:
  - The S corporation has AE & P at the close of its tax year.
  - Passive Investment Income (PII) is greater than 25% of Gross Receipts (GR).

  The S corporation tax on ENPI is equal to the maximum corporate rate for the year (35%) multiplied by the smaller of (1) ENPI and (2) Taxable Income (TI), where:
  - Net Passive Investment Income (NPII) is equal to PII reduced by allowable deductions directly connected with the production of such income.

- $ENPI = NPII \times \dfrac{PII - (25\% \text{ of } GR)}{PII}$

Further, each shareholder's pro rata share of NPII is proportionately reduced by the Section 1375 corporate level tax on ENPI.

6. F (p. 12-12; three years)

S corporations are *small business corporations* (as defined under Section 1361(b)) that have made a valid election under Section 1362. This election may be terminated under Section 1362(d) by either (1) voluntary revocation or (2) involuntary termination. Voluntary revocation of an S corporation election is accomplished when consent to such revocation is made by shareholders owning a majority of shares. In contrast, involuntary termination occurs by operation of law in the following instances.

- Where the S corporation fails to continue to satisfy the requirements of a *small business corporation*, the S corporation election is terminated effective on the day the S corporation ceases to meet the requirements of a *small business corporation*.
- Where the S corporation, for 3 consecutive taxable years, has both (1) Accumulated Earnings and Profits (AE & P) determined at the end of the taxable year and (2) Excess Passive Investment Income (EPII) [where EPII is equal to Passive Investment Income (PII) less 25% of Gross Receipts (GR)], the S corporation election is terminated as of the beginning of the fourth year.

7. F (p. 12-11; only if a voluntary revocation is filed)

S corporations are *small business corporations* (as defined under Section 1361(b)) that have made a valid election under Section 1362. This election may be terminated under Section 1362(d) by either (1) voluntary revocation or (2) involuntary termination. Voluntary revocation of an S corporation election is accomplished when consent to such revocation is made by shareholders owning a majority of shares.

In the instant case, the mere purchase of 51% of Omega stock by a new shareholder will not cause termination of Omega's S corporation election. If the new majority shareholder does not want Omega to be an S corporation, the new shareholder will need to cause a voluntarily revocation of Omega's S corporation election.

8. T (p. 12-11; termination of S on date event occurred)

In this case, a shareholder of Exodus sold her stock to Interferon Corporation on June 30, 2002. Even though Interferon subsequently sold such stock to its sole shareholder (Anthony) on July 1, 2002, Exodus was not a small business corporation on June 30, 2002. Accordingly:

STUDY GUIDE
CHAPTER 12
S Corporations

- Exodus' S corporation election is terminated effective June 30, 2002.
- Exodus must file short period tax returns for 2002: (1) one return for which the corporation is an S corporation (January 1, 2002–June 29, 2002) and (2) one return for which the corporation is a C corporation (June 30, 2002–Dec. 31, 2002).
- Exodus may re-elect S corporation status before the 5-year waiting period has expired because the event causing the termination was not reasonably within the control of Exodus or shareholders owning a majority of shares of Exodus.

9. F (p. 12–19; year-by-year election is made for all distributions during a particular tax year)

The tax treatment of a current distribution to an S corporation shareholder depends upon the interactive effects of (1) corporate Accumulated Earnings and Profits (AE & P), (2) the corporate Accumulated Adjustments Account (AAA), and (3) the shareholder's stock basis. Under Section 1368(c), if the S corporation has AE & P at the end of the taxable year (in contrast to no AE & P), the rules concerning the tax treatment of a current distribution are more complex and are discussed as follows.

10. T (p. 12–32)

In determining the Federal income tax of an S corporation shareholder for a particular tax year within which the S corporation tax year ends, such shareholder must take into account such shareholder's pro rata share (determined on a per share per day basis) of S corporation (1) separately stated items of income, deduction, gain, loss and credits and (2) nonseparately stated income or loss. However, family S corporations are accorded special treatment under Section 1366(e). Family S corporations are S corporations owned and controlled by members of the same family. Underlying the taxation of family S corporations is the following basic tenet:

Income is recognized by the person who performs the services or who owns the capital that generates income.

In the instant case, the salary to Son does not seem reasonable relative to the salary of Dad. Further, if there is no evidence of a bona fide indebtedness with respect to the transfer of $30,000 from Clover to Dad, the IRS may reclassify these transfers as follows.

- Loans to Dad are compensation. Consequently, Dad has additional gross income from wages and the S corporation has a similar increase in a deduction for wages.
- A portion of the salary to Son is unreasonable. Consequently, Son has a decrease in gross income from wages and the S corporation has a similar decrease in a deduction for wages.

Fill in the Blanks

1. reporting; paying (p. 12–2)

For Federal income tax purposes, the taxation of S corporations and their shareholders is *similar* to the taxation of partnerships and their partners. Consistent with the application of partnership aggregate theory, the incidence of taxation of an S corporation generally occurs at the shareholder level under Section 1366, rather than at the corporate level. However, there are exceptions, as follows.

- Under Section 1374, a tax is imposed at the corporate level on certain built-in gains.
- Under Section 1375, a tax is imposed at the corporate level on Excess Net Passive Income (ENPI).

In addition consistent with the application of partnership entity theory, the S corporation (1) reports S corporation items of income, deduction, gain, loss and credit and (2) files Form 1120S.

2. not included (p. 12–16)

The tax treatment of a current distribution from an S corporation to a shareholder depends upon the interactive effects of (1) corporate Accumulated Earnings and Profits (AE & P), (2) the corporate Accumulated Adjustments Account (AAA), and (3) the shareholder's stock basis. If the S corporation has no AE & P at the end of a taxable year, the shareholder's stock basis at the end of the S corporation's tax year exclusively determines the tax treatment of the current distribution. Under Section 1368(b), the distribution is treated as a tax-free return of capital to the extent that the amount does not exceed the shareholder's stock basis.

3. stock; loans (p. 12–24)

Under Section 1366, in determining the federal income tax of an S corporation shareholder for a particular tax year within which the S corporation tax year ends, such shareholder must take into account such shareholder's pro rata share (determined on a per share per day basis) of S corporation (1) separately stated items of income, deduction, gain, loss and credit and (2) nonseparately stated income or loss.

- However, under Section 1366(d), the aggregate amount of deductions and losses taken into account by such shareholder is limited to the sum of such shareholder's (1) adjusted basis in the stock and (2) adjusted basis in loans made by the shareholder to the corporation, where such aggregate amount first reduces such shareholder's adjusted basis in stock.

Generally, stock basis is determined only at the end of the S corporation's tax year. At that time, under Section 1367, stock basis is determined based upon a three-tiered analytical approach, as follows.

(a) Stock basis is increased by the sum of the following items:
   - Separately stated income or gain items.
   - Nonseparately computed income.
   - Tax-exempt income.
(b) Stock basis is decreased by:
   - Corporate distributions that constitute a return of capital.
(c) Stock basis is decreased by the sum of the following items:
   - Nondeductible expenses that are not properly charged to a capital account.
   - Separately stated loss or deduction items.
   - Nonseparately computed loss.

4. number of shareholders (p. 12–7)

S corporations are *small business corporations* that have made a valid election under Section 1362. Under Section 1361(b), a *small business corporation*:

- Is a domestic corporation (a U.S. corporation) that:
  - Is not an ineligible corporation (ineligible corporations include banks and insurance companies).
  - Has only one class of stock issued and outstanding.
  - Has only individuals, estates and certain trusts as shareholders,
    - But does not have a nonresident alien as shareholder.
    - But does not have more than 75 shareholders.

Accordingly, the term small refers to the ceiling limitation of 75 shareholders on the number of shareholders that can hold S corporation stock.

5. passive (p. 12–31)

Consistent with the application of the aggregate theory, the incidence of taxation of an S corporation generally occurs at the shareholder level, rather than at the corporate level. However, there are exceptions, as follows.

- Under Section 1374, a tax is imposed at the corporate level on certain built-in gains.
- Under Section 1375, a tax is imposed at the corporate level on Excess Net Passive Income (ENPI) if the following two conditions are satisfied:
  - The S corporation has AE & P at the close of its tax year.
  - Passive Investment Income (PII) is greater than 25% of Gross Receipts (GR). Generally, PII includes gross receipts derived from royalties, rents, dividends, interest, and annuities. Also, PII includes gains from sales or exchanges of stock or securities.

6. capital gains (p. 12–16)

   The tax treatment of a current distribution from an S corporation to a shareholder depends upon the interactive effects of (1) corporate Accumulated Earnings and Profits (AE & P), (2) the corporate Accumulated Adjustments Account (AAA), and (3) the shareholder's stock basis. If the S corporation has no AE & P at the end of a taxable year, the shareholder's stock basis at the end of the S corporation's tax year exclusively determines the tax treatment of the current distribution. Under Section 1368(b), the distribution is treated as a tax-free return of capital to the extent that the amount distributed does not exceed the shareholder's stock basis. An amount distributed in excess of such shareholder's stock basis is treated as gain from the deemed sale or exchange of stock (capital gain).

7. initial tax basis (p. 12–22)

   Generally, regular C corporation provisions apply to S corporations as long as such provisions are not inconsistent with a provision of Subchapter S. For example, regular C corporation provisions (Sections 351 & 358) determine the tax consequences relating to the formation of an S corporation, including determining the shareholder's initial stock basis.

8. the basis in loans from (p. 12–24)

   Under Section 1366, in determining the federal income tax of an S corporation shareholder for a particular tax year within which the S corporation tax year ends, such shareholder must take into account such shareholder's pro rata share (determined on a per share per day basis) of S corporation (1) separately stated items of income, deduction, gain, loss and credit and (2) nonseparately stated income or loss.

   - However, under Section 1366(d), the aggregate amount of deductions and losses taken into account by such shareholder is limited to the sum of such shareholder's (1) adjusted basis in the stock and (2) adjusted basis in loans made by the shareholder to the corporation, where such aggregate amount first reduces such shareholder's adjusted basis in stock.

Multiple Choice

1. d (p. 12–31)

   Consistent with the application of the aggregate theory, the incidence of taxation of an S corporation generally occurs at the shareholder level, rather than at the corporate level. However, there are exceptions, as follows.

   - Under Section 1374, a tax is imposed at the corporate level on certain built-in gains.
   - Under Section 1375, a tax is imposed at the corporate level on Excess Net Passive Income (ENPI) if the following two conditions are satisfied:
     - The S corporation has AE & P at the close of its tax year.
     - Passive Investment Income (PII) is greater than 25% of Gross Receipts (GR).
     The S corporation tax on ENPI is equal to the maximum corporate rate for the year (35%) multiplied by the smaller of (1) ENPI and (2) Taxable Income (TI), where:
   - Net Passive Investment Income (NPII) is equal to PII reduced by allowable deductions directly connected with the production of such income.
   - $\text{ENPI} = \text{NPII} \times \dfrac{\text{PII} - (25\% \text{ of GR})}{\text{PII}}$

   Further, each shareholder's pro rata share of NPII is proportionately reduced by the Section 1375 corporate level tax on ENPI. Thus, item d is correct since the at-risk rules are irrelevant to the application of the Section 1375 tax. Further, the following choice items are incorrect because each of the following items is relevant to the application of the Section 1375 tax.

- Item a is incorrect because had the corporation always been an S corporation, the corporation would have no AE & P and the Section 1375 tax would not apply.
- Item b is incorrect because if the corporation has AE & P at the end of the year, the Section 1375 tax may apply.
- Item c is incorrect because having Passive Investment Income (PII) greater than 25% of Gross Receipts (GR) is one of the requirements for application of the Section 1375 tax.

2. a (p. 12–13; $200,000 − $127,000 − $10,000)

   Under Section 1366, in determining the Federal income tax of an S corporation shareholder for a particular tax year within which the S corporation tax year ends, such shareholder must take into account such shareholder's pro rata share (determined on a per share per day basis) of S corporation (1) separately stated items of income, deduction, gain, loss and credit and (2) nonseparately stated income or loss. Within this context, separately stated items are items of income, deduction, gain or loss that can be treated differently across shareholders in the computation of a shareholder's income tax liability. Nonseparately stated income or loss is the aggregate of all undifferentiated (nonseparately stated) amounts.

   In the instant case, separately stated items include Rental Income (Passive Activity Income), Interest Income (Investment Income) and Net Long-term Capital Gain. Thus, the aggregate of all undifferentiated (nonseparately stated) amounts is $63,000 (Gross Receipts of $200,000 less Cost of Goods Sold and Commissions of $127,000 less Compensation paid to shareholder of $10,000). Thus, item a is correct.

3. b (p. 12–16; $65,000 − $50,000)

   The tax treatment of a current distribution from an S corporation to a shareholder depends upon the interactive effects of (1) corporate Accumulated Earnings and Profits (AE & P), (2) the corporate Accumulated Adjustments Account (AAA), and (3) the shareholder's stock basis. If the S corporation has no AE & P at the end of a taxable year, the shareholder's stock basis at the end of the S corporation's tax year exclusively determines the tax treatment of the current distribution. Under Section 1368(b), the distribution is treated as a tax-free return of capital to the extent that the amount distributed does not exceed the shareholder's stock basis. An amount distributed in excess of such shareholder's stock basis is treated as gain from the deemed sale or exchange of stock (capital gain).

   In the instant case, the amount distributed to Carlos by Twister is $65,000 (the fair market value of the property). Under Section 1368(b), the amount distributed of $65,000 is treated by Carlos as a tax-free return of capital to the extent of $50,000 (Carlos' stock basis) and as gain from the deemed sale or exchange of stock (capital gain) to the extent of $15,000 ($65,000 − $50,000). Thus, item b is correct.

4. b (p. 12–23; limited to basis)

   Under Section 1366, in determining the federal income tax of an S corporation shareholder for a particular tax year within which the S corporation tax year ends, such shareholder must take into account such shareholder's pro rata share (determined on a per share per day basis) of S corporation (1) separately stated items of income, deduction, gain, loss and credit and (2) nonseparately stated income or loss.

   However, under Section 1366(d), the aggregate amount of deductions and losses taken into account by such shareholder is limited to the sum of such shareholder's (1) adjusted basis in the stock and (2) adjusted basis in loans made by the shareholder to the corporation, where such aggregate amount first reduces such shareholder's adjusted basis in stock.

   In the instant case, Jon's pro rata share (determined on a per share per day basis) of Waite's ordinary loss is $80,000 ($160,000 × .5). However, under Section 1366(d), Jon can deduct only $75,000 (Jon's pro rata share of $80,000 ordinary loss to the extent of Jon's $75,000 adjusted basis in Waite stock). Thus, item b is correct.

5. c (p. 12–5; corporations are ineligible)

S corporations are *small business corporations* that have made a valid election under Section 1362. Under Section 1361(b), a *small business corporation*:

- Is a domestic corporation (a U.S. corporation) that:
  - Is not an ineligible corporation (ineligible corporations include banks and insurance companies).
  - Has only one class of stock issued and outstanding.
  - Has only individuals, estates and certain trusts as shareholders,
    - But does not have a nonresident alien as shareholder.
    - But does not have more than 75 shareholders.

In the instant case, item c is correct since a corporation cannot be a shareholder of an S corporation.

6. d (p. 12–22; income increases basis)

Stock basis is generally determined only at the end of the S corporation's tax year. At that time, under Section 1367, stock basis is determined based upon a three-tiered analytical approach, as follows.

(a) Stock basis is increased by the sum of the following items:
- Separately stated income or gain items.
- Nonseparately computed income.
- Tax-exempt income.

(b) Stock basis is decreased by:
- Corporate distributions that constitute a return of capital.

(c) Stock basis is decreased by the sum of the following items:
- Nondeductible expenses that are not properly charged to a capital account.
- Separately stated loss or deduction items.
- Nonseparately computed loss

In the instant case, item d is correct since stock basis is increased for a shareholder's pro rata share of income.

7. b (p. 12–17; $50,000 + $5,000 dividend; $100,000 − $5,000 dividend = $95,000 S distribution; $95,000 − $55,000 AAA − $10,000 PTI = $30,000 − basis of $25,000 = $5,000 capital)

Bryant's pro rata share of Valor's ordinary income is $50,000. Further, at the end of the year (before consideration of the distribution), Valor's AAA is $55,000 ($5,000 + $50,000), PTI is $10,000, and AE & P is $5,000. Bryant's stock basis is $90,000 ($40,000 + $50,000) at the end of the year (before consideration of the distribution). Thus, the amount distributed of $100,000 to Bryant is treated, under Section 1368(b), as:

- A tax-free return of capital to the extent of $65,000 (AAA of $55,000 plus PTI of $10,000), which reduces stock basis to $25,000 ($90,000 − $55,000 − $10,000),
- Dividend income to the extent of $5,000 (AE & P).
- Gain from the deemed sale or exchange of stock (capital gain) to the extent of $5,000 [($100,000 − $65,000 − $5,000) − Remaining Stock Basis of $25,000].

Thus, item b is correct.

8. b (p. 12–23; ($20,000 − 25%($90,000) + ($10,000 − 25%($60,000) = $7,500)

Under Section 1366, in determining the Federal income tax of an S corporation shareholder for a particular tax year within which the S corporation tax year ends, such shareholder must take into account such shareholder's pro rata share (determined on a per share per day basis) of S corporation (1) separately stated items of income, deduction, gain, loss and credit and (2) nonseparately stated income or loss.

However, under Section 1366(d), the aggregate amount of deductions and losses taken into account by such shareholder is limited to the sum of such shareholder's (1) adjusted basis in the stock and (2) adjusted basis in loans made by the shareholder to the corporation, where such aggregate amount first reduces such shareholder's adjusted basis in stock.

In the instant case, Kathy's pro rata share of Magnolia's ordinary loss for 2001 and 2002 is $22,500 ($90,000/4) and $15,000 ($60,000/4), respectively. At the end of 2001 (before consideration of Kathy's pro rata share of loss), Kathy has stock basis of $20,000 and debt basis of zero. On her 2001 income tax return, Kathy is able to deduct $20,000 (her pro rata share of loss of $22,500 to the extent of her stock basis of $20,000), which reduces her stock basis from $20,000 to zero. At the end of 2001, Kathy carries over to 2002 a disallowed loss of $2,500 ($22,500 − $20,000). At the end of 2002 (before consideration of Kathy's pro rata share of loss), Kathy has stock basis of zero and debt basis of $10,000 (payments made in connection with a guaranteed loan). On her 2002 income tax return, Kathy is able to deduct $10,000 (her pro rata share of loss of $15,000 to the extent of her debt basis of $10,000), which reduces her debt basis from $10,000 to zero. At the end of 2002, Kathy carries over to 2003 a disallowed loss of $7,500 [$2,500 + ($15,000 − $10,000)]. Thus, item b is correct.

9. b (p. 12–15; 50%($237,250)(30/366) + 50%($237,250) = $128,348)

Under Section 1366, in determining the federal income tax of an S corporation shareholder for a particular tax year within which the S corporation tax year ends, such shareholder must take into account such shareholder's pro rata share (determined on a per share per day basis) of S corporation (1) separately stated items of income, deduction, gain, loss and credit and (2) nonseparately stated income or loss.

However, under Section 1366(d), the aggregate amount of deductions and losses taken into account by such shareholder is limited to the sum of such shareholder's (1) adjusted basis in the stock and (2) adjusted basis in loans made by the shareholder to the corporation, where such aggregate amount first reduces such shareholder's adjusted basis in stock.

Moreover, for purposes of determining such shareholder's pro rata share in the year of acquisition, on the date of transfer, the transferor (and not the transferee) is considered to own the stock.

In the instant case, Wise's pro rata share of Cobra's ordinary loss for 2002 is $128,348 [($237,250 × ½) + ($237,250 × ½ × 30/366)]. Thus, item b is correct.

10. b (p. 12–22; $50,000 + $20,000 − $5,000)

Under Section 1366, in determining the Federal income tax of an S corporation shareholder for a particular tax year within which the S corporation tax year ends, such shareholder must take into account such shareholder's pro rata share (determined on a per share per day basis) of S corporation (1) separately stated items of income, deduction, gain, loss and credit and (2) nonseparately stated income or loss.

Further, the tax treatment of a current distribution from an S corporation to a shareholder depends upon the interactive effects of (1) corporate Accumulated Earnings and Profits (AE & P), (2) the corporate Accumulated Adjustments Account (AAA), and (3) the shareholder's stock basis. If the S corporation has no AE & P at the end of a taxable year, the shareholder's stock basis at the end of the S corporation's tax year exclusively determines the tax treatment of the current distribution. Under Section 1368(b), the distribution is treated as a tax-free return of capital to the extent that the amount distributed does not exceed the shareholder's stock basis. An amount distributed in excess of such shareholder's stock basis is treated as gain from the deemed sale or exchange of stock.

Further, stock basis is generally determined only at the end of the S corporation's tax year. At that time, under Section 1367, stock basis is determined based upon a three-tiered analytical approach, as follows.

(a) Stock basis is increased by the sum of the following items:
- Separately stated income or gain items.
- Nonseparately computed income.
- Tax-exempt income.

(b) Stock basis is decreased by:
- Corporate distributions that constitute a return of capital.

(c) Stock basis is decreased by the sum of the following items:
- Nondeductible expenses that are not properly charged to a capital account.
- Separately stated loss or deduction items.
- Nonseparately computed loss

In the instant case, assuming Computers has no AE & P, Lisa's stock basis in Computers is:

- Increased by $20,000 (Lisa's pro rata share of Computers' income) and
- Decreased by $5,000 (the portion of the current distribution of $5,000 that represents a nontaxable return of capital).

Thus, at the end of 2002, Lisa's stock basis is $65,000 ($50,000 + $20,000 − $5,000) and item b is correct. Note: Although the 2001 NOL cannot be used in a tax year for which the S corporation election is effective, such tax year counts as one year of the 20-year carry forward period.

11. c (p. 12–31)

Consistent with the application of the aggregate theory, the incidence of taxation of an S corporation generally occurs at the shareholder level, rather than at the corporate level. However, there are exceptions, as follows.

- Under Section 1374, a tax is imposed at the corporate level on certain built-in gains.
- Under Section 1375, a tax is imposed at the corporate level on Excess Net Passive Income (ENPI) if the following two conditions are satisfied:
  - The S corporation has AE & P at the close of its tax year.
  - Passive Investment Income (PII) is greater than 25% of Gross Receipts (GR). Generally, PII includes gross receipts derived from royalties, rents, dividends, interest, and annuities. Also, PII includes gains from sales or exchanges of stock or securities.

In the instant case, item c is correct because net operating losses are not PII.

12. c (p. 12–16)

The tax treatment of a current distribution from an S corporation to a shareholder depends upon the interactive effects of (1) corporate Accumulated Earnings and Profits (AE & P), (2) the corporate Accumulated Adjustments Account (AAA), and (3) the shareholder's stock basis. If the S corporation has no AE & P at the end of a taxable year, the shareholder's stock basis at the end of the S corporation's tax year exclusively determines the tax treatment of the current distribution. Under Section 1368(b), the distribution is treated as a tax-free return of capital to the extent that the amount distributed does not exceed the shareholder's stock basis. An amount distributed in excess of such shareholder's stock basis is treated as gain from the deemed sale or exchange of stock.

In the instant case, Oliver treats the amount distributed as a tax-free return of capital to the extent that such amount does not exceed Oliver's stock basis. The portion of such amount distributed in excess of Oliver's stock basis is treated as gain from the deemed sale or exchange of stock. Thus, item c is correct.

13. b (p. 12–27)

Under Section 1366, in determining the federal income tax of an S corporation shareholder for a particular tax year within which the S corporation tax year ends, such shareholder must take into account such shareholder's pro rata share (determined on a per share per day basis) of S corporation (1) separately stated items of income, deduction, gain, loss and credit and (2) nonseparately stated income or loss.

However, under Section 1366(d), the aggregate amount of deductions and losses taken into account by such shareholder is limited to the sum of such shareholder's (1) adjusted basis in the stock and (2) adjusted basis in loans made by the shareholder to the corporation, where such aggregate amount first reduces such shareholder's adjusted basis in stock.

Moreover, after application of Section 1366(d), shareholders are subject to the at-risk rules of Section 469. The at-risk rules apply at the shareholder level to each shareholder (i.e., to the deductible losses under Section 1366(d) that are passed through to each shareholder). Under the at-risk rules, a shareholder may deduct a loss only to the extent that such shareholder is at risk. A shareholder is generally at risk to the extent of the sum of (1) cash contributed, (2) the adjusted basis of property contributed, and (c) all or a portion of certain indebtedness. Thus, item b is correct.

14. d (p. 12–22; income increases basis)

Stock basis is generally determined only at the end of the S corporation's tax year. At that time, under Section 1367, stock basis is determined based upon a three-tiered analytical approach, as follows.

(a) Stock basis is increased by the sum of the following items:
- Separately stated income or gain items.
- Nonseparately computed income.
- Tax-exempt income.
(b) Stock basis is decreased by:
- Corporate distributions that constitute a return of capital.
(c) Stock basis is decreased by the sum of the following items:
- Nondeductible expenses that are not properly charged to a capital account.
- Separately stated loss or deduction items.
- Nonseparately computed loss

In the instant case, item d is correct since stock basis is increased for a shareholder's pro rata share of income.

15. d (p. 12–5; corporations are ineligible shareholders)

S corporations are *small business corporations* (as defined under Section 1361(b)) that have made a valid election under Section 1362. This election may be terminated under Section 1362(d) by either (1) voluntary revocation or (2) involuntary termination. Voluntary revocation of an S corporation election is accomplished when consent to such revocation is made by shareholders owning a majority of shares. In contrast, involuntary termination occurs by operation of law in the following instances.

- Where the S corporation fails to continue to satisfy the requirements of a *small business corporation*, the S corporation election is terminated effective on the day the S corporation ceases to meet the requirements of a *small business corporation*.
- Where the S corporation, for 3 consecutive taxable years, has both (1) Accumulated Earnings and Profits (AE & P) determined at the end of the taxable year and (2) Excess Passive Investment Income (EPII) [where EPII is equal to Passive Investment Income (PII) less 25% of Gross Receipts (GR)], the S corporation election is terminated as of the beginning of the fourth year.

In the instant case, item d is correct since a corporation cannot be a shareholder of a *small business corporation*.

16. b (p. 12–17; $300,000 − $264,000 = $36,000)

Paula's pro rata share of May's ordinary income is $204,000. Further, at the end of 2000 (before consideration of the distribution), May's AAA is $264,000 ($60,000 + $204,000), PTI is zero, and AE & P is $150,000. Paula's stock basis is $304,000 ($100,000 + $204,000) at the end of 2000 (before consideration of the distribution). Thus, the amount distributed of $300,000 to Paula is treated, under Section 1368(b), as:

- A tax-free return of capital to the extent of $264,000 (AAA of $264,000 plus PTI of zero), which reduces stock basis to $40,000 ($304,000 − $264,000).
- Dividend income to the extent of $36,000 [$36,000 ($300,000 − $264,000), but not to exceed AE & P of $150,000].

Thus, item b is correct.

CHAPTER 13

Comparative Forms of Doing Business

LEARNING OBJECTIVES

After completing Chapter 13, you should be able to:

1. Identify the principal legal forms for conducting a business.
2. Appreciate the relative importance of nontax factors in making business decisions.
3. Distinguish between the forms for conducting a business according to whether they are subject to single taxation or double taxation.
4. Identify techniques for avoiding double taxation and for controlling the entity tax.
5. Understand the applicability and the effect of the conduit and entity concepts on contributions to the entity, operations of the entity, entity distributions, passive activity loss and at-risk rules, and special allocations.
6. Analyze the effect of the disposition of a business on the owners and the entity for each of the forms for conducting a business.

KEY TERMS

Conduit concept
Entity concept

Limited liability company (LLC)

Thin capitalization

OUTLINE

I. **FORMS OF DOING BUSINESS**
   A. The principal legal forms of conducting a business entity.
      1. Sole proprietorship (as an extension of the sole proprietor)
      2. Partnership
      3. Corporation
   B. Generally, a taxpayer is bound by the legal form of business chosen; however, the IRS may, in some cases, apply the 'substance over form' doctrine to reclassify an entity for tax purposes.
   C. Limited Liability Company. A hybrid business form that combines the corporate characteristic of limited liability for the owners with the tax characteristics of a partnership.

II. **NONTAX FACTORS**
   A. Capital Formation
      1. Sole proprietorships depend upon the funds obtainable by the owner.
      2. Partnerships have a greater opportunity to raise capital because they pool the resources of the partners. Limited partnerships offer even greater potential because it can secure funds from investors.
      3. Corporations can issue additional stock to raise capital.
   B. Limited Liability
      1. The corporate form generally provides its owners with limited liability under state law.
         a. However, most states do not provide limited liability for the performance of professional services.
         b. In small corporations, shareholders often are required to personally guarantee loans made to the corporation.
      2. Limited partnerships provide limited liability to limited partners. The general partners have unlimited liability.
      3. LLCs generally limit the liability of all owners.
   C. Other Factors significant in selecting an organizational form include:
      1. estimated life of the business.
      2. number of owners and their role in the management of the business.
      3. freedom of choice in transferring ownership interests.
      4. organizational formality and the related cost and extent of government regulation.

III. **SINGLE VERSUS DOUBLE TAXATION**
   A. Overall Impact on Entity and Owners
      1. Sole proprietors and partners are taxed only at the owner level.
      2. Corporations are subject to double taxation. Earnings are taxed at the corporate level and distributions of corporate earnings are taxed at the shareholder level.
         a. Double taxation is frequently cited as the major tax disadvantage of the corporate form.
      3. S corporations generally avoid the corporate level tax and earnings are taxed at the shareholder level. However, the ownership structure of an S corporation is restricted in both the number and type of shareholders.
   B. All forms of business are directly or indirectly subject to the alternative minimum tax (AMT).
      1. Sole proprietors and corporations are taxed directly.
      2. Partnerships (LLCs) and S corporations pass through AMT preferences and adjustments to entity owners.
      3. The AMT does not apply to small corporations. A corporation having average annual gross receipts not more than $5 million for the 3-year period beginning after 12/31/93 (or any corporation in its first year of existence) is not subject to the corporate AMT.

a. A corporation will continue to be classified as a small corporation if its average annual gross receipts for the 3-year period preceding the current tax year (and any intervening 3-year period) do not exceed $7.5 million.
C. State and local income taxes also play a role in entity choice.

IV. **CONTROLLING THE ENTITY TAX**
   A. Favorable Treatment of Certain Fringe Benefits
      1. Some fringe benefits are deductible by the entity and excludable from the recipient's gross income.
      2. Of these excludable fringe benefits, some are available only to employees.
         a. For an owner to be an employee, the entity must be a corporation.
         b. For an S corporation, a more than 2% shareholder is treated as a partner.
      3. Qualified pension and profit sharing plans defer taxation for the recipient.
   B. Minimizing Double Taxation for a Corporation
      1. Double taxation occurs when a corporation distributes earnings.
      2. Deductible distributions include reasonable payments for:
         a. salary to shareholder-employees.
         b. rent to shareholder-lessors.
         c. interest to shareholder-creditors.
      3. The IRS scrutinizes these transactions carefully.
      4. Not making distributions carries the risk that the accumulated earnings tax will eventually apply.
      5. Double taxation can be reduced if distributions can qualify as a return of capital rather than a dividend. Stock redemptions are a tool that can be used for this purpose.
      6. Electing S status causes the tax to be levied at the shareholder, rather than at the corporate level, but all of the qualification/maintenance requirements of S status need to be considered.

V. **CONDUIT VERSUS ENTITY TREATMENT**
   A. Effect on Recognition at Time of Contribution to the Entity
      1. Contributions of personal use assets are valued at the lower of adjusted basis or fair market value.
      2. Partnerships (LLCs) have a carryover basis for contributed property and the partner (owner) has a substitute basis in his partnership interest.
      3. Corporations must satisfy the § 351 control requirements to obtain tax-free treatment; otherwise, the transfer will be a taxable event.
      4. Special allocation treatment is mandatory for partnerships when the adjusted basis and the fair market value of contributed property are not equal at the time of contribution.
   B. Effect on Basis of Ownership Interest
      1. A partner's basis in a partnership interest is affected by the partner's distributive share of partnership profits and losses by partnership liability changes. Similar rules apply to LLCs.
      2. A C corporation shareholder's basis is generally affected by neither corporate profit or loss, nor liability increases or decreases.
      3. An S corporation shareholder's basis is affected by the shareholder's allocative share of the corporation's profits and losses but not corporate liability increases or decreases.
   C. Effect on Results of Operations
      1. The entity concept of taxation is responsible for producing double taxation for the C corporation.
         a. Whether this is a disadvantage depends on whether the corporation produces positive taxable income, the tax rates that apply to the corporation and its shareholders, and the corporation's distribution policy.
         b. Under the entity concept of taxation, the earnings components of a C corporation lose their identity when passed through to the shareholder as dividends.

2. Under the conduit concept of taxation, any item that may be subject to special treatment on the taxpayer-owner's tax return is reported separately to the partner, LLC owner, or S corporation shareholder.
3. With regard to tax incidence, only the partnership and LLC exclusively recognize the conduit concept of taxation; an S corporation is subject to taxation at the entity level in some circumstances.

D. Effect on Recognition at Time of Distribution
1. Under the conduit concept, distributions made to partners, LLC owners, and S corporation shareholders are not taxed.
2. Distributions made to C corporation shareholders produce dividend treatment.
3. Special rules apply to S corporation distributions. Earnings distributions are covered by the conduit concept. Other distributions (e.g., property distributions) can trigger gain recognition by the S corporation (an application of the entity concept). Then the conduit concept is applied to pass-through the gain to the shareholders.

E. Effect on Passive Activity Losses
1. Passive activity loss rules apply to partnerships, LLCs, S corporations, and specific C corporations (personal service corporations and closely held corporations).
2. To be classified as a personal service corporation:
   a. the principal activity of the corporation must be the performance of personal services,
   b. the services must be substantially performed by owner-employees, and
   c. owner-employees must own more than 10% in value of the stock of the corporation.
3. In a closely held corporation more than 50% of the value of the outstanding stock at any time during the last half of the year must be owned by 5 or fewer individuals.
4. For personal service corporations, passive activity losses cannot be offset against either active or portfolio income.
5. For closely-held corporations, passive activity losses can be offset against active income but not against portfolio income.
6. The results of passive activities of a partnership, LLC, or an S corporation are separately stated and passed through to the partners, owners, or shareholders, respectively.

F. Effect of At-Risk Rules
1. The at-risk rules apply to a partnership, LLC, S corporation, or closely held C corporation.
2. These rules are harsher for partnerships and LLCs since they limit the use of leverage.

G. Effect of Special Allocations
1. An advantage of the conduit concept over the entity concept is the ability to make special allocations.
2. Special allocations are limited for S corporations.
3. Partnerships and LLCs have many opportunities to use special allocations.

VI. **DISPOSITION OF A BUSINESS OR OF AN OWNERSHIP INTEREST**
A. Sole Proprietorship
1. The sale of a sole proprietorship is treated as the sale of individual assets.
2. Classification as ordinary income or capital gain depends upon the nature and holding period of the individual assets.
3. If the amount realized exceeds the FMV of identifiable assets, the excess is identified as goodwill which produces capital gain for the seller.

B. Partnership and Limited Liability Company
1. If structured as a sale of assets, the treatment is the same as that of a sole proprietorship.
2. If structured as a sale of an ownership interest, it is treated as a sale of a capital asset under § 741 subject to ordinary income potential under § 751.

C. Corporation
1. A stock sale has the dual advantage to the seller of being less complex from both a legal and tax standpoint. It also avoids double taxation. The gain or loss on the sale is a capital gain or loss to the shareholder.

2. A stock sale may produce detrimental tax results for the purchaser.
   a. The basis of the corporate assets is not affected by the stock sale.
   b. If the fair market value of the stock exceeds the corporation's adjusted basis for its assets, the purchaser is denied the opportunity to step up the asset's basis (and, for example, get greater depreciation deductions).
3. In an asset sale, the corporation sells the assets, pays any debts not transferred, and makes a liquidating distribution to the shareholders.
   a. Alternatively, the corporation can distribute the assets to the shareholders in a liquidating distribution. The shareholders then sell the assets.
   b. In either case, double taxation will occur.
4. In an asset sale, the purchaser gets a stepped-up basis in the assets.
5. In summary, the stock sale is normally preferred by the seller; the asset sale is normally preferred by the purchaser.

D. S Corporation
1. S corporations are subject to the same rules as C corporations (above).
2. However, under the conduit concept, any gain recognized by the S corporation is taxed at the shareholder level.
3. Therefore, double taxation is avoided directly for a stock sale (only the shareholder is involved) and indirectly for an asset sale (the conduit concept ignores the involvement of the S corporation).

VII. **OVERALL COMPARISON OF FORMS OF DOING BUSINESS**
A. Overall comparison of forms of doing business. Concept Summary 13–2 of the text provides a detailed comparison of the tax consequences of different forms of business.
B. Considerations that should extend beyond the current tax period include:
   1. asset contributions.
   2. taxation of results of operations.
   3. distributions to owners.
   4. disposition of ownership interests.
   5. business termination.

TEST FOR SELF-EVALUATION—CHAPTER 13

True or False

Indicate which of the following statements is true or false by circling the correct answer.

T F 1. The capitalized costs of acquired goodwill or going concern value is amortized over a 15-year period, beginning with the month acquired. (IRS 95 2A-8)

T F 2. S Corporations are never taxed.

T F 3. The test in determining if the compensation paid to an officer of a corporation is reasonable is based on the total of salaries paid to all of the officers of that corporation.

T F 4. All forms of businesses are directly subject to AMT.

T F 5. Sole proprietors have the advantage over corporations when the alternative minimum tax applies.

T F 6. Fringe benefits which are not discriminatory are deductible by S Corporations.

T F 7. If a personal use asset is contributed to a corporation, the corporation's basis is the lower of adjusted basis or FMV when contributed.

Fill in the Blanks

Complete the following statements with the appropriate word(s) or amount(s).

1. _____ rules apply to personal service corporations and closely held corporations.

2. _____% or more of the stock value must be held by _____ or fewer individuals during the last half of the tax year for a corporation to meet the definition of a closely held corporation.

3. The At-Risk rules apply to both _____ and _____.

4. Under the _____ the business is an extension of the owners; under the _____ the business is distinct from the owners.

5. The ability to share profits and losses differently from the share in capital is a _____ allowed only to _____.

Multiple Choice

Choose the best answer for each of the following questions.

_____ 1. John bought land with a building on it that he planned to use in his business. His costs in connection with this purchase were as follows:

STUDY GUIDE
CHAPTER 13
Comparative Forms of Doing Business

13–7

Cash downpayment	$ 40,000
Mortgage on property	300,000
Survey costs	2,000
Transfer taxes	1,800
Charges for installation of gas lines	3,000
Back taxes owed by seller and paid by John	1,200

What is John's adjusted basis in the property? (IRS 95 1C-57)

a. $348,000
b. $346,800
c. $345,000
d. $343,000

_____ 2. In the current year, Robert sold a building used in his business. His books and records reflect the following information:

Original cost of building	$150,000
Improvements made to building	50,000
Broker's commissions paid on sale	10,000
Cash received on sale	100,000
Total property taxes for the year paid by Robert	3,000
Portion of property taxes imposed on purchaser and reimbursed in a separate payment to Robert by purchaser under IRC 164(d)	500
Mortgage assumed by buyer	80,000
Accumulated depreciation	70,000
Fair market value of other property received	20,000

What is the amount of gain Robert must recognize from the sale of the property? (IRS 95 1C-61)

a. $60,000
b. $61,000
c. $70,000
d. $71,000

_____ 3. Matt purchased a high-volume dry cleaning store for $960,000. No liabilities were assumed. The fair market values of the assets at the time of the purchase were as follows:

Cash in banks	$210,100
U. S. government securities	100,200
Building and land	312,200
Accounts receivable	100,000
Fixtures and equipment	202,000

Matt will not change the name of the cleaners. What is Matt's basis for goodwill or going concern value? (IRS 95 2C-46)

a. $0
b. $35,500
c. $91,300
d. $110,560

____ 4. In a sole proprietorship the liabilities of the business:

    a. extend to the owner's personal assets
    b. extend only to the assets of the business
    c. are limited to negligent acts of the owner personally, not employee actions
    d. both b and c

____ 5. Alisa purchased a day care center on December 10. The contract showed the following adjusted basis and fair market value of the assets:

	Adjusted Basis	Fair Market Value
Building	$150,000	$300,000
Land	40,000	50,000
Furniture & Fixtures	60,000	50,000

The contract provided that the agreed sale price was a lump sum $360,000. What is Alisa's basis in the building? (IRS 94 2C-52)

    a. $216,000
    b. $250,000
    c. $270,000
    d. $300,000

SOLUTIONS TO CHAPTER 13 QUESTIONS

True or False

1. T (p. 13–23)

    Within the context of the sale of a business, the excess of the sales price over the fair market value of identifiable assets is referred to as goodwill (or going-concern value). Prior to the Revenue Reconciliation Act (RRA) of 1993, an intangible (goodwill, patent, franchise, or covenant not to compete) was amortized for tax purposes only if such intangible had a limited life, where the amortization period was equal to such stated limited life. Thus, an intangible without a limited life was not amortized. After the effective date of RRA of 1993, under Section 197, all Section 197 intangibles are amortized over a 15-year statutory life, regardless of life (limited or not). In the instant case, goodwill is a Section 197 intangible. Accordingly, goodwill is amortized over a 15-year statutory period beginning with the month in which such intangible was acquired.

2. F (p. 13–8; S Corporations may be subject to taxation)

    S corporations are small business corporations (as defined under Section 1361(b)) that have made a valid election under Section 1362. The S corporation is a quasi-conduit; within many contexts, it is treated for tax purposes as a mere extension of its owners. For example, it is generally not a tax-paying entity, thereby avoiding double taxation of its income. Under Section 1366, an S corporation shareholder must recognize such shareholder's pro rata share (determined on a per share per day basis) of S corporation (1) separately stated items of income, deduction, gain, loss and credit and (2) non-separately stated income or loss. An S corporation shareholder recognizes such shareholder's pro rata share on the last day of the S corporation's tax year in determining the federal income tax liability of such shareholder for a particular tax year within which the S corporation tax year ends. However, an S corporation that was previously a C corporation may pay a tax, including:

    - A built-in gains tax under Section 1374.
    - A passive investment income tax under Section 1375.

3. F (p. 13–13; the test for reasonableness requires multiple inquiries)

    For a C corporation, various approaches may be taken to minimize the effect of double taxation. One approach is to eliminate (or reduce) corporate taxable income by paying reasonable compensation to a shareholder/employee. Such compensation is deductible by the corporation, unless found to be unreasonable. Under Treas. Reg. Sec. 1.162-7(b), the test for reasonableness within this context incorporates multi-dimensional inquiries, including:

    - Is the corporation closely held?
    - Are most shareholders also employees, thereby drawing salaries?
    - Are salaries of shareholders/employees in excess of those salaries ordinarily paid for similar services rendered?
    - Do excess salary amounts correlate with the stock holdings of shareholders/employees?

4. F (p. 13–10; all forms directly or indirectly subject to AMT)

    All forms of business are directly (or indirectly) subject to the Alternative Minimum Tax (AMT). The effect of the AMT on the C corporation is direct. For example, Alternative Minimum Taxable Income (AMTI) is calculated at the corporate level for the C corporation. However, for other forms of business organization (the partnership and S corporation), the effect of the AMT is indirect. Because these forms have conduit characteristics, AMT preferences and adjustments are passed through to the respective owners so that AMTI is calculated at the owner level. Similarly, if the sole proprietorship is viewed as a business entity (even though it is neither a legal entity nor a taxable entity), the effect of the AMT on the sole proprietorship is indirect. That is, AMT preferences and adjustments are passed through to the sole proprietor (owner) so that AMTI is calculated at the owner (individual) level. In contrast, if the sole proprietorship is viewed as being merely an extension of its owner, the effect of the AMT on the sole proprietorship is direct because AMTI is calculated at the owner (individual) level.

5.   F   (p. 13–10; C Corporations may have the advantage)

All forms of business are directly (or indirectly) subject to the Alternative Minimum Tax (AMT). If the sole proprietorship is viewed as a business entity (even though it is neither a legal entity nor a taxable entity), the effect of the AMT on the sole proprietorship is indirect. That is, AMT preferences and adjustments are passed through to the sole proprietor (owner) so that AMTI is calculated at the owner (individual) level. In contrast, the effect of the AMT on the C corporation is direct. Alternative Minimum Taxable Income (AMTI) is calculated at the corporate level. In two ways, the AMT may be viewed as applying more favorably to C corporations relative to individuals. First, AMTI is taxed at a rate of 20% for C corporations, as compared with a two-tier rate schedule (26% and 28%) for individuals. Second, as a percentage of the highest regular tax rate applicable to the respective entity, the AMT rate represents 72.5% (28%/38.6%) for individuals, but only 57% (20%/35%) for C corporations.

6.   T   (p. 13–12)

S corporations are small business corporations (as defined under Section 1361(b)) that have made a valid election under Section 1362. Regular C corporation provisions apply to S corporations as long as such provisions are not inconsistent with Subchapter S provisions.

For example, a fringe benefit is a benefit provided by the corporation/employer to the employee for the convenience of the corporation/employer. In general, the tax consequences of qualifying fringe benefits include being:

- Deductible by the corporation/employer but
- Excludible from the gross income of the employee.

Within this context, identifiable fringe benefits include:

- Amounts received from an accident and health plan excludible from the gross income of the employee under Section 105.
- Amounts paid by an employer to an accident and health plan excludible from the gross income of the employee under Section 106.
- The cost of up to $50,000 of group-term life insurance on an employee's life excludible from the gross income of the employee under Section 79.
- The cost of meals and lodging furnished for the convenience of the employer excludible from the gross income of the employee under Section 119.

Within the context of providing certain fringe benefits, to be a qualifying fringe benefit requires that the corporation/employer provide such fringe benefits on a nondiscriminatory basis. That is, in providing certain fringe benefits to employees, the corporation/employer is to give no preferential treatment to key employees, highly compensated individuals or highly compensated participants. Otherwise, such fringe benefits are not qualified and, accordingly, are not wholly excludible from the gross income of the employee. In any case (qualified or unqualified), the fringe benefit is deductible by the corporation/employer.

7.   T   (p. 13–17)

The conduit (or aggregate) theory is an underlying precept for determining the tax consequences of the formation of either the partnership or the corporation. Under this theory, the entity is viewed as a mere extension of its owners. Thus, upon the contribution of property to a new entity in exchange for an ownership interest in the new entity:

- The transferor of property generally recognizes no gain that is realized on the exchange.
- The transferee takes an adjusted basis in the transferred property, which is determined by reference to the adjusted basis of such property in the hands of the transferor.
  - However, if a personal use asset is contributed, the transferee's basis in the contributed property is the lower of (a) the transferor's adjusted basis and (b) the property's fair market value at the time of contribution. This rule ensures that the transferor will not receive a tax benefit for an unrealized loss that is otherwise nondeductible.

Fill in the Blanks

1. Passive activity loss (p. 13–20)

   The passive activity loss rules under Section 469 apply:

   - To partnerships and S corporations indirectly. Because these forms have conduit characteristics, income and losses of various passive activities are separately stated and are passed through to the respective owners so that the passive activity loss limitation rules are applied at the owner level.
   - To C corporations directly, but only to the extent of Closely Held Corporations and Personal Service Corporations (PSCs).
     - A PSC for purposes of Section 469 is a corporation whose principal activity is in the nature of providing personal services:
       - Where such personal services are performed substantially by owners/employees and
       - Where such owners/employees own in the aggregate more than 10% of the stock value of the corporation.
     - A Closely Held Corporation for purposes of Section 465 is a corporation that meets a 50% stock test. This test is met if at least 50% of the value of the outstanding stock of the corporation is owned by 5 or fewer individuals at any time during the last half of the taxable year.

2. 50; 5 (p. 13–20)

   The passive activity loss rules under Section 469 apply:

   - To partnerships and S corporations indirectly. Because these forms have conduit characteristics, income and losses of various passive activities are separately stated and are passed through to the respective owners so that the passive activity loss limitation rules are applied at the owner level.
   - To C corporations directly, but only to the extent of Closely Held Corporations and Personal Service Corporations (PSCs).
     - A PSC for purposes of Section 469 is a corporation whose principal activity is in the nature of providing personal services:
       - Where such personal services are performed substantially by owners/employees and
       - Where such owners/employees own in the aggregate more than 10% of the stock value of the corporation.
     - A Closely Held Corporation for purposes of Section 465 is a corporation that meets a 50% stock test. This test is met if at least 50% of the value of the outstanding stock of the corporation is owned by 5 or fewer individuals at any time during the last half of the taxable year.

3. partnerships; S Corporations (p. 13–21)

   The at-risk rules under Section 465 apply:

   - To partnerships and S corporations indirectly. Because these forms have conduit characteristics, losses of various activities are separately stated and are passed through to the respective owners so that the at-risk loss limitation rules are applied at the owner level.
   - To C corporations directly, but only to the extent of Closely Held Corporations (with isolated exceptions).

- A Closely Held Corporation for purposes of Section 469 is a corporation that meets a 50% stock test. This test is met if at least 50% of the value of the outstanding stock of the corporation is owned by 5 or fewer individuals at any time during the last half of the taxable year.

4. conduit concept; entity concept (p. 13–16)

    The conduit (or aggregate) theory is an underlying precept for determining the tax consequences of the formation of either the partnership or the corporation. Under this theory, the entity is viewed as a mere extension of the owners. Consistent with the application of the aggregate theory, the incidence of taxation of an S corporation (or a partnership) generally occurs at the owner level, rather than at the entity level.

    The entity theory is an underlying precept for determining the income tax consequences for most economic events of the C corporation. Under this theory, the C corporation is viewed as an entity, separate and distinct from its owners. Consistent with the application of the entity theory, the incidence of taxation of a C corporation generally occurs at the entity level.

5. special allocation; partnerships (p. 13–22)

    The owner of a partnership is a partner. Such partner's ownership interest constitutes an intangible asset incorporating:

    - An interest in partnership profits.
    - An interest in partnership losses.
    - An interest in partnership capital.
    - The power to manage and other powers enumerated under the Uniform Partnership Act.

    A partner's interest in partnership profits and losses can be specially allocated in terms of an overall percentage or in terms of a single item of partnership income, deduction, gain or loss. The allowance of special allocations (e.g., of a partnership item of income, deduction, gain or loss) is unique to the partnership form of business operation. Special allocations may be mandated (e.g., under Section 704(c)) or elected (e.g., under Section 754). For certain elected special allocations, as long as such allocations have substantial economic effect, these allocations will be respected regardless of the magnitude or timing of distributions and regardless of capital account balances.

Multiple Choice

1. a (p. 13–28; 40,000 + 300,000 + 2,000 + 1,800 + 3,000 + 1,200)

    John's adjusted basis in the land and building is determined under the cost rules of Section 1012, as follows.

Purchase Price ($40,000 + $300,000)	$340,000
Other Buyer's Costs ($2,000 + $1,800 + $1,200)	5,000
Costs to Place the Property into Service ($3,000)	3,000
Adjusted Basis (Cost)	$348,000

    Thus, item a is correct. Further, choice items b,c&d are incorrect because they each are inconsistent with item a.

2. a (p. 13–28; Amount Realized – Adjusted Basis; (100,000 + 80,000 + 20,000 – 10,000) – (150,000 + 50,000 – 70,000))

    Robert's adjusted basis in the land and building is determined under the cost rules of Section 1012, as follows.

Cost (for purchased property)	$150,000
Plus: Capital improvements	50,000
Less: Depreciation (Cost Recovery)	70,000
Equals: Adjusted Basis	$130,000

Robert's amount realized under Treas. Reg. Sec. 1.1001 is computed as follows:

Money received	$100,000
Plus: FMV of other property received	20,000
Plus: Liabilities discharged	80,000
Less: Liabilities assumed	
Less: Selling costs	10,000
Equals: Amount Realized	$190,000

Accordingly, Robert's realized and recognized gain or loss is computed under Section 1001 as follows:

Amount Realized	$190,000
Less: Adjusted Basis	130,000
Equals: Gain or Loss Realized	$ 60,000

Under Section 1012, current real estate taxes that are required to be apportioned between the buyer and the seller are not taken into account in determining the gain or loss realized on the sale of real property. Thus, item a is correct. Further, the other choice items are incorrect because they each are inconsistent with the correct answer.

3. b (p. 13–23; 960,000 − (210,100 + 100,200 + 312,200 + 100,000 + 202,000))

Within the context of the purchase or sale of a business, the excess of the purchase price over the fair market value of identifiable assets is referred to as goodwill (or going-concern value). Prior to the Revenue Reconciliation Act (RRA) of 1993, an intangible (goodwill, patent, franchise, or covenant not to compete) was amortized for tax purposes only if such intangible had a limited life, where the amortization period was equal to the stated limited life. Thus, an intangible without a limited life was not amortized. After the effective date of RRA of 1993, under Section 197, all Section 197 intangibles are amortized over a 15-year statutory life, regardless of life (limited or not). Goodwill is a Section 197 intangible. Accordingly, goodwill is amortized over a 15-year statutory period beginning with the month in which such goodwill is acquired.

In the instant case, Matt's purchase price for the dry cleaning store is $960,000. The fair market value of identifiable assets equals $924,400 ($210,000 + $100,200 + $312,200 + $100,000 + $202,000). Accordingly, goodwill is valued at $35,600 [the excess of the purchase price ($960,000) over the fair market value of identifiable assets ($924,400)]. Thus, item b is correct. Further, the other choice items are incorrect because they each are inconsistent with the correct answer.

4. a (p. 13–23; owner and business are same)

Operating a business through the sole proprietorship form of doing business is the most popular form of doing business. It is the most popular because it is the least burdensome in terms of administration.

The sole proprietorship is neither (a) a separate legal entity nor (b) a separate taxable entity. Instead, it is a pure conduit. For all purposes in all contexts, the sole proprietorship is merely extension of the individual. Accordingly, the sole proprietor has unlimited liability with respect to liabilities of the business. Thus, in the instant case, item a is correct. Further, choice items b,c&d are incorrect because each of these items implies that the sole proprietor has limited liability with respect to liabilities of the business.

5. c (p. 13–28; relative fair market value: (300,000/400,000) (360,000))

Alisa's adjusted basis in the depreciable building is determined under the cost allocation rules of Section 1012 and Treas. Reg. Sec. 1.61–6(a), as follows.

Purchase Price	$360,000
Building's Relative Fair Market Value ($300,000/$400,000)	75%
Adjusted Basis of Building	$270,000

Thus, item c is correct. Further, the other choice items are incorrect because they each are inconsistent with the correct answer.

CHAPTER 14

Exempt Entities

LEARNING OBJECTIVES

After completing Chapter 14, you should be able to:

1. Identify the different types of exempt organizations.
2. Enumerate the requirements for exempt status.
3. Know the tax consequences of exempt status, including the different consequences for public charities and private foundations.
4. Determine which exempt organizations are classified as private foundations.
5. Recognize the taxes imposed on private foundations and calculate the related initial tax and additional tax amounts.
6. Determine when an exempt organization is subject to the unrelated business income tax and calculate the amount of the tax.
7. List the reports exempt organizations must file with the IRS and the related due dates.
8. Identify tax planning opportunities for exempt organizations.

KEY TERMS

Debt-financed income
Excess lobbying expenditure
Exempt organization
Feeder organization

Grass roots expenditure
Intermediate sanctions
Lobbying expenditure
Private foundation

Unrelated business income
Unrelated business income tax (UBIT)

OUTLINE

I. **TYPES OF EXEMPT ORGANIZATIONS**
   A. To qualify for exempt status an organization must fit one of the categories provided in the Code. Exhibit 14–1 of the text contains many examples.

II. **REQUIREMENTS FOR EXEMPT STATUS**
   A. Requirements for exempt status include that the organization must:
      1. serve some type of common good,
      2. be a not-for-profit entity,
      3. allow no net earnings to be used for the benefit of any private shareholder or individual, and
      4. exert no political influence.

III. **TAX CONSEQUENCES OF EXEMPT STATUS: GENERAL**
   A. Though generally exempt, Federal taxes may be imposed on an organization classified as exempt if the organization:
      1. engages in prohibited transactions.
      2. is a feeder organization.
      3. is classified as a private foundation.
      4. has unrelated business income.
   B. Engaging in prohibited transactions can subject the organization's income to federal taxation. In addition, it can cause the organization to forfeit its exempt status.
      1. Prohibited transactions include:
         a. failure to sustain the initial requirements of exempt status.
         b. certain lobbying activities.
      2. Initial qualification requirements effectively become maintenance requirements.
      3. Most exempt organizations are prohibited from participating in lobbying activities. Any violation can result in forfeiture of exempt status.
      4. Qualifying § 501(c)(3) organizations may elect to participate in lobbying activities on a limited basis. These organizations may not exceed the ceiling amount statutorily imposed on lobbying expenditures.
      5. Two ceiling amounts apply. The grass roots ceiling limits the amount of expenditures incurred to influence general public opinion. The lobbying expenditures ceiling amount limits expenditures incurred to influence the formulation of legislation.
      6. Though not in excess of the ceiling amount, excess lobbying expenditures are subject to a 25% tax. The ceiling amounts are 150% of the grass roots or lobbying nontaxable amount; the excess lobbying expenditures are more than 100% of the grass roots or lobbying nontaxable amount. See Figure 14–1 of the text for calculations of the lobbying nontaxable amount.
   C. Intermediate sanctions can be applied to so-called public charities. These sanctions take the form of excise taxes imposed on "disqualified persons" (or exempt organization mangers) who engage in "excess benefit transactions."
   D. Feeder organizations carry on a trade or business activity for profit and pay all profits to one or more exempt organizations. These types of organizations are subject to Federal income tax with three exceptions. Feeder organizations not subject to Federal income tax include those engaged in activities:
      1. which generate rental income excluded from the definition of rent for unrelated business income tax purposes.
      2. for which substantially all work is performed by volunteers.
      3. which sell merchandise substantially all of which had been received as contributions or gifts.

IV. **PRIVATE FOUNDATIONS**
   A. Private foundations are so classified because these organizations generally do not have broad public support; they are formed to respond to the private interests of a limited number of persons.

STUDY GUIDE | CHAPTER 14 Exempt Entities | 14-3

B. Though generally exempt from Federal income tax, §§ 4940–4945 impose excise taxes on private foundations for certain actions or failures to act. Such taxes are levied only on private foundations and include a tax on:
   1. investment income.
   2. self-dealing (engaging in transactions with disqualified persons).
   3. failure to distribute income (for exempt purposes).
   4. excess business holdings (controlling unrelated businesses).
   5. investments that jeopardize charitable purposes (speculative investments).
   6. taxable expenditures (expenditures that should not be made by private foundations).
C. See Concept Summary 14–3 of the text.

V. **UNRELATED BUSINESS INCOME TAX**
A. An exempt organization may be subject to income tax on unrelated business income if:
   1. the organization conducts a trade or business,
   2. the trade or business is not substantially related to the exempt purpose of the organization, and
   3. the trade or business is regularly carried on by the organization.
B. Statutory exceptions to classification as unrelated trade or business apply even if all the above factors are present.
   1. All work is performed by volunteers.
   2. Substantially all merchandise being sold was received by gift.
   3. The business is conducted primarily for the convenience of the organization's members.
   4. Sales of work-related clothing and equipment to its members and items normally sold through vending machines, snack bars, or food-dispensing facilities.
C. Special rules apply for corporate sponsorship payments, bingo games, distribution of low-cost articles, and rental or exchange of membership lists.
D. If gross income from an unrelated business is less than $1,000, it is not necessary to file a return associated with the unrelated business income tax.
E. When applicable, the tax on unrelated business income is computed based on the application of corporate tax rates.

    Gross unrelated business income
  − Deductions
  = Net unrelated business income
  ± Modifications
  = Unrelated business taxable income

F. Special rules apply to unrelated debt-financed income.

VI. **REPORTING REQUIREMENTS**
A. Though only certain types of organizations are required to obtain IRS approval for exempt status, exempt organizations should apply to avoid potential disqualification by the IRS.
   1. Application is made on Form 1023 for § 501(c)(3) organizations.
   2. Form 1024 is used for most other types of exempt organizations.
B. Annual filings of Form 990 are required of exempt organizations other than:
   1. Federal agencies.
   2. churches.
   3. organizations having annual gross receipts that do not exceed $25,000.
   4. private foundations (private foundations are required to file Form 990–PF).
C. Form 990 is due on the 15th day of the 5th month after the end of the organization's tax year.
D. Exempt entities must make available to the general public Form 990 (three most recent returns) and Form 1023 (or Form 1024).

TEST FOR SELF-EVALUATION—CHAPTER 14

True or False

Indicate which of the following statements is true or false by circling the correct answer.

T F 1. Any organization that qualifies for tax-exempt status can receive contributions that are fully deductible by the donor. (IRS 97 4A-6)

T F 2. Exempt status is automatically lost if an exempt organization has any unrelated business income during the year.

T F 3. The ONLY organizations exempt from Federal income taxes are those organized and operated exclusively for religious, charitable, scientific or educational purposes. (IRS 96 4A-26)

T F 4. An organization recognized as a tax-exempt organization will NOT pay income tax on any income it earns, but is still responsible for withholding, social security taxes, and Federal unemployment tax for wage payments. (IRS 94 4A-26)

T F 5. A partnership may qualify as an organization exempt from Federal income tax if it is organized and operated exclusively for one or more of the purposes found in Section 501(c)(3) of the Internal Revenue Code. (IRS 91 4A-39)

T F 6. An exempt organization with $4,999 of gross income from an unrelated business is required to file Form 990–T, Exempt Organization Business Income Tax Return. (IRS 91 4A-40)

T F 7. Organizations recognized as tax-exempt are not responsible for withholding, depositing, paying and reporting federal income tax withholding, FICA and FUTA associated with wages paid to their employees. (IRS 91 4A-41)

T F 8. A church, its integrated auxiliaries, or a convention or association of churches is not required to file Form 1023, Application for Recognition of Exemption under Section 501(c)(3) of the Internal Revenue Code, in order to be tax exempt or to receive tax deductible contributions. (IRS 91 4A-42)

Fill in the Blanks

Complete the following statements with the appropriate word(s) or amount(s).

1. The underlying rationale for all exempt organizations is to _____.

2. Ceiling amounts on lobbying expenditures for Section 501(c)(3) exempt organizations are calculated for _____ expenditures and for _____ expenditures.

3. Failure to continue to qualify as a type of exempt organization is a _____.

4. A _____ carries on a trade or business for the benefit of an exempt organization.

5. _____ or _____ includes any activity conducted for the production of income through the sale of merchandise or the performance of services.

Multiple Choice

Choose the best answer for each of the following questions.

_____ 1. Which of the following statements is correct in respect to tax-exempt organizations? (IRS 97 4B-44)

    a. A private foundation may qualify for exemption from Federal income tax if it is organized for the prevention of cruelty to animals.
    b. A partnership may qualify as an organization exempt from Federal income tax if it is organized and operated exclusively for one or more of the purposes found in section 501(c)(3).
    c. An individual can qualify as an organization exempt from Federal income tax.
    d. In order to qualify as an exempt organization, the organization must be a corporation.

_____ 2. Which of the following organizations, which are exempt from Federal income tax, must generally file an annual information report? (IRS 97 4B-45)

    a. An organization, other than a private foundation, with annual gross receipts that normally are not more than $25,000.
    b. A private foundation.
    c. A church.
    d. A religious order.

_____ 3. If applicable, the tax on unrelated business income is:

    a. computed at corporate tax rates
    b. computed at trust tax rates
    c. computed at single individual tax rates
    d. computed at special exempt organization tax rates

_____ 4. Private foundation status of a Section 501(c)(3) organization terminates if it:

    a. invests in a functionally related business
    b. becomes a public charity
    c. receives less than 1/3 of its support from a governmental unit
    d. becomes an exempt operating foundation

_____ 5. To qualify as a tax-exempt organization, an entity:

    a. can never engage in lobbying activities
    b. cannot have a nonresident shareholder
    c. must fit into one of the categories provided for in the Code
    d. can be a feeder organization

_____ 6. Income derived from conducting bingo games will be exempt if:

    a. allowed by state law only to exempt organizations
    b. the games are legal under state and local law
    c. both of the above
    d. neither of the above

_____ 7. A generally tax-exempt private foundation may be subject to taxes imposed on:

    a. investment income
    b. self dealing
    c. undistributed income
    d. all of the above
    e. none of the above

_____ 8. In determining whether a Section 501(c)(3) organization is broadly supported and not classified as a private foundation, two tests must be satisfied:

    a. more than one-third support test (External)
    b. not more than one-third support test (Internal)
    c. $5,000 or 1% support, the greater, test
    d. a and c
    e. a and b

_____ 9. Low cost items distributed incidental to solicitation for charitable contributions are not considered unrelated trade or business when:

    a. the item is requested by the recipient
    b. the item is returned in lieu of a donation
    c. the items cost less than $7.60 each for 2002
    d. all of the above
    e. none of the above

_____ 10. An exempt organization will be subject to the tax on unrelated business income if:

    a. the trade or business is not regularly carried on
    b. the trade or business is not substantially related to the exempt purpose of the organization
    c. the trade or business is substantially related to the exempt purpose of the organization
    d. the trade or business is conducted primarily for the convenience of members of a Section 501(c)(3) organization

_____ 11. Which of the following might be considered an unrelated trade or business for a hospital:

    a. cafeteria
    b. pharmacy
    c. gift shop
    d. all of the above
    e. none of the above

_____ 12. A tax-exempt organization that is required to file Form 990, Return of Organization Exempt From Income Tax, must do so by what date (do NOT consider any extensions, weekends, or holidays)? (IRS 96 4B-67)

    a. The last day of the month following the end of the organization's accounting period.
    b. The 15th day of the 3rd month following the end of the organization's accounting period.
    c. The 15th day of the 4th month following the end of the organization's accounting period.
    d. The 15th day of the 5th month following the end of the organization's accounting period.

_____ 13. Which of the following organizations, exempt from Federal income tax under Section 501(a) of the Internal Revenue Code (IRC), must file an annual information return on Form 990 or Form 990–PF? (IRS 94 4B-68)

    a. A private foundation exempt under § 501(c)(3) of the IRC.
    b. An organization, other than a private foundation, having gross receipts in each year that normally are NOT more than $5,000.
    c. A stock bonus, pension, or profit-sharing trust that qualifies under § 401 of the IRC.
    d. A school BELOW college level, affiliated with a church or operated by a religious order, that is NOT an integrated auxiliary of a church.

SOLUTIONS TO CHAPTER 14 QUESTIONS

True or False

1. F   (p. 14–6; only certain tax-exempt organizations)

    After comparing these two sets of organizations, it is apparent that not all tax-exempt organizations are qualified charitable organizations. For example, a qualified trust under Section 401 (a tax-exempt organization) is not a qualified charitable organization under Section 170(c).

2. F   (p. 14–15; exempt status not lost, UBIT may apply)

    Within the context of ensuring that the activities of a tax-exempt organization are not similar to an entity engaged in an activity for-profit, the Unrelated Business Income Tax (UBIT) applies to many (but not all) tax-exempt organizations. This tax is imposed on certain tax-exempt organizations that engage in substantial commercial activities (a trade or business regularly carried on), where these activities are not related to the exempt purpose of such organization. The UBIT regime attempts to neutralize the tax-exempt organization's tax advantage by treating such organization as if it were a corporation. That is, the UBIT regime utilizes the corporate income tax rate schedule and applies such rate schedule against Unrelated Business Taxable Income (UBTI).

    UBTI is modified net unrelated business income (gross unrelated business income less deductions). In the instant case, if a tax-exempt organization has net unrelated business income, the consequence to it is application of the UBIT regime, not termination of its tax-exempt status. In this case, Congress recognizes the need for a tax-exempt organization to be adequately funded but (at the same time) does not want the tax law to unfairly discriminate against for-profit organizations (in favor of tax-exempt organizations).

3. F   (Exhibit 14–1; Section 501(c)(3) organization only one type of exempt organization)

    After comparing these two sets or organizations, it is apparent that not all tax-exempt organizations are qualified charitable organizations. For example, a qualified trust under Section 401 (a tax-exempt organization) is not a qualified charitable organization under Section 170(c), including (more specifically) an organization operated exclusively for religious, charitable, scientific or educational purposes under Section 170(c)(2)(B).

4. F   (p. 14–15; may pay on unrelated business income)

    Within the context of ensuring that the activities of a tax-exempt organization are not similar to an entity engaged in an activity for-profit, the Unrelated Business Income Tax (UBIT) applies to many (but not all) tax-exempt organizations. This tax is imposed on certain tax-exempt organizations that engage in substantial commercial activities (a trade or business regularly carried on), where these activities are not related to the exempt purpose of such organization. The UBIT regime attempts to neutralize the tax-exempt organization's tax advantage by treating such organization as if it were a corporation. That is, the UBIT regime utilizes the corporate income tax rate schedule and applies such rate schedule against Unrelated Business Taxable Income (UBTI). UBTI is modified net unrelated business income (gross unrelated business income less deductions).

    In the instant case, if a tax-exempt organization has net unrelated business income, the organization may pay a UBIT. In this case, Congress recognizes the need for a tax-exempt organization to be adequately funded but (at the same time) does not want the tax law to unfairly discriminate against for-profit organizations (in favor of tax-exempt organizations). In any case, a tax-exempt organization may employ employees and, as a result, must pay employment taxes (FICA and FUTA) and must withhold FICA tax and federal and state income taxes from wages paid.

5. F (p. 14–4; net earnings must not benefit members)

   In the instant case, net earnings of a partnership inure to member partners. Thus, the tax law does not allow the partnership to qualify for tax-exempt status, even though it is organized and operated exclusively for a charitable purpose that is identified in Section 501(c)(3).

6. T (p. 14–27)

   If a tax-exempt organization has gross unrelated business income of at least $1,000, the organization must file Form 990–T (Exempt Organization Business Income Tax Return) and may be required to pay a UBIT. The due date for the return is the fifteenth day of the fifth month after the end of the taxable year. In this case, Congress recognizes the need for a tax-exempt organization to be adequately funded but (at the same time) does not want the tax law to unfairly discriminate against for-profit organizations (in favor of tax-exempt organizations).

7. F (p. 14–6; exempt from Federal income tax only)

   The primary purpose of the federal income tax system is revenue collection. However, the Federal income tax system serves many purposes other than revenue collection. Further, much of the complexity of the tax laws can be attributed to these other purposes. For example, many provisions of the Internal Revenue Code serve Congress' social agenda. In one instance where social policy considerations affect the tax law, an organization may receive tax-exempt status if such organization is devoted to charitable or other purposes. Congress allows this exemption because additional appropriations would be needed for the promotion of the general welfare, but for this type of organization.

   In the instant case, the tax-exempt organization is generally exempt from paying an entity income tax. Nevertheless, such tax-exempt organization may employ employees. As a result, it must pay employment taxes (FICA and FUTA) and must withhold FICA tax and Federal and state income taxes from wages paid. Its (income) tax-exempt status will not obviate these burdens.

8. T (p. 14–25)

   The primary purpose of the Federal income tax system is revenue collection. However, the Federal income tax system serves many purposes other than revenue collection. Further, much of the complexity of the tax laws can be attributed to these other purposes. For example, many provisions of the Internal Revenue Code serve Congress' social agenda. In one instance where social policy considerations affect the tax law, an organization may receive tax-exempt status if such organization is devoted to charitable or other purposes. Congress allows this exemption because additional appropriations would be needed for the promotion of the general welfare, but for this type of organization.

   Even though it may be most prudent for the organization to apply for tax-exempt status, not all organizations are statutorily required to apply for such status. In general, Section 501(c)(3) type organizations are required to file Form 1023 (Application for Recognition of Exemption under Section 501(c)(3) of the Internal Revenue Code). However, as an exception to this general rule, churches, their auxiliaries, and an association (or convention) of churches are not required to file Form 1023, even though they qualify as Section 501(c)(3) organizations.

Fill in the Blanks

1. serve some type of common good (p. 14–4)

   The primary purpose of the Federal income tax system is revenue collection. However, the Federal income tax system serves many purposes other than revenue collection. Further, much of the complexity of the tax laws can be attributed to these other purposes. For example, many provisions of the Internal Revenue Code serve Congress' social agenda. In one instance where social policy considerations affect the tax law, an organization may receive tax-exempt status if such organization is devoted to charitable or other purpose that serves some type of common good. Congress allows this exemption because additional appropriations would be needed for the promotion of the general welfare, but for this type of organization.

Although certain organizations receive tax-exempt status, severe limitations are placed on such status to ensure compliance with congressional social policy. These limitations ensure that the activities of certain tax-exempt organizations:

- Do not result in net earnings, which benefit its members.
- Do not exert political influence.
- Are not similar to an activity for-profit.
- Serve a common good.

2. lobbying; grass roots (p. 14–8)

As an exception to the general rule prohibiting political lobbying, certain Section 501(c)(3) organizations (organizations that make an affirmative election to lobby) may engage in political lobbying to a limited extent (up to a ceiling amount), where exceeding the ceiling amount can be the basis for termination of the Section 501(c)(3) organization's tax-exempt status. Further, even though the ceiling is not exceeded, political lobbying expenditures may give rise to a tax on a portion of such expenditures. The political lobbying ceiling is multi-dimensional and is determined by reference to separate ceilings of (a) lobbying expenditures and (b) grass roots expenditures. Grass roots expenditures are expenditures made for the purpose of attempting to affect the opinions of the general public. Lobbying expenditures (which include grass roots expenditures) are expenditures made for the purpose of influencing legislation through (a) attempting to affect the opinions of the general public or (b) communicating with any government office that may participate in the formulation of legislation.

3. prohibited transaction (p. 14–6)

The primary purpose of the Federal income tax system is revenue collection. However, the Federal income tax system serves many purposes other than revenue collection. Further, much of the complexity of the tax laws can be attributed to these other purposes. For example, many provisions of the Internal Revenue Code serve Congress' social agenda. In one instance where social policy considerations affect the tax law, an organization may receive tax-exempt status if such organization is devoted to charitable or other purposes. Congress allows this exemption because additional appropriations would be needed for the promotion of the general welfare, but for this type of organization.

Although certain organizations receive tax-exempt status, severe limitations are placed on such status to ensure compliance with congressional social policy. These limitations ensure that the activities of certain tax-exempt organizations:

- Serve a common good.
- Do not result in net earnings, which benefit its members.
- Do not exert political influence (political lobbying).
- Are not similar to an activity for-profit.

Within the context of ensuring that the activities of a tax-exempt organization continue to qualify the organization for tax-exempt status, if the organization fails to continue to qualify as a tax-exempt organization by reference to the nature of its activities, such organization will forfeit its tax-exempt status.

4. feeder organization (p. 14–10)

Although certain organizations receive tax-exempt status, severe limitations are placed on such status to ensure compliance with congressional social policy. These limitations ensure that the activities of certain tax-exempt organizations:

- Serve a common good.
- Do not result in net earnings, which benefit its members.
- Do not exert political influence (political lobbying).
- Are not similar to an activity for-profit.

Within the context of ensuring that the activities of a tax-exempt organization are not similar to an entity engaged in an activity for-profit, Section 502 prohibits tax-exempt status for feeder organizations. Feeder organizations are organizations operated for the primary purpose of engaging in a for-profit, trade or business, where profits feed into tax-exempt organizations.

5. trade, business (p. 14–15)

Although certain organizations receive tax-exempt status, severe limitations are placed on such status to ensure compliance with congressional social policy. These limitations ensure that the activities of certain tax-exempt organizations:

- Serve a common good.
- Do not result in net earnings, which benefit its members.
- Do not exert political influence (political lobbying).
- Are not similar to an activity for-profit.

Within the context of ensuring that the activities of a tax-exempt organization are not similar to an entity engaged in an activity for-profit, Section 502 prohibits tax-exempt status for feeder organizations. Feeder organizations are organizations operated for the primary purpose of engaging in a for-profit, trade or business, where profits feed into one or more tax-exempt organization. Within this context, a trade or business includes a merchandising, manufacturing or service-oriented activity for-profit.

Multiple Choice

1. a (p. 14–11)

Although certain organizations receive tax-exempt status, severe limitations are placed on such status to ensure compliance with congressional social policy. These limitations ensure that the activities of certain tax-exempt organizations:

- Do not result in net earnings, which benefit its members.
- Do not exert political influence (political lobbying).
- Are not similar to an activity for-profit.
- Serve a common good.

Within the context of ensuring that the activities of a tax-exempt organization promote the general welfare (serve some type of common good), although generally tax-exempt, private foundations may be subject to a tax on:

- Investment income under Section 4940.
- Self-dealing under Section 4941.
- The failure to distribute income under Section 4942.
- Excess business holdings under Section 4943.
- Investments that jeopardize its charitable purpose under Section 4944.
- Taxable expenditures under Section 4945.

These taxes necessarily restrict the activities of a private foundation. The activities of private foundations are more closely scrutinized because they:

- generally define common good more narrowly and
- are not broadly supported by the general public.

In the instant case, a foundation organized and operated exclusively for the prevention of cruelty to animals is tax-exempt under Section 503(c)(3). If such a foundation is a private foundation, it is also generally tax-exempt. Thus, item a is correct. Further, the following items are incorrect.

- Item b is incorrect because the tax law does not allow a partnership to qualify for tax-exempt status, even though it is organized and operated exclusively for a charitable purpose that is identified in Section 501(c)(3), since the net earnings of such partnership inure to member partners.
- Item c is incorrect because an individual is not an organization described as a tax-exempt organization in:
  - Section 501(c)(1)–(27),
  - Section 501(d): Religious organizations, and
  - Section 401(a): Qualified trusts.
- Item d is incorrect because there are organizations (other than corporations) that are described as tax-exempt organizations in:
  - Section 501(c)(1)–(27),
  - Section 501(d): Religious organizations, and
  - Section 401(a): Qualified trusts.

2. b (p. 14–26)

   Even though tax-exempt, most tax-exempt organizations are required to file an annual informational return by the fifteenth day of the fifth month after the end of the taxable year. Form 990 (Return of Organization Exempt from Income Tax) is required most often. However:

   - Private foundations are required to file Form 990–PF (Return of Private Foundation).
   - Some tax-exempt organizations are exempt from the annual informational return filing requirement under Section 6033(a)(2), including:
     - Churches, their integrated auxiliaries, and conventions or associations of churches.
     - Organizations that have annual gross receipts that do not exceed $25,000.

   Thus, in the instant case, item b is correct. Further, items a, c, and d are incorrect because each of these tax-exempt organizations are exempt from the annual informational return filing requirement.

3. a (p. 14–15)

   Within the context of ensuring that the activities of a tax-exempt organization are not similar to an entity engaged in an activity for-profit, the Unrelated Business Income Tax (UBIT) applies to many (but not all) tax-exempt organizations. This tax is imposed on certain tax-exempt organizations that engage in substantial commercial activities (a trade or business regularly carried on), where these activities are not related to the exempt purpose of such organization. The UBIT regime attempts to neutralize the tax-exempt organization's tax advantage by treating such organization as if it were a corporation. That is, the UBIT regime utilizes the corporate income tax rate schedule and applies such rate schedule against Unrelated Business Taxable Income (UBTI). Thus, in the instant case, item a is correct.

4. b (p. 14–11)

   Private foundations do not include Section 501(c)(3) organizations that are broadly supported by the general public, since these organizations are assumed to be responsive to the general public, rather than a small group of individuals with a private agenda. Section 501(c)(3) organizations are broadly supported by the general public, if the following two tests are met.

   - External support test. The external support test is met if more than one-third of the organization's support generally originates from either (1) the general public, (2) governmental units, or (3) other Section 501(c)(3) organizations.
   - Internal support test. The internal support test is met if no more than one-third of the organization's support generally originates from either (1) gross investment income or (2) unrelated business taxable income (less the associated tax).

   Thus, in the instant case, item b is correct, assuming both the external support test and the internal support test are met. Further, items a, c, and d are incorrect because each of these items will not cause the Section 501(c)(3) organization to avoid its private foundation status by meeting both the internal and external support tests under the being broadly supported by the general public rationale.

5. c (p. 14-4)

Under Section 501(a), organizations that are tax-exempt are described in:

- Section 501(c)(1)–(27),
- Section 501(d): Religious organizations, and
- Section 401(a): Qualified trusts.

Although certain organizations receive tax-exempt status, severe limitations are placed on such status to ensure compliance with congressional social policy. These limitations ensure that the activities of certain tax-exempt organizations:

- Serve a common good.
- Do not result in net earnings, which benefit its members.
- Do not exert political influence (political lobbying).
- Are not similar to an activity for-profit.

Within the context of ensuring that the activities of a tax-exempt organization are not similar to an entity engaged in an activity for-profit, Section 502 prohibits tax-exempt status for feeder organizations. Feeder organizations are organizations operated for the primary purpose of engaging in a for-profit, trade or business, where profits feed into one or more tax-exempt organizations. Within this context, a trade or business includes a merchandising, manufacturing or service-oriented activity for-profit. Furthermore, within the context of ensuring that certain tax-exempt organizations do not engage in political lobbying, tax-exempt organizations under Section 501(c)(3) [organizations operated exclusively for religious, charitable, scientific or educational purposes] are generally prohibited from engaging in political lobbying. Violation of this prohibition can be the basis for termination of the Section 501(c)(3) organization's tax-exempt status. The prohibition against political lobbying is absolute with respect to churches and private foundations.

However, as an exception to this general rule prohibiting political lobbying, certain Section 501(c)(3) organizations (organizations that make an affirmative election to lobby) may engage in political lobbying to a limited extent (up to a ceiling amount), where exceeding the ceiling amount can be the basis for termination of the Section 501(c)(3) organization's tax-exempt status. Further, even though the ceiling is not exceeded, political lobbying expenditures may give rise to a tax on a portion of such expenditures.

Thus, in the instant case, item c is correct. Further, the following items are incorrect.

- Item a is incorrect because certain Section 501(c)(3) organizations may engage in political lobbying.
- Item b is incorrect because tax-exempt organizations do not have shareholders.
- Item d is incorrect because feeder organizations are not tax-exempt.

6. c (p. 14-18)

Within the context of ensuring that the activities of a tax-exempt organization are not similar to an entity engaged in an activity for-profit, the Unrelated Business Income Tax (UBIT) applies to many (but not all) tax-exempt organizations. This tax is imposed on certain tax-exempt organizations that engage in substantial commercial activities (a trade or business regularly carried on), where theses activities are not related to the exempt purpose of such organization. The UBIT regime attempts to neutralize the tax-exempt organization's tax advantage by treating such organization as if it were a corporation. That is, the UBIT regime incorporates the corporate income tax rate schedule and applies such rate schedule against Unrelated Business Taxable Income (UBTI). UBTI is modified net unrelated business income (gross unrelated business income less deductions).

In the instant case, if a tax-exempt organization has net unrelated business income, the organization may pay a UBIT. In this case, Congress recognizes the need for a tax-exempt organization to be adequately funded but (at the same time) does not want the tax law to unfairly discriminate against for-profit organizations (in favor of tax-exempt organizations). Generally, income from bingo games constitutes gross unrelated business income. However, income from qualified bingo games does not constitute gross unrelated business income. A qualified bingo game is a bingo game where:

- the bingo game is legal under both state and local law and
- commercial bingo games (engaged in for profit) generally are not permitted within the jurisdiction.

Thus, item c (constituting items a and b) is correct. Further, item d is incorrect because it is inconsistent with item c.

7. d (p. 14–13)

Within the context of ensuring that the activities of a tax-exempt organization promote the general welfare (serve some type of common good), although generally tax-exempt, private foundations may be subject to a tax on:

- Investment income under Section 4940.
- Self-dealing under Section 4941.
- The failure to distribute income under Section 4942.
- Excess business holdings under Section 4943.
- Investments that jeopardize its charitable purpose under Section 4944.
- Taxable expenditures under Section 4945.

These taxes necessarily restrict the activities of a private foundation. The activities of private foundations are more closely scrutinized because they:

- generally define common good more narrowly and
- are not broadly supported by the general public.

Thus, in the instant case, item d (constituting items a, b, and c) is correct. Further, item e is incorrect because it is inconsistent with item d.

8. e (p. 14–11)

The activities of private foundations are closely scrutinized because they:

- generally define common good more narrowly and
- are not broadly supported by the general public.

Consequently, private foundations do not include Section 501(c)(3) organizations that are broadly supported by the general public, since these organizations are assumed to be responsive to the general public, rather than a small group of individuals with a private agenda. Section 501(c)(3) organizations are broadly supported by the general public, if the following two tests are met.

- External support test. The external support test is met if more than one-third of the organization's support generally originates from either (1) the general public, (2) governmental units, or (3) other Section 501(c)(3) organizations.
- Internal support test. The internal support test is met if no more than one-third of the organization's support generally originates from either (1) gross investment income or (2) unrelated business taxable income (less the associated tax).

Thus, in the instant case, item e (constituting items a and b) is correct. Further, items c and d are incorrect because they are each inconsistent with item e.

9. c (p. 14–19)

In the instant case, if a tax-exempt organization has net unrelated business income, the organization may pay a UBIT. In this case, Congress recognizes the need for a tax-exempt organization to be adequately funded but (at the same time) does not want the tax law to unfairly discriminate against for-profit organizations (in favor of tax-exempt organizations). In soliciting for charitable contributions, if a tax-exempt organization incidentally distributes qualifying low-cost articles, such distributions do not constitute conduct associated with an unrelated trade or business. Qualifying low-cost articles are items of personal property that cost at most $7.90 each for 2002. Thus, item c is correct. Further, choice items a and b are not relevant to the determination as to whether the distribution of articles, within the context

10. b (p. 14–15)

Within the context of ensuring that the activities of a tax-exempt organization are not similar to an entity engaged in an activity for-profit, the Unrelated Business Income Tax (UBIT) applies to many (but not all) tax-exempt organizations. This tax is imposed on certain tax-exempt organizations that engage in substantial commercial activities (a trade or business regularly carried on), where these activities are not related to the exempt purpose of such organization. The UBIT regime attempts to neutralize the tax-exempt organization's tax advantage by treating such organization as if it were a corporation. That is, the UBIT regime utilizes the corporate income tax rate schedule and applies such rate schedule against Unrelated Business Taxable Income (UBTI). UBTI is modified net unrelated business income (gross unrelated business income less deductions).

In the instant case, if a tax-exempt organization has net unrelated business income, the consequence to it is application of the UBIT regime. In this case, Congress recognizes the need for a tax-exempt organization to be adequately funded but (at the same time) does not want the tax law to unfairly discriminate against for-profit organizations (in favor of tax-exempt organizations). Thus, item b is correct. Further, the following choice items are incorrect.

- Item a is incorrect because the UBIT regime applies only if an unrelated trade or business is regularly carried on.
- Item c is incorrect because the UBIT regime applies only if the trade or business is unrelated to the exempt purpose of the organization.
- Item d is incorrect because the UBIT regime applies only if the trade or business (even though unrelated to the exempt purpose of the organization) is not conducted primarily for the convenience of the members of a Section 501(c)(3) organization.

11. c (p. 14–15; if not found to be for the convenience of members)

Within the context of ensuring that the activities of a tax-exempt organization are not similar to an entity engaged in an activity for-profit, the Unrelated Business Income Tax (UBIT) applies to many (but not all) tax-exempt organizations. This tax is imposed on certain tax-exempt organizations that engage in substantial commercial activities (a trade or business regularly carried on), where these activities are not related to the exempt purpose of such organization. The UBIT regime attempts to neutralize the tax-exempt organization's tax advantage by treating such organization as if it were a corporation. That is, the UBIT regime utilizes the corporate income tax rate schedule and applies such rate schedule against Unrelated Business Taxable Income (UBTI). UBTI is modified net unrelated business income (gross unrelated business income less deductions).

In the instant case, if a tax-exempt organization has net unrelated business income, the consequence to it is application of the UBIT regime. In this case, Congress recognizes the need for a tax-exempt organization to be adequately funded but (at the same time) does not want the tax law to unfairly discriminate against for-profit organizations (in favor of tax-exempt organizations). Thus, item c is correct, since the gift shop constitutes an unrelated trade or business. Further, the following choice items are incorrect.

- Items a and b are incorrect because the UBIT regime does not apply to either the cafeteria or the pharmacy, since these trades or businesses are conducted primarily for the convenience of the members of a Section 501(c)(3) organization.
- Items d and e are incorrect because they are inconsistent with item c.

12. d (p. 14–26)

The primary purpose of the Federal income tax system is revenue collection. However, the Federal income tax system serves many purposes other than revenue collection. Further, much of the complexity of the tax laws can be attributed to these other purposes. For example, many provisions of the Internal

Revenue Code serve Congress' social agenda. In one instance where social considerations affect the tax law, an organization may receive tax-exempt status if such organization is devoted to charitable or other purposes. Congress allows this exemption because additional appropriations would be needed for the promotion of the general welfare, but for this type of organization.

Under Section 501(a), organizations that are tax-exempt are described in:

- Section 501(c)(1)–(27),
- Section 501(d): Religious organizations, and
- Section 401(a): Qualified trusts.

Even though tax-exempt, most tax-exempt organizations are required to file an annual, informational return by the fifteenth day of the fifth month after the end of the taxable year. Form 990 (Return of Organization Exempt from Income Tax) is required most often. Thus, in the instant case, item d is correct.

13.   a (p. 14–26)

Under Section 501(a), organizations that are tax-exempt are described in:

- Section 501(c)(1)–(27),
- Section 501(d): Religious organizations, and
- Section 401(a): Qualified trusts.

Even though tax-exempt, most tax-exempt organizations are required to file an annual, informational return by the fifteenth day of the fifth month after the end of the taxable year. Form 990 (Return of Organization Exempt from Income Tax) is required most often. However:

- Private foundations are required to file Form 990–PF (Return of Private Foundation).
- Some tax-exempt organizations are exempt from the annual, informational return, filing requirement under Section 6033(a)(2), including:
  - Churches, their integrated auxiliaries, and conventions or associations of churches.
  - Certain organizations (other than private foundations) that have annual gross receipts that do not exceed $25,000.

Thus, in the instant case, item a is correct. Further, the following items are incorrect.

- Item b is incorrect because such tax-exempt organizations are exempt from the annual, informational return, filing requirement under Section 6033(a)(2).
- Item c is incorrect because such tax-exempt organizations are not tax-exempt under Section 501(a).
- Item d is incorrect because such tax-exempt organizations are exempt from the annual, informational return, filing requirement under Treas. Reg. Sec.1.6033–2(g).

CHAPTER 15

Multistate Corporate Taxation

LEARNING OBJECTIVES

After completing Chapter 15, you should be able to:

1. Illustrate the computation of a multistate corporation's state tax liability.
2. Define nexus and its role in state income taxation.
3. Distinguish between allocation and apportionment of a multistate corporation's taxable income.
4. Describe the nature and tax treatment of business and nonbusiness income.
5. Discuss the sales, payroll, and property apportionment factors.
6. Apply the unitary method of state income taxation.
7. Discuss states' income tax treatment of S corporations.
8. Describe other commonly encountered state and local taxes on businesses.
9. Recognize tax planning opportunities available to minimize a corporation's state and local tax liability.

KEY TERMS

Allocate
Apportion
Dock sales
Multistate Tax Commission (MTC)
Nexus
Passive investment company
Payroll factor
Property factor
Public Law 86–272
Sales factor
Throwback rule
UDITPA
Unitary theory
Water's edge election

OUTLINE

I. **OVERVIEW OF CORPORATE STATE INCOME TAXATION**
   A. Currently, forty-six states and the District of Columbia impose a tax based on a corporation's income.
   B. Generally, states require use of the same accounting periods and methods as those used on the corporation's Federal return.
   C. In a majority of states, state taxable income is determined by reference to the corporation's Federal return, with modification. State modifications (see Figure 15-1):
      1. reflect differences between state and Federal statutes.
      2. remove income that a state is constitutionally prohibited from taxing.
      3. eliminate the recovery of income for which the state did not permit a deduction on an earlier return.
   D. The Uniform Division of Income for Tax Purposes Act (UDITPA) is a model law relating to the assignment of income among the states in which a corporation operates.
      1. The Multistate Tax Commission (MTC) writes regulations and other rules that interepret the UDITPA.
   E. Jurisdiction to Impose Tax: Nexus and Public Law 86–272
      1. The state within which a business is incorporated has taxing jurisdiction.
      2. For a corporation operating in a state other than its state of incorporation, sufficient nexus must be established (see Exhibit 15-2).
         a. Nexus describes the degree of business activity that must be present before a tax can be imposed.
         b. The criteria by which nexus is measured depends on state statute; thus, the definition and sufficiency of nexus vary across states.
      3. Public Law 86–272 limits the states' right to impose an income tax on interstate activities.

II. **ALLOCATION AND APPORTIONMENT OF INCOME**
   A. Apportionment is a means by which a corporation's business income is divided among the states in which it conducts business.
      1. A specific apportionment procedure is followed, although states are free to modify the general procedure.
      2. As a result, a corporation may be subject to state income tax on more or less than 100 percent of its income.
   B. Allocation assigns specific components of corporate net income to a certain state.
   C. Allocable income generally includes:
      1. income or loss derived from sale of nonbusiness real or tangible property.
      2. income or loss derived from rentals and royalties from nonbusiness real or tangible property.
   D. Business and Nonbusiness Income
      1. Business income arises from the taxpayer's regular course of business or an activity that constitutes an integral part of the taxpayer's regular business.
      2. Nonbusiness income is "all income other than business income."
      3. Business income is apportioned; nonbusiness income may be apportioned or allocated to the state in which the property is located.
   E. Apportionment Factors
      1. Each state chooses the type and number of factors used to establish its apportionment formula.
      2. Most states use a three-factor formula which assigns equal weight to sales, payroll and property.
      3. Variations in the state's definition of allocable and apportionable income and in apportionment formulas may cause a corporation to be subject to state income tax on more or less than 100% of its Federal taxable income after modifications.
      4. To determine the apportionment factor for each state, a ratio is calculated by comparing the level of a specific activity (sales, payroll, property) within a state to the total corporate activity

of that type. The ratios are then summed, averaged, and appropriately weighted (if required) to determine the corporation's apportionment percentage for a specific state.

F. Sales Factor
1. The sales factor is determined by comparing the corporation's total sales in the state during the period to the corporation's total sales everywhere during the period.
2. In determining in-state sales, total sales:
    a. includes sales that generate business income.
    b. excludes income on federal obligations.
    c. may or may not include sales of capital assets, depending on the particular state.
3. In determining in-state sales, most states apply the ultimate destination concept, which assumes a sale takes place at the point of delivery (not where the shipment originates).
4. Most states apply the ultimate destination concept to dock sales.
5. In determining in-state sales, if an origination state has adopted a throwback rule, out-of-state sales not subject to tax in the destination state (or sales to the U.S. government) are treated as sales in the state of origination.

G. The Payroll Factor
1. The payroll factor is determined by comparing the compensation paid for services rendered within a state to the corporation's total compensation.
2. In determining in-state compensation, total compensation:
    a. generally includes compensation includible in an employees' Federal gross income.
    b. may or may not include certain fringe benefits that are excluded from Federal income tax under § 401(k), depending on the particular state.
    c. does not include payments to non-employee, outside contractors in most states.
3. In determining in-state compensation, compensation of an employee is not, normally, split between states unless the employee is transferred or changes position during the year.
4. In determining in-state compensation, when services are performed in more than one state, that employee's compensation is allocated based upon the following hierarchical ordering, to the state in which:
    a. the services are primarily performed.
    b. the employee's base of operations is located and the services are performed.
    c. the services are directed (or controlled) and performed.
    d. the employee resides.
5. In determining in-state compensation, only compensation related to the production of apportionable income is included in the payroll factor.

H. The Property Factor
1. The property factor is determined by comparing the average value of the corporation's real property and its tangible personal property owned and used (or rented and used) in the state during the period to the average value of the corporation's real property and its tangible personal property owned and used (or rented and used) everywhere.
2. In determining in-state property, total property is based on the average value of the corporation's real and tangible personal property owned (or rented) and used during the year.
3. In determining in-state property, owned property is usually valued at historic cost plus additions and improvements.
4. In determining in-state property, rented property is usually valued at 8 times its annual rent.
5. In determining in-state property, only property used to produce apportionable income is included in the property factor.

III. **THE UNITARY THEORY**
A. The unitary approach, adopted by many states, requires a corporation to file a combined or consolidated return, which includes the operating results of certain affiliated corporations.

B. The unitary theory:
1. ignores the separate legal existence of the entities and focuses on practical business realities, including:
   a. unity of ownership.
   b. unity of operations.
   c. unity of use.
2. treats the separate entities as a single business for state income tax purposes.
3. applies the apportionment formula to the combined income of the unitary business.
C. Water's Edge Election:
1. permits a multinational corporation to elect to limit a state's taxing jurisdiction over out-of-state affiliates to activities occurring within the U.S.
2. generally cannot be revoked for a number of years without permission.
3. may subject the corporation to an additional tax for the privilege of excluding out-of-state entities from the combined report.

IV. **TAXATION OF S CORPORATIONS**
A. Many of the states that recognize S corporations automatically treat them as conduits if a valid Federal election is effective. However, certain states impose additional eligibility requirements.
B. Most states that impose corporate income taxes have special provisions for S corporations.
C. When an S corporation has nonresident shareholders:
1. a corporate-level tax may be imposed.
2. the corporation may be required to withhold tax on the portion of taxable income attributable to nonresident shareholders.
3. nonresident shareholders may have to agree to pay a state income tax.

V. **OTHER STATE AND LOCAL TAXES**
A. State and Local Sales and Use Taxes
1. Sales and use taxes are imposed on the final consumer of the taxable item.
2. The seller of taxable property or services acts as an agent of the state in collecting the sales tax.
3. The use tax is designed to prevent consumers from evading sales tax by purchasing goods out-of-state for in-state use.
4. States apply a separate set of nexus rules to the sales/use tax.
5. Many states provide exemptions from the sales/use tax for sales of inventory, groceries, and medical products.
6. Some states are attempting to place the sales/use tax on services rendered, e.g., by physicians, attorneys, etc.
B. Property Taxes
1. Property taxes are ad valorem taxes because they are based on the value of the property.
2. Property taxes may be assessed on real property and/or personal property.
   a. Different tax rates and assessment methods apply to the two classes.
   b. Most states limit personal property taxes to tangible property.

IV. **TAX PLANNING CONSIDERATIONS**
A. Redirection of Corporate Activities within various states
B. Selecting the Optimal State in Which to Operate
1. Disconnect activities from undesirable states.
2. Create nexus in a desirable state.
C. Use passive income holding companies

TEST FOR SELF-EVALUATION—CHAPTER 15

True or False

Indicate which of the following statements is true or false by circling the correct answer.

T F 1. The portion of a corporation's tax base that is allocated is included in the amount that a corporation apportions by formula.

T F 2. Corporations cannot be subject to tax on more than 100% of their income.

T F 3. States uniformly define business net income.

T F 4. Double weighting the sales factor in a state apportionment formula favors corporations domiciled within the state.

T F 5. An employee's salary is always attributed to his state of residence.

T F 6. A unitary business cannot be segregated into independent operating divisions.

T F 7. Generally, if a greater weight is assigned to the sales factor of an apportionment formula, a greater tax burden is imposed on out-of-state taxpayers.

T F 8. States are prohibited from imposing an income tax on U.S. government obligations.

T F 9. States generally accept an organization's classifications of income as active or passive to be business or nonbusiness income respectively.

T F 10. Sales made to a retailer by a manufacturer are generally exempt from sales tax.

Fill in the Blanks

Complete the following statements with the appropriate word(s) or amount(s).

1. _____ describes the degree of business activity that must be present before a tax can be imposed on a corporation's income.

2. Apportionment formulas are generally based on three factors: _____, _____, and _____.

3. Under the _____, sales are assumed to take place at point of delivery.

4. To simplify the filing of tax returns, more than 40 states _____ onto the Federal income tax base.

5. _____ apportions a corporation's business income among states.

6. _____ directly assigns specific income components to a certain state.

Multiple Choice

Choose the best answer for each of the following questions.

Use the following data to answer questions 1–3:

Zack Corporation owns and operates two manufacturing facilities, one in State I and one in State W. Zack had $400,000 of taxable income this year from its manufacturing activities. Zack Corporation had no other income.

	I	W
Sales	$750,000	$500,000
Property	500,000	400,000
Payroll	225,000	150,000

_____ 1. Assuming both states use an equally weighted three factor apportionment formula, what is Zack's taxable income in State W?

    a. $160,000
    b. $165,926
    c. $234,075
    d. $240,000

_____ 2. Assuming State W uses a double weighted sales factor in its three factor apportionment formula, what would Zack's taxable income be in State W?

    a. $165,926
    b. $160,000
    c. $164,444
    d. $139,259

_____ 3. Assume I uses a single-factor sales only formula and W uses an equally weighted three factor formula, what will Zack's total taxable income be?

    a. $400,000
    b. $405,926
    c. $474,075
    d. $440,000

_____ 4. Generally, sales are allocated to the state

    a. where the shipment originates
    b. at point of delivery
    c. of ultimate destination

_____ 5. Under UDITPA, compensation is treated as paid in the state if:

    a. service is performed entirely within the state
    b. the base of operations is within the state
    c. neither of the above
    d. both of the above

STUDY GUIDE
CHAPTER 15
Multistate Corporate Taxation

_____ 6. A furniture store purchased 20 desks for $500 each. One desk was taken from the inventory and used by the storekeeper. Assuming a 5% use tax rate, how much tax does the store owe?

    a. $0
    b. $4
    c. $25
    d. $50

Zinc, a multistate S corporation, apportioned its $500,000 of ordinary income 40% to state A and 60% to state B. Zinc is owned equally by Larry and Mike. Larry resides in State A; Mike resides in state B.

_____ 7. On their resident income tax returns, Larry and Mike will each report income of:

    a. $500,000
    b. $300,000
    c. $250,000
    d. $200,000

_____ 8. On his state B return, Larry will report income of:

    a. $250,000
    b. $150,000
    c. $125,000
    d. $100,000

_____ 9. On Mike's state A return, he will report income of:

    a. $250,000
    b. $150,000
    c. $125,000
    d. $100,000

Wren Corporation owns property in States A and B. A values property at its historical cost, B values property at its net book value, both use the average value of assets.

	January 1, 2002		December 31, 2002	
	State A	State B	State A	State B
Inventories	$ 125,000	$ 100,000	$ 150,000	$ 175,000
Buildings & Machinery	225,000	400,000	225,000	400,000
Accumulated Depreciation	(75,000)	(50,000)	(100,000)	(100,000)
Land	25,000	50,000	25,000	50,000
Totals	$ 300,000	$ 500,000	$ 300,000	$ 525,000

_____ 10. Compute the property factor for State A.
_____ 11. Compute the property factor for State B.
_____ 12. What is the aggregate of Wren's property factors?

    a. 97%
    b. 100%
    c. 103%

SOLUTIONS TO CHAPTER 15 QUESTIONS

True or False

1. F (p. 15–11; allocable income removed, not included).

    Under the state tax structure of many jurisdictions, components of the tax base are allocated (e.g., non-business income) and a portion of the tax base is apportioned by formula (business income). Thus, the portion of a corporation's tax base that is allocated to particular jurisdictional units (states) is NOT included in the portion of the corporation's tax base that is apportioned by formula.

2. F (p. 15–12; apportionment of more or less than 100%).

    Under the state tax structure of many jurisdictions, components of the tax base are allocated (e.g., non-business income) and a portion is apportioned by formula (business income). Furthermore, uncertainty, ambiguity and complexity lie not in the variety of apportionment methods but rather in identifying the contours of what constitutes business activities for apportionment across the various states within which an enterprise is doing business. The interactive effects of:

    (a) different combinations of apportionment methods being applied across states and
    (b) different contours of what constitutes business activities for apportionment purposes being drawn across states,

    may result in a corporation being subject to tax on more than (or less than) 100% of such corporation's tax base.

3. F (p. 15–13; definition of business income varies across states).

    Under the state tax structure of many jurisdictions, components of the tax base are allocated (e.g., non-business income) and a portion is apportioned by formula (business income). Furthermore, uncertainty, ambiguity and complexity lie not only in identifying the contours of what constitutes business activities for apportionment across the various states within which an enterprise is doing business but also in defining business net income (non-business net income) for apportionment (allocation) purposes. States do not uniformly define business or non-business net income.

4. T (p. 15–15).

    In imposing a tax on a multi-state enterprise, states are limited by the Commerce Clause and the Due Process Clause of the U.S. Constitution. That is, a state generally does not impose a tax on a foreign corporation based upon the entire amount of the tax base (some form of net income), if such foreign corporation conducts business activities (e.g., maintains offices and employees, owns property and/or derives income) in some other state. Similarly, the state of incorporation generally does not impose a tax on a domestic corporation based upon the entire amount of the tax base (some form of net income), if such domestic corporation conducts business activities (e.g., maintains offices and employees, owns property and/or derives income) in some other state.

    The process by which the tax base (or components of the tax base) is (are) segregated and allocated to a particular state is called apportionment. Further, apportionment is accomplished by various methods, which vary across states, and include:

    - Separate accounting: A process by which (a) the business is first separated into activities by state and then (b) the tax base is allocated to such separate activities across the various states within which the corporation is doing business.
    - Allocation: A process by which the components of the tax base are associated with property, receipts or income, which is then traced to particular jurisdictional units (states).

- Apportionment by formula: A process by which the tax base is assigned to the various states within which the corporation is doing business, based on one or more attribution factors that are appropriately weighted. Typical attribution factors include:
  - Sales.
  - Average property.
  - Payroll.

Some states weight more heavily the sales factor. If the sales factor is weighted more heavily (in comparison with payroll and average property), more of the tax burden will be borne by foreign corporations. That is, the tax will favor corporations domiciled within the state, assuming corporations domiciled within the state have larger average property and payroll ratios.

5. F (p. 15–20; salary attributed to place dependent on facts).

The payroll factor is determined by comparing the compensation paid for services rendered within a state to total compensation paid by the corporation. For these purposes, compensation generally includes wages, salaries, commissions and any fringe benefit that is included in the employee's gross income. States differ as to whether items of income that are excluded from the employee's gross income are included for purposes of determining the payroll factor.

Generally, the compensation of an employee is not assigned to different states. Under the Uniform Division of Income for Tax Purposes Act (UDITPA), the following hierarchical rules determine the state to which compensation is attributed in situations where services are performed in more than one state.

Where services are performed in more than one state, compensation is treated as paid in the state:

- In which such services are primarily performed.
- In which the employee has a base of operations:
  - if some services are performed in such state and
  - if such services are not primarily performed in any one state.
- In which such services are directed and controlled:
  - if such services are not primarily performed in any one state and
  - if no services are performed in the state within which the employee's base of operations exists.
- In which the employee resides:
  - if such services are not primarily performed in any one state,
  - if no services are performed in the state within which the employee's base of operations exists and
  - no state serves as a jurisdiction where such services are directed and controlled.

6. T (p. 15–24).

The process by which the tax base (or components of the tax base) is (are) segregated and allocated to a particular state is called apportionment. Further, apportionment is accomplished by various methods, which vary across states, and include:

- Separate accounting: A process by which (a) the business is first separated into activities by state and then (b) the tax base is allocated to such separate activities across the various states within which the corporation is doing business.
- Allocation: A process by which the components of the tax base are associated with property, receipts or income, which is then traced to particular jurisdictional units (states).
- Apportionment by formula: A process by which the tax base is assigned to the various states within which the corporation is doing business, based on one or more attribution factors that are appropriately weighted. Typical attribution factors include:
  - Sales.
  - Average property.
  - Payroll.

In response to the difficulties raised with respect to allocating and apportioning the tax base of multi-state business enterprises, some states have applied a unitary theoretical approach. Under this approach, multiple operating activities that are an integral part of a unitary business enterprise are required to be combined for purposes of allocating and apportioning such combined tax base to states within which such enterprise conducts its activities.

7. T (p. 15–14).

The process by which the tax base (or components of the tax base) is (are) segregated and allocated to a particular state is called apportionment. Further, apportionment is accomplished by various methods, which vary across states, and include:

- Separate accounting: A process by which (a) the business is first separated into activities by state and then (b) the tax base is allocated to such separate activities across the various states within which the corporation is doing business.
- Allocation: A process by which the components of the tax base are associated with property, receipts or income, which is then traced to particular jurisdictional units (states).
- Apportionment by formula: A process by which the tax base is assigned to the various states within which the corporation is doing business, based on one or more attribution factors that are appropriately weighted. Typical attribution factors include:
  - Sales.
  - Average property.
  - Payroll.

Some states weight more heavily the sales factor. If the sales factor is weighted more heavily (in comparison with payroll and average property), more of the tax burden will be borne by foreign corporations. That is, the tax will favor corporations domiciled within the state, assuming corporations domiciled within the state have larger average property and payroll ratios.

8. T (p. 15–6).

Consistent with the doctrine of intergovernmental immunity, states are prohibited from imposing the legal incidence of taxation on the federal government. Accordingly, state tax provisions typically include a provision eliminating interest on federal obligations from a tax base that is defined in terms of net income.

9. F (p. 15–13; states use a variety of approaches to determine income classification).

Under the state tax structure of many jurisdictions, components of the tax base are allocated (e.g., non-business income) and a portion is apportioned by formula (business income). Furthermore, uncertainty, ambiguity and complexity lie not only in identifying the contours of what constitutes business activities for apportionment across the various states within which an enterprise is doing business but also in defining business net income (non-business net income) for apportionment (allocation) purposes. States do not uniformly define business or non-business net income.

10. T (p. 15–30).

A vast majority of states impose a tax that is a sales tax or that has characteristics similar to a sales tax. Such a tax is imposed on retail sales of tangible personal property for use or consumption. It is generally imposed on the final consumer. Accordingly, sales by manufacturers, producers and processors are generally exempt since these sellers are typically not selling to a final consumer.

Fill in the Blanks

1. Nexus (p. 15–9).

Under the state tax structure of many jurisdictions, components of the tax base are allocated (e.g., non-business income) and a portion is apportioned by formula (business income). Furthermore, uncertainty, ambiguity and complexity lie not in the variety of apportionment methods but rather in identifying the contours of what constitutes business activities for apportionment across the various states within which an enterprise is doing business. Nexus is the term used to denote sufficient presence of a multi-state enterprise within a state that warrants apportionment of such enterprise's tax base to such state.

2. property, payroll, sales (p. 15–15).

The process by which the tax base (or components of the tax base) is (are) segregated and allocated to a particular state is called apportionment. Further, apportionment is accomplished by various methods, which vary across states, and include:

- Separate accounting: A process by which (a) the business is first separated into activities by state and then (b) the tax base is allocated to such separate activities across the various states within which the corporation is doing business.
- Allocation: A process by which the components of the tax base are associated with property, receipts or income, which is then traced to particular jurisdictional units (states).
- Apportionment by formula: A process by which the tax base is assigned to the various states within which the corporation is doing business, based on one or more attribution factors that are appropriately weighted. Typical attribution factors include:
  - Sales.
  - Average property.
  - Payroll.

3. ultimate destination concept (p. 15–17).

The process by which the tax base (or components of the tax base) is (are) segregated and allocated to a particular state is called apportionment. Further, apportionment is accomplished by various methods, which vary across states, and include:

- Separate accounting: A process by which (a) the business is first separated into activities by state and then (b) the tax base is allocated to such separate activities across the various states within which the corporation is doing business.
- Allocation: A process by which the components of the tax base are associated with property, receipts or income, which is then traced to particular jurisdictional units (states).
- Apportionment by formula: A process by which the tax base is assigned to the various states within which the corporation is doing business, based on one or more attribution factors that are appropriately weighted. Typical attribution factors include:
  - Sales.
  - Average property.
  - Payroll.

The sales factor weights the sales in a particular state to total sales. In many jurisdictions, the term sales is defined as net sales (gross sales less returns, allowances and discounts) plus interest, taxes, service charges, and carrying charges. Further, under the Uniform Division of Income for Tax Purposes Act (UDITPA), sales attributable to a particular state are determined by applying the ultimate destination concept. Under this concept, sales of tangible personal property are attributed to the state to which the goods are shipped to the customer (rather than the origination point).

4. piggyback (p. 15–4).

Under the state tax structure of many jurisdictions, components of the tax base are allocated (e.g., non-business income) and a portion is apportioned by formula (business income). Furthermore, uncertainty, ambiguity and complexity lie not only in identifying the contours of what constitutes business activities for apportionment across the various states within which an enterprise is doing business but also in defining business net income (non-business net income) for apportionment (allocation) purposes. States do not uniformly define business or non-business net income. Many jurisdictions piggyback (with modifications) onto the Federal income tax definition of gross income and taxable income.

5. An apportionment formula (p. 15–15).

The process by which the tax base (or components of the tax base) is (are) segregated and allocated to a particular state is called apportionment. Further, apportionment is accomplished by various methods, which vary across states, and include:

- Separate accounting: A process by which (a) the business is first separated into activities by state and then (b) the tax base is allocated to such separate activities across the various states within which the corporation is doing business.
- Allocation: A process by which the components of the tax base are associated with property, receipts or income, which is then traced to particular jurisdictional units (states).
- Apportionment by formula: A process by which the tax base is assigned to the various states within which the corporation is doing business, based on one or more attribution factors that are appropriately weighted. Typical attribution factors include:
  - Sales.
  - Average property.
  - Payroll.

6. allocation (p. 15–10).

The process by which the tax base (or components of the tax base) is (are) segregated and allocated to a particular state is called apportionment. Further, apportionment is accomplished by various methods, which vary across states, and include:

- Separate accounting: A process by which (a) the business is first separated into activities by state and then (b) the tax base is allocated to such separate activities across the various states within which the corporation is doing business.
- Allocation: A process by which the components of the tax base are associated with property, receipts or income, which is then traced to particular jurisdictional units (states).
- Apportionment by formula: A process by which the tax base is assigned to the various states within which the corporation is doing business, based on one or more attribution factors that are appropriately weighted. Typical attribution factors include:
  - Sales.
  - Average property.
  - Payroll.

Multiple Choice

The following information relates to Zack Corporation.

Sales (W):		$ 500,000
Sales (Total):	$750,000 + $500,000 =	$1,250,000
Average property (W):		$ 400,000
Average property (Total):	$500,000 + $400,000 =	$ 900,000
Payroll (W):		$ 150,000
Payroll (Total):	$225,000 + $150,000 =	$ 375,000

Zack's taxable income of $400,000 is apportioned by a three-factor formula to State W.

1. b (p. 15–16; (((500,000/1,250,000) + (400,000/900,000) + (150,000/375,000))/3) times 400,000)

Assuming Zack's apportionment formula equally weights the three factors, $165,926 is apportioned to State W, calculated as follows.

[($500,000/$1,250,000) + ($400,000/$900,000) + ($150,000/$375,000)]/3 = .4148148

.4148148 ($400,000) = $165,926

Thus, item b is correct. Further, the other choice items are incorrect because they each are inconsistent with the correct answer.

2. c (p. 15–16; (((500,000/1,250,000)2 + (400,000/900,000) + (150,000/375,000))/4) times 400,000)

Assuming Zack's three factor apportionment formula uses a double weighted sales factor, $164,444 is apportioned to State W, calculated as follows.

[2($500,000/$1,250,000) + ($400,000/$900,000) + ($150,000/$375,000)]/4 = .4111111

.4111111 ($400,000) = $164,444

Thus, item c is correct. Further, the other choice items are incorrect because they each are inconsistent with the correct answer.

3. b (p. 15–16; (750,000/1,250,000)(400,000) + 165,926)

Zack's total taxable income is calculated as follows. Assuming Zack uses a single factor apportionment formula, with sales as the only factor, $240,000 is apportioned to State I, calculated as follows.

($750,000/$1,250,000) ($400,000) = $240,000

Assuming Zack's apportionment formula equally weights the three factors, $165,926 is apportioned to State W, calculated as follows.

[($500,000/$1,250,000) + ($400,000/$900,000) + ($150,000/$375,000)]/3 = .4148148

.4148148 ($400,000) = $165,926

Thus, Zack's total taxable income is $405,926 ($160,000 + $165,926). and item b is correct. Further, the other choice items are incorrect because they each are inconsistent with the correct answer.

4. c (p. 15–17)

The sales factor weights the sales in a particular state to total sales. In many jurisdictions, the term sales is defined as net sales (gross sales less returns, allowances and discounts) plus interest, taxes, service charges, and carrying charges. Further, under the Uniform Division of Income for Tax Purposes Act (UDITPA), sales attributable to a particular state are determined by applying the ultimate destination concept. Under this concept, sales of tangible personal property are attributed to the state to which the goods are shipped to the customer (rather than the origination point). Thus, item c is correct. Further, the following choice items are incorrect.

- Item a is incorrect because it is inconsistent with item c.
- Item b is incorrect because the point of delivery does not denote that such point is necessarily the point to which goods have been shipped to the customer.

5. a (p. 15–19)

Generally, the compensation of an employee is not assigned to different states. Under the Uniform Division of Income for Tax Purposes Act (UDITPA), the following hierarchical rules determine the state to which compensation is attributed in situations where services are performed in more than one state.

Where services are performed in more than one state, compensation is treated as paid in the state:

- In which such services are primarily performed.
- In which the employee has a base of operations:
  - if some services are performed in such state and
  - if such services are not primarily performed in any one state.
- In which such services are directed and controlled:
  - if such services are not primarily performed in any one state and
  - if no services are performed in the state within which the employee's base of operations exists.

- In which the employee resides:
  - if such services are not primarily performed in any one state,
  - if no services are performed in the state within which the employee's base of operations exists and
  - no state serves as a jurisdiction where such services are directed and controlled.

In the instant case, since under the hierarchical rules of UDITPA item a comes before item b, item a is correct, which means item b is incorrect. Further, choice items c&d are incorrect because they are inconsistent with item a being the only correct answer.

6. c (p. 15–30; ($500 × 5%))

A vast majority of states impose a tax that is a sales tax or that has characteristics similar to a sales tax (e.g., a use tax). Such a tax is imposed on retail sales of tangible personal property for use or consumption. It is generally imposed on the final consumer. Accordingly, sales by manufacturers, producers and processors are generally exempt, since these sellers are typically not selling to a final consumer. The sales tax (or facsimile thereof) is calculated by applying a proportionate tax rate structure against the tax base. In this case, the tax base is measured by the sales price.

In the instant case, item c is correct. The use tax is $25 (the use tax rate of 5% applied against the sales price of only one desk at $500). The use tax applies to only one desk because the furniture store was:

- A retailer not subject to the use tax with respect to the 19 desks that it will sell in the ordinary course of its business.
- A final consumer subject to the use tax with respect to the one desk that it uses in its business operations.

The following information relates to Zinc Corporation.

State A Apportionment:	40% of $500,000	$200,000
Larry's (Mike's) Share	(40% of $500,000)/2	$100,000
State B Apportionment:	60% of $500,000	$300,000
Larry's (Mike's) Share	(60% of $500,000)/2	$150,000

7. c (p. 15–27; ($500,000 × 50%))

On the resident returns of Larry and Mike, each reports income of $250,000, calculated as follows.

Larry's (Mike's) Share	(40% of $500,000)/2	$100,000
Larry's (Mike's) Share	(60% of $500,000)/2	$150,000
Total		$250,000

Thus, item c is correct. Further, the other choice items are incorrect because they each are inconsistent with the correct answer.

8. b (p. 15–27; ($500,000 × 60% × 50%))

On Larry's state B return, Larry reports income of $150,000, calculated as follows.

| State B Apportionment: | 60% of $500,000 | $300,000 |
| Larry's (Mike's) Share | (60% of $500,000)/2 | $150,000 |

Thus, item b is correct. Further, the other choice items are incorrect because they each are inconsistent with the correct answer.

9. d (p. 15–27; ($500,000 × 40% × 50%))

    On Mike's state A return, Mike reports income of $100,000, calculated as follows.

    | State A Apportionment: | 40% of $500,000 | $200,000 |
    | Larry's (Mike's) Share | (40% of $500,000)/2 | $100,000 |

    The following information relates to Wren Corporation.

    | Average Property (A): | |
    | ($300,000 + $100,000 + $300,000 + $75,000)/2 | $387,500 |
    | Average Property (B): | |
    | ($525,000 + $100,000 + $500,000 + $50,000)/2 | $587,500 |
    | Average Property (Total): | $975,000 |

    Thus, item d is correct. Further, the other choice items are incorrect because they each are inconsistent with the correct answer.

10. 39.7436% (Example 19) (387,500/975,000)

    The property factor for State A is computed as follows.

    | Average Property Factor (A): | $387,500/$975,000 | 39.7436% |

11. 63.0769% (Example 19) 587,500/975,000)

    The property factor for State B is computed as follows.

    | Average Property Factor (B): | $587,500/$975,000 | 63.0769% |

12. c (p. 15–22, 23; Example 19) (39.7436 + 63.0769)

    The aggregate of Wren's average property factors is computed as follows.

    | Aggregate Average Property Factor: | 39.7436% + 63.0769% | 102.8205 |

    Thus, item c is correct. Further, the other choice items are incorrect because they each are inconsistent with the correct answer.

CHAPTER 16

Tax Administration and Practice

LEARNING OBJECTIVES

After completing Chapter 16, you should be able to:

1. Describe the organization and structure of the IRS.
2. Identify the various administrative pronouncements issued by the IRS and explain how they can be used in tax practice.
3. Describe the audit process, including how returns are selected for audit and the various types of audits.
4. Explain the taxpayer appeal process, including various settlement options available.
5. Determine the amount of interest on a deficiency or a refund and when it is due.
6. Discuss the various penalties that can be imposed on acts of noncompliance by taxpayers and return preparers.
7. Understand the rules governing the statute of limitations on assessments and refunds.
8. Summarize the legal and ethical guidelines that apply to those engaged in tax practice.

KEY TERMS

Accuracy-related penalty
Closing agreement
Determination letter
Enrolled agent (EA)
Fraud
Letter ruling

Negligence
Ninety-day letter
Offer in compromise
Reasonable cause
Revenue Agent's Report (RAR)

Statute of limitations
Substantial authority
Technical advice memorandum (TAM)
Thirty-day letter

OUTLINE

I. **TAX ADMINISTRATION**
   A. IRS responsibilities include (Figure 16–1 displays the current structure of the IRS):
      1. providing adequate information to taxpayers so that they can comply with tax laws.
      2. identifying delinquent taxpayers and their related tax payments.
      3. carrying out assessment and collection procedures.
   B. IRS Procedures—Letter Rulings
      1. Letter Rulings, issued by the National Office, are written statements of the IRS' current position on the tax consequences of a course of action contemplated by a taxpayer.
      2. Rulings are issued only on uncompleted, actual transactions or on transactions which have been completed prior to filing the tax return for the year in question.
      3. Rulings are not issued in cases essentially involving a question of fact (e.g., whether compensation is reasonable).
      4. Rulings may be revoked if substantial discrepancies are found between the facts in the ruling request and the actual situation.
      5. A letter ruling may be relied on only by the taxpayer who requested and received it.
      6. Rulings must be attached to the tax return for the year in question.
   C. IRS Procedures—Other Issuances
      1. Determination Letters are issued by a Director and cover completed transactions when the issue involved is covered by judicial or statutory authority, regulations or rulings.
      2. A Technical Advice Memorandum is issued by the National Office to a Director and/or Regional Commissioner in response to a specific request from either an agent, an Appellate Conferee or a Director. Technical Advice requests arise within the audit process.
   D. Administrative Powers of the IRS
      1. The Code empowers the IRS to examine the taxpayer's books and records in determining the correct amount of tax due.
         a. The IRS may also require the person(s) responsible for the return to appear and to produce any necessary books and records.
         b. Generally taxpayers have the burden of proof regarding amounts disclosed on a tax return.
      2. The Code also permits the IRS to assess a deficiency and demand a payment for the tax.
         a. No collection effort can begin until 90 days after a deficiency notice is sent to the taxpayer (a 90-day letter).
         b. Following assessment, the taxpayer is usually given 30 days to pay the tax due.
      3. The IRS can place a lien on all taxpayer property if payment is not made.
   E. The Audit Process
      1. Selection of returns for audit
         a. A computer-assisted procedure, through the use of mathematical formulas, attempts to select returns likely to contain errors.
         b. Taxpayers with gross income in excess of $100,000, self-employed individuals and cash businesses, are subject to audit more frequently than other taxpayers.
         c. If corresponding information returns (e.g., Form 1099) are not in substantial agreement with the taxpayer's return, the return may be audited.
         d. Itemized deductions in excess of norms may trigger an audit.
         e. Filing a refund claim may trigger an audit.
         f. Some returns are selected because the IRS has targeted a specific industry.
         g. Other returns are selected on a random sampling basis.
      2. An initial review corrects math errors or failures to comply with deduction limitations. These matters are usually settled through correspondence without a formal audit (a *correspondence audit*).

3. *Office audits* usually require substantiation of a particular item on an individual's return having few or no items of business income.
4. *Field audits* generally entail a more complete examination of a taxpayer's transactions. Field audits usually deal with corporate returns and individuals engaged in business or professional activities.
5. Taxpayer Rights
   a. Prior to or at the initial interview, the IRS must provide an explanation of the audit process and describe the taxpayer's rights under that process.
   b. Upon advance request, the IRS must allow an audio recording of any in-person interview.
6. Settlement with the Revenue Agent
   a. The IRS agent may accept the return as filed or recommend certain adjustments following an audit. A Revenue Agent's Report (RAR) summarizes the audit.
   b. Usually, questions of fact can be resolved at the agent level. Agents must adhere strictly to published IRS policy.
   c. If agreement is reached, Form 870, Waiver of Restrictions on Assessment and Collection of Deficiency in Tax, is signed by the taxpayer. Form 870 generally closes the case; however, the IRS may assess additional deficiencies if deemed necessary.

F. The Taxpayer Appeal Process (see Figure 16–2)
1. If agreement cannot be reached at the agent level, the taxpayer receives a copy of the Revenue Agent's Report and a letter which grants the taxpayer 30 days to request an administrative appeal (a 30-day letter).
2. If an appeal is not requested, a statutory notice of deficiency, a 90-day letter, will be issued.
3. A request for appeal must be made to the Appeals Division and must be accompanied by a written protest unless:
   a. the proposed tax deficiency does not exceed $10,000 or
   b. the deficiency resulted from a correspondence or office audit.
4. The Appeals Division of the IRS has authority to settle all tax disputes based on the hazards of litigation (the probability of losing a court case).
5. If agreement is reached, Form 870–AD is signed by the taxpayer. This agreement is usually binding upon both parties.
6. If agreement is not reached, the IRS issues a statutory notice of deficiency (a 90-day letter) which gives the taxpayer 90 days to file a petition with the Tax Court or to pay the tax and file a claim for refund.

G. Offers in Compromise and Closing Agreements
1. Offers in Compromise are generally used only in extreme cases where the taxpayer's ability to pay the total amount of tax is doubtful.
2. Closing Agreements are used in situations when disputed issues involve future years. A Closing Agreement is generally binding on both parties.

H. Interest
1. Interest accrues on tax underpayments and overpayments. Interest compounds daily.
2. Interest usually accrues from the unextended due date of the return until 30 days after the taxpayer agrees to the deficiency by signing Form 870.
3. Quarterly adjustments to the interest rates are based on the average market yield of outstanding U.S. marketable obligations maturing in 3 years or less.
4. If an overpayment is refunded within 45 days, no interest is allowed.
   a. When a return is filed after the due date, interest accrues from the date of filing.

I. Taxpayer Penalties
1. Penalties are additions to tax liability and are not tax-deductible.
2. "Ad valorem" penalties are based on a percentage of the tax owed and are subject to the same deficiency procedures that apply to the underlying tax.
3. "Assessable penalties" are typically a flat dollar amount.

4. Failure to file penalty is 5% per month up to 25% of the tax liability; a minimum penalty of $100 may be imposed. If fraud is demonstrated, the penalty is 15% per month, with a maximum of 75% of the tax liability.
5. Failure to pay penalty is 0.5% per month up to 25% of the tax liability.
6. If both the failure to file and the failure to pay penalties apply in any month, the failure to file penalty is reduced by the failure to pay penalty amount.
   a. These penalties can be avoided if the taxpayer shows that the failure to file or failure to pay tax was due to a "reasonable cause."
   b. The Code and Regulations provide little guidance as to what is "reasonable cause," so the courts have been the arbiter of the term.
7. "Accuracy-related" penalties are applied when the taxpayer fails to show reasonable cause for the underpayment or a good faith effort to comply with the tax law. The penalty is 20% of the underpayment attributable to:
   a. negligence or disregard of rules or regulations. Negligence includes any failure to make a reasonable attempt to comply with tax law.
   b. substantial understatement of tax liability (when the understatement exceeds the larger of 10% of the tax due or $5,000 ($10,000 for a C corporation)).
   c. substantial valuation overstatement (when the valuation is 200% or more of the correct amount).
   d. substantial valuation understatement (when the valuation is 50% or less than the correct amount).
8. Fraud occurs when a taxpayer is found to have intended specifically to evade a tax.
   a. Civil fraud must be proved by a preponderance of evidence. The civil fraud penalty is equal to 75% of that underpayment resulting from such fraud.
   b. Criminal fraud must be proved beyond the shadow of any reasonable doubt. The criminal fraud penalty varies, depending upon the severity of the infraction, but may be no more than $100,000 ($500,000 in the case of a corporation) and 5 years in jail.
9. Penalties may be imposed for failure to pay estimated income taxes.
10. Penalties may also be imposed if the taxpayer provides false information on taxes withheld or fails to make tax deposits as required.

J. Statute of Limitations
   1. Generally, any tax imposed must be assessed within three years of the filing of the return. Exceptions to the above rule are:
      a. If no return was filed (or if a fraudulent return was filed), an assessment may be made at any time.
      b. The statute is increased to six years if the taxpayer omits from gross income an amount in excess of 25% of the gross income as stated on the return.
      c. The statute may be extended by mutual consent of a Director and the taxpayer (Form 872 is used for this purpose).
   2. If after the IRS issues a statutory notice of deficiency, the taxpayer, within the allotted time, files a Tax Court petition, the statute of limitations is suspended on both the assessment and period of collection until 60 days after the court's final decision.
   3. A taxpayer who wishes to file a tax refund claim must file the appropriate form within three years of the filing of the original tax return, or within two years following the payment of the tax, whichever is later. Individuals use Form 1040X, and corporations use Form 1120X.

II. **TAX PRACTICE**
   A. While anyone can prepare a tax return or give tax advice, practice before the IRS is usually limited to CPA's, attorneys, and persons who have passed an IRS-administered examination (called enrolled agents).
   B. Rules governing tax practice (Circular 230) require the tax preparer:
      1. to not take a position on a tax return unless there is a realistic possibility that the position will be sustained on its merits.

2. to not take frivolous tax return positions.
3. to inform taxpayers of penalties likely to apply to return positions and how to avoid such penalties.
4. to make known to a client any error or omission on any return (or document) submitted to the IRS.
5. to submit records or information lawfully requested by the IRS.
6. to exercise due diligence in preparing and filing returns.
7. to not delay matters before the IRS, charge the taxpayer "unconscionable fees," or represent clients if there is a conflict of interest.

D. Preparer penalties include:
1. A $250 penalty for the understatement of tax liability due to an unrealistic position.
2. A $1,000 penalty for willful and reckless conduct.
3. A $1,000 ($10,000 for corporations) penalty per return (or document) is imposed against any person who aids in the preparation of a return (or other document), where such person knows that there exists an understatement of tax liability.
4. A $50 penalty is assessed for each of the following:
   a. failure to sign the return.
   b. failure to furnish preparer's identifying number.
   c. failure to furnish the taxpayer with a copy of the return.
5. A $500 penalty may be assessed if a preparer endorses a check for a tax refund which is issued to the taxpayer.

E. Communications between a taxpayer and tax practitioner are privileged communications when involving tax advice.

F. The AICPA has issued statements to guide CPAs in resolving ethical questions related to tax practice. Some of these statements are summarized below.
- *Positions Contrary to IRS Interpretations*: The CPA must believe the position has a realistic possibility of being accepted if challenged and must advise the client of the risks and penalties if the position is not accepted.
- *Questions on Returns*: Reasonable efforts should be made to provide answers to all questions on a tax return.
- *Procedural Aspects of Preparing Returns*: The CPA must inform the client of any applicable expenditure verification rules and must make reasonable inquiries if client representations appear to be incorrect, incomplete or inconsistent.
- *Estimates*: Estimates may be used in preparing a tax return if reasonable and indicated as such if it is impracticable to obtain exact data.
- *Recognition of Administrative Proceeding*: A CPA is not bound by proceedings involving a prior year but is to use his/her own judgment depending on the facts and circumstances of the particular situation.
- *Knowledge of Error*: The CPA should promptly advise the client and recommend corrective measures of any errors or omissions on returns.
- *Advice to Clients*: The CPA must use judgment in advising clients. His advice should be professionally competent and appropriate for the particular client.

TEST FOR SELF-EVALUATION—CHAPTER 16

True or False

Indicate which of the following statements is true or false by circling the correct answer.

T F 1. Trusts, receiverships, guardianships, or estates may be represented before any office of the Internal Revenue Service by their trustees, receivers, guardians, administrators, or executors. (IRS 97 4A-5)

T F 2. A check drawn on the United States Treasury for a refund of Internal Revenue Service taxes, penalties or interest cannot be mailed to the recognized representative of the taxpayer even if there is a valid power of attorney containing specific authorization. (IRS 97 4A-10)

T F 3. Doyle, an enrolled agent, knows that his client has not complied with the revenue laws of the United States. Doyle has the responsibility to advise his client promptly of such noncompliance. (IRS 97 4A-18)

T F 4. A taxpayer, during an interview conducted by the preparer, stated that he paid $6,500 in doctor bills and $5,000 in deductible travel and entertainment expenses during the tax year, when in fact he had paid smaller amounts. On the basis of this information, the preparer properly calculated the deductions for medical expenses and for travel and entertainment expenses which resulted in an understatement of tax liability. The preparer had no reason to believe that the medical expenses and the travel and entertainment expense information was incorrect or incomplete. The preparer did not ask for underlying documentation of the medical expenses but inquired about the existence of travel and entertainment expense records. The preparer was reasonably satisfied by the taxpayer's representations that the taxpayer had adequate records (or other corroborative evidence) for the deduction of $5,000 for travel and entertainment expenses. The preparer is not subject to a penalty under section 6694. (IRS 97 4A-25)

T F 5. A revenue ruling holds that certain expenses incurred in the purchase of a business must be capitalized. The Code is silent as to whether these expenses must be capitalized or may be deducted currently, but several cases from different courts hold that these particular expenses may be deducted currently. There is no other authority. Under these circumstances, a return preparer taking a position contrary to the revenue ruling would not be subject to the penalty for understatement due to willful or reckless conduct (IRC § 6694(b)). (IRS 97 4A-26)

T F 6. If the proposed increase or decrease in tax resulting from an IRS examination, conducted at the taxpayer's place of business, exceeds $2,500, but not more than $10,000, the taxpayer or the taxpayer's representative who wishes to appeal, must provide a brief written statement explaining the disputed issues. (IRS 97 4A-31)

T F 7. The trust fund recovery penalty may be imposed against any person who is responsible for collecting or paying withheld income and employment taxes and who willfully fails to collect or pay them. (IRS 96 4A-32)

T F 8. A taxpayer can only submit an Offer in Compromise if it is submitted based on doubt as to the liability owed and doubt as to the ability of the taxpayer to fully pay the amount owed. (IRS 96 4A-33)

T F 9. Audrey's 2000 income tax return is under examination by the Internal Revenue Service. She agrees with several proposed changes by the examiner. Audrey thinks that she will owe additional tax of $3,000 and deposits a cash bond in that amount with the IRS. This deposit will stop the further accrual of interest on both the tax and on the interest accrued to that point. (IRS 96 4A-12)

T F 10. If you are filing a claim for credit or refund based on contested income tax issues considered in previously examined returns and do not want to appeal within the IRS, you should request in writing that the claim be immediately rejected. (IRS 96 4A-10)

Fill in the Blanks

Complete the following statements with the appropriate word(s) or amount(s).

1. When agreement cannot be reached between the taxpayer and the Appeals Division, the IRS issues a ________.
2. The ________ defines the period of time during which one party may pursue legal action against another party.
3. The position of Commissioner of the Internal Revenue Service is an ________ position.
4. In addition to issuing Letter Rulings and Revenue Rulings, the IRS also issues ________, and ________.
5. The AICPA has issued ________, the purpose of which is to guide the conduct of CPAs in tax practice.
6. ________ of ________ is a term used to describe the possibility of winning or losing a tax issue if the case goes to court.
7. An ________ in ________ gives the IRS the authority to negotiate a compromise settlement if there is doubt as to the amount or ability to collect a tax liability.
8. ________ are additions to the tax liability and are not deductible as itemized or business expense deductions.
9. The statement which is filed following an audit which recommends acceptance of adjustment of the tax return is known as the ________.

Multiple Choice

Choose the best answer for each of the following questions.

______ 1. Which of the following is not practice before the Internal Revenue Service? (IRS 97 4B-41)

a. Preparing the tax return, furnishing information at the request of the IRS, or appearing as a witness for a taxpayer.
b. Communicating with the IRS for a taxpayer regarding the taxpayer's rights, privileges, or liabilities under laws and regulations administered by the IRS.
c. Preparing and filing necessary documents with the IRS for the taxpayer whose tax returns were prepared by a different practitioner.
d. Representing a taxpayer at conferences, hearings, or meetings with the IRS.

_____ 2. All of the following can practice before the Internal Revenue Service except: (IRS 97 4B-43)

    a. An individual family member representing members of his or her immediate family without compensation.
    b. An individual convicted of any offense involving dishonesty or lack of trust.
    c. A regular full-time employee representing his or her employer.
    d. A bona fide officer of a corporation, association or organized group representing the corporation, association or group, respectively.

_____ 3. Late payments by a taxpayer on an installment agreement to pay a tax liability will: (IRS 97 4B-48)

    a. Necessitate payment by certified check.
    b. Extend the statute of limitations.
    c. Generate a Notice of Intent to Levy.
    d. Generate a 30-day notice as to the cessation of the agreement.

_____ 4. Which of the following statements with respect to taxpayers' offers in compromise on unpaid tax liabilities is correct? (IRS 97 4B-55)

    a. A taxpayer does not have the right to submit an offer in compromise on his/her tax bill but is given the opportunity in order to increase voluntary compliance with the tax law.
    b. Doubt as to the liability for the amount owed must be supported by evidence and the amount acceptable under the offer in compromise will depend on the degree of doubt found in the particular case.
    c. Submission of an offer in compromise automatically suspends the collection of an account.
    d. If the offer in compromise is made on the grounds that there is doubt as to the taxpayer's ability to make full payment on the amount owed, the amount offered must give sufficient consideration only to the taxpayer's present earning capacity.

_____ 5. With regard to an installment agreement with the IRS to pay a federal tax due, all of the following statements are correct except: (IRS 97 4B-56)

    a. Once an installment payment plan has been approved, the IRS will not continue to charge the taxpayer's account with interest on the taxpayer's unpaid balance of penalties and interest.
    b. Installment payments may be paid by electronic transfers from the taxpayers' bank account.
    c. While the taxpayer is making installment payments, the IRS may require the taxpayer to provide financial information on his/her financial condition to determine any change in his/her ability to pay.
    d. The IRS may file a Notice of Federal Tax Lien to secure the government's interest until the taxpayer makes the final installment payment.

_____ 6. Which of the following situations describes a disclosure of tax return information by a tax return preparer which would subject the preparer to a penalty? (IRS 97 4B-63)

    a. Grandfather's tax information is made available to his granddaughter to inform her she will be claimed as a dependent on the grandfather's return.
    b. Employee of the tax return preparer makes corporate return information available to shareholders.
    c. After a client files for bankruptcy, the tax return preparer provides a copy of the last return filed to the court-appointed fiduciary without written permission.
    d. None of the above.

STUDY GUIDE | CHAPTER 16 | 16–9
Tax Administration and Practice

_____ 7. In which of the following situations may the tax return preparer disclose the tax return information requested without first obtaining consent of the taxpayer/client? (IRS 97 4B-64)

    a. The preparer receives a state grand jury subpoena requesting copies of federal and state income tax returns.

    b. An IRS agent, in his or her official capacity, makes a visit to the preparer and requests copies of state and federal income tax returns, related returns, schedules and records of the taxpayer used in the preparation of the tax returns.

    c. A partner in a partnership, who was not involved with the return preparation or partnership records, requests a copy of the partnership return including the schedule K–1s for ALL partners.

    d. All of the above.

_____ 8. Mr. Congenial's 2000 income tax return was examined by the IRS and he agreed with the proposed changes. He has several ways by which he may settle his account and pay any additional tax that is due. All of the following statements with respect to this situation are correct except: (IRS 97 4B-65)

    a. If he pays when he signs the agreement, the interest is generally figured from the due date of the return to the date of his payment.

    b. If he does not pay the additional tax when he signs the agreement, he will receive a bill. The interest on the additional tax is generally figured from the due date of the return to the billing date.

    c. If the bill is delayed, he will not be billed for additional interest for more than 60 days from the date he signed the agreement.

    d. If he pays the amount due within 10 days of the billing date, he will not have to pay more interest or penalties.

_____ 9. Which of the following persons would be subject to the penalty for improperly negotiating a taxpayer's refund check? (IRS 97 4B-73)

    a. An income tax return preparer who operates a check-cashing agency that cashes, endorses, or negotiates income tax refund checks for returns he prepared.

    b. An income tax return preparer who operates a check-cashing business and cashes checks for his clients as part of a second business.

    c. The firm which prepared the tax return and is authorized by the taxpayer to receive an income tax refund, but not to endorse or negotiate the check.

    d. A business manager who prepares income tax returns for clients who maintain special checking accounts against which the business manager is authorized to sign certain checks on their behalf. The clients' federal income tax refunds are mailed to the business manager, who has the clients endorse the checks and deposits them in the special accounts.

SOLUTIONS TO CHAPTER 16 QUESTIONS

True or False

1. T (p. 16–25)

    Under Circular 230, the following persons are allowed to practice before the I.R.S.

    - C.P.A.
    - Attorney.
    - Enrolled Agent (EA).

    However, Circular 230 also allows the following persons to practice before the I.R.S., under certain limited circumstances.

    - A taxpayer representing himself or an immediate family member (if no compensation is received).
    - A regular, full-time employee representing his employer.
    - An officer representing his corporation.
    - A partner representing his partnership.
    - The respective fiduciary (trustee, receiver, guardian, administrator or executor) representing the trust, receivership, guardianship or estate.
    - The tax practitioner representing the taxpayer for whom the return was prepared.

    All activities related to the making of presentations before the I.R.S. concerning a taxpayer's rights, privileges, or liabilities are within the scope of the phrase "Practice before the I.R.S." Such activities include the preparation and filing of necessary documents and the representation of a client.

2. F (p. 16–25; may be an enumerated power of tax practitioner)

    To practice before the I.R.S. (e.g., representation of a particular taxpayer), the practitioner must be properly authorized by the taxpayer. If the practitioner intends to act on behalf of the taxpayer, the taxpayer must file with the I.R.S. Form 2848 (The Power of Attorney). Such authorization by the taxpayer gives the practitioner/representative the general right to:

    - Receive confidential information.
    - Perform any and all acts with respect to the tax matters enumerated within Form 2848 (The Power of Attorney).

    However, such general authority does not specifically extend to either signing tax returns or receiving refund checks on behalf of the taxpayer. If a taxpayer intends for the practitioner/representative to either sign tax returns or receive refund checks on behalf of the taxpayer, such authority must be specifically expressed on Form 2848 (The Power of Attorney). In any case, the practitioner/representative is not allowed to endorse or negotiate a taxpayer's refund check.

3. T (p. 16–29)

    The conduct of tax practitioners/representatives is guided by codes (or cannons) of professional ethics as issued by their respective professional groups. For example:

    - Subpart B of Circular 230 sets forth a code of conduct to which practitioners who represent taxpayers must adhere. Specifically, Section 10.21 states that a practitioner who knows that a client has not complied with a tax law (or has made an error in or omission from any return) must promptly advise the client of such noncompliance (error or omission).
    - The American Institute of Certified Public Accountants (AICPA) periodically issues statements attempting to guide its membership in the area of ethical responsibilities within various contexts of the

professional environment. Under one of these statements, a CPA should promptly advise a client upon learning of:
- an error in a previously filed return or
- a client's failure to file a required return.

4. T (p. 16–27; preparer acted in good faith)

To promote taxpayer (and tax practitioner) compliance, a vast array of penalties (civil and criminal) can be imposed upon a finding of culpable conduct. For example:

- Under Section 6694(a), a $250 civil penalty is imposed on tax practitioners for understatements arising from unrealistic positions. An unrealistic position is a position that:
  - Was known (or should have been known) by the practitioner and
  - Does not have a realistic possibility of being sustained on its merits.
- Under Section 6694(b), a $1,000 civil penalty is imposed on tax practitioners for willful and reckless conduct, which includes the practitioner's:
  - Willful attempt to understate the taxpayer's tax liability in any manner.
  - Reckless or intentional disregard of an administrative rule or regulation.

In the instant case, the tax practitioner is not subject to the penalties under Section 6694 because the facts indicate that there was reasonable cause for the understatement and the practitioner acted a good faith. The tax practitioner is not generally required to verify information furnished by the taxpayer but is required to ask questions to determine the existence of certain facts that are required by the tax law.

5. T (p. 16–27; not willful or reckless conduct)

To promote taxpayer (and tax practitioner) compliance, a vast array of penalties (civil and criminal) can be imposed upon a finding of culpable conduct. For example:

- Under Section 6694(a), a $250 civil penalty is imposed on tax practitioners for understatements arising from unrealistic positions. An unrealistic position is a position that:
  - Was known (or should have been known) by the practitioner and
  - Does not have a realistic possibility of being sustained on its merits.
- Under Section 6694(b), a $1,000 civil penalty is imposed on tax practitioners for willful and reckless conduct, which includes the practitioner's:
  - Willful attempt to understate the taxpayer's tax liability in any manner.
  - Reckless or intentional disregard of an administrative rule or regulation.

In the instant case, the tax practitioner is not subject to the penalty under Section 6694(b) because the facts indicate that the practitioner did not recklessly or intentionally disregard an administrative rule (Revenue Ruling). Here, there were judicial rulings (precedential authority) contrary to such ruling's position. In other words, there was a realistic possibility that the taxpayer's position would be sustained on its merits (a position for which a reasonable and well-informed analysis by a person knowledgeable in the tax law would conclude as having at least a one-in-three chance of being sustained on its merits).

6. T (p. 16–12; field audit Appeals Division requirement)

If a case is unagreed, the examination audit has not been settled at the revenue agent level. In this case, the report of the revenue agent is more extensive. The Examination Division Review Staff reviews the report of the revenue agent. If approved, the 30-day letter is sent to the taxpayer along with Form 4549–A (Income Tax Examination Changes) as supporting documentation. The 30-day letter provides the following options for the taxpayer exercisable within the prescribed period.

- The taxpayer can accept the findings incorporated within Form 4549–A (Income Tax Examination Changes).
- The taxpayer can request a conference with the Appeals Office. However, if the deficiency is more than $2,500 (but less than $10,000) resulting from a field examination, such request must be in writing and

be accompanied by a brief statement of the disputed issues outlining the taxpayer's position regarding such issues.

7. T (p. 16–22)

To promote taxpayer (and tax practitioner) compliance, a vast array of penalties (civil and criminal) can be imposed upon a finding of culpable conduct. Penalties imposed on the taxpayer are additions to tax and are not deductible.

For example, within the context of an employee-employer relationship, the employer acts as the employee's agent in withholding from the employee's salary amounts representing F.I.C.A. tax and Federal income tax. If the employer does not timely deposit these withheld amounts, civil penalties are imposed. For example, a 100% penalty is assessed against any responsible person who willfully fails to make timely deposits of tax.

8. F (p. 16–13; too restrictive, IRS has liberal acceptance policy in compromising)

The I.R.S. may accept an Offer in Compromise in situations when, based upon the evidence submitted, the I.R.S. finds:

(a) It is unlikely that the tax liability will be collected in full.
(b) The amount offered reasonably reflects the collection potential, based on the taxpayer's net worth, current income and future income potential.

In addition, the I.R.S. may accept an Offer in Compromise when, based upon the evidence submitted, the I.R.S. finds doubt as to the amount of assessed liability. This situation may have arisen because of the taxpayer's failure to take advantage of mechanisms within the audit process to dispute a proposed deficiency.

The Offer in Compromise process begins with the taxpayer filing a Form 656 (Offer in Compromise), which must be accompanied by a detailed set of financial statements. The form and supporting documentation is reviewed by a revenue agent from the Collection Division (Examination Division), if the basis for the offer is doubt as to collectibility (liability).

The Offer in Compromise is a reasonable alternative to the I.R.S. declaring an account as currently non-collectible. One objective of this procedure is to provide the taxpayer with a fresh start and a further incentive for prospective compliance with the tax laws. This objective is accomplished by accepting the offer conditioned upon the taxpayer's prospective compliance (5 years) with all filing and paying requirements.

9. F (p. 16–14; interest stops only on amount remitted)

The alleged deficiency, deficiency or assessed deficiency includes not only an increase in tax but also an interest component. For this purpose, interest is calculated for the period starting with the due date of the tax until the payment date. However:

- If the taxpayer agrees with an alleged deficiency and files Form 870 (Waiver on Restrictions and Collection of Deficiency in Tax and Acceptance of Overassessment):
  - the alleged deficiency is immediately assessed and
  - interest is suspended for a period beginning 30 days after the filing of Form 870 until the date of the notice and demand of the deficiency. Further, interest does not begin accruing on the date of the notice and demand of the deficiency if the taxpayer pays within 30 days of such date.
- Even though interest is not suspended while a taxpayer sues the I.R.S. in U.S. Tax Court, interest on a deficiency can be stopped if payment is made either as against the tax (including interest) or as a bond.

In the instant case, Audrey's cash bond of $3,000 will stop interest from accruing only on $3,000 of the total amount of tax plus interest due. For example, if the amount paid does not take into account the

STUDY GUIDE • CHAPTER 16 • Tax Administration and Practice • 16–13

interest accrued to the date of payment, Section 6622 requires that interest accrue on the interest due at the date of payment.

10. T (Figure 16–2)

Under Section 7422, no suit for the recovery of any tax shall be maintained unless a formal claim for refund has been filed with the I.R.S. Further, to file a claim alleging an overpayment of tax in either the U.S. Court of Federal Claims or the U.S. District Court, the claim for refund filed with the I.R.S. must have been either:

- disallowed by the I.R.S. in a statutory notice of claim disallowance or
- filed at least 6 months ago without any I.R.S. action being taken.

However, to enable the taxpayer to more quickly file a claim alleging an overpayment of tax in either the U.S. Court of Federal Claims or the U.S. District Court, the taxpayer may request in writing that the I.R.S. immediately issue a statutory notice of claim disallowance. Otherwise, the taxpayer may be waiting 6 months after the claim for refund is filed with the I.R.S.

Fill in the Blanks

1. 90 day letter: statutory notice of deficiency (p. 16–11)

   Even though the I.R.S. authority to examine arises from its mandate from Congress to administer the tax laws, the I.R.S. examination audit is best viewed as an adversarial proceeding. However, unlike a civil or criminal proceeding, within many contexts, the procedural burden of going forward with the evidence generally rests with the taxpayer.

   If the examination audit has not been settled at the revenue agent level, the 30-day letter is sent to the taxpayer along with Form 4549–A (Income Tax Examination Changes) as supporting documentation. The 30-day letter provides the following options for the taxpayer within the prescribed period.

   - The taxpayer can accept the findings incorporated within Form 4549–A (Income Tax Examination Changes).
   - The taxpayer can request a conference with the Appeals Office.

   If no action is taken by the taxpayer, a Statutory Notice of Deficiency (the 90-day letter) is issued. The 90-day letter states that the tax liability will be assessed if the taxpayer does not file a petition in the United States Tax Court during the prescribed period. If this statutory 90-day period expires, the tax is assessed. Assessment of the tax is a condition precedent for the collection process to begin.

2. statute of limitations (p. 16–22)

   The statute of limitations is a statutory rule of law prescribing the maximum time period during which a cause of action can be brought or a right enforced. Such period may vary depending on the facts and circumstances (e.g., 3 years in one instance and 6 years in another).

3. appointed (p. 16–4)

   The organizational structure of the I.R.S. is summarized as follows.

   - The I.R.S. is a branch of the U.S. Treasury Department.
   - The head of the I.R.S. is the Commissioner of Internal Revenue, who reports to the Secretary of the Treasury and is appointed by the President.
   - To carry out its administrative functions, the I.R.S. is organized based upon a type-of-taxpayer approach. Under such approach, the I.R.S. uses 4 core divisions, as follows: (1) Large and Mid-Size Business Division, (2) Small Business and Self-Employed Division, (3) Wage and Investment Division, and (4) Tax-Exempt and Government Entities Division.

4. Determination Letters, and Technical Advice Memoranda (p. 16–6)

   During an examination audit, the taxpayer can seek official advice from the I.R.S. concerning a disputed tax issue:

   - In the form of a Determination Letter. A Determination Letter is issued by a Director's Office that has jurisdiction over the taxpayer's audit. Such letter is written only if the response to the issue presented is one within the specific scope of statutory, administrative or judicial tax law.
   - In the form of a Technical Advice Memorandum. A Technical Advice Memorandum is issued by the National Office to a Director or Regional Commissioner in connection with a disputed tax issue with a view toward maintaining consistent positions within the IRS. It applies statutory, administrative or judicial tax law to the facts at issue.

5. "Statements on Standards for Tax Services" (p. 16–28)

   Under Circular 230, the following persons are allowed to practice before the I.R.S.

   - CPA.
   - Attorney.
   - Enrolled Agent (EA).

   All activities related to the making of presentations before the I.R.S. concerning a taxpayer's rights, privileges, or liabilities are within the scope of the phrase "Practice before the I.R.S." Such activities include the preparation and filing of necessary documents and the representation of a client.

   To practice before the I.R.S. (e.g., representation of a particular taxpayer), the practitioner must be properly authorized by the taxpayer. If the practitioner intends to act on behalf of the taxpayer, the taxpayer must file with the I.R.S. Form 2848 (The Power of Attorney). Such authorization by the taxpayer gives the practitioner/representative the general right to:

   - Receive confidential information.
   - Perform any and all acts with respect to the tax matters enumerated within Form 2848 (The Power of Attorney).

6. "Hazards; litigation" (p. 16–12)

   Even though the I.R.S. authority to examine arises from its mandate from Congress to administer the tax laws, the I.R.S. examination audit is best viewed as an adversarial proceeding. However, unlike a civil or criminal proceeding, within many contexts, the procedural burden of going forward with the evidence generally rests with the taxpayer.

   In an examination audit, the revenue agent does not have the technical authority to settle issues of dispute. An agreement between the revenue agent and the taxpayer is not binding on the I.R.S. However, for the revenue agent, certain areas of discretion exist, which may eventually be approved by the agent's group supervisor or Review Staff. The function of review by the Examination Division Review Staff is to ensure that the treatment recommended by the agent and agreed to by the taxpayer is consistent with all I.R.S. rules. If the Examination Division Review Staff approves of the agent's treatment, the agent's office will issue a report notifying the taxpayer as such.

   If the examination audit has not been settled at the revenue agent level, the 30-day letter is sent to the taxpayer.

   If no action is taken by the taxpayer, a Statutory Notice of Deficiency (the 90-day letter) is issued. The 90-day letter states that the tax liability will be assessed if the taxpayer does not file a petition in the United States Tax Court during the prescribed period.

7. offer; compromise (p. 16–13)

   The I.R.S. may accept an Offer in Compromise in situations when, based upon the evidence submitted, the I.R.S. finds:

STUDY GUIDE | **CHAPTER 16** | 16–15
Tax Administration and Practice

(a) it is unlikely that the tax liability will be collected in full and
(b) the amount offered reasonably reflects the collection potential, based on the taxpayer's net worth, current income and future income potential.

In addition, the I.R.S. may accept an Offer in Compromise when, based upon the evidence submitted, the I.R.S. finds doubt as to the amount of assessed liability. This situation may have arisen because of the taxpayer's failure to take advantage of mechanisms within the audit process to dispute a proposed deficiency.

The Offer in Compromise process begins with the taxpayer filing a Form 656 (Offer in Compromise), which must be accompanied by a detailed set of financial statements. The form and supporting documentation are reviewed by a revenue agent from the Collection Division (Examination Division), if the basis for the offer is doubt as to collectibility (liability).

The Offer in Compromise is a reasonable alternative to the I.R.S. declaring an account as currently non-collectible. One objective of this procedure is to provide the taxpayer with a fresh start and a further incentive for prospective compliance with the tax laws. This objective is accomplished by accepting the offer conditioned on the taxpayer's prospective compliance (5 years) with all filing and paying requirements.

8. Penalties (p. 16–15)

To promote taxpayer (and tax practitioner) compliance, a vast array of penalties (civil and criminal) can be imposed upon a finding of culpable conduct. Penalties imposed on the taxpayer are additions to tax and are not deductible.

For example, within the context of an employee-employer relationship, the employer acts as the employee's agent in withholding from the employee's salary amounts representing F.I.C.A. tax and Federal income tax. If the employer does not timely deposit these withheld amounts, penalties are imposed. For example, a 100% civil penalty is assessed against any responsible person who willfully fails to make timely deposits of tax.

9. Revenue Agent's Report (p. 16–10)

Even though the I.R.S.' authority to examine arises from its mandate from Congress to administer the laws of the Internal Revenue Code, the I.R.S.' examination audit is best viewed as an adversarial proceeding. However, unlike a civil or criminal proceeding, within many contexts, the procedural burden of going forward with the evidence generally rests with the taxpayer.

In an examination audit, execution of the Revenue Agent's Report is different depending on whether the case is agreed or unagreed. If the case is agreed, the revenue agent generally prepares Form 4549 (Income Tax Examination Changes).

If the case is unagreed, the examination audit has not been settled at the revenue agent level.

Multiple Choice

1. a (p. 16–25)

All activities related to the making of presentations before the I.R.S. concerning a taxpayer's rights, privileges, or liabilities are within the scope of the phrase "Practice before the I.R.S." Such activities include the preparation and filing of necessary documents and the representation of a client.

Thus, in the instant case, item a is correct because each of the activities identified in item a does not represent practice before the I.R.S. Neither:

- preparing the tax return,
- furnishing information at the request of the I.R.S., nor
- appearing as a witness for a taxpayer

reflects either the preparation and filing of necessary documents or the representation of a client. Further, choice items b, c and d are incorrect because each of these items do reflect activities that do represent practice before the I.R.S., incorporating either the preparation and filing of necessary documents or the representation of a client.

2. b (p. 16–25)

Under Circular 230, the following persons are allowed to practice before the I.R.S.

- CPA.
- Attorney.
- Enrolled Agent (EA).

However, Circular 230 also allows the following persons to practice before the I.R.S., under certain limited circumstances.

- A taxpayer representing himself or an immediate family member (if no compensation is received).
- A regular, full-time employee representing his employer.
- An officer representing his corporation.
- A partner representing his partnership.
- The respective fiduciary (trustee, receiver, guardian, administrator or executor) representing the trust, receivership, guardianship or estate.
- The tax practitioner representing the taxpayer for whom the return was prepared.

Thus, in the instant case, item b is correct if, in fact, the Secretary of the Treasury has found the individual to be disreputable and has suspended or disbarred such individual from practicing before the I.R.S. Further, items a, c and d are incorrect because each of these items do reflect persons that may conduct a limited practice before the I.R.S. under Section 10.7(c) of Subpart A (Rules Governing Authority to Practice) of Circular 230.

3. d (p. 16–13)

There are several types of installment agreements that differ depending upon the needs of the parties. Generally, within the context of an installment agreement, revenue officers have discretion as to whether the I.R.S. files a Notice of Federal Tax Lien to protect the interests of the government.

Under Section 6159(b), the installment agreement remains in effect unless:

- The Secretary of the Treasury (Secretary) determines:
  - Information provided to the Secretary is inaccurate or incomplete.
  - The collection of the tax is in jeopardy.
  - The financial condition of the taxpayer has significantly changed.
- The taxpayer fails:
  - To timely pay any installment.
  - To timely pay any tax.
  - To comply with the Secretary's request for a financial condition update to determine whether the taxpayer has had a change in his/her ability to pay.

In these cases, the Secretary may terminate the installment agreement. However, under Section 6159(b)(5), the Secretary may not take any action to alter, modify or terminate the agreement until 30 days after notice of such action is communicated to the taxpayer. Such communication shall include an explanation for the intended action.

Thus, in the instant case, item d is correct. Further, items a, b and c are incorrect because they are each inconsistent with item d, which has statutory authority as to the effect of a taxpayer's late payment.

4. b (p. 16–13; taxpayer's rights include a right to submit an offer)

The I.R.S. may accept an Offer in Compromise in situations when, based upon the evidence submitted, the I.R.S. finds:

(a) it is unlikely that the tax liability will be collected in full and
(b) the amount offered reasonably reflects the collection potential, based on the taxpayer's net worth, current income and future income potential.

In addition, the I.R.S. may accept an Offer in Compromise when, based upon the evidence submitted, the I.R.S. finds doubt as to the amount of assessed liability. This situation may have arisen because of the taxpayer's failure to take advantage of mechanisms within the audit process to dispute a proposed deficiency. The extent to which an offer is found acceptable depends on the extent to which doubt is found.

The Offer in Compromise process begins with the taxpayer filing a Form 656 (Offer in Compromise), which must be accompanied by a detailed set of financial statements. The form and supporting documentation is reviewed by a revenue agent from the Collection Division (Examination Division), if the basis for the offer is doubt as to collectibility (liability).

The Offer in Compromise is a reasonable alternative to the I.R.S. declaring an account as currently non-collectible. One objective of this procedure is to provide the taxpayer with a fresh start and a further incentive for prospective compliance with the tax laws. This objective is accomplished by accepting the offer conditioned upon the taxpayer's prospective compliance (5 years) with all filing and paying requirements.

Thus, in the instant case, item b is correct. Further, the following choice items are incorrect.

- Item a is incorrect because under Section 7122 the taxpayer has an implicit right to submit an offer. Section 7122(a) states "The Secretary may compromise ..." Section 7122(c) states "The Secretary shall prescribe guidelines..."
- Item c is incorrect because submission of an offer does not necessarily suspend collection activities. Submission generally suspends collection activity unless the offer is deemed frivolous, the filing is deemed made for the sole purpose of delaying collection, or collection is in jeopardy.
- Item d is incorrect because the amount offered must reasonably reflect the collection potential, based on the taxpayer's net worth and current income, as well as future income potential.

5. a (p. 16–14; interest is charged on unpaid balance during installment period)

There are several types of installment agreements that differ depending upon the needs of the parties. Generally, within the context of an installment agreement, revenue officers have discretion as to whether the I.R.S. files a Notice of Federal Tax Lien to protect the interests of the government.

Under Section 6159(b), the installment agreement remains in effect unless:

- The Secretary of the Treasury (Secretary) determines:
  - Information provided to the Secretary is inaccurate or incomplete.
  - The collection of the tax is in jeopardy.
  - The financial condition of the taxpayer has significantly changed.
- The taxpayer fails:
  - To timely pay any installment.
  - To timely pay any tax.
  - To comply with the Secretary's request for a financial condition update to determine whether the taxpayer has had a change in his/her ability to pay.

In these cases, the Secretary may terminate the installment agreement. However, under Section 6159(b)(5), the Secretary may not take any action to alter, modify or terminate the agreement until 30 days after notice of such action is communicated to the taxpayer. Such communication shall include an explanation for the intended action.

Thus, in the instant case, item a is the right answer because interest does not stop accruing. Rather, it continues to accrue on a taxpayer's unpaid balance of tax, interest and some penalties. Further, items b, c and d are the wrong answers because each is correct within the context of an installment agreement.

For example, to minimize the administrative burden to the taxpayer, the I.R.S. allows installment payments to be made by electronic transfer from the taxpayer's bank account.

6. d   (p. 16–27; not third parties)

To promote taxpayer (and tax practitioner) compliance, a vast array of penalties (civil and criminal) can be imposed upon a finding of culpable conduct. Penalties imposed on the taxpayer are additions to tax and are not deductible. For example, under Section 6713, a $250 civil penalty is imposed on any tax practitioner who makes an unauthorized disclosure of tax return information. Under Section 6713(b), the rules under Section 7216(b) provide exceptions. Section 7216 is the criminal penalty equivalent of Section 6713.

Under Treas. Reg. Sec. 301.7216–2(a), a tax practitioner (or his agent) may disclose tax return information of a taxpayer (without the formal consent of such taxpayer) pursuant to a request made by an officer or employee of the I.R.S. of books, papers, records, or other data, which may be relevant to the determination of such taxpayer's tax liability.

Under Treas. Reg. Sec. 301.7216–2(c), a tax practitioner (or his agent) may disclose tax return information of a taxpayer (without the formal consent of such taxpayer) pursuant to:

- A court order.
- A subpoena issued by a grand jury.
- An administrative order, demand, summons or subpoena.
- A request by a State agency, body or commission.
- A request by a political subdivision of the State charged with the licensing, registration or regulation of tax practitioners.

Under Treas. Reg. Sec. 301.7216–2(b), a tax practitioner (or his agent) may disclose tax return information of one taxpayer (without the formal consent of such taxpayer) to a second taxpayer if all of the following conditions are satisfied.

- The two taxpayers are related. Related parties include:
  - Husband and wife.
  - Parent and child.
  - Partner and partnership.
  - Corporation and shareholder.
  - Bankruptcy estate and fiduciary trustee.
- The first taxpayer's tax interest is not adverse to the second taxpayer's tax interest.
- The first taxpayer has not expressly prohibited such disclosure.

Thus, in the instant case, item d is correct, because the disclosure penalty does not apply to any of the situations in items a, b and c, assuming the first taxpayer's tax interest is not adverse to the second taxpayer's tax interest and the first taxpayer has not expressly prohibited such disclosure. Items a, b and c all involve a related party situation such that disclosure of tax information by the tax practitioner (or his agent) from one party to the other party is exempted from penalty application under Treas. Reg. Sec. 301.7216–2(b).

7. d   (p. 16–27)

Under Treas. Reg. Sec. 301.7216–2(c), a tax practitioner (or his agent) may disclose tax return information of a taxpayer (without the formal consent of such taxpayer) pursuant to:

- A court order.
- A subpoena issued by a grand jury.
- An administrative order, demand, summons or subpoena.
- A request by a State agency, body or commission.
- A request by a political subdivision of the State charged with the licensing, registration or regulation of tax practitioners.

| STUDY GUIDE | **CHAPTER 16**
Tax Administration and Practice | 16–19 |

Under Treas. Reg. Sec. 301.7216–2(b), a tax practitioner (or his agent) may disclose tax return information of one taxpayer (without the formal consent of such taxpayer) to a second taxpayer if all of the following conditions are satisfied.

- The two taxpayers are related. Related parties include:
  - Husband and wife.
  - Parent and child.
  - Partner and partnership.
  - Corporation and shareholder.
  - Bankruptcy estate and fiduciary trustee.
- The first taxpayer's tax interest is not adverse to the second taxpayer's tax interest.
- The first taxpayer has not expressly prohibited such disclosure.

Thus, in the instant case, item d is correct, because the disclosure penalty does not apply to any of the situations in items a, b and c Items a, b and c all involve a disclosure of tax information by the tax practitioner (or his agent) that is exempt from the civil penalty under Treas. Reg. Sec. 301.7216–2 as follows.

- Item a: Treas. Reg. Sec. 301.7216–2(c).
- Item b: Treas. Reg. Sec. 301.7216–2(a).
- Item c: Treas. Reg. Sec. 301.7216–2(b).

8. c (p. 16–10; interest stops 30 days after form is filed)

In an examination audit, execution of the Revenue Agent's Report is different depending on whether the case is agreed or unagreed. If the case is agreed, the revenue agent generally prepares Form 4549 (Income Tax Examination Changes). This form summarizes the audit adjustments to income and/or deductions and computes the additional tax and penalties. The taxpayer may consent to Form 4559 (Income Tax Examination Changes) or sign Form 870 (Waiver of Restrictions on Assessment and Collection of Deficiency in Tax). The consent or waiver effectively waives the taxpayer's right to:

- Receive a Statutory Notice of Deficiency (the 90-day letter).
- File a petition in the United States Tax Court.
- Request a conference with the Appeals Office.

In this case, the deficiency can be immediately assessed. For this purpose, interest is generally calculated from the due date of the return to the date of payment. However, under Section 6601(c), interest is suspended from accruing on the agreed deficiency for a period beginning 30 days after the consent or waiver is filed until the date of the notice and demand of the deficiency. Further, interest does not begin accruing on the date of the notice and demand of the deficiency, if the taxpayer pays the deficiency within 30 days of such date.

Thus, in the instant case, item c is the right answer because it is not true the taxpayer will not be billed for additional interest more than 60 days from the date he signed the agreement. Instead, interest is suspended from accruing on the agreed deficiency for a period beginning 30 days after the consent or waiver is filed until the date of the notice and demand of the deficiency. Further, the following items are wrong.

- Item a is wrong because it is true that interest is generally calculated from the due date of the return to the date of payment.
- Item b and d are wrong because it is true that interest is suspended from accruing on the agreed deficiency for a period beginning 30 days after the consent or waiver is filed until the date of the notice and demand of the deficiency. Further, interest does not begin accruing on the date of the notice and demand of the deficiency if the taxpayer pays the deficiency within 30 days of such date.

9. a (p. 16–27; preparer endorses in his preparer capacity)

    To promote taxpayer (and tax practitioner) compliance, a vast array of penalties (civil and criminal) can be imposed upon a finding of culpable conduct. Penalties imposed on the taxpayer are additions to tax and are not deductible. For example, under Section 6695, a $500 civil penalty is imposed on any tax practitioner who endorses or negotiates, either directly or through an agent, a refund check of a taxpayer, a person for whom such practitioner prepared a return. Thus, in the instant case, item a is correct because the tax practitioner through an agent (his check-cashing agency) is endorsing or negotiating a refund check of a taxpayer, a person for whom such practitioner prepared a return. Further, the following items are incorrect.

    - Item b is incorrect because merely cashing a refund check is neither endorsing nor negotiating a refund check. The proscribed conduct is endorsing or negotiating.
    - Item c is incorrect because merely receiving a refund check is neither endorsing nor negotiating a refund check. The proscribed conduct is endorsing or negotiating.
    - Item d is incorrect because merely depositing refund checks (endorsed by the taxpayer) into special accounts of the taxpayer does not constitute either endorsing or negotiating a refund check. The proscribed conduct is endorsing or negotiating.

CHAPTER 17

The Federal Gift and Estate Taxes

LEARNING OBJECTIVES

After completing Chapter 17, you should be able to:

1. Understand the nature of the Federal gift and estate taxes.
2. Work with the Federal gift tax formula.
3. Work with the Federal estate tax formula.
4. Explain the operation of the Federal gift tax.
5. Illustrate the computation of the Federal gift tax.
6. Review the components of the gross estate.
7. Describe the components of the taxable estate.
8. Determine the Federal estate tax liability.
9. Appreciate the role of the generation skipping transfer tax.

KEY TERMS

Alternate valuation date
Annual exclusion
Disclaimers
Exclusion amount
Exemption equivalent
Future interest
Gross estate
Inheritance tax

Joint tenants
Marital deduction
Power of appointment
Probate estate
Qualified family-owned business interest (QFOBI)
Qualified terminable interest property (QTIP)

Taxable estate
Taxable gift
Tenants by the entirety
Tenants in common
Terminable interests
Unified tax credit
Unified transfer tax

OUTLINE

I. **TRANSFER TAXES**
   A. Nature of the Taxes
      1. Transfer taxes are based on the value of the property transferred, not the income derived from the property.
      2. The Unified Transfer Tax covers all gratuitous transfers.
         a. The gift tax is a tax on transfers during the donor's lifetime.
         b. The estate tax is a tax on transfers at death.
      3. Persons subject to the tax
         a. The Federal gift tax applies to:
            1. all transfers of property by individuals who, at the time of the gift, were citizens or residents of the U.S.
            2. gifts of property located in the U.S. for individuals who were neither citizens nor residents.
         b. The Federal estate tax applies to:
            1. the entire estate of decedents who, at the time of death, were U.S. citizens or residents.
            2. property located in the U.S. for decedents who were neither citizens or residents.
         c. For nonresidents and/or noncitizens, application of these taxes may be different under treaties between the U.S. and various foreign countries.
      4. Formulas
         a. The Gift Tax

            Current year's taxable gifts (net of any deductions allowed and any exclusions available)
            + All prior years' taxable gifts
            = Total taxable gifts
            Compute tax on total taxable gifts (see Appendix A)
            − Tax paid or deemed paid on prior years' taxable gifts
            − The unified tax credit
            = Gift tax due on current year's taxable gifts

         b. The Estate Tax

            Gross estate
            − Deductions allowed (e.g., charitable bequests, marital deduction)
            = Taxable estate
            + Post-1976 adjusted taxable gifts
            = Tax base
            Tentative tax on tax base
            − Unified transfer tax on post-1976 taxable gifts (paid or deemed paid)
            − Tax credits, including: unified tax credit, state death tax credit, credit for certain gift taxes actually paid on post-1976 taxable gifts
            = Estate tax due

   B. Valuation for Estate and Gift Tax Purposes
      1. The fair market value of property on *the date of transfer* is generally the amount subject to the gift or estate tax.
      2. An estate may elect the alternate valuation date if:
         a. the estate is required to file an Estate Tax Return (Form 706), and
         b. the election would decrease *both* the value of the gross estate and the estate tax liability.
      3. If the alternate valuation date is properly elected, all property is valued either six months after the date of death or on the date of disposition, whichever is earlier.

C. Key Property Concepts
   1. Undivided ownership
      a. Joint tenants and tenants by the entirety have rights of survivorship.
      b. Tenants in common or community property interests held by the decedent at death will pass to the estate or heirs.
   2. Partial interests are interests in assets divided as to rights to either the income or principal.

II. THE FEDERAL GIFT TAX
A. General Considerations
   1. Under state law, for a gift to be complete, the following conditions must be present.
      a. A donor must be competent to make the gift.
      b. A donee must be capable of receiving and possessing the gifted property.
      c. Donative intent on behalf of the donor must be present.
      d. Actual or constructive delivery of the property to the donee or donee's representative must have been accomplished.
      e. Acceptance of the gift by the donee must have occurred.
   2. Incomplete transfers (e.g., when transferor retains the right to reclaim the property) are not covered by the Federal gift tax.
   3. Gifts are unlikely to occur in a business setting.
   4. Certain transfers are exempt from the Federal gift tax, including:
      a. transfers to political organizations.
      b. payments made on another's behalf for tuition and medical care, if made directly to the provider (e.g., college, doctor, hospital).
B. Transfers Subject to the Gift Tax
   1. Gift loans
      a. A gift loan is any below-market interest rate loan where foregone interest is in the nature of a gift. Under the Code, the lender has given a gift and has received interest income; the borrower has received a gift and may have an interest expense deduction.
      b. The gross gift is calculated as the difference between actual interest charged and the market rate of interest (the interest element).
      c. Special limitations apply if the gift loan does not exceed $100,000 (unless tax avoidance is a principal purpose of the loan).
         1. If the borrower's net investment income does not exceed $1,000, the interest element is disregarded.
         2. If the borrower's net investment income is $1,000 or more, the interest income element may not exceed the borrower's net investment income.
   2. Generally, the settlement of certain marital rights is subject to the Federal gift tax. However, settlement of marital or property rights is not subject to the Federal gift tax when:
      a. a written agreement between spouses is executed and
      b. a final divorce is obtained within the three-year period beginning on the date one year before such agreement is entered into.
C. Disclaimers
   1. A disclaimer is a formal refusal by a person to accept property that is designated to pass to him or her.
   2. The effect of the disclaimer is to pass the property to someone else, thereby avoiding the transfer tax payment.
   3. The requirements of Code Section 2518 must be met to avoid the Federal gift tax.
D. Annual Exclusion
   1. The first $11,000 of gifts made to any one person during any calendar year are excluded from the gift tax (i.e., not included in total taxable gifts).
   2. The exclusion does not apply to future interests in property (an interest that will come into being at some point in the future).
   3. For a gift in trust, the annual exclusion applies to each beneficiary of the trust.

E. An exception to the future interest rule applies to gifts to minors. A gift to a minor is considered a gift of a present interest (i.e., not a future interest) if all of the following conditions are met:
   1. Both the property and its income may be expended by or for the benefit of the minor before the minor attains the age of 21.
   2. If the property is not expended, it will pass to the minor once the minor reaches the age of 21.
   3. If the minor dies before reaching the age of 21, the property will pass either to the minor's estate or as the minor may designate under a general power of appointment.
F. Deductions
   1. A deduction is allowed for transfers to certain qualified charitable organizations.
   2. A marital deduction may be available for transfers between spouses.
G. Computing the Federal Gift Tax
   1. The top rate for the unified transfer tax rate is 50 percent (see Appendix A).
   2. The unified transfer rate schedule applies to all transfers (by gift or death) after 1976 and before 2010.
   3. A "deemed paid adjustment" is allowed on all pre-1977 taxable gifts.
   4. Married couples can utilize gift splitting to minimize gift tax consequences. Both spouses must indicate their consent to split gifts on their separate gift tax returns (Form 709).
H. Procedural Matters.
   1. Form 709 must be filed whenever the gifts to one person for one calendar year exceed the annual exclusion or involve a gift of a future interest.
   2. A Form 709 is not required for transfers between spouses that are offset by the unlimited marital deduction (regardless of the transfer amount).
   3. The gift tax return must be filed by April 15 following the year of the gift.

III. **THE FEDERAL ESTATE TAX**
   A. The Gross Estate
      1. The gross estate is composed of the value of all property owned by the decedent at the time of death. The nature of the property has no significance for estate tax purposes.
      2. Certain gifts made within three years of death are included in the gross estate. Examples include:
         a. any gift tax paid on gifts made within 3 years of death.
         b. a completed transfer of a property interest transferred by gift within 3 years of death, where such property interest would have been included in the decedent's gross estate because the donor retained rights in the interest. Examples include:
            1. a retained life estate.
            2. a revocable transfer.
            3. life insurance.
      3. The value of any property transferred by the deceased during lifetime for less than adequate consideration is included in the gross estate if either of the following was retained (a retained life interest):
         a. The possession or enjoyment of, or the right to the income from, the property.
         b. The right to designate the person(s) who possess, or receive income from, the property.
      4. The value of property interests transferred by the decedent are included in the gross estate if the decedent maintained the power to alter, amend, revoke or terminate the transfer (a revocable transfer).
      5. Survivorship annuities are included in the gross estate. In general, the amount included in the estate is the cost of a comparable annuity covering the survivor at his or her age on the date of the deceased annuitant's death.
      6. Certain property held in joint tenancy is included in the decedent's gross estate unless (and to the extent) it can be proved that the surviving co-owners contributed to the cost of the property.
         a. Funds received as a gift from the deceased co-owner and applied to the cost cannot be counted as funds provided by a surviving co-owner.
         b. For married persons, one-half of the value of the property is included in the gross estate of the spouse who dies first.

7. In joint ownership cases, where there is equal ownership but disproportionate contributions to the cost of the property, generally a gift has been made.
   a. For a joint bank account, a gift occurs only when the noncontributing party withdraws funds provided by the other joint tenant.
   b. For U.S. savings bonds, a gift occurs when the noncontributing party uses some or all of the proceeds for his or her individual use.
8. Property over which the decedent possessed a general power of appointment is included in the gross estate.
9. Life insurance proceeds on the decedent's life are included in the gross estate if:
   a. they are receivable by the estate,
   b. they are receivable by another for the benefit of the estate, or
   c. the decedent possessed an incident of ownership in the policy.

B. Taxable Estate
1. Deductions are allowed for certain expenses, indebtedness, and taxes, including:
   a. funeral expenses.
   b. expenses incurred in administering property (e.g., attorney fees, accountant fees, court costs, selling expenses)
   c. unpaid mortgages and other charges.
   d. claims against the estate (e.g., property taxes accrued before the decedent's death, unpaid income and gift taxes until date of death).
2. Casualty or theft losses incurred while administering the estate may be deducted.
3. Deductions are allowed for charitable transfers to:
   a. the United States or any of its political subdivisions.
   b. any corporation or association organized and operated exclusively for religious, charitable, scientific, literary, or educational purposes.
   c. various veterans' organizations.
4. A marital deduction is allowed property included in the decedent's gross estate and that passes (or has passed to) the surviving spouse.
   a. The deduction includes any interest received as:
      1. the decedent's heir.
      2. the decedent's surviving tenant by the entirety or joint tenant.
      3. the appointee under the decedent's exercise, lapse or release of a general power of appointment.
      4. the beneficiary of insurance on the life of the decedent.
   b. Certain interests passing from the deceased spouse to the surviving spouse will not qualify for the marital deduction.
      1. A terminable interest (an interest which terminates after the passage of time) will not qualify if another interest in the same property passed from the decedent to a person other than the spouse.
      2. The terminable interest rule can be avoided if the surviving spouse is granted a general power of appointment over the property.
      3. A qualified terminable interest property (QTIP) qualifies for the marital deduction. A QTIP exists if the person is entitled to a specific portion of the property's income for life and no person has a power to appoint any part of the property to a person other than the surviving spouse.
5. A qualified family-owned business interest (QFOBI) deduction is available for taxable years before 2004.
   a. This deduction (of up to $675,000) is intended to keep the business intact for the benefit of the deceased owner's family.
   b. This deduction applies when:
      1. at date of death, the decedent was a citizen or resident of the U.S.
      2. the value of the business interest exceeds 50% of the adjusted gross estate.

3. the decedent (or a family member) owned and materially participated in the business for at least 5 of the 8 years prior to death.
4. a qualified heir (a family member) must materially participate in the business for at least 5 years in an 8 year period during the 10 years following the decedent's death.
   c. Tax savings are recaptured when any of the following events occur:
      1. the qualified heir ceases to meet the material participation requirements.
      2. the business is disposed of to outsiders.
      3. the business is moved outside of the U.S. or the qualified heir loses U.S. citizenship.
   d. Full recapture (100%) is required if the disqualifying act occurs during the first six years after the owner's death. The recapture percentage declines by 20 percent each year thereafter.
   e. The deduction is elective and is made by the executor. The election must include an agreement that the qualified heir(s) will accept liability for recapture tax consequences should they arise.

C. Computing the Federal Estate Tax
1. Determine the taxable estate
2. Add post-1976 taxable gifts
3. Compute the tentative tax
4. Subtract available estate tax credits

D. Estate Tax Credits
1. The unified tax credit reduces the tentative estate tax. An adjustment to the unified tax credit is necessary if any portion of the specific exemption was utilized on gifts made after September 8, 1976, and before January 1, 1977.
2 The Code allows a limited credit for state death taxes paid (see Appendix A for the maximum amounts). The credit phases out over the next several years (75% of the credit is allowed in 2002, 50% in 2003, 25% in 2004, and none thereafter).
4. If a decedent received property from an estate and the estate paid taxes on the transfer, a credit may be available.
   a. The transfer must have occurred within the 10 year period before the decedent's death.
   b. The credit is limited to the lesser of:
      1. The amount of the Federal estate tax attributable to the transferred property in the transferor's estate,
      2. The amount of the Federal estate tax attributable to the transferred property in the decedent's estate.
   c. The credit is allowed in full if the transferor died within two years of the decedent. The credit phases-out as the length of time increases (80% if transferor died three or four years prior to decedent; 60% if within five or six years; 40% if within seven or eight years; 20% if within nine or ten years)
5. A credit is allowed for foreign death taxes paid. The credit is limited to the lesser of:
   a. The amount of the foreign death tax attributable to the property situated in the country imposing the tax and included in the decedent's Federal gross estate,
   b. The amount of the Federal estate tax attributable to the property.

E. Procedural Matters
1. If required, the Federal estate tax return (Form 706) is due nine months after the date of death.
2. An automatic six-month extension of time to file the estate tax return is available.
3. Filing requirements parallel the exclusion amounts of the unified tax credit available for each year (see Table 17–1).

IV. **THE GENERATION SKIPPING TRANSFER TAX (GSTT)**
   A. The GSTT is imposed when a younger generation is bypassed in favor of a transfer to a later generation.
   B. The GSTT applies to lifetime transfers by gift and to transfers by death. The tax rate imposed is the highest rate under the gift and estate tax schedule (currently 50%).
   C. Every grantor is allowed a GSTT exemption ($1,100,000 in 2002).

TEST FOR SELF-EVALUATION—CHAPTER 17

True or False

Indicate which of the following statements is true or false by circling the correct answer.

T F 1. Mr. Goulart, a U.S. resident alien, died on July 1, 2002. As the executor of the estate, you must file an estate tax return if the value of the gross estate at the date of death was $150,000 or more. (IRS 97 3A-2)

T F 2. During 2002, Bethany gave $5,000 to her mother; $6,000 to her father; and $3,000 to her aunt. Bethany must file Form 709, United States Gift and Generation Skipping Transfer Tax Return. (IRS 97 3A-7)

T F 3. In January 2002, Jon gave an interest free loan of $10,500 to his son so that he could buy a boat. His son repaid the entire $10,500 in December 2002. In addition, Jon gave other gifts to his son during 2002 totaling $85,000. Jon must include an amount for the forgone interest on the boat loan on his gift tax return for 2002. (IRS 97 3A-8)

T F 4. Mr. Hodges, a U. S. citizen, died on August 1, 2002. As the personal representative of the estate, you must file Form 706, United States Estate (and Generation-Skipping Transfer) Tax Return if the value of the gross estate at the date of death was $1,700,000. (IRS 96 3A-13)

T F 5. The gross estate includes property owned by a decedent at the time of his death and transferred by will or intestacy laws. (IRS 96 3A-15)

T F 6. Taxable gifts for the current year are total gifts for the current year reduced by the cumulative number and amount of applicable annual exclusions, the charitable deduction and the marital deduction. (IRS 96 3A-19)

T F 7. An extension of time to file an income tax return for any tax year that is a calendar year automatically extends the time for filing the annual gift tax return for that calendar year until the extended due date of the income tax return. (IRS 95 3A-18)

T F 8. Herman, as executor of the estate of his deceased father, must sell his father's house to make distributions to all beneficiaries. Herman pays $9,000 to paint and carpet the house to enhance its marketability. The $9,000 Herman pays is deductible from the gross estate to compute the taxable estate. (IRS 94 3A-13)

T F 9. If the alternate valuation method is elected in valuing the decedent's property, any property not disposed of within 6 months after the decedent's death is valued as of 6 months after the date of the decedent's death. (IRS 93 3A-14)

Fill in the Blanks

Complete the following statements with the appropriate word(s) or amount(s).

1. A transfer subject to the Federal gift tax is a transfer of property from one person to another for less than _____ and _____ consideration in money or money's worth.

2. The Federal gift tax is _____ in effect.

3. The deductions and exclusions which are allowed in arriving at the taxable gifts are _____, _____, and _____.

4. Gift splitting must be between _____.

5. The _____ comprises all property which is subject to the Federal estate tax.

6. _____ is a right that a surviving husband has in his deceased wife's property.

7. An _____ is defined as "one or more payments extending over a period of time."

8. The three things that can happen to a power of appointment are _____, _____ and _____.

9. Powers of appointment fall into two categories: _____ power of appointment and _____ power of appointment.

10. A _____ power of appointment is one in which the decedent could have appointed himself, his creditors, his estate, or the creditors of his estate.

11. The Federal estate tax is imposed on the decedent's right to _____ at death.

Multiple Choice

Choose the best answer for each of the following questions.

_____ 1. Eileen, a U.S. citizen, died on June 28, 2002. The value of her gross estate as of the date of death was determined to be in excess of $1,000,000. Without regard to extensions, what is the due date of Form 706, United States Estate and Generation Skipping Transfer Tax Return? (IRS 97 3B-26)

    a. September 15, 2002
    b. December 31, 2002
    c. March 28, 2003
    d. June 30, 2003

_____ 2. Form 706, United States Estate (and Generation Skipping Transfer) Tax Return, was filed for the estate of Erik Cage in 2002. The gross estate tax was $350,000. All of the following items are credited against the gross estate tax to determine the net estate tax payable, except: (IRS 97 3B-27)

    a. Marital deduction.
    b. Credit for state and foreign death taxes.
    c. Unified Transfer Tax Credit.
    d. Credit for gift taxes deemed payable on post-1976 taxable gifts.

_____ 3. Nancy's books and records reflect the following for 2002. Which transaction would require filing Form 709, United States Gift (and Generation Skipping Transfer) Tax Return? (IRS 97 3B-27)

    a. Gratuitously transferred a vehicle with a fair market value of $20,000 to her fiance a month before they were married.
    b. Donated $12,000 to a qualified political organization.
    c. Paid $20,000 to St. Francis Hospital for her aunt's unreimbursed medical expenses.
    d. Paid $11,000 to State University for her brother's tuition.

_____ 4. All of the following statements concerning gift-splitting are true except: (IRS 97 3B-29)

    a. To qualify for gift-splitting, a couple must be married at the time the gift is made to a third party.
    b. Both spouses must consent to the use of gift-splitting.

c. For gift tax purposes, a husband and wife must file a joint income tax return to qualify for the gift-splitting benefits.
d. The annual gift tax exclusion allows spouses who consent to split their gifts to transfer up to $22,000 to any one person during any calendar year without gift tax liability, if the gift qualifies as a present interest.

_____ 5. Listed below are gifts Joan made during 2002.

Gift to a nonprofit home for the underprivileged	$26,000
Gift to her daughter	11,000
Contributions to an historical museum	11,000
Gift to her spouse	41,000

What is the amount of taxable gifts to be reported on Form 709 for 2002? (IRS 97 3C-50)

a. $0
b. $37,000
c. $48,000
d. $78,000

_____ 6. What amount of a decedent's taxable estate is effectively tax-free if the maximum unified estate and gift tax credit is taken, in 2002? (IRS 96 3B-34)

a. $11,000
b. $345,800
c. $675,000
d. $1,000,000

_____ 7. On June 15, 2002, Marlo made a transfer by gift in an amount sufficient to require the filing of a gift tax return. If Marlo does not request an extension of time for filing the 2002 gift tax return, the due date for filing is (IRS 96 3B-37)

a. December 31, 2002
b. March 15, 2003
c. April 15, 2003
d. June 15, 2003

_____ 8. For transfers by gift during 2002, one must file a gift tax return for which of the following? (IRS 96 3B-38)

a. a transfer of $18,000 to a son for which one's spouse has agreed to gift-splitting.
b. A qualified transfer for educational or medical expenses.
c. A transfer of a present interest in property that is not more than the annual exclusion.
d. A transfer to one's spouse that qualified for the unlimited marital deduction.

_____ 9. Valerie and Dino, who were married in 1993, made a gift to their son Michael on January 2, 2002. In July 2002, Valerie and Dino were legally divorced. Valerie married Scott on December 20, 2002. Which answer below best describes this situation? (IRS 96 3B-39)

a. The gift-splitting benefits are available to Valerie and Dino if Valerie consents.
b. The gift-splitting benefits are NOT available to Valerie and Dino because they were divorced in 2002.
c. The gift-splitting benefits are NOT available to Valerie and Dino because Valerie remarried in 2002.
d. The gift-splitting benefits ARE available to Valerie and Dino because they were married at the time the gift was made.

CHAPTER 17
The Federal Gift and Estate Taxes

_____ 10. Jason died on October 1, 2002. The alternate valuation method was not elected. The assets in his estate were valued as of the date of death as follows:

Home	$300,000
Car	20,000
Stocks, bonds, and savings	250,000
Jewelry	50,000
Dividends declared July 1, 2002, not paid as of October 1, 2002	1,000
Accrued interest on savings as of October 1, 2002	6,500

What is the amount of Jason's gross estate? (IRS 96 3C-73)

a. $570,000
b. $620,000
c. $621,000
d. $627,500

_____ 11. Ellie died on June 15, 2002. The assets in her estate were valued on the date of her death and the alternate valuation date, respectively, as follows:

Asset	Date of Death Valuation	Alternate Valuation
Home	$250,000	$300,000
Stock	425,000	450,000
Bonds	200,000	125,000
Furnishings	100,000	100,000

The executor sold the home on August 1, 2002, for $275,000. If Ellie's executor elects the alternate valuation date method, what is the value of Ellie's estate? (IRS 96 3C-74)

a. $895,000
b. $945,000
c. $950,000
d. $970,000

_____ 12. Chris, who is single and a U.S. citizen, made the following gifts in 2002:

Cash to nephew	$100,000
Cash to sister	100,000
Property to brother	200,000
Cash to local university building fund	100,000

Chris had not made any gifts in prior years. What is the amount of taxable gifts? (IRS 96 3C-75)

a. $367,000
b. $467,000
c. $478,000
d. $500,000

_____ 13. In 2002, Linda gave her daughter a gift of land that had a fair market value of $1,000,000. She made no gifts in years 1988 through 2001. In 1987, she used $121,800 of her unified credit to offset gift tax otherwise due. What amount of unified credit can Linda use to offset gift tax due on the 2002 gift? (IRS 96 3C-76)

    a. $345,800
    b. $224,000
    c. $11,000
    d. $0

14. During 2002, Wellington made the following gifts:

Cash to son Willis	$ 42,000
Land to wife Paula	100,000
Painting to niece Marlene	16,000

Wellington and Paula elect gift-splitting. Paula's only gift in 2002 was a $52,000 cash gift to her mother. What is the amount of the taxable gifts to be reported by Wellington in 2002? (IRS 96 3C-77)

    a. $25,000
    b. $36,000
    c. $158,000
    d. $210,000

15. All of the following provisions with respect to the election of the alternate valuation method for property included in the decedent's gross estate are correct except: (IRS 96 3B-33)

    a. The election must be made on a return filed within one year of the due date, including extensions, for filing the return.
    b. The election may be changed after filing the return by filing an amended return.
    c. The election may be made only if it will decrease the value of the gross estate and the sum of the estate tax and the generation skipping transfer tax (reduced by any allowable credits).
    d. The election applies to all of the property in the estate and does not preclude you from electing the special-use valuation for qualified real property.

SOLUTIONS TO CHAPTER 17 QUESTIONS

True or False

1. F (p. 17-7; in excess of exclusion amount of $1,000,000 for calendar year 2002)

    The Federal estate tax is an excise tax that applies to transfers of property by reason of a decedent's death. The tax is calculated (in part) by applying a progressive tax rate structure to the cumulative value of property transferred either during life or at death. The progressive estate tax rate structure ranges from 18 percent to 55 percent.

    The estate tax is imposed on a person who (at the time of his/her death) is:

    - A citizen of the U.S.
    - A resident alien of the U.S. (i.e., a person domiciled in the U.S.).
    - A nonresident alien to the extent that property is situation in the U.S.

    The estate tax return (Form 706) must be filed by the decedent's representative for decedents dying in a particular year with a gross estate of more than the applicable exemption equivalent amount. In 2002, the exclusion amount was $1,000,000. However, for purposes of determining the filing requirement of the estate tax return, the exemption equivalent amount is reduced by post-1976 adjusted taxable gifts.

    In the instant case, Mr. Goulart is a resident alien of the U.S. Thus, the executor of Mr. Goulart's estate must file an estate tax return (Form 706) if Mr. Goulart's gross estate is more than the exemption equivalent amount of $675,000 for 2001, assuming the amount of post-1976 adjusted taxable gifts is zero.

2. F (p. 17-14; annual exclusion is $11,000 per donee)

    The gift tax return (Form 706) must be filed by the donor for any particular calendar year in which the donor made a transfer to any donee (other than the donor's spouse) that was not entirely excluded from being subject to the gift tax. Transfers that are excluded from being subject to the gift tax include annual transfers of present interests to any donee, where the cumulative amount of such transfers does not exceed $11,000. A present interest is an interest that is not a future interest. A future interest is an interest in real or personal property in which possession or enjoyment of such property will come into being at some future point in time.

    In the instant case:

    - Transfers of cash are transfers of present interests.
    - Each of the Bethany's transfers:
        - to Mother ($5,000),
        - to Father ($6,000), and
        - to Aunt ($3,000)
      are excluded from the gift tax.

    Consequently, Bethany does not have to file a gift tax return (Form 706) for calendar year 2002.

3. T (p. 17-12)

    Congress has carved out three exceptions to the rules for interest-free and below-market loans under Section 7872, as follows.

    (a) No income or gift consequences will result if gift loans do not exceed $10,000 during the year and the loan proceeds are not used to purchase income-producing property.

    (b) There is no deemed interest income when loans between individuals do not exceed $100,000 and the net investment income of the borrower does not exceed $1,000. However, the lender is still deemed to have made a gift of the foregone interest, which is computed based upon a statutory rate of interest. That is, a taxable gift is attributable to the lender to the extent that the gift of the foregone interest exceeds the $10,000 annual gift tax exclusion.

(c) When loans between individuals do not exceed $100,000 but the borrower's net investment income exceeds $1,000, the deemed interest income reported by the lender is limited to the borrower's actual net investment income. However, the lender is still deemed to have made a gift of the foregone interest, which is computed based upon a statutory rate of interest. That is, a taxable gift is attributable to the lender to the extent that the gift of the foregone interest exceeds the $10,000 annual gift tax exclusion. There is no deemed interest income when loans between individuals do not exceed $100,000 and the net investment income of the borrower does not exceed $1,000. However, the lender is still deemed to have made a gift of the foregone interest, which is computed based upon a statutory rate of interest. That is, a taxable gift is attributable to the lender to the extent that the gift of the foregone interest exceeds the $10,000 annual gift tax exclusion.

In the instant case, Jon's free loan to his son exceeds $10,000. Thus, Jon is still deemed to have made a gift of the foregone interest to his son, which is computed based upon a statutory rate of interest.

4. T (p. 17–7; value of gross estate exceeds $1,000,000 exclusion amount for calendar year 2002)

The Federal estate tax is an excise tax that applies to transfers of property by reason of a decedent's death. The tax is calculated (in part) by applying a progressive tax rate structure to the cumulative value of property transferred either during life or at death. The progressive estate tax rate structure ranges from 18 percent to 55 percent.

The estate tax is imposed on a person who (at the time of his/her death) is:

- A citizen of the U.S.
- A resident alien of the U.S. (i.e., a person domiciled in the U.S.).
- A nonresident alien to the extent that property is situation in the U.S.

The estate tax return (Form 706) must be filed by the decedent's representative for decedents dying in a particular year with a gross estate of more than the applicable exemption equivalent amount. In 2002, the exclusion amount was $1,000,000. However, for purposes of determining the filing requirement of the estate tax return, the exemption equivalent amount is reduced by post-1976 adjusted taxable gifts.

In the instant case, Mr. Hodges is a citizen of the U.S. Thus, the executor of Mr. Hodges' estate must file an estate tax return (Form 706) since Mr. Hodges' gross estate of $1,700,000 is more than the exclusion amount of $1,000,000 in 2002.

5. T (p. 17–18)

The estate tax return (Form 706) must be filed by the decedent's representative for decedents dying in a particular year with a gross estate of more than the applicable exemption equivalent amount. The gross estate incorporates the value of all interests in property that are transferred by reason of the decedent's death. Such interests in property that are included in the gross estate are described in Section 2033 through Section 2044, inclusive. For example, under Section 2033, the gross estate includes all interests in property that the decedent owned at the time of his death. Generally, such interests in property encompass the probate estate (i.e., interests in property administered in a probate proceeding by an executor or administrator) for the purpose of distributing such interests in property to the decedent's heirs. The decedent's heirs are identified either by the intestacy statutes, of the decedent's state of residence (if the decedent died intestate) or by will (if the decedent died testate).

6. T (p. 17–6)

The gift tax return (Form 709) must be filed by the donor for any particular calendar year in which the donor made a transfer to any donee (other than the donor's spouse) that was not entirely excluded from being subject to the gift tax. Transfers that are excluded from being subject to the gift tax include annual transfers of present interests to any donee, where the cumulative amount of such transfers does not exceed $11,000. A present interest is an interest that is not a future interest. A future interest is an interest in real or personal property in which possession or enjoyment of such property will come into being at some future point in time.

The taxable gift is the portion of a transferred interest in property to which the progressive gift tax rate structure is applied. Total taxable gifts for the current year is calculated as follows.

- Gross Gifts for the current period (the cumulative fair market value of all gifts made during the current period subject to the gift tax).
- Less:
  - The cumulative value of all applicable annual exclusions.
  - The marital deduction.
  - The charitable deduction.
- Equals: Total taxable gifts for the current year.

7. T (p. 17–18; footnote 27)

The due date for the filing of Form 709 is April 15 of the year following the year of taxable transfer. However, an automatic or approved extension for the filing of the same year's calendar Federal income tax return automatically extends the due date of the gift tax return until the extended due date of the Federal income tax return.

8. F (p. 17–29; not an administrative expense)

Administrative expenses under Section 2053 include selling expenses necessarily incurred to:

- Pay debts.
- Preserve the estate.
- Make final distributions.

For this purpose, brokers fees, survey fees, or transfer stamps are administrative expenses under Treas. Reg. Sec. 2053–3(d)(2).

In the instant case, the estate incurred an expense of $9,000 to paint and carpet a house to enhance such house's marketability. However, the estate must sell this house to make its final distributions to its beneficiaries. The expense is not an administrative expense under Section 2054 since the painting and carpeting expense was not necessarily incurred to sell the house.

9. T (p. 17–8)

The estate tax return (Form 706) must be filed by the decedent's representative for decedents dying in a particular year with a gross estate of more than the applicable exemption equivalent amount. The gross estate incorporates the value of all interests in property that are transferred by reason of the decedent's death. Such valuation is generally measured as of the date of the decedent's death. However, under Section 2032, the executor (administrator) may elect the Alternate Valuation Date as the date upon which an interest in property included in the gross estate is valued. Such date is the earlier of either:

- Six (6) months after the date of such decedent's death.
- Date of distribution or sale of the interest in property.

The Alternate Valuation Date may be elected only if as a result of such election:

- The gross estate is reduced.
- The estate tax liability decreases

Fill in the Blanks

1. full; adequate (p. 17–3)

    The Federal gift tax is an excise tax that applies to certain transfers of property, where property is transferred for less than a full and adequate consideration in money or money's worth.

2. cumulative (p. 17–5)

    The Federal gift tax is an excise tax that applies to certain transfers of property. The tax is calculated by applying a progressive tax rate structure to the cumulative value of such property transferred during life.

3. charitable deductions; marital deductions; annual exclusions (p. 17–6)

    The taxable gift is the portion of a transferred of an interest in property to which the progressive gift tax rate structure is applied. Total taxable gifts for the current year is calculated as follows.

    - Gross gifts for the current period (the cumulative fair market value of all gifts made during the current period subject to the gift tax).
    - Less:
        - The cumulative value of all applicable annual exclusions.
        - The marital deduction.
        - The charitable deduction
    - Equals: Total taxable gifts for the current year.

4. married persons (p. 17–16)

    With respect to a transfer of a present interest in property to a third party by either a husband or a wife, effective utilization of the annual exclusion can be accomplished by having the husband and wife elect to gift split under Section 2513. In this case, the husband and wife each file a gift tax return and elect to treat gifts made by either as if made one-half by each. In this way, they effectively double the annual exclusion available for each of their gifts.

5. gross estate (p. 17–19)

    The Federal estate tax is an excise tax that applies to transfers of property by reason of a decedent's death. The tax is calculated (in part) by applying a progressive tax rate structure to the cumulative value of property transferred either during life or at death.

    The estate tax return (Form 706) must be filed by the decedent's representative for decedents dying in a particular year with a gross estate of more than the applicable exclusion amount. The gross estate incorporates the value of all interests in property that are transferred by reason of the decedent's death.

6. curtesy (p. 17–20)

    The gross estate incorporates the value of all interests in property that are transferred by reason of the decedent's death. Under Section 2034, the value of the decedent spouse's gross estate includes the value of any interest in property held by the surviving spouse as dower or curtesy. Curtesy is the interest in real property owned by the wife during marriage that arises in the husband upon the death of his wife.

7. annuity (p. 17–23)

    The gross estate incorporates the value of all interests in property that are transferred by reason of the decedent's death. Under Section 2039, the value of the decedent's gross estate includes the value of any annuity that is received by a beneficiary by reason of the decedent's death, if such decedent at the time of his death possessed the right to receive such annuity. An annuity is a fixed sum payable to a person either for a fixed term (term annuity) or for life (life annuity).

CHAPTER 17
The Federal Gift and Estate Taxes

8. exercise; lapse; release (p. 17-27)

    Under Treas. Reg. Sec. 20.2041-1(c)(1), a general power of appointment is any power of appointment that is exercisable in favor of the decedent, his estate, his creditors or the creditors of his estate.

    The holder of a power of appointment may cause such power:

    - To be exercised. To exercise the power is to execute the terms of it.
    - To lapse. Lapse is the failure to execute a right during a period of time because of the occurrence or nonoccurrence of an event.
    - To be released. Release is the voluntary abandonment of a right.

9. general; special (p. 17-26)

    Under Treas. Reg. Sec. 20.2041-1(c)(1), a general power of appointment is any power of appointment that is exercisable in favor of the decedent, his estate, his creditors or the creditors of his estate. However, a general power of appointment does not include a special power of appointment. A special power of appointment is any power of appointment if by its terms it is either:

    - exercisable only in favor of one or more designated persons (or classes of persons) or
    - limited by an ascertainable standard.

    A power is limited by an ascertainable standard if the extent of the holder's duty to exercise (or not to exercise) is reasonably measurable in terms of his needs for health, education, support, or maintenance. For example, a power to consume, invade, or appropriate income or corpus (or both) for the benefit of the decedent, which is limited by an ascertainable standard (relating to the health, education, support, or maintenance of the decedent) is a special power of appointment.

10. general (p. 17-26)

    Under Treas. Reg. Sec. 20.2041-1(c)(1), a general power of appointment is any power of appointment that is exercisable in favor of the decedent, his estate, his creditors or the creditors of his estate. However, a general power of appointment does not include a special power of appointment. A special power of appointment is any power of appointment if by its terms it is either:

    - exercisable only in favor of one or more designated persons (or classes of persons) or
    - limited by an ascertainable standard.

11. pass property (p. 17-3)

    The Federal estate tax is an excise tax that applies to transfers of property by reason of a decedent's death. The tax is calculated (in part) by applying a progressive tax rate structure to the cumulative value of property transferred either during life or at death.

Multiple Choice

1. c (p. 17-40; nine months after decedent's death)

    The estate tax return (Form 706) must be filed by the decedent's representative for decedents dying in a particular year with a gross estate of more than the applicable exclusion amount ($1,000,000 in 2002). The estate tax return is due 9 months after the date of death.

    Eileen's estate tax return is due on March 28, 2003 (9 months after the date of her death of June 28, 2002). Thus, item c is correct.

2. a (p. 17-37; marital deduction reduces gross estate not estate tax)

Interests in property that are included in the gross estate are described in Section 2033 through Section 2044, inclusive.

The taxable estate is the portion of the gross estate to which the progressive estate tax rate structure is applied. The Unified Transfer Tax Credit, credit for state and foreign death taxes, and the credit for gift taxes deemed payable on post-1976 taxable gifts are all credited against the estate tax liability.

Thus, in the instant case, item a is correct, because the marital deduction is not a credit.

3. a (p. 17-11; transfer not for full consideration in excess of annual exclusion)

The gift tax return (Form 709) must be filed by the donor for any particular calendar year in which the donor made a transfer to any donee (other than the donor's spouse) that was not entirely excluded from being subject to the gift tax. Transfers that are excluded from being subject to the gift tax include:

- Annual transfers of present interests to any donee, where the cumulative amount of such transfers does not exceed $11,000.
- Transfers to a qualified political organization.
- Transfers for which a qualified disclaimer is made.
- Transfers directly to an educational institution on behalf of a donee for tuition.
- Transfers directly to health care providers on behalf of a donee for medical services.

Thus, in the instant case, item a is correct, because Nancy's transfer of property to her fiance is subject to the gift tax. Nancy's fiance is not her spouse. Further, the $20,000 value exceeds the $11,000.

4. c (p. 17-16; no requirement for filing joint income tax return)

With respect to a transfer of a present interest in property to a third party by either a husband or a wife, effective utilization of the annual exclusion can be accomplished by having the husband and wife elect to gift split under Section 2513. In this case, the husband and wife each file a gift tax return and elect to treat gifts made by either as if made one-half by each. In this way, they effectively double the annual exclusion available for each of their gifts.

Thus, in the instant case, item c is correct; filing a joint income tax return is not a requirement to gift split.

5. a (p. 17-6; transfers ($25,000 + $10,000 + $10,000 + $40,000) less deductions ($15,000 + $30,000) less exclusions ($40,000))

The taxable gift is the portion of a transferred interest in property to which the progressive gift tax rate structure is applied.

The amount of Joan's taxable gifts for 2002 is computed as follows.

Gross gifts ($26,000 + $11,000 + $11,000 + $41,000)	$89,000
Less:	
The cumulative value of all applicable annual exclusions ($11,000 + $11,000 + $11,000 + $11,000)	44,000
Marital deduction	30,000
Charitable deduction ($15,000)	15,000
Equals: Total taxable gifts for 2002	$ –0–

Thus, item a is correct.

6. d (p. 17–7; unified credit exclusion amount)

The estate tax return (Form 706) must be filed by the decedent's representative for decedents dying in a particular year with a gross estate of more than the applicable exclusion amount ($1,000,000 in 2002). Thus, item d is correct.

7. c (p. 17–18; April 15 of the following year)

The gift tax return (Form 709) must be filed by the donor for any particular calendar year in which the donor made a transfer to any donee (other than the donor's spouse) that was not entirely excluded from being subject to the gift tax. The due date of the return is April 15 of the subsequent year. Thus, in the instant case, item c is correct. The due date of the return (without extension) is April 15, 2003.

8. a (p. 17–16; must file to elect gift-splitting)

The gift tax return (Form 709) must be filed by the donor for any particular calendar year in which the donor made a transfer to any donee (other than the donor's spouse) that was not entirely excluded from being subject to the gift tax.

With respect to a transfer of a present interest in property to a third party by either a husband or a wife, effective utilization of the annual exclusion can be accomplished by having the husband and wife elect to gift split under Section 2513. In this case, the husband and wife each file a gift tax return and elect to treat gifts made by either as if made one-half by each.

Thus, in the instant case, item a is correct, because both spouses must individually file a gift tax return so that each spouse may elect and consent to gift splitting. Each of the other items do not require the filing of a gift tax return.

9. c (p. 17–16; Valerie remarried before the end of the year of the gift)

In order to elect and consent to gift splitting:

- spouses must be married to each other at the time of the transfer to the third party and
- if the spouses divorce later in the same year, remarriage of either spouse is precluded before year-end.

Thus, in the instant case, item c is correct because the remarriage of Valerie in 2002 (the year of the transfer) precludes Valerie and Dino from gift splitting.

10. d (p. 17–19; gross estate includes all property owned at death)

The gross estate incorporates the value of all interests in property that are transferred by reason of the decedent's death.

In the instant case, Jason's gross estate is calculated as follows.

Included in the value of the gross estate under Section 2033— ($300,000 + $20,000 + $250,000 + $50,000 + $1,000 + $6,500)	$627,500

Thus, item d is correct.

11. c (p. 17–8)

The gross estate incorporates the value of all interests in property that are transferred by reason of the decedent's death. The valuation is generally measured as of the date of the decedent's death. However, under Section 2032, the executor (administrator) may elect the alternate valuation date as the date upon which an interest in property included in the gross estate is valued. This date is the earlier of either:

- Six (6) months after the date of the decedent's death.
- Date of distribution or sale of the interest in property.

Ellie's gross estate is calculated as follows.

Included in the value of the gross estate (using the alternate valuation date) under Section 2033— ($275,000 (value when sold) + $450,000 + $125,000 + $100,000)	$950,000

Thus, item c is correct.

12. a (p. 17–6)

The taxable gift is the portion of a transferred interest in property to which the progressive gift tax rate structure is applied.

The amount of Chris' taxable gifts for 2002 is computed as follows.

Gross gifts ($100,000 + $100,000 + $200,000 + $100,000)	$500,000
Less:	
The cumulative value of all applicable annual exclusions ($11,000 + $11,000 + $11,000 + $11,000)	44,000
Charitable deduction	89,000
Equals: Total taxable gifts for 2002	$367,000

Thus, item a is correct. Further, items b, c, and d are incorrect because they are each inconsistent with item a.

13. b (p. 17–7; 2002 unified credit $345,800 − $121,800)

In the instant case, the 2002 unified transfer tax credit is $345,800 and the unified transfer tax credit available is $224,000 ($345,800 − $121,800). Thus, item b is correct.

14. a (p. 17–6,16)

The amount of Wellington's taxable gifts for 2002 (assuming Wellington and Paula elect and consent to gift splitting) is computed as follows.

Gross gifts ($42,000/2 + $100,000 + $16,000/2 + $52,000/2)	$155,000
Less:	
The cumulative value of all applicable annual exclusions ($11,000 + $11,000 + $8,000 + $11,000)	41,000
The marital deduction	89,000
Equals: Total taxable gifts for 2002	$ 25,000

Thus, item a is correct.

15. b (p. 17–8; irrevocable election)

The gross estate incorporates the value of all interests in property that are transferred by reason of the decedent's death. Such valuation is generally measured as of the date of the decedent's death. However, under Section 2032, the executor (administrator) may elect the alternate valuation date as the date upon which all interests in property included in the gross estate are valued, including the special use valuation of farmland. The election must be made on the original estate tax return. However, the election is ineffective where the original estate tax return is filed more than one year after the time prescribed by law (including extensions) for filing such return. If made, the election is irrevocable.

The alternate valuation date is the earlier of either:

- Six (6) months after the date of the decedent's death.
- Date of distribution or sale of such interest in property.

The alternate valuation date may be elected only if as a result of such election:

- The gross estate is reduced.
  - However, decreases in valuation due only to the lapse of time are ignored.
- The estate tax liability decreases.

Thus, in the instant case, item b is the right answer. The alternate valuation date, once elected, is irrevocable.

CHAPTER 18

Family Tax Planning

LEARNING OBJECTIVES

After completing Chapter 18, you should be able to:

1. Use various established concepts in carrying out the valuation process.
2. Apply the special use valuation method in appropriate situations.
3. Identify problems involved in valuing an interest in a closely held business.
4. Compare the income tax basis rules apply to property received by gift and by death.
5. Plan gifts so as to minimize gift taxes and avoid estate taxes.
6. Make gifts so as to avoid income taxes for the donor.
7. Reduce probate costs in the administration of an estate.
8. Apply procedures to reduce estate tax consequences.
9. Obtain liquidity for an estate.

KEY TERMS

Blockage rule
Buy-sell agreement
Conservation easements
Cross-purchase buy-sell
   agreement
Entity buy-sell agreement
Estate freeze
Living trust
Probate costs
Special use value
Step-down in basis
Step-up in basis

OUTLINE

I. **VALUATION CONCEPTS**
   A. Valuation in General
      1. Fair Market Value (FMV) is "the price at which property would change hands between a willing buyer and a willing seller, neither being under any compulsion to buy or sell and both having reasonable knowledge of relevant facts."
      2. FMV is not determined by a forced sale price.
      3. FMV is not determined by the sale price of the item in a market other than that in which the item is most commonly sold to the public.
      4. FMV is based on what the general public would pay; thus, sentiment should not play a part in its determination.
   B. Valuation of Specific Assets
      1. Stocks and bonds that are:
         a. traded on valuation date: mean between highest and lowest quoted prices on that date.
         b. recently traded: the inverse weighted-average of the mean between the highest and lowest prices quoted on the nearest dates before and after the valuation date.
      2. Notes receivable
         a. Receivables are generally valued at unpaid principal plus accrued interest.
         b. However, a lower value may be established due to:
            1. a low interest rate.
            2. distant maturity date.
            3. proof of entire or partial worthlessness.
      3. Insurance policies and annuity contracts
         a. The value of a life insurance policy on the life of a person other than the decedent, or the value of an annuity contract issued by a company regularly engaged in selling annuities, is the cost of a comparable contract.
         b. For noncommercial annuity contracts, special tables are issued by the IRS to assist in the determination of FMV.
      4. Life estates, terms for years, reversions, and remainders involve using IRS tables to assist in the determination of FMV.
   C. Real Estate and the Special Use Valuation Method
      1. Section 2032A permits an executor to elect to value certain classes of real estate at "current" use value, rather than "best" use value. The election is intended to protect heirs from having to sell a portion of a business to pay estate taxes.
      2. The special use valuation procedure permits a reduction of no more than $820,000 in 2002 ($800,000 for 2001).
      3. All of the following conditions must be satisfied.
         a. At least 50% of the adjusted value of the gross estate must consist of real or personal property devoted to the qualifying use (used in farming or a closely held business).
         b. At least 25% of the adjusted value of the gross estate must consist of the real property devoted to qualifying use, where qualifying property is considered at its "most suitable use" value for purposes of the 25% and 50% tests.
         c. For both the 50% and 25% tests, qualifying property is considered at its "most suitable use" value.
         d. A qualifying heir of the decedent is the recipient of qualifying property.
         e. The real property has been owned by the decedent or the decedent's family for five out of the eight years ending on date of decedent's death, and the property was being used for its qualifying purpose during that period.
         f. The decedent or a member of his family has participated materially in the operation of the qualifying purpose during the qualifying period.

4. Estate tax savings are recaptured from the heir if the property is sold or withdrawn from its qualifying use within 10 years.
D. Valuation Problems With a Closely Held Business
1. Goodwill may be present if the corporation's past earnings are higher than usual for the industry.
2. A discounted valuation may be justified if a minority interest is involved and the corporation has a poor dividend paying record.
3. The "blockage rule" permits a discount from the amount at which smaller lots are selling recognizing that, when a controlling interest is held, the per unit value may fall if a large block of shares are marketed at one time.
4. A discount may be recognized for lack of marketability of shares not traded in a market.
5. Buy-Sell Agreements and Valuation
   a. The main objective of a buy-sell agreement is to transfer a business without the risk of outsiders taking control. There are two types of buy-sell agreements: entity and cross-exchange agreements.
   b. In an entity buy-sell agreement, the business buys the interest of the withdrawing owner.
   c. In a cross-purchase buy/sell agreement, the surviving owners buy out the withdrawing owner.
   d. The purchase price will be included in the deceased owner's estate and will control for valuation purposes if:
      1. the price is the result of a bona fide business agreement.
      2. the agreement is not a device to transfer property to family members.
      3. the agreement is comparable to other arrangements entered into by persons dealing at arm's length.
6. Estate freezes are attempts by closely held corporation owners to maintain control over their business while minimizing estate tax consequences. The owners retain preferred stock and give common stock to family members. Under current law, this technique will not be successful as the full value of the business is attached to the common stock given away.
7. Family limited partnerships have become popular as tools to minimize estate tax consequences. Here, a partnership is formed to hold the stock of a closely held corporation. The owners are general partners, and make gifts of limited partnership interests to their children or grandchildren.

II. **INCOME TAX CONCEPTS**
A. Basis of Property Acquired by Gift
1. Basis determination depends upon when the gift was made and whether the property was subsequently sold for a gain or loss.
   a. After 1920 and before 1977
      1. Basis for gain is the donor's adjusted basis plus any gift tax paid.
      2. Basis for gain cannot be higher than FMV on the date of the gift.
      3. Basis for loss is the lower of the basis for gain or the FMV at the date of the gift.
   b. After 1976
      1. Basis for gain is the donor's adjusted basis plus the gift tax attributable to any appreciation up to the date of the gift.
      2. Basis for loss is the lower of the gain basis or the FMV at the date of the gift.
2. The donee's holding period includes the holding period of the donor.
B. Basis of Property Acquired by Death
1. Generally property acquired from a decedent is valued at its FMV on the date of death or alternate valuation date and the holding period automatically qualifies as long-term.
2. The surviving spouse's half of community property takes the same basis as the half included in the deceased spouse's gross estate.

3. Under the Section 1014(e) exception to the FMV at valuation date rules, decedent's basis in the property determined immediately before the death of the decedent, carries over to the donor/heir of the property. For Section 1014(e) to apply, the following conditions must be satisfied.
    a. The decedent must have received appreciated property as a gift during the one-year period ending with his or her death.
    b. The property is acquired from the decedent by the donor or the donor's spouse.
4. Income in respect of a decedent (IRD) is income which was earned by a decedent prior to his death but not recognized due to his/her method of accounting.
    a. For estate tax purposes income in respect of a decedent is valued at fair market value on the valuation date.
    b. For income tax purposes, the decedent's basis in IRD and the character of such IRD, determined immediately before the death of the decedent carries over to the estate or heirs.

III. **GIFT PLANNING**
   A. A plan of lifetime giving can minimize transfer taxes and income taxes through use of the annual exclusion by:
      1. spacing gifts over several years.
      2. making successive gifts of partial interests to effect the transfer of real property.
   B. Gifts of property expected to appreciate in value effectively remove subsequent appreciation from the donor's gross estate.
   C. Lifetime gifts may also minimize state gift/death taxes.
   D. Transferring income-producing assets from high-bracket taxpayers to low-bracket taxpayers can minimize income taxes for the family unit.

IV. **ESTATE PLANNING**
   A. Estate planning considers both the nontax and tax aspects of death.
   B. An estate plan should consider reducing the probate estate through:
      1. holding property in joint ownership with rights of survivorship.
      2. naming a life insurance beneficiary other than the estate.
      3. using a revocable living trust which at death becomes irrevocable.
   C. Estate taxes can be reduced either by decreasing the size of the gross estate or increasing the total allowable deductions. The lower the taxable estate, the less estate tax is generated. The following items should be considered:
      1. Making proper use of the marital deduction.
      2. Working effectively with the charitable deduction.
      3. Optimizing other deductions and losses allowed under § 2053 and § 2054.
   D. The liquidity of an estate is often strained between the date of death and the final disposition of the estate assets. The following should be considered for purposes of estate liquidity:
      1. Life insurance payable to the estate.
      2. A carefully drawn will.
      3. The judicious use of trust arrangements.
      4. Qualifying for the extension of time for the payment of death taxes.

STUDY GUIDE
CHAPTER 18
Family Tax Planning

TEST FOR SELF-EVALUATION—CHAPTER 18

True or False

Indicate which of the following statements is true or false by circling the correct answer.

T   F   1. If a Federal estate tax return does not have to be filed, an individual's basis in inherited property is the property's adjusted basis to the decedent at the date of death. (IRS 97 1A-7)

T   F   2. When a taxpayer dies, no gain is reported on depreciable personal property or real property that is transferred to his or her estate or beneficiary. (IRS 97 3A-3)

T   F   3. On February 1, 2002, John Smith, a cash basis taxpayer, sold his machine for $5,000, payable March 1 of the same year. His adjusted basis in the machine was $4,000. Mr. Smith died on February 15, 2002, before receiving payment. The gain to be reported as income in respect of the decedent is the $1,000 difference between the decedent's basis in the property and sales proceeds. (IRS 96 3A-12)

T   F   4. There are provisions that allow additional time for paying the estate tax. The usual extension of time to pay is up to 12 months from the date the payment is due. However, if you can show reasonable cause why it is impractical for you to pay the full amount of the tax due on the due date, the IRS may extend the time for payment up to 10 years. (IRS 96 3A-14)

T   F   5. Generally, any income generated by the property after the owner's death must be accounted for separately.

T   F   6. Generally, the income tax basis of property acquired from a person who died will be its fair market value on the date of death, or, if elected, on the alternate valuation date.

T   F   7. As it is possible to have a "step-up" in basis, it is also possible to have a "step-down" in basis for property received as the result of a death transfer.

T   F   8. When income must be included in both the gross income and the gross estate of a decedent, the individual is allowed a credit on his final income tax return in order to avoid double taxation.

T   F   9. To determine your basis in the property you receive as a gift, it is sometimes necessary to add all or part of the gift tax paid on the property. (IRS 94 1A-11)

T   F   10. The only importance in properly determining the value of property is to correctly compute the possible gift or estate tax.

T   F   11. Due to the conservative nature of the IRS, taxpayers are required to use wholesale prices when determining the value of property.

T   F   12. Shares in a mutual fund should be valued at the redemption or bid price of the security.

T   F   13. The value of property reflected on the estate tax return and subsequently accepted by the IRS is presumed to be correct; thus, any future change to that valuation by an heir requires the heir to rebut such presumption of correctness.

T   F   14.   The special valuation method allows certain classes of real estate to be valued at their "most suitable" use.

T   F   15.   Buy-sell agreements are useful tools in planning for estate liquidity.

Fill in the Blanks

Complete the following statements with the appropriate word(s) or amount(s).

1. The special use valuation procedure permits a reduction in estate tax valuation of no more than $_____.

2. To qualify for the special use valuation method, at least _____% of the adjusted value of the gross estate must consist of real or personal property devoted to a qualifying use.

3. The concept that recognizes that the per unit value of shares may fall when a large number of shares are sold at one time is called the "_____."

4. To meet the requirements of Section 6166, a decedent's interest in a farm or closely-held business must be more than _____ of his or her adjusted gross estate.

Multiple Choice

Choose the best answer for each of the following questions.

_____ 1. In 2002, Darryl received several acres of land from his father as a gift. At the time of the gift, the land had a fair market value of $85,000. The father's adjusted basis in the land was $105,000. Two years later, Darryl sold the land for $90,000. No events occurred that increased or decreased Darryl's basis in the land. What was Darryl's gain or (loss) on the sale of the land? (IRS 97 1C-49)

    a. ($15,000)
    b. $5,000
    c. $20,000
    d. $0

_____ 2. Jack received 50 shares of stock as an inheritance on July 15, 2002 from his father who died April 25, 2002. His father's adjusted basis in the stock was $65,000. The stock's fair market value on April 25, 2002, was $75,000. On October 25, 2002, its value was $85,000 and on the date Jack received the stock, it was $70,000. The alternative valuation date was not selected for filing the Federal estate tax return. Jack's basis in the inherited stock is: (IRS 97 1C-50)

    a. $65,000
    b. $70,000
    c. $75,000
    d. $85,000

_____ 3. Mr. Fitch died on December 1, 2002. The alternate valuation method was not elected. The assets in his estate were valued as of the date of death as follows:

Home		$400,000
Car		30,000
Stocks, bonds, and savings		350,000
Jewelry		25,000
Dividends, declared November 15, 2002, not paid as of December 1, 2002		5,000
Accrued interest on savings as of December 1, 2002		2,500
Life insurance (proceeds receivable by the estate)		300,000

What is the value of Mr. Fitch's gross estate? (IRS 97 3C-48)

   a. $1,112,500
   b. $1,110,000
   c. $1,105,000
   d. $812,500

_____ 4. Loretta died on January 20, 2002. The assets included in her estate were valued as follows:

	1-20-02	7-20-02	10-20-02
House	$900,000	$800,000	$700,000
Stocks	850,000	600,000	1,000,000

The executor sold the house on October 20, 2002 for $700,000. The alternative valuation date was properly elected. What is the value of Loretta's gross estate? (IRS 97 3C-49)

   a. $1,750,000
   b. $1,700,000
   c. $1,400,000
   d. $1,300,000

_____ 5. In 2002, Donna received land as a gift from her grandfather. At the time of the gift, the land had a fair market value of $80,000 and an adjusted basis of $100,000 to Donna's grandfather. Donna's grandfather paid no gift tax. One year later, Donna sold the land for $105,000. What was her gain or (loss) on this transaction? (IRS 96 1C-55)

   a. $5,000
   b. $15,000
   c. $20,000
   d. No gain or loss

_____ 6. During 2002, Juan received a gift of property from his uncle. At the time of the gift, the property had a fair market value of $100,000 and an adjusted basis to his uncle of $40,000. Juan's uncle paid a gift tax on the transfer of $18,000. What is Juan's basis in the property? (IRS 96 1C-56)

   a. $40,000
   b. $50,800
   c. $60,000
   d. $128,000

_____ 7. Mr. Hill inherited 1,000 shares of Pro Corporation stock from his father who died on March 8, 2002. His father paid $10 per share for the stock on September 1, 1975. The fair market value of the stock on the date of death was $50 per share. On September 8, 2002, the fair market value of the stock was $60 per share. Mr. Hill sold the stock for $75 a share on December 5, 2002. The estate qualified for, and the executor elected, the alternate valuation method. A Federal estate tax return was filed. What was Mr. Hill's basis in the stock on the date of sale? (IRS 96 1C-57)

    a. $50,000
    b. $60,000
    c. $75,000
    d. $150,000

_____ 8. On June 1, 2002, Kirk received a gift of income-producing real estate having a donor's adjusted basis of $50,000 at the date of the gift. The fair market value of the property at the date of the gift was $40,000. Kirk sold the property for $46,000 on August 1, 2002. How much gain or loss should Kirk report for 2002? (IRS 96 1C-67)

    a.   No gain or loss
    b. $4,000 short-term capital loss
    c. $4,000 ordinary loss
    d. $6,000 short-term capital gain

_____ 9. In 2002, Daniel inherited 100% of Candy Corporation's outstanding stock from his mother. The stock had a fair market value of $250,000 at the date of death and was reflected on Candy's balance sheet as:

Cash	$250,000
Capital stock	150,000
Accumulated earnings & profits	100,000

Daniel immediately withdrew $50,000 out of Candy Corporation as a dividend distribution. Later in 2002, pursuant to a plan of liquidation, Daniel withdrew the remaining $200,000 out of Candy. For 2002, how much will Daniel be required to report as ordinary dividend income and capital gain or (loss)? (IRS 96 3C-63)

	Ordinary Dividend	Capital Gain or (Loss)
a.	$ 0	$ 0
b.	$ 50,000	($ 50,000)
c.	$100,000	($100,000)
d.	$ 50,000	($250,000)

_____ 10. Mrs. Butler, a cash method taxpayer, died on July 31, 2002. A review of her records reflected that, as of July 31, 2002, she had received interest of $500 and wages of $80,000. Also, on stock that she owned, an $800 dividend was declared on June 20, 2002, and was payable on July 31, 2002. The dividend check was not received until August 3, 2002. What is the amount of income to be reported on Mrs. Butler's final income tax return? (IRS 96 3C-71)

    a. $80,000
    b. $80,500
    c. $80,800
    d. $81,300

STUDY GUIDE | CHAPTER 18
Family Tax Planning

SOLUTIONS TO CHAPTER 18 QUESTIONS

True or False

1. F   (p. 18–15; FMV on date of death)

    Generally, under Section 1014, the income tax basis of property in the hands of a person who acquires property from a decedent is the fair market value of such property on the date of the decedent's death. The determination of income tax basis within this context does not depend upon whether or not an estate tax return is filed.

2. T   (p. 18–15)

    The taxpayer's death does not trigger the realization and recognition of unrealized gains that would otherwise be reported on the decedent's last income tax return.

3. T   (p. 18–16)

    Generally, under Section 1014, the income tax basis of property in the hands of a person who acquires property from a decedent is the fair market value of such property on the date of the decedent's death. If property is received that was appreciated (depreciated) immediately before the decedent's death, a step-up (step-down) in income tax basis occurs automatically.

    However, the income tax basis of property acquired from a decedent that represents (in part) income in respect of a decedent (IRD) is not such property's fair market value on the date of the decedent's death. Rather, such property has an income tax basis equal to the decedent's adjusted basis immediately before his or her death, even though the decedent's estate tax return records the property at its fair market value. IRD is income earned by a decedent at the time of death but not recognized by the decedent under his/her method of accounting (e.g., accrued salary or installment sale gain).

    In the instant case, John Smith's estate tax return reflects an account (or note) receivable in the amount of $5,000. However, the income tax basis of such receivable in the hands of the estate (or heir) is $4,000. Thus, when the estate (or heir) receives payment of $5,000 in satisfaction of the receivable, the estate (or heir) realizes and recognizes a gain of $1,000 (amount realized of $5,000 – adjusted basis of $4,000) as income in respect of a decedent.

4. T   (p. 18–30)

    The estate tax return (Form 706) must be filed by the decedent's representative for decedents dying in a particular year with a gross estate of more than the automatically exemption equivalent amount. The estate tax return is due 9 months after the date of death. In addition, the estate tax is payable at the same time that the estate tax return is due. However, an extension of time to pay may be granted.

    Under Section 6161(a)(1), based on a showing of reasonable cause, the District Director may grant the executor an extension of time to pay the estate tax of up to 12 months from the time such tax is due. Also, under Section 6161(a)(2), based on a showing of undue hardship, the District Director may grant the executor an extension of time to pay the estate tax of up to 10 years from the time such tax is due.

5. T   (p. 18–4)

    The estate tax return (Form 706) must be filed by the decedent's representative for decedents dying in a particular year with a gross estate of more than the exemption equivalent amount. The gross estate incorporates the value of all interests in property that are transferred by reason of the decedent's death. Such interests in property that are included in the gross estate are described in Section 2033 through Section 2044, inclusive. For example, under Section 2033, the gross estate includes all interests in property that the decedent owned at the time of his death. Generally, such interests in property encompass the probate estate (i.e., interests in property administered in a probate proceeding by an executor or administrator) for the purpose of distributing such interests to the decedent's heirs. Examples of property included in the gross estate under Section 2033 include:

- Installment sale note.
- Accrued interest receivable.
- Accrued salary receivable.
- Accrued rent receivable.

Thus, interests in property included in the gross estate include receivables arising from income earned (but not yet paid) at the date of the decedent's death. However, income earned post date of death is the income and property of either the estate or an heir. It is not reported on the decedent's estate tax return.

6. T (p. 18–16)

The estate tax return (Form 706) must be filed by the decedent's representative for decedents dying in a particular year with a gross estate of more than the applicable exemption equivalent amount. The gross estate incorporates the value of all interests in property that are transferred by reason of the decedent's death. Such valuation is generally measured as of the date of the decedent's death. However, under Section 2032, the executor (administrator) may elect the alternate valuation date as the date upon which an interest in property included in the gross estate is valued. Such date is the earlier of either:

- six (6) months after the date of the decedent's death or
- date of distribution or sale of such interest in property.

7. T (p. 18–16)

Under Section 1014, the income tax basis of property in the hands of a person who acquires property from a decedent is the fair market value of such property on the date of the decedent's death. If property is received that was appreciated (depreciated) immediately before the decedent's death, a step-up (step-down) in income tax basis occurs automatically.

8. F (p. 18–4; transfer tax and income tax are separate and distinct, therefore no double taxation)

Interests in property included in the gross estate include receivables arising from income earned (but not yet paid). Even though these interests are subject to the estate tax as interests in property that are transferred by reason of the decedent's death, some of these interests may represent earned income that is included in the taxable income for the period ending with the decedent's death. Accordingly, the same interest in property may:

- Reflect earnings (and be subject to the Federal income tax).
- Be the subject of a transfer by reason of the decedent's death (and be subject to the Federal estate tax).

If the same interest in property is (in fact) subject to both the Federal income tax and the Federal estate tax, a mitigating benefit (e.g., a credit) does not arise because the nature of the two taxes is qualitatively different (transfer vs. income). Accordingly, the issue of double taxation does not arise.

9. T (p. 18–14)

Generally, under Section 1015, the income tax basis of property in the hands of a taxpayer who acquires property by gift depends upon the amount realized by such person upon a subsequent sale of such property. If the amount realized on a subsequent sale exceeds the gain basis, the income tax basis of the property is the gain basis of such property and the taxpayer realizes and recognizes a gain. Here, gain basis is equal to the donor's adjusted basis immediately before the gift, increased by the portion of the gift tax paid (if any) that is attributable to the property's appreciation (if any) at the time of the gift. On the other hand, if the amount realized on a subsequent sale is less than the loss basis, the income tax basis of the property is the loss basis of such property and the taxpayer realizes and recognizes a loss. Here, loss basis is equal to the lesser of either:

- the donor's gain basis or
- the fair market value of the property at the time of the gift.

Further, if the amount realized on a subsequent sale is greater than the loss basis but less than the gain basis, no gain or loss is recognized.

10.   F   (p. 18–14, 15; basis for depreciation or later disposition)

For property transferred by reason of the decedent's death, determining the fair market value of such property at the date of the decedent's death is important not only for estate tax purposes, but also for subsequent income tax purposes. Such determination is important for income tax purposes because, generally, under Section 1014, the income tax basis of property in the hands of a person who acquires property from a decedent is the fair market value of such property at the date of the decedent's death. If property is received that is appreciated (depreciated) immediately before the decedent's death, a step-up (step-down) in income tax basis occurs automatically. Accordingly, the determination of income tax basis within this context does not depend upon whether or not an estate tax return is filed.

11.   F   (p. 18–2; fair market value)

The estate tax return (Form 706) must be filed by the decedent's representative for decedents dying in a particular year with a gross estate of more than the applicable exemption equivalent amount. The gross estate incorporates the fair market value of all interests in property that are transferred by reason of the decedent's death. Such interests in property that are included in the gross estate are described in Section 2033 through Section 2044, inclusive. For example, under Section 2033, the gross estate includes the fair market value of all interests in property that the decedent owned at the time of his death. Under Treas. Reg. Sec. 20.2031–1(b), fair market value is defined as the price at which an interest in property would change hands between a willing buyer and a willing seller where:

- Neither person is under a compulsion to buy or sell.
- Both persons have reasonable knowledge of the relevant facts.

Further, under Treas. Reg. Sec. 20.2031–1(b), the appropriate market for such determination is the market within which the interest in property is sold to the public, rather than a wholesale market or a forced sales market.

12.   T   (p. 18–3)

Under Treas. Reg. Sec. 20.2031–1(b), the appropriate market for such determination is the market within which the interest in property is sold to the public, rather than a wholesale market or a forced sales market. In particular, under Treas. Reg. Sec. 20.2031–8(b), the fair market value of shares in a mutual fund (open-end investment company) should be determined based upon such shares' public redemption or bid price.

13.   T   (p. 18–18)

Under Rev. Rul. 54–97, if an estate tax return is filed, values attributed to interests in property as reflected on the estate tax return are presumed to be correct for estate tax and income tax purposes. However, an heir who disagrees with the valuation of a particular interest in property as reflected on the estate tax return has the following two options.

- If the statute of limitations has not expired to preclude amending the estate tax return, then the executor can amend the estate tax return, subject to approval by the IRS.
- The heir can rebut the presumption of the estate tax return's correctness with respect to the valuation of a particular interest in property as reflected on the return.

14.   F   (p. 18–6; current use)

Under Treas. Reg. Sec. 20.2031–1(b), the appropriate market for such determination is the market within which the interest in property is sold to the public, rather than a wholesale market or a forced sales market. In particular, under Section 2032A, qualifying real property used either as a family farm or in a closely held business may be valued for estate tax purposes based upon its current business use, rather than upon its highest and best use. This special valuation method may effectively reduce the value associated with the qualifying real property for both estate tax and income tax purposes, at least relative to such property's value at its highest and best use. However, the reduction is limited to $820,000 for decedents dying in 2002.

15. T (p. 18–10)

Under Treas. Reg. Sec. 20.2031–1(b), the appropriate market for such determination is the market within which the interest in property is sold to the public, rather than a wholesale market or a forced sales market. In particular, with respect to a business interest, a buy-sell agreement will generally be respected for estate tax purposes. In general, a buy-cell agreement functions to effectuate the disposition of a business interest consistent with the intentions of all associates and conditioned upon the occurrence or nonoccurrence of some event. Positive indirect effects of such agreement include:

- A mechanism for the determination of the fair market value of such interest for estate tax purposes.
- Liquidity for the estate.

Fill in the Blanks

1. $820,000 for 2002 (p. 18–6)

   This special valuation method may effectively reduce the value associated with the qualifying real property for both estate tax and income tax purposes at least relative to such property's value at its highest and best use. However, the reduction is limited to $820,000 for decedents dying in 2002 ($800,000 for 2001).

2. 50 (p. 18–6)

   Under Section 2032A, qualifying real property used either as a family farm or in a closely held business may be valued for estate tax purposes based upon its current business use, rather than upon its highest and best use. This special valuation method may effectively reduce the value associated with the qualifying real property for both estate tax and income tax purposes at least relative to such property's value at its highest and best use. In order to qualify, at least 50% of the adjusted value of the gross estate must consist of real or personal property devoted to the qualifying use. However, the reduction is limited to $820,000 for decedents dying in 2002.

3. blockage rule (p. 18–8)

   Under Treas. Reg. Sec. 20.2031–1(b), the appropriate market for such determination is the market within which the interest in property is sold to the public, rather than a wholesale market or a forced sales market. In particular, within the context of valuing stock representing a controlling interest of a corporation (where a market for such stock exists), the price at which smaller lots are sold within the established market can be used to calculate the value of the controlling interest. However, such value is discounted under the blockage rule. The blockage rule recognizes the effect (a downward shift in the per unit price of stock) of the interaction of supply and demand factors when a large block of shares is offered for sale.

4. 35% (p. 18–30)

   Under Section 6166, the executor (of an estate of a decedent owning a qualifying closely held business interest on the date of his death) may elect to pay the estate tax associated with such interest in installments. Specifically, installment payments of estate tax and associated interest may be paid over 14 years as follows.

   - For the first 4 years, interest only.
   - For the next 10 years, estate tax and associated interest.

   A qualifying closely held business interest is an interest where the value of such interest represents more than 35% of the adjusted gross estate.

Multiple Choice

1. d (p. 18–14; gain basis is adjusted basis + gift tax on appreciation; loss basis is lesser of gain basis or FMV, when amount realized is between gain basis and loss basis—no gain or loss)

    In the instant case,

    - Gain basis is $105,000 (the father's adjusted basis immediately before the gift).
    - Loss basis is $85,000 (the lesser of either the donor's gain basis of $105,000 or the fair market value of the property of $85,000 at the time of the gift).

    Since the amount realized of $90,000 is greater than the loss basis but less than the gain basis, no gain or loss is recognized. Thus, item d is correct.

2. c (p. 18–15; FMV on date of death)

    Under Section 1014, the income tax basis of property in the hands of a person who acquires property from a decedent is the fair market value of such property on the date of the decedent's death. If property is received that was appreciated (depreciated) immediately before the decedent's death, a step-up (step-down) in income tax basis occurs automatically.

    In the instant case, Jack's income tax basis for the 50 shares of stock is $75,000 (the fair market value of the stock on the date of Jack's father's death). Thus, item c is correct.

3. a (p. 18–2; all listed assets are included)

    Under Section 2033, the gross estate includes the fair market value of all interests in property that the decedent owned at the time of his death.

    In addition, under Section 2042, the gross estate includes the insurance proceeds receivable by the executor under policies on the life of the decedent.

    In the instant case, the value of the gross estate includes:

Under 2033: ($400,000 + $30,000 + $350,000 + $25,000 + $5,000 + $2,500)	$ 812,500
Under 2042:	300,000
Total Gross Estate	$1,112,500

    Thus, item a is correct.

4. c (p. 18–2; 6 months after death, prior to house sale)

    The gross estate incorporates the value of all interests in property that are transferred by reason of the decedent's death. Such valuation is generally measured as of the date of the decedent's death. However, under Section 2032, the executor (administrator) may elect the alternate valuation date as the date upon which an interest in property included in the gross estate is valued. Such date is the earlier of either:

    - six (6) months after the date of the decedent's death or
    - date of distribution or sale of such interest in property.

    In the instant case, the value of the gross estate includes:

Under 2033:		
	House (7/20/02)	$ 800,000
	Stocks (7/20/02)	600,000
Total		$1,400,000

    Thus, item c is correct.

5. a (p. 18–14; $105,000 − $100,000 = $5,000; gain basis is $100,000)

Generally, under Section 1015, the income tax basis of property in the hands of a taxpayer that acquires property by gift depends upon the amount realized by such person upon a subsequent sale of such property.

In the instant case,

- Gain basis is $100,000 (the grandfather's adjusted basis immediately before the gift).
- Loss basis is $80,000 (the lesser of either the donor's gain basis of $100,000 or the fair market value of the property of $80,000 at the time of the gift).

Since the amount realized of $105,000 is greater than the gain basis, gain is realized and recognized as follows.

Amount Realized	$105,000
Less: Adjusted Basis (Gain Basis)	100,000
Equals: Gain Realized and Recognized	$ 5,000

Thus, item a is correct.

6. b (p. 18–14; 60% of gift tax (appreciation) + donor's adjusted basis)

Generally, under Section 1015, the income tax basis of property in the hands of a taxpayer that acquires property by gift depends upon the amount realized by such person upon a subsequent sale of such property.

In the instant case,

- Gain basis is $50,800 (the uncle's adjusted basis immediately before the gift of $40,000 increased by the portion of the gift tax paid of $18,000 that is attributable to the property's appreciation ($60,000/$100,000) at the time of the gift.
- Loss basis is $50,800 (the lesser of either the donor's gain basis of $50,800 or the fair market value of the property of $100,000 at the time of the gift).

Thus, Juan's basis in the property is $50,800 and item b is correct.

7. b (p. 18–2; 1,000 shares @ $60 per share, alternate valuation date, September 8)

Under Section 1014, the income tax basis of property in the hands of a person who acquired property from a decedent is the fair market value of such property at the date of the decedent's death. However, if the executor makes an election under Section 2032, the income tax basis is the fair market value of such property on the appropriate alternate valuation date. Such date is the earlier of either:

- six (6) months after the date of the decedent's death or
- date of distribution or sale of such interest in property.

In the instant case, Mr. Hill's income tax basis for the 1,000 shares of stock is $60,000 [the fair market value per share of stock of $60 (valued as of the appropriate alternate valuation date: six (6) months after the date of the father's death) multiplied by 1,000 shares].

Thus, item b is correct.

8. a (p. 18–14; donor's basis = gain basis, loss basis is lesser of FMV, $40,000, or gain basis, $50,000, when amount realized is between gain basis and loss basis—no gain or loss)

Generally, under Section 1015, the income tax basis of property in the hands of a taxpayer that acquires property by gift depends upon the amount realized by such person upon a subsequent sale of such property.

In the instant case,

- Gain basis is $50,000 (the donor's adjusted basis immediately before the gift).
- Loss basis is $40,000 (the lesser of either the donor's gain basis of $50,000 or the fair market value of the property of $40,000 at the time of the gift).

Since the amount realized of $46,000 is greater than the loss basis of $40,000 but less than the gain basis of $50,000, no gain or loss is recognized.

Thus, item a is correct.

9. b (p. 18–15; $50,000 dividend is ordinary, amount realized of $200,000 less basis of $250,000)

Under Section 1014, the income tax basis of property in the hands of a person who acquired property from a decedent is the fair market value of such property at the date of the decedent's death. If property is received that was appreciated (depreciated) immediately before the decedent's death, a step-up (step-down) in income tax basis occurs automatically.

To the extent that a Section 301 distribution is made from corporate earnings and profits (E & P), the distribution is a dividend, taxed as ordinary income under Section 301(c)(1).

Under Section 331(a), a distribution from a corporation to a shareholder in complete liquidation of the corporation is treated as a sale or exchange of the shareholder's stock.

In the instant case:

- The income tax basis of Candy Corporation's stock in the hands of Daniel is $250,000 (the fair market value of such stock on the date of the decedent's death).
- Under Section 301, the current dividend of $50,000 is ordinary dividend income.
- Under Section 331, the $200,000 liquidating distribution is treated as an amount realized in exchange for Candy Corporation's stock. Thus, Daniel's realized and recognized capital gain (or loss) is calculated as follows.

Amount Realized	$200,000
Less: Adjusted Basis	250,000
Equals: Gain (or Loss) Realized and Recognized	($ 50,000)

Thus, item b is correct.

10. b (p. 18–17; $80,000 + $500, dividend is IRD)

The income tax basis of property acquired from a decedent that represents (in part) income in respect of a decedent (IRD) is not such property's fair market value at the date of the decedent's death. Rather, such property has an income tax basis equal to the decedent's adjusted basis, even though the decedent's estate tax return reports the property at its fair market value. IRD is income earned by a decedent at the time of death but not recognized by the decedent under his/her method of accounting (e.g., accrued salary or installment sale gain).

Further, under Section 2033, the gross estate includes all interests in property that the decedent owned at the time of death, including interest, salary, and rent receivables.

In the instant case:

- As Mrs. Butler was a cash method taxpayer, the $800 dividend check is IRD since it was received after the date of Mrs. Butler's death. Thus, the $800 dividend is reported by either the estate or an heir and not reported on Mrs. Butler's final income tax return.
- The interest of $500 and wages of $80,000 were received by Mrs. Butler. Thus, the executor of Mrs. Butler's estate (as Mrs. Butler was a cash method taxpayer) reports $80,500 of wages and interest on Mrs. Butler's final income tax return.

CHAPTER 19

Income Taxation of Trusts and Estates

LEARNING OBJECTIVES

After completing Chapter 19, you should be able to:

1. Use working definitions with respect to trusts, estates, beneficiaries, and other parties
2. Identify the steps in determining the accounting and taxable income of a trust or estate and the related taxable income of the beneficiaries.
3. Illustrate the uses and implications of distributable net income.
4. Use the special rules that apply to trusts where the creator (grantor) of the trust retains certain rights.

KEY TERMS

Complex trust
Corpus
Distributable net income (DNI)
Expenses in respect of a decedent

Grantor
Grantor trust
Income in respect of a decedent (IRD)

Reversionary interest
Simple trust
Sprinkling trust

OUTLINE

I. **AN OVERVIEW OF SUBCHAPTER J**
   A. A trust refers to an arrangement created by a will or by an inter vivos declaration through which the trustee takes title to property for the purpose of protecting or conserving it for the benefit of named beneficiaries.
   B. Typically, three parties are involved in the creation and operation of a trust.
      1. The grantor transfers property which becomes the principal or corpus of the trust.
      2. The trustee manages the trust according to the terms of the trust document and applicable local law.
      3. The beneficiary receives the income or property from the trust.
      4. Certain trusts are not recognized for income tax purposes.
         a. Grantor trusts (where the grantor is also the trustee).
         b. Trusts where the same individual is grantor, trustee and sole beneficiary.
   C. Trusts typically have two types of beneficiaries:
      1. The beneficiary with an *income interest* receives the accounting income.
      2. The beneficiary with a *remainder interest* receives the trust property (called corpus) when the trust terminates.
   D. If the grantor retains the remainder interest, the interest is known as a *reversionary interest*.
   E. If the trustee can determine the timing of the income or corpus distributions, or the beneficiaries who will receive them, the trust is known as a *sprinkling trust*.
   F. Each year a trust must be classified as either simple or complex.
      1. A simple trust:
         a. is required to distribute its entire accounting income each year.
         b. does not have a qualified charitable organization as a beneficiary.
         c. makes no distribution of corpus during the year.
      2. A complex trust is any trust that is not a simple trust.
   G. An estate is created upon the death of every individual to:
      1. collect and conserve the decedent's assets,
      2. satisfy the decedent's liabilities, and
      3. distribute the remaining assets to the decedent's heirs.

II. **NATURE OF TRUST AND ESTATE INCOME TAXATION**
   A. The taxable income of an estate or trust is taxed to the entity (or beneficiaries) to the extent that each receives accounting income.
   B. Income Taxation Filing Requirements
      1. Form 1041, U.S. Fiduciary Income Tax Return, is used by trusts and estates.
      2. An estate must file if it has $600 or more gross income for the tax year.
      3. A trust must file if it has $600 or more gross income and/or any taxable income.
      4. The return is due on the 15th day of the fourth month after the close of the entity's tax year.
   C. Tax Accounting Periods and Payments
      1. An estate or trust may use many of the tax accounting methods available to individuals.
      2. An estate may select any fiscal year (including a calendar year).
      3. A trust, other than a tax-exempt trust, must use the calendar year.
      4. Trusts and estates having tax years ending 2 or more years after the death of the decedent, are required to make quarterly estimated tax payments.
   D. Tax Rates and Personal Exemptions
      1. Trusts and estates use a compressed tax rate schedule as compared with individuals.
      2. Tax on net capital gains is subject to the same limitations as those that apply to individuals.
      3. The alternative minimum tax may apply (but is unusual, except where the exercise of stock options is involved).

STUDY GUIDE / CHAPTER 19 / Income Taxation of Trusts and Estates

4. Trusts and estates are allowed a personal exemption, as follows:
   a. simple trusts, $300.
   b. complex trusts, $100.
   c. estates, $600.

III. **TAXABLE INCOME OF TRUSTS AND ESTATES**
   A. Trust and estate taxable income computation involves 5 steps.
      1. Determine the accounting income of the entity.
      2. Compute entity taxable income before the distribution deduction.
      3. Determine distributable net income (DNI) and the distribution deduction.
      4. Compute entity taxable income (step 2 less step 3).
      5. Allocate DNI to the beneficiaries and identify the character of such allocated amounts.
   B. Entity Accounting Income
      1. Accounting income is the amount that an income beneficiary of a trust or estate is eligible to receive.
      2. Accounting income may be defined in the will or trust agreement; however, if not, state law prevails.
      3. The calculation of accounting income must take into account allocations of specific items of income and expenditure to income or corpus.
   C. Gross Income
      1. Gross income of a trust or estate is determined in a manner similar to that of an individual.
      2. The basis of assets:
         a. acquired from a decedent = FMV on date of death or alternate valuation date.
         b. acquired by gift = donor's basis.
         c. acquired by purchase = cost.
      3. Income in respect of decedent (IRD) is included in the gross income of an estate or trust.
         a. Examples include accrued salary, interest, rent and other income that were not constructively received before death.
         b. Expenses related to the IRD that were not reported on the final income tax return of the decedent (e.g., interest and taxes) may be claimed by the recipient.
         c. The fair market value of the right to IRD is also included in the decedent's gross estate.
   D. Ordinary Deductions
      1. Deductions are:
         a. determined in a manner similar to that of an individual, where many deductions are subject to the 2% of AGI floor.
         b. allowed for reasonable administration expenses.
         c. allowed for expenses in respect of a decedent.
   E. Deductions for Losses
      1. Eligible deductions include:
         a. casualty or theft losses not covered by insurance.
         b. NOLs, where trade or business income is generated.
         c. net capital losses that are taken into account on the fiduciary income tax return.
   F. Charitable Contributions
      1. To be eligible for deduction, the charitable contribution:
         a. must be made pursuant to the will (or trust agreement) and such amount must be reasonably determinable from the document.
         b. must be made to a qualified organization.
         c. generally, must be paid in the year claimed.
      2. The deduction is limited to the entity's gross income in the year of contribution.
   G. Deductions for Distributions to Beneficiaries
      1. Distributable net income (DNI) is used in computing the amount of the entity's distribution deduction.
      2. DNI is the maximum amount of the distribution on which the beneficiaries may be taxed.

3. DNI is the maximum amount that can be used by the entity as a distribution deduction for the year.
4. The composition of DNI carries over to the beneficiaries.
5. The DNI computation begins by determining the entity's taxable income before the distribution deduction. This amount is modified by:
   a. adding back the personal exemption.
   b. adding back net tax-exempt interest.
   c. adding back net capital losses.
   d. subtracting any net capital gains allocable to corpus.

IV. TAXATION OF BENEFICIARIES
A. Distributions by Simple Trusts
   1. The maximum amount taxable is the trust's DNI. However, since DNI may include net tax-exempt income, the taxable amount may be less than DNI.
   2. When there is more than one income beneficiary, the elements of DNI are apportioned ratably according to the amount required to be distributed.
B. Distributions by Estates and Complex Trusts
   1. Distributions are divided into two tiers, as follows:
      a. First tier distributions: income that is required to be distributed currently, even if not distributed.
      b. Second tier distributions: all other amounts properly paid, credited, or required to be distributed.
   2. If first tier distributions exceed DNI, second tier distributions are not taxed. A pro-rata formula is used to allocate DNI among the first-tier beneficiaries.

$$\frac{\text{First-tier distribution to Beneficiary A}}{\text{First-tier distributions to all Beneficiaries} - \text{DNI}} = \text{Beneficiary A's share of DNI}$$

   3. If first tier distributions do not exceed DNI, second tier distributions are taxed to the extent of such excess DNI. A pro-rata formula is used to allocate DNI among second-tier beneficiaries.

$$\frac{\text{Second-tier distributions to Beneficiary A}}{\text{Second-tier distributions to all Beneficiaries} - \text{Remaining DNI}} = \text{Beneficiary A's Share of DNI}$$

C. Character of Income
   1. The character of income distributed retains its same character in the hands of the beneficiary. Distributions are treated as consisting of the same proportion as the DNI items.
   2. A special allocation is permitted to the extent required in the trust agreement (or local law) and to the extent that such allocation has an economic effect independent of income tax consequences.
D. Losses in the Termination Year
   1. A negative taxable income incurred in the last year of an entity's existence is allowed to the beneficiaries as a deduction *from* AGI.
      a. The deduction amount is in proportion to the corpus assets that each beneficiary receives.
      b. The deduction is a miscellaneous itemized deduction, subject to the 2% of AGI floor.
   2. Carryovers of other losses (NOLs and net capital losses) flow through to the beneficiaries in the termination year and may be used as deductions for AGI.
E. The Sixty-Five Day Rule
   1. Amounts paid or credited to beneficiaries in the first 65 days of the estate or trust's tax year may be treated as paid on the last day of the previous year.
   2. This allows the trustee some flexibility in timing distributions.

V. GRANTOR TRUSTS
A. The creation of a reversionary trust is subject to the Federal gift tax. If the grantor dies before the income interest expires, the present value of the reversionary interest will be included in his gross estate.

- B. Moreover, Section 674 provides that the grantor will be treated as the owner of any portion of a trust and taxed on its income, if he or she retains:
    1. the beneficial enjoyment of the corpus, or
    2. the power to dispose of the trust income without the approval or consent of any adverse party.
- C. There are exceptions to the above rule that, when considered, will not cause the income to be taxed to the grantor. These include the power to:
    1. apply the income toward the support of the grantor's dependents.
    2. allocate trust income or corpus among charitable beneficiaries.
    3. invade corpus on behalf of a designated beneficiary.
    4. withhold income from a beneficiary during his or her minority or disability.
    5. allocate receipts and disbursements between income and corpus.
- D. If certain administrative powers are retained by the grantor (or a nonadverse party), the income from the trust will be taxed to the grantor. These powers include:
    1. the power to deal with the trust income or property for less than full and adequate consideration.
    2. the power to borrow from the trust without adequate interest or security.
    3. the power to revoke the trust.
- E. A grantor is taxed on all or part of the income of a trust when, at the discretion of the grantor or a non-adverse party (without the consent of any adverse party), the income is or may be:
    1. distributed to the grantor (or the grantor's spouse).
    2. accumulated for future distribution to the grantor (or the grantor's spouse).
    3. applied to premium payments on life insurance policies on the life of the grantor (or the grantor's spouse).

TEST FOR SELF-EVALUATION—CHAPTER 19

True or False

Indicate which of the following statements is true or false by circling the correct answer.

T F 1. Les, as executor of the estate of his deceased father, must sell his father's house to make distributions to all beneficiaries. Les paid $9,000 to paint and carpet the house to enhance its marketability. The $9,000 Les paid is deductible from the gross estate to compute the taxable estate. (IRS 97 3A-4)

T F 2. The beneficiaries succeeding to the estate's property are not permitted to claim unused net operating loss carryovers from the estate's last tax year. (IRS 97 3C-6)

T F 3. A beneficiary of a complex trust must include in his taxable income the income that is required to be distributed only if the income is actually distributed during the tax year. (IRS 97 3C-11)

T F 4. If the estate has unused capital loss carryovers or excess deductions for its last tax year, they are allowed to those beneficiaries who succeed to the estate's property. (IRS 96 3A-18)

T F 5. A trust may be a simple trust for one year and a complex trust for another year. (IRS 96 3A-20)

Fill in the Blanks

Complete the following statements with the appropriate word(s) or amount(s).

1. A trust involves three parties: a _____, a _____, and a _____.

2. A _____ is the transferor of the property and the creator of the trust.

3. Beneficiaries fall into two categories: those entitled to _____ from the trust and those entitled to the _____ upon the expiration of the _____ interest.

4. The fiduciary return is due not later than the fifteenth day of the _____ month following the close of the entity's taxable year.

5. _____ is the maximum amount that can be used by the entity as a distribution deduction for the year.

6. For estates and complex trusts, income required to be distributed currently, whether distributed or not, is classified as a _____ distribution.

7. The creation of a reversionary trust is subject to the Federal _____ tax.

8. When an income interest in a trust is based on a beneficiary's life, such beneficiary is known as the _____.

STUDY GUIDE
CHAPTER 19
Income Taxation of Trusts and Estates

Multiple Choice

Choose the best answer for each of the following questions.

_____ 1. Joan died on August 18. All of the following statements are correct except: (IRS 97 3B-23)

   a. Joan's death did not close the tax year of a partnership in which she was a partner before it would normally end.
   b. Medical expenses paid by Joan before her death are deductible on her final income tax return if deductions are itemized.
   c. On Joan's final return, all income is reported on the accrual method of accounting regardless of the accounting method that Joan employed.
   d. Any tax credits that applied to Joan before her death may be claimed on her final income tax return.

_____ 2. In which circumstance must an estate of a decedent make estimated tax payments? (IRS 97 3B-24)

   a. The estate has a tax year ending 2 or more years after the date of the decedent's death.
   b. The estate has income in excess of $400.
   c. The estate has a first tax year that covers 12 months.
   d. None, since an estate is not required to make estimated tax payments.

_____ 3. Stuart died on May 15, 2002. After his death, his estate received interest of $500, dividends of $700, salary of $4,000 and life insurance proceeds of $35,000. How much should Stuart's estate include in income on its 2002 income tax return? (IRS 97 3B-25)

   a. $40,200
   b. $36,200
   c. $5,200
   d. $1,200

_____ 4. With regard to a trust, all of the following statements are correct except: (IRS 97 3B-30)

   a. A trust is a separate taxable entity.
   b. The income allocated to a beneficiary retains the same character in his hands as it had in the hands of the trust.
   c. If income is required to be distributed currently or is properly distributed to a beneficiary, the trust is regarded as a conduit with respect to that income.
   d. Generally, the trust is effectively taxed on income currently distributed and on the remaining portion accumulated.

_____ 5. A trust which is required to distribute all of its income currently, does not make a distribution other than of current income and does NOT make charitable contributions is called a (IRS 97 3B-31)

   a. Complex trust
   b. Simple trust
   c. Estate
   d. Totten trust

_____ 6. Which of the following is a characteristic of a "simple" trust? (IRS 97 3B-32)

   a. A trust in the final year of administration.
   b. A trust which is partially liquidated during the taxable year.
   c. A trust which is allowed a personal exemption of $300.
   d. A trust which distributes an amount out of corpus.

_____ 7. Dave, the grantor, set up two irrevocable trusts, Trust D and Trust G. The income of Trust D is to be accumulated for distribution to Dave's spouse after Dave's death. The income of Trust G is to be accumulated for Dave's children, whom Dave is legally obligated to support. The trustee has the discretion to use any part of the income for the children's support. Half of the income was so used this year. Based on this information, which of the following statements is correct? (IRS 97 3B-33)

    a. None of the income from either trust is taxed to Dave.
    b. No income from Trust D is taxed to Dave and half of the income from Trust G is taxed to Dave.
    c. All the income from Trust D and half the income from Trust G is taxed to Dave.
    d. All the income from both trusts is taxed to Dave.

_____ 8. Under terms of the will of Rick Waters, $6,000 a year is to be paid to his widow and $3,000 a year to his daughter out of the estate's income during the period of administration. There are no charitable contributions. For the year, the estate's distributable net income is only $6,000. How much must the widow and the daughter include in their gross income? (IRS 97 3C-47)

	Widow	Daughter
a.	$6,000	$3,000
b.	$4,000	$2,000
c.	$3,000	$3,000
d.	$2,000	$1,000

_____ 9. Trust C, a simple trust, has taxable interest of $8,000, tax-exempt interest of $12,000 and a short-term capital gain of $16,000. The trust instrument provides that capital gains are allocable to corpus. There are two equal beneficiaries. How much gross income does each beneficiary have from Trust C? (IRS 97 3C-51)

    a. $4,000
    b. $6,000
    c. $10,000
    d. $12,000

_____ 10. Under the terms of the trust agreement, the income of Murphy Trust is required to be currently distributed to Kathy during her life. Capital gains are allocable to corpus, and all expenses are charged against corpus. During the taxable year, the trust had the following items of income and expense:

Dividends	$35,000
Taxable interest	25,000
Nontaxable interest	10,000
Long-term capital gains	15,000
Commissions and miscellaneous expenses allocable to corpus	7,000

The Murphy Trust's distributable net income is: (IRS 97 3C-52)

    a. $70,000
    b. $63,000
    c. $60,000
    d. $53,000

_____ 11. Trust D, a complex trust, is required to distribute $20,000 to its beneficiary under the terms of the trust instrument. The trust's distributable net income is $40,000. The $20,000 is deemed to have been paid from the following items of income (all expenses have been allocated):

Rent	$ 2,000
Taxable interest	14,000
Dividends	16,000
Tax-exempt interest	8,000
Total	40,000

What is the trust's distribution deduction? (IRS 97 3C-53)

    a. $15,000
    b. $16,000
    c. $19,000
    d. $20,000

SOLUTIONS TO CHAPTER 19 QUESTIONS

True or False

1. **F** (p. 19–14; not an administrative expense, but may be deductible as production of income expense (rental))

    Administrative expenses under Section 2053 are deductible from the gross estate to compute the taxable estate. Administrative expenses include selling expenses necessarily incurred to:

    - Pay debts.
    - Preserve the estate's assets.
    - Make final distributions.

    For this purpose, brokers fees, survey fees or transfer stamps are administrative expenses under Treas. Reg. Sec. 2053-3(d)(2).

    The estate incurred an expense of $9,000 to paint and carpet a house to enhance such house's marketability. This expense is not an administrative expense under Section 2054 (since the painting and carpeting expense was not necessarily incurred to sell the house).

    However, if the executor decided to rent the house until the house was sold, the expense of $9,000 to paint and carpet the house would be deductible on Schedule E (as a rental expense).

2. **F** (p. 19–26; unused net operating loss carryovers flow through to the beneficiaries in the year of termination)

    In the year that an estate terminates, tax attributes that are passed through to the beneficiaries succeeding to the property of the estate include:

    - Unused Net Operating Loss (NOL) carryovers.
    - Unused capital loss carryovers.
    - The excess of deductions over gross income attributable to the termination year, adjusted for:
      - The personal exemption.
      - A charitable deduction.

    Tax attributes that are passed through to the beneficiaries are allocated to the beneficiaries succeeding to the property of the estate based upon the extent to which each beneficiary bears either the loss or deduction.

3. **F** (p. 19–22; income required to be distributed recognized by beneficiary even though not paid)

    The rules regarding the taxation of beneficiaries (for distributions made to beneficiaries during a trust's tax year) depend upon whether such trust is a complex or simple trust for a particular year.

    If the trust is a complex trust, a hierarchical system is established for the purpose of taxing categories of beneficiaries. These categories are identified as follows.

    - First, income that is required to be distributed currently, whether or not a distribution is actually made, constitutes the first-tier distribution category.
    - Second, amounts (other than income that is required to be distributed currently) that are properly paid or credited constitute the second-tier distribution category.

4. **T** (p. 19–26; losses apportioned based upon relative amounts of corpus received)

    In the year that an estate terminates, certain tax attributes that are passed through to the beneficiaries.

    Tax attributes that are passed through to the beneficiaries are allocated to the beneficiaries succeeding to the property of the estate based upon the extent to which each beneficiary bears either the loss or deduction.

5. T (p. 19–5)

The trust is a legal entity. Under governing state law and a valid trust instrument, the trust is created by either a grantor (inter vivos trust) or testator (testamentary trust) for the benefit of enumerated beneficiaries.

The designation of a trust as either simple or complex is made on a year-by-year basis.

Fill in the Blanks

1. grantor; trustee; beneficiary (p. 19–4)

    The trust is a legal entity. Under governing state law and a valid trust instrument, the trust is created by either a grantor (inter vivos trust) or testator (testamentary trust) for the benefit of enumerated beneficiaries. The trustee of a trust has fiduciary responsibilities in administering the trust under governing state law and the trust instrument.

2. grantor (p. 19–4)

    The grantor is the creator of the trust.

3. income; principal; income (p. 19–4)

    The trust is a legal entity. A present interest in trust is an interest that allows the owner to the immediate use, possession, or enjoyment (e.g., an income interest) of trust property. A future interest in trust is an interest where possession or enjoyment of trust property will occur in the future (e.g., a remainder interest where the owner receives the principal of the trust upon the expiration of the income interest).

4. fourth (p. 19–6)

    A trust determines gross income and deductions on an annual basis similar to that of an individual and files Form 1041 (U.S. Income Tax Return for Estates and Trusts). The trust income tax return is due by the fifteenth day of the fourth month after the end of the trust's tax year.

5. distributable net income (p. 19–18)

    The trust is a legal entity.

    Trust income is calculated based upon the trust agreement in conjunction with local law. DNI is the maximum amount of the distribution that can be taxed to the beneficiaries.

6. first-tier (p. 19–22)

    Income that is required to be distributed currently, whether or not a distribution is actually made, constitutes the first-tier distribution category.

7. gift (p. 19–27)

    If the trust property reverts to the grantor upon the expiration of the income interest (e.g., the death of the life tenant), the grantor holds a reversionary interest. A trust that has this characteristic is called a reversionary trust because the grantor has transferred a present interest while retaining a reversionary interest. The present value of the reversionary interest is subject to the gift tax.

8. life tenant (p. 19–4)

    A person (the life tenant) holding a life estate in trust owns an income interest in trust for the life of such person. Such beneficiary is entitled to trust income for life.

Multiple Choice

1. c (p. 19–6; accounting methods available to individuals are generally available to estates)

    The person responsible for administering the estate is the executor (if appointed by the testator to carry out the provisions of a valid will) or an administrator (if appointed by the court). The executor/administrator is a fiduciary and owes fiduciary duties to the beneficiaries to carry out the provisions of a valid will and conserve the assets of the decedent for the benefit of the beneficiaries. As the fiduciary of the estate, the executor/administrator is also responsible for filing Form 706 (the estate tax return) and Form 1041 (U.S. Income Tax Return for Estates and Trusts), if required. For an estate, the filing of Form 1041 is required if the estate has gross income of more than $600. The estate determines gross income and deductions on an annual basis based upon the estate's elected methods of accounting. Such methods are similar to those available to an individual. Thus, the methods of accounting used by the decedent do not carry over to the decedent's estate.

    In addition, the fiduciary of the estate is also responsible for filing Form 1040 (U.S. Individual Income Tax Return) for the decedent as the decedent's final return for the short period ending on the date of his/her death. Accordingly, by employing the decedent's various methods of accounting, the fiduciary must recognize the decedent's gross income, deductions, gains and losses for the short period ending on the date of his/her death. Income earned and received post date of death is the income and property of either the estate or an heir. It is not reported on the decedent's final income tax return. This separation of tax attributes (between the period after the date of death versus on or before such date) is exemplified by the partnership tax rule relating to the death of a partner. Under Section 706(c)(2)(A), the taxable year of a partnership closes with respect to a partner whose entire interest in the partnership terminates by reason of death. This closing allows tax attributes to be easily separated between the period after the date of death versus on or before such date.

    Thus, in the instant case, item c is the right answer because it is not true that the fiduciary of Joan's estate must employ the accrual method of accounting in determining Joan's gross income, deductions, gains and losses for the short period ending on the date of her death. In fact, the fiduciary must employ various methods of accounting consistent with Joan's previous use.

2. a (p. 19–6)

    For an estate, the filing of Form 1041 is required if the estate has gross income of more than $600. The estate determines gross income and deductions on an annual basis based upon the estate's elected methods of accounting. The estate is required to make estimated tax payments using the same quarterly schedule that applies to individuals, but only for tax years that end two or more years after the date of decedent's death.

    Thus, in the instant case, item a is correct.

3. c (p. 19–11; 500 + 700 + 4,000; life insurance proceeds are excluded from gross income)

    For an estate, the filing of Form 1041 is required if the estate has gross income of more than $600. The estate determines gross income and deductions on an annual basis based upon the estate's elected methods of accounting. In general, income earned and received post date of death is the income and property of either the estate or an heir.

    However, Income in Respect of a Decedent (IRD) must be recognized as income by the estate when received on behalf of a cash basis decedent. IRD is income earned by a decedent at the time of death but not recognized by the decedent under his/her method of accounting (e.g., accrued salary or installment sale gain).

    In the instant case (assuming the interest, dividends and salary constitute IRD), gross income is $5,200 ($500 + $700 + $4,000). The life insurance proceeds are excluded from the gross income of the estate under Section 101. Thus, item c is correct.

4. d (p. 19–18; under the modified conduit approach of Subchapter J, the trust claims a distribution deduction)

The trust is a legal entity.

For tax purposes, the trust is a conduit. Under the governing trust instrument or state law:

- The trust may either be required to or voluntarily distributes income.
- The character of the income flows through to the beneficiary.
- The trust gets a deduction for distributions made to a beneficiary to the extent that such distribution represents the taxable income portion of Distributable Net Income (DNI).

The rules regarding the taxation of beneficiaries (for distributions made to beneficiaries during a trust's tax year) depend upon whether such trust is a complex or simple trust for a particular year. If the trust is a simple trust:

- Whether or not a distribution is actually made, a beneficiary is taxed on the income that is required to be distributed currently under the trust instrument, limited to the amount of Distributable Net Income (DNI) for the year. The elements of DNI are ratably apportioned across beneficiaries if there are multiple income beneficiaries.

If the trust is a complex trust, a hierarchical system is established for the purpose of taxing categories of beneficiaries. These categories are identified as follows.

- First, income that is required to be distributed currently, whether or not a distribution is actually made, constitutes the first-tier distribution category.
- Second, amounts (other than income that is required to be distributed currently) that are properly paid or credited constitute the second-tier distribution category.

Thus, in the instant case, item d is the right answer because it is not true that the trust is effectively taxed on both (a) the income currently distributed and (b) the remaining portion accumulated.

5. b (p. 19–5)

A simple trust is a trust that makes no distribution other than that of income and has a trust agreement which:

- requires that all income be distributed currently and
- does not provide for any amount to be either:
  - paid,
  - permanently set aside, or
  - used for a charitable purpose.

Thus, in the instant case, item b is correct.

6. c (p. 19–5)

A simple trust is a trust that makes no distribution other than that of income and has a trust agreement which:

- requires that all income be distributed currently and
- does not provide for any amount to be either
  - paid,
  - permanently set aside, or
  - used for a charitable purpose.

Thus, in the instant case, item c is correct. Further, items a, b and d are incorrect because each of these items (final year, partial liquidation and corpus distribution) necessarily requires that there be a distribution other than that of income, thereby being inconsistent with the definition of a simple trust.

7. **c** (p. 19–27; income accumulated for future distribution to grantor's spouse taxed to the grantor)

   A grantor trust is not recognized for tax purposes because the grantor has retained beneficial enjoyment or substantial control over either trust income or corpus. In this case, the grantor is treated as the owner of the trust, including the owner over trust income and property. Accordingly, tax attributes of the trust (income, deductions, gains, losses and credits) are entirely allocable to the grantor.

   In the instant case:

   - With respect to Trust D, Dave is treated as owner of the entire trust, since all of the income of such trust may be distributed to his wife. Accordingly, the income, deductions, gains, losses and credits of Trust D are entirely allocable to Dave.
   - With respect to Trust G, Dave is deemed to have received a distribution of one-half of the income of Trust G, since one-half of the income of Trust G was used to support Dave's children for whom Dave is legally obligated to support.

   Thus, item c is correct.

8. **b** (p. 19–22; elements of DNI apportioned ratably)

   The rules regarding the taxation of beneficiaries (for distributions made to beneficiaries during a trust's tax year) depend upon whether such trust is a complex or simple trust during such year.

   If the trust is a complex trust, a hierarchical system is established for the purpose of taxing categories of beneficiaries. These categories are identified as follows.

   - First, income that is required to be distributed currently, whether or not a distribution is actually made, constitutes the first-tier distribution category.
   - Second, amounts (other than income that is required to be distributed currently) that are properly paid or credited constitute the second-tier distribution category.

   When income (which is required to be distributed currently) exceeds DNI, DNI is ratably allocated across beneficiaries, as follows.

   $$\frac{\text{First-tier distribution to Beneficiary A}}{\text{First-tier distributions to all Beneficiaries}} \times \text{DNI} = \text{Beneficiary A's share of DNI}$$

   In the instant case, each of the beneficiaries (widow and daughter) include in her gross income such beneficiary's share of DNI (assuming the trust has no tax-exempt income). The daughter's share of DNI is calculated as follows.

   $$(\$3,000/\$9,000) \times \$6,000 = \$2,000$$

   The widow's share of DNI is calculated as follows.

   $$(\$6,000/\$9,000) \times \$6,000 = \$4,000$$

   Thus, item b is correct.

9. **a** (p. 19–22; DNI (20,000), 50% (8,000) taxable interest)

   In the instant case, DNI of Trust C is $20,000 ($8,000 + $12,000). DNI includes tax-exempt interest but does not include capital gains attributable to corpus. Each one of two equal beneficiaries (B1 and B2) shares equally in the elements of DNI as follows.

	DNI	B1	B2
Taxable Interest	$ 8,000	$4,000	$4,000
Tax-Exempt Interest	$12,000	$6,000	$6,000

   Thus, the gross income of each of B1 and B2 is $4,000 and item a is correct.

STUDY GUIDE | **CHAPTER 19** | 19–15
Income Taxation of Trusts and Estates

10. b (p. 19–18; DNI is reduced by expenses allocated to corpus; 35,000 + 25,000 + 10,000 − 7000))

- DNI is calculated as follows:
  - Taxable income before the distribution deduction
  - Plus: Tax-exempt income
  - Plus: The personal exemption
  - Less: Capital gains attributable to corpus
  - Equals: DNI

In the instant case, DNI of the Murphy Trust (a simple trust) is $63,000 ($35,000 + $25,000 − $7,000 + $10,000). Taxable income before the distribution deduction (and therefore DNI) includes the deduction for all of the expenses of the Murphy Trust, notwithstanding the fact that the trust instrument allocates all trust expenses to corpus. Thus, item b is correct.

11. b (p. 19–18; tax-exempt interest is removed from DNI to calculate the deduction; (20,000/40,000) × (40,000 − 8,000))

If the trust is a complex trust, a hierarchical system is established for the purpose of taxing categories of beneficiaries, as follows.

- First, income that is required to be distributed currently, whether or not a distribution is actually made, constitutes the first-tier distribution category.
- Second, amounts (other than income that is required to be distributed currently) that are properly paid or credited constitute the second-tier distribution category.

When income (required to be distributed currently) does not exceed DNI, the extent to which an element of DNI is distributed is determined as follows.

$$\frac{\text{Total distribution}}{\text{DNI}} \times \text{Class of DNI} = \text{Portion of an Element of DNI Deemed Distributed}$$

- DNI is calculated as follows:
  - Taxable income before the distribution deduction
  - Plus: Tax-exempt income
  - Plus: The personal exemption
  - Less: Capital gains attributable to corpus
  - Equals: DNI

In the instant case, the extent to which an element of DNI is distributed is determined as follows.

Rent Deemed Distributed	($20,000/$40,000) × $ 2,000 =	$ 1,000
Taxable Interest Deemed Distributed	($20,000/$40,000) × $14,000 =	$ 7,000
Dividends Deemed Distributed	($20,000/$40,000) × $16,000 =	$ 8,000
Tax-Exempt Interest Deemed Distributed	($20,000/$40,000) × $ 8,000 =	$ 4,000
		$20,000

Further, the extent to which the distribution of $20,000 reflects the taxable income portion of DNI is $16,000 ($1,000 + $7,000 + $8,000). Thus, Trust D's distribution deduction if $16,000 and item b is correct.